Rewriting the Soul

Rewriting the Soul

MULTIPLE PERSONALITY AND THE SCIENCES OF MEMORY

Ian Hacking

PRINCETON UNIVERSITY PRESS

PRINCETON, NEW JERSEY

Library of Congress Cataloging-in-Publication Data

Hacking, Ian.
Rewriting the soul : multiple personality and the sciences
of memory / Ian Hacking.
p.   cm.
Includes bibliographical references (p.   ) and index.
ISBN 0-691-03642-X (cloth : alk. paper)
1. Multiple personality—Philosophy.   2. Memory—Social aspects.
3. Multiple personality—Social aspects.   4. Multiple personality—
History.   5. Soul—Psychological aspects.   I. Title.
RC569.5.M8H33   1995
153.1′2—dc20   94-41975

This book has been composed in Galliard

Princeton University Press books are
printed on acid-free paper and meet the guidelines
for permanence and durability of the Committee
on Production Guidelines for Book Longevity
of the Council on Library Resources

Printed in the United States of America

1   2   3   4   5   6   7   8   9   10

FOR OLIVER

Contents

CONTENTS

Acknowledgments

MANY PEOPLE have helped me, but here I would like to speak for all the members of a seminar on multiple personality that met on Monday evenings during the winters of 1992 and 1993. We thank our guests who came on those cold dark nights for no reward, except love of their subject, to share their experience, knowledge, and opinions: Paul Antze, medical anthropologist, York University; John Beresford, psychiatrist; Adam Crabtree, clinical psychologist; Toby Gelfand, Hannah Professor of History of Medicine, University of Ottawa; Peter Keefe, psychiatrist at the Clarke Institute of Psychiatry and Mount Sinai Hospital, Toronto; Michael Kenny, anthropologist, Simon Fraser University; Danny Kaplan and Stanley Klein, Community Head Injury Rehabilitation Services; Michael Lambek, anthropologist, University of Toronto; Ruth Leys, Humanities Center, The Johns Hopkins University; Harold Merskey, psychiatrist, London Psychiatric Hospital, and professor of psychiatry at the University of Western Ontario; Margo Rivera, clinical psychologist and director of Education/Dissociation. Special thanks to Paul Antze who worked with us throughout the winter of 1992, and to Stanley Klein, who did the same in 1993.

At another level I have to thank the Social Sciences and Humanities Research Council of Canada for a small grant to cover research expenses, which enabled me to enlist the splendid help of André Leblanc.

I owe a special debt of gratitude to my editor, Ann Himmelberger Wald.

Rewriting the Soul

Introduction

MEMORY is a powerful tool in quests for understanding, justice, and knowledge. It raises consciousness. It heals some wounds, restores dignity, and prompts uprisings. What better motto for automobile license plates in Québec than *Je me souviens?*—I remember. Memories of the holocaust and of slavery must be passed on to new generations. Severe and repeated child abuse is said to be a cause of multiple personality disorder; the illness is to be treated through a recovery of lost memories of pain. An aging population is scared of Alzheimer's disease, which it regards as a disease of memory. In a most extraordinary venture into the mind by way of biochemistry, the central focus of research in brain science is memory. An astonishing variety of concerns are pulled in under that one heading: memory.

My curiosity is piqued exactly when something seems inevitable. Why are such diverse interests grouped under *memory?* One senior American philosopher, Nelson Goodman, as committed to the arts as to the sciences, has called himself skeptical, analytical, and constructionalist. I have those tendencies too. I wonder skeptically: why has it been essential to organize so many of our present projects in terms of memory? I wonder analytically: what are the dominating principles that lock us into memory as an approach to so many of the problems of life, from child rearing to patriotism, from aging to anxiety? And I wonder, what constructions underlie these principles? I am not looking for the trite wisdom that there are different kinds of memory. I wonder why there is one creature, "memory," of which there are so many different kinds.

I do not want, now, a grand reflection on memory, or its associated horrors such as genocide and child abuse. Skeptics are unenthusiastic about systems, about theories of everything. I propose to examine an entirely specific case of memory-thinking. Multiple personality is perfect for the purpose. This illness, which seemed as nothing twenty-five years ago, is flourishing all over North America. Amnesia has been built in to the official diagnostic criteria for what has just been renamed dissociative identity disorder. Dissociation into personality fragments is caused (on current theorizing) by abuse in childhood that had long been forgotten. Multiple personality is a paradigmatic, if tiny, memory-concept.

We can get some perspective on the question of how memory came into play, because multiple personality, though florid now, is not new. One of its previous incarnations, beginning in 1876, took place when a whole new discourse of memory came into being. People have always been fascinated by memory. In classical Greece, and in the High Middle Ages, mastery of *the art of memory* was one of the most admired of skills. But the sciences of memory arose only in the second half of the nineteenth century. One of these sciences, especially developed in France, fixed on pathological memory, and multiple personality is a part of that new science. I argue that the way in which the sciences of memory evolved has much to do with the frontline memory confrontations of today.

As a research strategy I have always been much taken by what Michel Foucault named archaeology. I think that there are sometimes fairly sharp mutations in systems of thought and that these redistributions of ideas establish what later seems inevitable, unquestionable, necessary. I hold that whatever made possible the most up-to-the-moment events in the little saga of multiple personality is strongly connected to fundamental and long-term aspects of the great field of knowledge about memory that emerged in the last half of the nineteenth century. I can use multiple personality, then and now, as a microcosm of thinking-and-talking-about-memory, then and now. Hence in the middle of the book I open a narrow window looking out onto memory—and multiple personality—long ago. The venue is France 1874–1886. I choose it because that was the center of the span of time when the structure of the modern sciences of memory came into being.

It is by no means an accident that in precisely that period the word *trauma* acquired a new meaning. It had always meant a lesion or wound, but its meaning was limited to the physical, the physiological. Then suddenly the word got its most common and compelling meaning, a psychological hurt, a spiritual lesion, a wound to the soul. Some historical dictionaries direct us to Freud, in the early 1890s, for the first usage of the word in that sense. We must go back further than that, for Freud only deployed what had already become current. He did so in connection with memory, for it is memories of psychic trauma that transfix us. The idea of trauma was already intimately connected with multiple personality. So many striking changes in ideas occur in my chosen two decades that I become convinced that we are looking at a radically formative moment, even for the idea of memory itself. The very fact that we do not think about these changes—who wonders how trauma became a lesion of the soul?—shows that we have come to think of them as inevitable, invisible, a priori.

In preparing this work, feeling the tentacles of madness surround me, I was brought sharply to my senses in The Musical Offering, a café in Berkeley, California, which displayed a large and handsome poster of a rainy Paris street, "The World of the Impressionists, 1874–1886." I had become so caught up in my strange tales that I had forgotten what all of us know about that time and place. We all have a vision of what that world looked like, at least to the chosen few. Let their world be my base-line. I ask you to imagine that I am talking about the world of the impressionists. Visually it was a new world, created not only by artists but also by the camera. The camera was truly objective because no human observer intervened between the object and the record. Alongside the impressions made with paint we must place the reproducible images captured by the lens. Toward the end of my chosen twelve years Jean-Martin Charcot, master neurologist, became fascinated by pictorial representations of hysteria, old and new. He and his students made this illness visual. Hysterics had to have some affliction that could be photographed. Multiple personality was thought to be a bizarre form of hysteria. The very first *multiple* personality—multiple meaning *more than two*—was photographed in each of ten personality states. Here they are in my hand, among the pages of a printed book, as faithful today as in 1885, when the poses were captured on the photographic plate.

Multiple personality became an object of knowledge in many ways. Photography was part of the initial rhetoric of multiplicity. Today quantitative tests of dissociation fill a similar role. My chief topic, toward the end of the book, will become the way in which a new science, a purported knowledge of memory, quite self-consciously was created in order to secularize the soul. Science had hitherto been excluded from study of the soul itself. The new sciences of memory came into being in order to conquer that resilient core of Western thought and practice. That is the bond that connects, under the heading of *memory*, all those different kinds of knowledge and rhetoric I have mentioned. When the family falls apart, when parents abuse their children, when incest obsesses the media, when one people tries to destroy another, we are concerned with defects of the soul. But we have learned how to replace the soul with knowledge, with science. Hence spiritual battles are fought, not on the explicit ground of the soul, but on the terrain of memory, where we suppose that there is such a thing as knowledge to be had.

Talk of the soul sounds old-fashioned, but I take it seriously. The soul that was scientized was something transcendental, perhaps immortal. Philosophers of my stripe speak of the soul not to suggest something eternal, but to invoke character, reflective choice, self-understanding, values that include honesty to others and oneself, and several types of freedom and responsibility. Love, passion, envy, tedium, regret, and quiet contentment are the stuff of the soul. This may be a very old idea of the soul, pre-Socratic. I do not think of the soul as unitary, as an essence, as one single thing, or even as a thing at all. It does not denote an unchanging core of personal identity. One person, one soul, may have many facets and speak with many tongues. To think of the soul is not to imply that there is one essence, one spiritual point, from which all voices issue. In my way of thinking the soul is a more modest concept than that. It stands for the strange mix of aspects of a person that may be, at some time, imaged as inner—a thought not contradicted by Wittgenstein's dictum, that the body is the best picture of the soul.

I am not writing about the soul in the way that you might expect in a book about multiple personality. I am preoccupied by attempts to scientize the soul through the study of memory. Some philosophers, and not a few clinicians, have wanted to make a quite different use of multiple personality. They argue that it shows something about what it is to be a person, or the limits of personal identity. Some have gone so far as to say that this disorder provides a window on the relation between brain and mind, or even contributes to solving the mind-body problem. I have no such illusions, no such intentions, no such problem.

I came to this topic when thinking about how kinds of people come into being. How do systems of knowledge about kinds of people interact with the people who are known about? The story of multiple personality is, in all too many different ways, a story about what I have called making up people.[1] I am fascinated by the dynamics of the relation between people who are known about, the knowledge about them, and the knowers. That is a public dynamics. There is also a more private one. The theory and practice of multiple personality today is bound up with memories of childhood, memories that are to be not only recovered but also redescribed. New meanings change the past. It is reinterpreted, yes, but more than that, it is reorganized, repopulated. It becomes filled with new actions, new intentions, new events that caused us to be as we are. I have to discuss not only making up people but making up ourselves by reworking our memories.

I dwell on these difficult matters at the end of the book. In the middle I excavate the sciences of memory that provide the ground for so many present concerns. I begin by describing some recent dynamics. I tell how multiples, theories of multiple personality, and experts on the disorder have been interacting in the past few years. I tell only enough to set my stage. The whole field of multiple personality is ripe for participant observation and sociological analysis. But that is a task for others. I have scrupulously limited myself to matters of public record.

Is It Real?

AS LONG AGO as 1982 psychiatrists were talking about "the multiple personality epidemic."[1] Yet those were early days. Multiple personality—whose "essential feature is the existence within the individual of two or more distinct personalities, each of which is dominant at a particular time"—became an official diagnosis of the American Psychiatric Association only in 1980.[2] Clinicians were still reporting occasional cases as they appeared in treatment. Soon the number of patients would become so overwhelming that only statistics could give an impression of the field.

Ten years earlier, in 1972, multiple personality had seemed to be a mere curiosity. "Less than a dozen cases have been reported in the last fifty years."[3] You could list every multiple personality recorded in the history of Western medicine, even if experts disagreed on how many of these cases were genuine. None? Eighty-four? More than one hundred, with the first clear description given by a German physician in 1791?[4] Whatever number you favored, the word for the disorder was *rare*.

Ten years later, in 1992, there were hundreds of multiples in treatment in every sizable town in North America. Even by 1986 it was thought that six thousand patients had been diagnosed.[5] After that, one stopped counting and spoke about an exponential increase in the rate of diagnosis since 1980. Clinics, wards, units, and entire private hospitals dedicated to the illness were being established all over the continent. Maybe one person in twenty suffered from a dissociative disorder.[6]

What has happened? Is a new form of madness, hitherto almost unknown, stalking the continent? Or have multiples always been around, unrecognized? Were they classified, when they needed help, as suffering from something else? Perhaps clinicians have only recently learned to make correct diagnoses. It is far easier, they say, now that we know the most common cause of dissociated personalities—early and repeated sexual abuse in childhood. Only a society prepared to acknowledge that family violence is everywhere could find multiple personalities everywhere.

Or, as a majority of psychiatrists still contend, is there simply no such thing as multiple personality disorder? Is the epidemic the work of a small but committed band of therapists, unwittingly aided and abetted by sensational stories in the tabloids and afternoon TV talk shows?

We at once arrive at what sounds like the big question: *Is it real?* That is the first question people ask me when they hear I am interested in multiple personality. It is not only amateurs who ask. The American Psychiatric Association staged a debate at its annual meeting of 1988: "Resolved That Multiple Personality Is a True Disease Entity." For: Richard Kluft and David Spiegel. Against: Fred Frankel and Martin Orne. The debaters, all leading professionals, remain in bitter disagreement today. The rest of us, once we see how vehemently the two camps of experts oppose each other, are bewildered. Multiple personality has become the most contested type of diagnosis in psychiatry. So we bystanders repeat, rather helplessly: Is it real?

What is "it," this controversial multiple personality? Not schizophrenia. Schizophrenia is often called split personality, so we reason that multiple personality = split personality = schizophrenia. Not so. The name *schizophrenia* was introduced at the beginning of the twentieth century. It is Greek for "split brain." The metaphor of splitting has been used in many different ways—Freud, for example, used it in three distinct ways at different stages in his career.[7] The idea behind the name schizophrenia was that a person's thoughts, emotions, and physical reactions are split off from each other, so that the emotional reaction to a thought, or the physical response to an emotion, is completely inappropriate or bizarre. There are delusions, thought disorders, and a terrible range of suffering. It is unclear whether schizophrenia is one disease or several. One form of it develops in the late teens or early twenties, so that this disease was once called *dementia praecox*, or premature senility. Schizophrenia probably has neurochemical causes; some forms of it might be genetic. Since the 1960s there has been an increasing battery of drugs that radically improve the quality of life for many schizophrenics.

None of the things I have just said about schizophrenia is true of multiple personality. No medication has specific effects on multiple personality as such, although switches in personality, like any other exceptional behavior, can be damped down by mood-altering drugs. Multiple personality has most commonly been first diagnosed in patients over thirty years of age, not in adolescence. It is not characterized by a splitting of thought, emotion, and bodily response. Multiple personality may mimic schizophrenia, in that there may be short periods of "schizophreniform" behavior, but these episodes do not endure. I shall return to schizophrenia, but for the present we must put it to one side.

So what is multiple personality? I will begin by being quite formal, using official guidelines. There are two widely used standard classifications of mental illness. One is part of the International Classification of Diseases, published by the World Health Organization in Geneva. The tenth edition of 1992, called *ICD-10*, does not have a separate category for multiple personality, although it does have an extended classification of types of dissociation.[8] *ICD-10* is used primarily in Europe, where most psychiatric establishments are disdainful of the multiple personality diagnosis. Another classification is the *Diagnostic and Statistical Manual of Mental Disorders*, authorized by the American Psychiatric Association. It sets the standard in North America and, despite *ICD-10*, is widely used overseas. In its third edition of 1980, called *DSM-III*, the diagnostic criteria for multiple personality disorder were:

A. The existence within the individual of two or more distinct personalities, each of which is dominant at a particular time.

B. The personality that is dominant at any particular time determines the individual's behavior.

C. Each individual personality is complex and integrated with its own unique behavior pattern and social relationships.[9]

These criteria, abstract as they are, matter to both research and practice. The great American psychiatric journals require that results be written up according to the classification of the current *Diagnostic and Statistical Manual*. Insurance companies and publicly funded health plans reimburse doctors, hospitals, and clinics according to a schedule coded by the current *DSM*.

The criteria were made less restrictive in the revised *Manual* of 1987, *DSM-III-R*, where condition C was deleted. The personalities no longer had to be complex and integrated, or to manifest distinct social relationships.[10] Hence more individuals could be diagnosed with multiple personality. But in research at the National Institute of Mental Health, Frank Putnam insisted on criteria more stringent than *DSM-III*, not less. "The diagnosing clinician must: (1) witness a switch between two alter personality states; (2) must meet a given alter personality on at least three separate occasions to assess the degree of uniqueness and stability of the alter personality state; and (3) must establish that the patient has amnesias, either by witnessing amnesic behavior or by the patient's report."[11] The amnesia condition, as we shall see, was built in to the criteria of *DSM-IV* in 1994.

The changes do not seem to matter to the pressing question: whether there is such a thing as multiple personality. The straightforward answer is plainly yes. There were patients who satisfied the criteria of 1980. More satisfied the criteria of 1987. Some satisfy Putnam's more stringent protocol. No matter what criteria are used, the rate of diagnosis has been growing apace. There are plenty of questions about what multiple personality is, and how to define it, but the simple conclusion is that there is such a disorder.

So that's the answer? There really is such a thing as multiple personality, because this or that book of rules lists some symptoms, and some patients have those symptoms? We should be more fastidious than that. To begin with, the question "Is it real?" is not of itself a clear one. The classic examination of the word "real" is due to the doyen of ordinary language philosophers, J. L. Austin. As he insisted, you have to ask, "A real *what*?" Moreover, "a definite sense attaches to the assertion that something is real, a real such-and-such, only in the light of a specific way in which it might be, or might have been *not* real."[12] Something may fail to be real cream because the butterfat content is too low, or because it is synthetic creamer. A man may not be a real constable because he is impersonating a police officer, or because he has not yet been sworn in, or because he is a military policeman, not a civil one. A painting may fail to be a real Constable because it is a forgery, or because it is a copy, or because it is an honest work by one of John Constable's students, or simply because it is an inferior work of the master. The moral is, if you ask, "Is it real?" you must supply a noun. You have to ask, "Is it a real *N*?" (or, "Is it real *N*?"). Then you have to indicate how it might fail to be a real *N*, "a real *N* as opposed to what?" Even that is no guarantee that a question about what's real will make sense. Even with a noun and an alternative, we may not have a real anything: there is no such thing as the "real" color of a deep-sea fish.

The American Psychiatric Association debate asked whether multiple personality "is a true disease entity." Colin Ross, a leading advocate of multiple personality, says that "the APA debate was incorrectly titled because MPD is not a true *disease* entity in the biomedical sense. It is a true psychiatric entity and a true disorder, but not a biomedical disease."[13] The APA provided a noun phrase ("disease entity"), and Ross offered two more terms ("psychiatric entity" and "disorder"). Do they help? We need to know what a true or real psychiatric entity *is*. A true or real disorder *as opposed to what?*

One question would be: Is multiple personality a real disorder as opposed to a kind of behavior worked up by doctor and patient? If we have

11

to answer yes-or-no, the answer is yes, it is real—that is, multiple personality is not usually "iatrogenic."[14] That answer of course allows for some skepticism, for it might still be that many of the more florid bits of multiple behavior are iatrogenic.

A second question would be: Is multiple personality a real disorder as opposed to a product of social circumstances, a culturally permissible way to express distress or unhappiness? That question makes a presupposition that we should reject. It implies that there is an important contrast between being a real disorder and being a product of social circumstances. The fact that a certain type of mental illness appears only in specific historical or geographical contexts does not imply that it is manufactured, artificial, or in any other way not real. This entire book is about the relationships between multiplicity, memory, discourse, knowledge, and history. It must allow a place for historically constituted illness.

Throughout the history of psychiatry, that is, since 1800, there have been two competing ways to classify mental illness. One model organizes the field according to symptom clusters; disorders are sorted according to how they look. Another organizes according to underlying causes; disorders are sorted according to theories about them. Because of the enormous variety of doctrine among American psychiatrists, it seemed expedient to create a merely symptomatic classification. The idea was that people of different schools could agree on the symptoms, even if disagreeing on causes or treatment. From the very beginning, American *DSM*s have tried to be purely symptomatic. That is one reason for their limited relevance to the question of whether multiple personality is real. A mere collection of symptoms may leave us with the sense that the symptoms may have different causes.

We need to go beyond symptoms, and hence beyond the *DSM*, to settle a reality debate. In all the natural sciences, we feel more confident that something is real when we think we understand its causes. Likewise we feel more confident when we are able to intervene and change it. The questions about multiple personality seem to come down to two issues, familiar in all the sciences: intervention and causation.

Intervention is serious indeed. Does it help a sizable number of clients, who satisfy suitable criteria, to treat them as if they suffer from multiple personality disorder? At present such therapy often involves coming to know numerous personality states, and working with each in order to achieve some sort of integration. Or is that strategy virtually always a bad one—even when someone walks in off the street and claims to be controlled, successively, by three different personalities? The skeptics say that fragmenting should be discouraged from the start. Instead of eliciting more alter personalities and thus causing the patient to disintegrate further, we should focus on the whole individual and help one person deal responsibly with immediate crises, dysfunction, confusion, and despair. Advocates call that "benign neglect" and say it is ineffective in the long run. But more cautious multiple clinicians do discourage fragmenting, even when they are willing to diagnose multiple personality in the long haul.[15]

The argument is not only about how to interact with some troubled people. The working clinician is seldom a total empiric; disease and disorder are identified according to an underlying vision of health and of humanity, of what kinds of being we are, and what can go wrong with us. That is why, as we shall see, the multiple personality field is so full of models of dissociation. We want to understand as well as to heal: practice demands theory. One kind of theory is causal, and so we pass from intervention to causation. The multiple personality field has been solidified by the causal idea that multiplicity is a coping mechanism, a response to early and repeated trauma, often sexual in nature.

When seen to be connected with child abuse, multiple personality prompts strong opinions about the family, about patriarchy, about violence. Many therapists of multiples are also feminists who are convinced that the roots of a patient's trouble came from the home, from neglect, from cruelty, from overt sexual assault, from male indifference, from oppression by a social system that favors men. It is no accident, they say, that most multiples are women, for women have had to bear the brunt of family violence from the time they were infants. Dissociation begins when babies and children are abused. A commitment to multiple personality becomes a social commitment. What kind of healer do you want to be? That is not only a question about how you conduct your practice: it is a question about how you want to live your life.

We hear moral conviction on all sides. Psychiatrists who reject multiple personality are accused of complacently dismissing the victims, the abused, the women and children. Is that true? Do the majority of doctors need to have their consciousness raised? There are less inflammatory explanations for their opposition. One has to do with institutions, training, and power. There has been a populist, grassroots air to the multiple personality movement. Many of the clinicians are not M.D.'s or Ph.D. psychologists but hold another credential—a master of social work degree, a nursing qualification, right down (in the pecking order) to people who have taken a couple of weekend courses in memory regression and are in no strict sense qualified at all. There is a motley of believers drawn from the rich mixture of eclectic therapies that run rampant in America. Hence the more skeptical psychiatrists distrust the feminism, the populism, the New-Age babble that they hear. These doctors, most of whom are men, not only are at the top of their profession's power structure but also see themselves as scientists, dedicated to objective fact, not social movements. They resent the media hype that surrounds multiple personality. They are dubious about the sheer scope of the epidemic. How can a mental disorder be so at the whim of place and time? How can it disappear and reappear? How can it be everywhere in North America and nonexistent in the rest of the world until it is carried there by missionaries, by clinicians who seem determined to establish beachheads of multiple personality in Europe and Australasia? The only place that multiples flourish overseas is in the Netherlands, and that florescence, say skeptics, was nourished by intensive visiting by the leading American members of the movement.[16]

There are further grounds for professional caution. In the course of some types of therapy, multiples have been encouraged to recover ghastly scenes of long ago, painfully reliving them. Each alter, it is argued, was created to cope with some appalling incident, usually in childhood, and often involving sexual assault by father, stepfather, uncle, brother, baby-sitter. Any supportive therapist committed to multiple personality would, at least during therapy, accept such memories as they surface. But increasingly bizarre events are recalled: cults, rituals, Satan, cannibalism, innocents programmed to do terrible things later in life, adolescent girls used as breeders of babies intended for human sacrifice. These memories include allegations about real people, relatives or neighbors. The resulting accusations seldom stand up to police inquiry, or charges collapse when brought to trial. The credibility of the memory structure of multiples in therapy has thus become suspect, and hence the alters themselves come to look more like a way to act out fantasies.

Such doubts are now institutionalized in a False Memory Syndrome Foundation, established in 1992. This action group is dedicated to supporting accused parents, to litigation, and to publicizing the dangers of irresponsible psychotherapy. It accuses gullible clinicians, including those who work with multiple personality, of generating memories of child abuse that never happened. In return, activists on the other side say that the foundation is a support group for child abusers.

These events are unfolding day by day, but we should not ignore an older complaint about multiple personality. Multiples have always been associated with hypnosis and hypnotic therapy. Some people are more readily hypnotized than others. Multiples are at the top of the scale. They are terribly suggestible. Isn't the elaborate personality structure of multiples unwittingly (or worse, wittingly) encouraged by all-too-willing therapists who use hypnosis or related techniques? Hypnosis is, and has always been, a notorious problem area for psychiatry and the allied arts. Doctors who have favored the use of hypnosis in therapy have tended to be marginalized. It does no good for advocates of multiple personality therapy to protest that multiples seem to develop in therapy in much the same way whether or not the clinician uses hypnosis, for multiple personality is irrevocably tainted with hypnosis. Advocates protest: the suggestibility of the patients is an important clue to their disorder. Multiple personality is only one extreme in a continuum of what are called *dissociative* disorders. Opposition scientists who study hypnosis reply that hypnosis is too complex to be arranged on a linear scale of hypnotizability, and there is no one continuum of dissociation to range alongside of it.[17]

The debate rages. We are not on purely medical terrain. We are deeply involved in morality. Susan Sontag has movingly described how tuberculosis, and then cancer, and then AIDS have been relentlessly inscribed with judgments about the characters of the diseased. Childhood trauma gives a whole new dimension to the morality of the disorder. The most sensational trauma of recent times is child abuse. Abuse, as trauma, enters the equations of morality and medicine. It exculpates, or passes the guilt up to the abuser. Not only is a person with multiple personality genuinely ill: someone else is responsible for the illness. Lest you think that I exaggerate the emphasis on morality and metaphor, consider the opening words at the 1993 annual conference on multiple personality: "AIDS is a plague which attacks individuals. *Child abuse* damages individuals and is the cancer of our society: all too often it flourishes unrecognized and metastasizes across families and generations."[18] AIDS, plague, cancer, metastasizes: we do not need Susan Sontag to help us notice the hyperbolic moral metaphors of multiple personality.

Now let us complete the circle back from morality to causation. It is common, in some psychiatric practice, to diagnose a patient as suffering from several different *DSM* disorders. If we had a system of classification based on causes, that would mean that a person had problems arising from two or more distinct and logically unrelated causes. But *DSM* is symptomatic, so it is not surprising that the life and behavior of a patient should exhibit several different symptom clusters, such as depression,

15

substance abuse, and panic disorder, say. Now the clinician may suspect that one of these clusters gets at the heart of the problem. For example, a classical psychiatrist may give a primary diagnosis of schizophrenia and hold that other behavior—including, perhaps, multiple personality behavior—is subordinate to that underlying cause. Hence he will treat the patient with some cocktail of neuroleptic drugs. The real disorder, he may say, is schizophrenia. The disorder to which all the other disorders are subordinate is sometimes called superordinate. Primary treatment is for the superordinate disorder, and other symptoms are expected to remit, to some extent, as the superordinate disorder is relieved. Is multiple personality disorder a superordinate diagnosis? Is it the problem to be treated, in the expectation that other problems such as depression, or bulimia, or panic disorder are subordinate to it? Advocates are affirmative.[19] Skeptics completely disagree. In the skeptical opinion, patients who evince multiple personality have problems, but the mutually amnesic personality fragments are mere symptoms of some underlying disorder. "The diagnosis of MPD represents a misdirection of effort which hinders the resolution of serious psychological problems in the lives of the patients."[20]

You may be beginning to think I'm of two minds, just a little bit split myself, when it comes to multiple personality. One moment I am sketching part of the general theory proposed by experts who take for granted that multiple personality is a real disorder. The next moment I am repeating grounds for skepticism about the very idea of multiple personality. What do *I* think? Is it real, or is it not?

I am not going to answer that question. I hope that no one who reads this book will end up wanting to ask exactly that question. This is not because I have some hang-up about reality or the idea of reality. There is a current fashion, among intellectuals who identify themselves as postmodern, to surround the word *reality* with a shower of ironical quotation marks. That is not my fashion. I do not use scare-quotes, and I am not ironical about reality. I expect that both advocates and opponents of multiple personality will find some of my discussion distasteful. I have no inclination to take sides. My concern is not, directly, with uncovering a fundamental timeless truth about personality or the relationship of fragmentation to psychic pain. I want to know how this configuration of ideas came into being, and how it has made and molded our life, our customs, our science.

My very neutrality makes me cautious about even the name of our topic. Names organize our thoughts. Between 1980 and 1994 the official diagnosis was "Multiple Personality Disorder." Most people involved in the field said or wrote simply "MPD." I never do that, except when quoting—because there is nothing like an acronym to make something permanent, unquestioned. (I use only two acronyms systematically throughout this book, both for very real entities. One is *DSM*, abbreviating the name of the manual. The other is ISSMP&D, which stands for the original name of the multiple movement's professional society, the International Society for the Study of Multiple Personality and Dissociation.) I shall talk about multiple personality, but very seldom do I even say "multiple personality disorder." That is partly because I am wary of the word "disorder." It is the standard all-purpose word used in the *DSM*. It is a good choice but it cannot help being loaded with values. The word is code for a vision of the world that ought to be orderly. Order is desirable, it is healthy, it is a goal. Truth, the true person, is disrupted by disorder. I am cautious about that picture of pathology. Others actively protest the very word "disorder" for multiple personality. These radicals suggest that perhaps we are all multiples really. A few established clinicians have gone almost that far, and one hears the same thing in some patient support groups.[21]

Another word has attracted more criticism than "disorder"—"personality." In fact Multiple Personality Disorder has just gone out of existence. The official heading in the *DSM-IV* of 1994 is "Dissociative Identity Disorder (*formerly* Multiple Personality Disorder)." Personality has been bracketed. What is happening?

As early as 1984 Philip Coons warned, in one of the most scrupulous essays on the topic during that decade, that "it is a mistake to consider each personality totally separate, whole or autonomous. The other personalities might best be described as personality states, other selves, or personality fragments."[22] That was not at first agreed. In 1986 B. G. Braun suggested a nomenclature distinguishing alter personalities from "fragments."[23] The meaning was that, yes, there are fragments, but there are also personalities.[24]

There is one textbook of our subject, *Diagnosis and Treatment of Multiple Personality Disorder*, by Frank Putnam. It is humane and clear; at its appearance in 1989 it was up-to-the-minute. I shall occasionally take issue with Putnam's work, but that is a sign of real respect, for he is the clearest and most careful authority in the field. In his textbook he emphasized a treatment that involves intensive interaction with all the alters in a personality system. These alters, in his account, have very distinct characters and behaviors. One does get the picture of rather rounded "personalities." He nevertheless issued a salutary warning:

> Overemphasis on multiplicity per se is a common mistake made by therapists new to the disorder. MPD is a fascinating phenomenon that makes one question most of what one has learned about the human mind. A reading of the case report literature from the earliest cases to the present shows that one of the common impulses on the part of therapists is an attempt to document the differences among the alter personalities of their patients. This fascination with the differences of the alters sends a clear message to patients that these are what makes them interesting to therapists and to others.[25]

In a 1992 talk Putnam candidly stated that "very little is known about the alter personalities and what they represent."[26] His increasing reservations about alter personalities are shared by an influential group of psychiatrists within the multiple movement who have long held that the emphasis on personalities is wrongheaded. In 1993 David Spiegel, chair of the dissociative disorders committee for the 1994 *DSM-IV*, wrote that "there is a widespread misunderstanding of the essential psychopathology in this dissociative disorder, which is failure of integration of various aspects of identity, memory, and consciousness. The problem is not having more than one personality; it is having less than one personality."[27] Spiegel asked who originated this aphorism on being less than one personality. One is reminded of Alice (in Wonderland), "for this curious child was very fond of pretending to be two people. 'But it's no use now,' thought poor Alice, 'to pretend to be two people! Why, there is hardly enough of me left to make *one* respectable person!'"[28]

The emphasis on treating alter personalities almost as persons has not, however, gone away. In 1993, the same year that Spiegel made the comment I have just quoted, a clinician and a clergyman were describing the problems of treating a patient who was a devout Christian. Her alters were not. "Because some alter personalities have experienced so little religious involvement, their questions often require very basic religious education."[29] Although there is no inconsistency, it is hard to think in terms of giving religious instruction to a mere fragment.

An emphasis on fragments as opposed to whole personalities is having its effects. The replacement name "Dissociative Identity Disorder" is intended to dispel simplistic ideas that go along with "multiple personality." As Spiegel put it,

I want to in a sense mainstream this disorder—I don't want it to be seen as some kind of circus sideshow. I want it to be considered as seriously as any other mental disorder. And we took great pains to make the language consistent with that of other disorders. But I felt that the important thing was to emphasize that the main problem is the difficulty in integrating disparate elements of memory, identity and consciousness, rather than the proliferation of personalities.[30]

Spiegel has been strongly criticized for railroading the name change. "The primary constituency of the Dissociative Disorders field is abused men, women and children, and the professionals who treat them."[31] And that constituency was not consulted! Will not the American Psychiatric Association be accused of "acting in a sexist and/or political manner"? The leaders in the movement quickly acknowledged the lay of the land. There was no longer such a thing as multiple personality to study, so the International Society for the Study of Multiple Personality and Dissociation had to change its name. This was done by overwhelming vote at the spring meeting in May 1994; we now have the International Society for the Study of Dissociation.

According to Spiegel, "the name change does not correspond to any change in diagnostic criteria."[32] Yet that is not strictly true. In 1994 the criteria became:

A. The presence of two or more distinct identities or personalities or personality states (each with its own relatively enduring pattern of perceiving, relating to and thinking about the environment and self).

B. At least two of these identities or personality states recurrently take control of the person's behavior.

C. Inability to recall important personal information that is too extensive to be explained by ordinary forgetfulness.

D. The disturbance is not due to the direct physiological effects of a substance (e.g., blackouts or chaotic behavior during Alcohol Intoxication) or a general medical condition (e.g., complex partial seizures). *Note:* In children the symptoms are not attributable to imaginary playmates or other fantasy play.[33]

The final "note" has a subtext. Many advocates wanted a new diagnostic category of childhood multiple personality disorder. They did not succeed but got their foot in the door. They hope to open the door wider in *DSM-V*.

Subtle differences in definition can be a surprisingly useful way to begin to understand how the disorder itself is changing.[34] *DSM-III* required the *existence* of more than one personality or personality state. In 1994 we require only the *presence*. What's the difference between existence and presence? Spiegel explained, "We felt that *existence* conveys some belief that there really are twelve people, when really what we want to underscore is that they experience themselves that way."[35] This tiny change in wording moves us away from actual multiple personalities to an experience that the patient has. Second, "presence" is the word used for the delusions characteristic of the schizophrenias. The parallelism was deliberate. Thus the alters of a multiple personality are, through the change of a mere word, made more analogous to delusions. Spiegel is, in effect, saying that multiple personality is not the main disturbance. The problem is disintegration of the sense of identity. We shall find over and over again that multiple personality is a moving target. Perhaps it has just moved out of sight.

Yet two things are constantly in view, memory and psychic pain. Whether the illness involves more than one personality or less than one, whether we have dissociation or disintegration, the disorder is supposed to be a response to childhood trauma. Memories of the early cruelties are hidden and must be recalled to effect a true integration and cure. Multiple personality and its treatment are grounded upon the supposition that the troubled mind can be understood through increased knowledge about the very nature of memory. I do not intend to question beliefs in multiple personality. I intend instead to find out why it is so taken for granted, by both sides, that memory is the key to the soul.

What Is It Like?

WHAT IS IT LIKE to be a multiple? The formal criteria of the diagnostic manuals are too impersonal. Nineteenth-century patients with "double consciousness" fit the criteria, but their experience, their ways of getting on (or not), the resulting family and social life—all those are quite unlike the life of a modern multiple. To start with, there was usually only one well-defined alter; today, sixteen alters is the norm. In France, a century or so ago, cases of doubling had the symptoms then associated with florid hysteria—partial paralyses, partial anesthesia, intestinal bleeding, restricted field of vision. English cases of double consciousness were more restrained but regularly went into a trance—an intervening period of unconsciousness or confusion—between the two personalities. In addition, the second state was often described as trance, even though the person seemed normal enough to an outsider.

Times change, and so do people. People in trouble are not more constant than anyone else. But there is more to the change in the lifestyle of multiples than the passage of time. We tend to behave in ways that are expected of us, especially by authority figures—doctors, for example. Some physicians had multiples among their patients in the 1840s, but their picture of the disorder was very different from the one that is common in the 1990s. The doctors' vision was different because the patients were different; but the patients were different because the doctors' expectations were different. That is an example of a very general phenomenon: the looping effect of human kinds.[1] People classified in a certain way tend to conform to or grow into the ways that they are described; but they also evolve in their own ways, so that the classifications and descriptions have to be constantly revised. Multiple personality is an almost too perfect illustration of this feedback effect.

I shall later describe the double consciousness of old, but first we need to see what it is like to be a multiple, today. This presents a problem. People in therapy go through many stages, some of which are very painful. Nowhere is this more striking than in a clinic for dissociative disorders. The most distinctive symptoms become fully evident only in the course of treatment. Hence the published descriptions of multiples best fit patients in therapy. Thanks to very recent publicity, some people do now walk in to a doctor's office claiming to have a number of personalities, but during the 1980s only a clinician well versed in detecting certain signs was likely to spot a multiple. All too many clinicians actively sought out alters, but there was always a core of more cautious practitioners who wanted multiplicity to lie dormant until the patient was well enough to grapple with it and its causes.

I shall present a picture of multiple personality that was current during the 1980s. Notice that it is internal to the multiple personality movement. Skeptics would describe the phenomena very differently, and even people diagnosed as multiples usually portrayed themselves very differently before diagnosis. Before trying to say what it is like to be a multiple, we should do a little logical spadework. We know how to describe individuals, even though few of us are as deft as novelists, gifted biographers, or insightful journalists. We are not so clear when we move to one level of abstraction, when we try to characterize not an individual but a *kind* of person. It is often thought that a class, such as a class of people suffering from an illness, is best defined by necessary and sufficient conditions. This means that to be in the class a person must satisfy all the conditions (necessary); anyone who satisfies all the conditions is automatically in the class (sufficient). The *DSM* tries to define disorders that way, even though it does not always succeed. Schizophrenia was characterized in a confusing way, as befits that cruel but complex disease. The definition read like a menu. You had to pick and choose within sets of criteria, and no one criterion was strictly necessary. We need not worry about that here, because the *DSM* entries for multiple personality look like necessary and sufficient conditions.

They are not always used in that way. For example, *DSM-IV* added an explicit amnesia condition. Yet many authors agree that there are multiples for whom amnesia is not apparent, even though in the most florid and complex multiples one will always find some amnesia.[2] Amnesia shows up, it is said, in at least 90 percent of known cases. But 90 percent is not 100 percent. The condition is not treated as necessary after all. Should clinicians be more strict in using their diagnostic manuals? Frank Putnam fears that the *DSM* criteria are too weak. They allow too easy a diagnosis of multiple personality. Even the stricter *DSM-IV* is not good enough for him. "Recent corrective efforts to increase the specificity of the *DSM-IV* criteria were only partially successful."[3] Putnam thinks that overdiagnosis is a real danger, especially when the diagnosis itself is under attack. I have mentioned the criteria used by his unit at the

National Institute of Mental Health. Before diagnosing multiple personality a clinician must actually witness switches between two alter personality states, must meet specific alters more than twice, and must encounter amnesias. Contrast this demand for more careful diagnosis, checked by tighter necessary conditions, with a breezy statement by Colin Ross, a recent president of the ISSMP&D. "I have never encountered a false positive diagnosis of MPD made by another clinician, so a requirement for more rigorous criteria has never arisen."[4] Has the president of any other professional society of medical specialists ever averred that he has never encountered a mistaken diagnosis?

Putnam's supplementary criteria are part of a research protocol. When his group evaluates or tests a procedure, it demands strict controls on the individuals assessed as multiples for research purposes. Although my sympathies are entirely with Putnam, rigor may not be so essential to day-to-day clinical practice. For example, a patient might be helpfully treated as multiple even though she had no amnesia. This point is a logical one. Disorders are constituted by a clustering of symptoms, and not, in general, by necessary and sufficient conditions. This is true of most ordinary kinds of things as well. As the great English philosopher of science William Whewell wrote in 1840, "Anyone can make true assertions about dogs, but who can define a dog?"[5] Labels often work well without strict necessary and sufficient conditions. Linguists and cognitive psychologists have recently proposed one way in which to explain this fact. They take a hint from Wittgenstein, who suggested that many words connect things by "family resemblances."[6] There is no one feature that runs through all members of a family. Father and daughter and niece have snub noses; niece, son, and two cousins have sandy hair; mother and just one cousin have small feet; and so forth. Only the niece has both a snub nose and sandy hair; no one has all the family features. Wittgenstein also compared names of classes to an old-fashioned hemp rope: it is very strong, but no one fiber runs through one hundred meters of rope. There need be no one bunch of things in common—necessary and sufficient conditions—for the same general word ("dog" or "multiple personality") to apply to a class of individuals.

Theoretical linguists find more structure in classes than mere family resemblance. Each class has best examples (of dogs, or of multiples), and then other examples that radiate away from the best examples. Thus many people, asked to give an example of a bird, apparently say, "Robin." People seldom offer "ostrich" or "pelican" straight off. The robin is a best example. The robin is what the psycholinguist Eleanor

Rosch calls a *prototype*.[7] Ostriches differ from robins in some ways; pelicans differ from robins in others. We cannot arrange all birds in a single linear order of birdiness, saying that pelicans are more birdy than ostriches but less birdy than robins. If we must draw a diagram, it should be a circle or sphere, with ostriches and pelicans farther from robins than hawks and sparrows, but not in one straight line. The class of birds may be thought of as *radial*, with different birds related by different chains of family resemblances, the chains leading in to a central prototype.[8] Likewise for mental illness, individual patients cannot be simply arranged as more "close to" or "distant from" standard cases. This is because the ways in which a patient differs from the standard may themselves be structured. A patient with no amnesia will also not be remarkable for gaps in personal history, or for having several distinct wardrobes that she does not understand. A patient with malicious persecutor alters will be expected also to be self-destructive and to have injured herself. The nonamnesic patient is not closer to or more distant from the prototype for multiple personality than is the self-destructive patient. There is a set of family resemblances among the patients, with some patients, prototypes, being best examples.

This idea of a prototype is implicit in psychiatry. For example, one of the companion publications to the *DSM* is the *Casebook*.[9] Under each coded disorder it gives, in plain prose, an example of a patient suffering from that disorder. These vignettes flesh out the formal criteria given in the *DSM*. Neither the *DSM* nor the *Casebook* is a substitute for clinical experience, but a reader might gain a better understanding of a disorder from the *Casebook* than from the *Manual*. Prototypes, and radial classes, whether for birds or for mental disorders, are not mere supplements to definitions. They are essential to comprehension. One can make a very strong argument, in the philosophy of language, that what people understand by a word is not a definition, but a prototype and the class of examples structurally arranged around the prototype. In chapter 7, I examine the idea that dissociation is distributed among people along a *linear* continuum. That is, there is one thing, dissociation, and everyone is slightly dissociative, some are more so, and multiples are the most dissociative of all. This hypothesis might prove less attractive if we thought of both multiple personality and dissociation as radial concepts. Just as it makes little sense to say that a pelican is birdier than an ostrich, so it may make little sense to say, of any two people, that one is more dissociative than the other.

We can easily distill, from the research and clinical literature, the prototype of a multiple during the 1980s. The point is not to give colorful examples, but to show what multiple personality meant to insiders during that decade. To begin with, many multiples came for help because they suffered from severe depression. Perhaps this is the most common symptom, but unfortunately it goes with a great many illnesses. When we start looking for something more specific, one early warning sign is missing time—the patient has no idea what she was doing for a couple of hours yesterday afternoon. Janice recalls leaving the café where she had a pleasant midday snack with her friend, and strolling back to her job as receptionist for a dentist. But she got a dressing-down when she arrived, because she did not walk in until just after 3:30. She has no idea what happened in between. Thus there may be gaps in the recent past (it turns out) because the main, public, personality has been replaced by an alter, of whose activities the host has no memory.

There are less blatant clues about time. After taking a life history, the clinician may notice that the narrative does not hang together very well. The patient is hazy about the past, and cannot recall what happened when, or is confused about the sequence of life events. Perhaps that is because unknown alters have taken control from time to time, and the host personality has no idea what they did or when they did it. We may suspect that an alter was in control for a whole year of a patient's life, a year that is at odds with the rest of the case history. For example, Steve's scholastic record may show that he was wildly erratic at school, doing wonderfully until seventh grade. At that point he got Ds in everything except a course that the transcript of his progressive school calls "Food" (i.e., home economics, or good old uneuphemistic cooking). He got an A in Food. In eighth grade he once again became the A student. Is this because Steve's female alter had come out in seventh grade? It turns out that Steve, now employed by the World Bank, had said, "I hate math" in seventh grade, just like a talking Barbie doll. So a clinician may start attending carefully to these two very different sides of Steve's life and in the end find two alternating personalities that persist today.

Obviously missing time is closely connected with the amnesia familiar to clinicians and now encoded in the criteria for multiplicity. Amnesia can be embarrassing for all sorts of reasons. You meet someone at a party who claims to know you; you have no idea who this is. Some patients say they are accused of being liars, for they deny doing something that other people saw them do. Perhaps an alter is the culprit.

Many of the presenting symptoms of multiples are common to many other disorders: bad headaches, sleepwalking, nightmares, and sometimes foggy memories of what seem to be troubling events long ago. Or a patient may complain of sharp and uncontrollable flashbacks, vivid and terrifying images of the past, of childhood. There may be severe mood swings every day. There can be horrible hallucinations, neither dream nor fantasy, during long twilight times that precede falling asleep, or in the drowsy periods before the patient awakens (in psychiatric jargon, hypnogenic and hypnopompic phenomena are common).

Many multiples have a history of alcoholism and drug addiction, although sometimes it is only an alter who drinks to excess. There have been stories of an alter who gets drunk on a drop, while another makes it through a whole bottle with decorum. One should be wary of such folklore, just as one should be wary of the claims made of some alters that they speak languages of which the host is ignorant—a phenomenon quite distinct from the case of a person who is genuinely bilingual and who uses one language for one persona, the second language for another. There has been the suggestion that obsessions and addictions are reactions to or results of early child abuse. For example, the resistance of many anorexics to therapy is elucidated by the fact that one alter personality is telling the host personality not to eat, while another is telling it to binge-eat; the obsession with oral intake is explained by forced oral sex in childhood.[10]

Stormy marriages or love affairs are the rule rather than the exception. What the clinician may see, on a first visit, is someone coming for help with these familiar matters of depression, addiction, or marital breakdown. In some florid cases, a multiple comes in because she is terrified—she wakes up, or comes to, in a strange place, a hotel room, or on a subway train, with no idea of how she got there or what she was doing. She may report hearing voices, not from outside, not from God, but inside her head. More commonly, however, there is a rambling report of assorted symptoms, a few of which, like auditory hallucinations, resemble the symptoms of schizophrenia. It is standard multiple gossip now to say: "Never tell the hospital you hear voices; otherwise they'll say you are schizophrenic. If you must talk about voices, make clear they are *inside* your head!"

The *DSM* symptom profile for multiple personality has one highly unusual entry: "The patient has long been diagnosed with many other psychiatric disorders." During the 1980s, investigators found that the average number of years a multiple spent in the mental health system prior to diagnosis was almost seven. Even today, only a committed clinician may be confident enough to diagnose multiple personality. To do so one must recognize and establish contact with alter personalities: you must see them come out and take control.

What are these alters like? In 1980 the *DSM-III* put it this way: "The individual personalities are nearly always quite discrepant and frequently seem to be opposites." When the presenting individual, the host, is conservative, cautious, and shy, one of the more prominent alters may be lively, flirtatious, and coarse. The *DSM* mentions "a quiet and retiring spinster" and "a flamboyant promiscuous bar habituée." The trait most clearly shared by the prototype of the modern multiple and the old double consciousness of over a century ago is that the host personality is reserved and inhibited, while an alter is lively and vivacious. But that is only the beginning. Unlike the old days of double consciousness, nowadays a multiple who never goes beyond two personalities is almost never encountered. A dozen alters is a common configuration; in some samples twenty-five per individual is the mean. People with more than a hundred alters are reported, although in these cases fewer than twenty will regularly assume executive control. Inevitably the more alters that are elicited, the more they seem to be mere personality fragments.

There is a language of multiplicity. *DSM-III* says that "transition from one personality to another is sudden," but in the multiple community this is called *switching*. Talk of an alter's taking executive control reeks of the business school; in real life, multiples say that an alter is *out*, or is coming out. Sometimes an alter may leave for *another place* to be alone. As multiple personality becomes more socially acceptable, some multiples prefer to refer to themselves as *we*, at least when speaking with a therapist, a family member, another multiple, or *themselves*.

Many alters are unaware that others exist within the same individual. This is especially true of the host, who at the beginning of treatment commonly denies being a multiple. On the other hand, some alters may know about other alters and actually be acquainted with them, talk with them, or jointly engage in some activity. This is called co-consciousness. The alters argue with each other, snarl, or console. One alter may be out and yet have another alter yammering away beside the left ear, telling her what a ninny she is. Many therapists try to introduce different alters to each other, believing that thoroughgoing co-consciousness is a necessary step toward integration. I should not give the impression that alters just come out as soon as a diagnosis is made. One clinician remarked that the experience is more like watching a few cats fighting underneath a blanket—a lot of noise, movement, and pain, but you can't make out the individual cats. Alters are encouraged and cultivated as therapist and patient come into a trusting relationship with one another.

A first step in therapy may be getting alters to respect each other. This is especially necessary because there are vicious, cruel alters, evil even to the point that they will threaten suicide in order to murder other alters whom they loathe. A psychiatrist may have to make contracts with such persecutors, getting them to agree that they will not go beyond certain limits. Alters are said to be literal but litigious. They abide by their promises, but the contract must be ironclad; if there is a loophole, an alter will find it and take advantage of it.[11]

Just to balance the sheet, there are also helpful alters, which some clinicians look for and encourage as assistants in the therapy. The most valuable of all may be an Inner Self-Helper, who knows all the alters, and who can encourage them to cooperate with the therapist and each other. And there are protector alters of various kinds. Cornelia Wilbur— a founding figure of the modern multiple movement and the doctor whose treatment was described in a famous multobiography of 1973, *Sybil*—had such a patient.[12] Jonah, an African American in Lexington, Kentucky, had three alters: Sammy, King Young, and Usoffa Abdulla. Sammy had formed when Jonah was six, after an incident when Jonah's mother had stabbed his father. King Young arose when his mother had dressed him in girl's clothes. The fourth character was a protector. When Jonah was nine or ten a gang of white boys was beating him up; suddenly Usoffa Abdulla sprang into action and demolished the gang. He was available for emergencies from that time on. And unlike Sammy and King Young, who had fairly rich characters, Usoffa Abdulla was very much a fragment, with little emotion or involvement with anyone else. Like the original Superman, he had no interest in sex. He was there to serve and protect. He is one of the most dignified and sympathetic fig- ures in the literature.[13]

Jonah was a man of the late sixties, an era of black pride and the Black Panthers. Even though he had only four personalities, he foreshadowed later prototypes in that the alters were traced back to childhood events. The alters coped with insult and violence. The theory of the alter as a coping device was coming into being, in part thanks to the work of Wilbur herself. But there was also a global change in sensibility, pro- duced by the hard work of activists in the women's movement. During the 1970s the public conception of child abuse and neglect was shifted to sexual abuse and incest. The theory of multiple personality followed in train. By 1986 a questionnaire survey of clinicians treating multiple personality produced a sample of one hundred patients, ninety-seven of whom reported experiencing significant trauma in childhood, most often sexual in nature.[14] This result has been repeatedly corroborated. By 1990 there was no firmer item of knowledge about multiple personality than the fact that it was caused by childhood trauma, usually repeated acts of sexual abuse. There are two mutually reinforcing aspects of this knowledge. On the one hand, virtually all multiples in therapy now have child alters. On the other hand, these child alters become, in treatment, witnesses to the abuse that brought them into being.

Very roughly there are two trajectories for an alter formed in childhood. Some remain child alters, forever locked in time. Others grow up and cope with incidents in later life that are reminiscent of the initial trauma. The alters of a single individual differ not only in age, but also in race, sexual inclination, and even sex. That is, a person whose body is of one sex may, when an alter is in control, resolutely claim the opposite physiology, rejecting all ordinary evidence to the contrary. I am not here speaking of a wish to be of the opposite sex, which some analysts might see as the root of the problem. The alter simply is of the opposite sex. "But what do you do when you go to the bathroom?" asks the doctor, who is a man, attempting to cast some light of reality on this delusion. "Same thing as you do, jerk." There is, then, an immense amount of gender confusion, and often, in therapy, it turns out to be connected with early incidents of incest, rape, sodomy. This or that alter may display mild versions of symptoms of old-fashioned hysteria. These are now called conversion symptoms: the patient is insensitive to pain in some region of the body, but without any neurological cause. There may even be temporary paralysis of a limb. Often these effects can be traced back to some assault, on that part of the body, during childhood.

In many respects multiples are conformists—they are so far from being "mad" that some of the alters are different types of normal people. You can learn a lot about contemporary culture from the life of a multiple. I mentioned Jonah and the Black Panthers; in another old case, the promiscuous alter of a very proper host was the first to wear miniskirts in her small town in Iowa. More recently, "shop till you drop" is not a bad joke but sound sociology. A prudent penny-pinching host has an alter who shops endlessly and extravagantly. Or there is the cool, brisk administrative assistant of a rising executive. She dresses impeccably in tailored suits. She has a small closet where sensible clothes hang neatly on padded hangers. But there is another wardrobe that she stays away from, packed messily with glitzy sequined garments she has seen only in late-night reruns of old B movies. When she last looked into the wardrobe she shut it in a hurry; the stuff in there was repugnant, frivolous, lewd. She has endless credit cards. Even when she destroys unwanted cards new ones appear. Bills from strange shops in another part of town keep coming in. She pays them.

Many diagnosed multiples work in service industries—including teaching, nursing, and the law, as well as waiting tables, processing driver's licenses, and retailing in the mall. Alters are a nuisance at work because an antagonistic alter will burst in and take over when you're talking to your boss or a customer. Multiples develop strategies to cover up the gross gaffes committed by misbehaving alters. In this respect they are a bit like maintenance alcoholics. Marie, a heavyset woman, is serving from a street-side stall in Ottawa where she sells hot dogs and *poutine*, a Québec dish of fried potatoes and cottage cheese smothered in gravy. Two men drive up and ask for hot dogs. These men and their wieners remind her of her uncle and his drunken crony who would take her for rides and abuse her. She gives a little cry and shrinks to the size of a four-year-old, or so it seems to her. She is crouched under the countertop, whimpering to herself; Esther has come out but as quickly retreats. Then Marie is standing up again, smiling—"Merde, I spilled some *poutine*, had to clean it up."

But this is only one side of the story. Some multiples use their alters to take care of different jobs. One takes dictation, meekly producing letter after letter, while the host has withdrawn to another place. A woman who wants to have nothing to do with sex has an alter who does it with her husband. A mother would never do anything to harm her children. But she does slap them around, they say, and there are bruises to show for it. Only the mother's alter could express that anger. A long-running court case in Columbia, South Carolina, has to do with alimony. In that state, if a wife can be proven to have committed adultery, she will not be awarded alimony in divorce proceedings. One woman's psychologist clinician, Larry Nelson, testifies in court that his client was faithful; it was an alter who slept with other men.[15]

Different alters may use different handwriting.[16] Older multiples who wear glasses say that they need different prescription glasses for different personalities, and they may carry several pairs around with them. Some clinicians believe that physiological or biochemical differences are associated with switches from one alter to another. That is a good research project, but at present there is no reproducible evidence that these differences are even as great as occur during changes of moods in healthy people.[17] Autonomic nervous system responses to noxious stimuli are known to carry over from alter to alter, unhindered by switching.[18] It is nevertheless to be expected that there will be all sorts of what are called objective differences between alters. Anger often shows up in high blood pressure; fear makes you sweat. It would be astounding to learn that there is no detectable physiological change when a persecutor alter is out, or when a brusque waitress has turned into a terrified child.

Multiples are incredibly suggestible and are easily hypnotized. Often in a therapeutic session an alter will be in a trancelike state, in which memories come in and out and switches occur rapidly. Eugene Bliss, another founding figure of the multiple personality movement, wrote in 1980 that "to enter the domain of the personalities is childishly simple, for the key to the door is hypnosis and these patients are excellent hypnotic subjects. This is the world of hypnosis. Personalities hidden for decades may be accosted and interviewed, or forgotten memories can be encountered and relived by the subject with all the emotional intensity of a contemporary event."[19] What with all the current talk of suggestion and false memories, few today would be as incautious as Bliss. Yet his innocent enthusiasm is not to be dismissed. Trance states are one of the very few common denominators in a majority of individuals who, in the course of the past two hundred years or so, have satisfied the *DSM* criteria for multiple personality.

Observers have always reported a different "look" to different alters, and have sometimes included drawings or photographs in their reports in order to suggest the change. This practice is over a century old. We have a set of photographs of the very first *multiple* personality in history—the first clinical case of an individual said to have more than two stable and distinct alters. That was Louis Vivet, first presented as a multiple in 1885, whom I describe in chapter 12. Likewise the very first individual whose dissociative fugues were studied at length—Albert Dad., in 1887—was recorded photographically in three states, namely, normal, hypnotized, and during a fugue.[20] Thus multiplicity was made visual from the very beginning, and faithfully followed new technologies. After movies had been invented, they were used to record switches.[21] And now there are innumerable videos. However, even videos do not seem to the casual observer as striking as they do to experienced therapists. To counteract this, some exponents offer us scenes of very radical changes in demeanor. On several occasions I have watched videos after which the presenter said, "Not even the most gifted actress could

31

change roles so well, so abruptly." My impression was that any ham could have done better. I'm not saying that the patient was faking, only that the roles were poorly done. And why not? Why should we expect an anorexic woman from Chicago, who is severely upset and in a florid state, to act at one moment just like a two-hundred-pound male truck driver from Alabama, and at the next just like a scared three-year-old in a blizzard? No, we are offered sharply distinguished caricatures. In order for it to be clear that the alters are distinct personalities, it does help to have them of different ages, races, sizes, voices.

Some really dysfunctional multiples going through a bad patch switch personalities very rapidly, each time assuming a new stock character. The effect is similar to that of switching TV channels by channel surfing. This impression is enhanced because patients with a great many alters often choose, for some of their personalities, the names of characters in sitcoms, soaps, and crime series. It happens that TV remote controls became widely available in America just about the time that today's florid multiples became abundant. I am not saying that multiples self-consciously act out television fantasies—or, at any rate, that they do so any more than the rest of us. We constantly mimic others. Art, from great to tawdry, presents us with a selection of stylized characters from whom we acquire bits of our own ever-evolving personal style—and on whom, selectively, we mold our own character. It is very important not to think that there is a special kind of truth about multiples, that each alter is revealing a secret soul, hidden since childhood as an escape from cruelty, but profoundly real. No. The alters are, in this respect, just like the rest of us, if a little more circumscribed in their range of emotions. They too respond to their environment, the people they meet, the stories they watch.

I must repeat that I am describing a prototype. Many patients and their symptoms radiate away from the prototype, but that does not show they are not true multiples any more than the oddities of an ostrich make it any the less a bird. Here is one newly published account: "To me, having multiple personalities does not feel like I have lots of people living inside my body. Rather I find myself thinking and talking to myself in different tones and accents. Some of the voices that talk in my mind sound like children. When I allow them to talk to other people they don't talk like children to impress anyone or be dramatic. I have to talk like that sometimes in order to express what I need to say. I can't say it from my adult voice. . . . Then there are the deep-raspy intent voices that say the meanest things you could imagine. When they talk, I feel hard inside, I feel cold and calculating."[22] The writer describes herself as a victim of extremely severe ritual abuse. Most of the time she is, as you can see, very much in control; she *permits* the child voices to speak. But when the topic of cults comes up, other voices flow uncontrollably out of her mouth. Clearly this author is at some distance from the prototype I have been describing, especially in that the illness is expressed almost entirely in terms of talking, and not of discordant actions or lost time. This does not show that I have misdescribed the prototype. On the contrary, a radial class has a central prototype and a large number of examples some distance from the prototype, which vary from the prototype, all with their own characteristic idiosyncrasies.

There is now no difficulty in summarizing the 1980s prototype for multiple personality: a middle-class white woman with the values and expectations of her social group. She is in her thirties, and she has quite a large number of distinct alters—sixteen, say. She spent a large part of her life denying the very existence of these alters. The alters include children, persecutors, and helpers, and at least one male alter. She was sexually abused on many occasions by a trusted man in her family when she was very young. She has suffered many other indignities from people from whom she needs love. The needs are, among other things, part of her class values, which may be abetted or taken advantage of by her abuser. She has previously been through parts of the mental health system and has been diagnosed with many complaints, but her treatments have not helped her in the long run until she came to a clinician sensitive to multiple personality. She has amnesia for parts of her past. She has the experience of "coming to" in a strange situation with no idea of how she got there. She is severely depressed and has quite often thought about suicide.

That is the prototype, the typical multiple as presented in expositions by mental health professionals all over North America, an increasingly regular part of the education of anyone training to be a therapist. It is not something stated in official manuals but rather part of the culture, part of the specialized language of multiplicity. Every special branch of knowledge has just such prototypes. It is not a defect in the multiple personality movement that the prototype is not spelled out exactly in any textbook, for prototypes are the carriers of meaning before textbooks are written or understood. Full mastery comes only in clinical experience. This is not because psychiatry is somehow a "soft" or nebulous science; the case is much the same in physics. T. S. Kuhn insisted in his famous book *The Structure of Scientific Revolutions* that you can't learn

33

physics from the texts—you have to do the problems at the back of the book.

How then do we know what the prototype is? By looking and listening. All the features that I have mentioned recur in the literature, but a prototype is more general than that. It is part of what people understand by a concept, what they point to when they want to explain it. When I casually meet someone who is in training for some sort of eclectic lay therapy, I will hear, "Oh, we had a class on multiples last week." And on inquiry I get something like the prototype I have just described.

There is no doubt that prototypes can be misused. They can be presented in such a way as to have dramatic effects on susceptible listeners. As we shall see in chapter 8, a radical wing of the multiple movement believes that many patients have been programmed by ritualistic cults. Yet we can find something very much like cult initiation, with many of the trappings of dubious religion, within the multiple movement itself. It relies heavily on presenting the prototype in a compelling narrative, and inviting each listener to feel that prototype awakening within herself. A striking example is furnished by a July 1994 newsletter from North Carolina. It is written by Gary Peterson, an influential psychiatrist at the forefront of research on child multiple personalities. He urges fellow students of dissociation in his region to spread the word—that is, inculcate the prototype. He says that far too many people still rely on Eve or Sybil or Oprah Winfrey for their information.

> Where can one find these uninitiated? Many places.
>
> We can find them in our churches and other places of worship, at Women's and Men's Centers, at Rape Crises, at mental health centers, at schools, at local self help and business organizations, and many other local institutions.

Peterson urges his followers to work with any such group. He suggests one approach. Begin a presentation "with a life course story." First of all, warm up audience members by asking them to go through a time regression back to the moment of their birth. Then ask "them to consider what it would be like to have a life such as the one about to be described." He next provides a script. He tells his acolytes to "read the story deliberately and emotionally, stopping at appropriate places to let the audience absorb the impact of what has just been said." The age-regression just conducted is reversed: it begins at birth and goes up year by year. It gradually brings out every aspect in the prototype of the multiple, including all the features I have mentioned, plus a rich life history of abuse and confusion. The script concludes at the age of twenty-eight, when the wretched woman whose life course is enacted—and which is to be felt and experienced by the audience—has gone through two divorces, much missing time, many therapies.[23] Members of the audience are urged to feel like that . . . to become like that. This is a powerful way to create mental illness in susceptible auditors. In this book I refrain from personal criticism, as opposed to analysis of texts, but it would be wrong not to state that this procedure seems thoroughly pernicious.

But there is nothing wrong with characterizing an illness by a prototype. A prototype, to repeat, is not an average. Many multiples are as ostriches to birds; I have offered the examples of Jonah, an African-American man, and Marie, an underpaid Québecoise who daily crosses the river from the French-speaking slums of Hull (Québec) to the polished streets of Ottawa (Ontario) to sell *poutine*. Jonah, Marie, and the victim of cult abuse whom I quoted earlier are all on the edges of that classification, multiple personality; each differs from the prototype in his or her own way. There is nothing linear about radial classifications.

Far from being fuzzy, the use of prototypical examples is sound science and is often essential to conveying meaning. For that very reason, it distances us from real people. Even when the prototypes of which we are told are colorful—nay, florid—they are used only to fix ideas. They don't tell us what it feels like to be a multiple. How does it feel? That is a natural question, but be cautious. Multiples asked to say how they feel give perfectly good answers, and they don't say anything very special. They tend to pick up the current lingo and talk about themselves much as anyone else does. That is how language works. When the multiples are not emphasizing the alters, their most notable feature besides depression may be a sort of confusion, daze, haziness, unclarity about bits of the past, an inability to fit together memories and current unhappiness. But how does it feel! Miserable, scary, that's how it feels. What is it like to be in a daze? Or drunk? Or lost in thought? Can you say very much by way of describing how it feels to be in those states, except by using those very words? Most of us cannot, but the words suffice. The teetotaler may not know exactly how I feel when drunk, any more than the man of whole limbs knows exactly how it felt when I broke my arm, but there is no special problem about mental states. Many therapists believe it helps their clients to get them to talk about their feelings; when they do talk, there is no difficulty understanding what they say.

Now we are in philosophical country, the problem of other minds.[24] It is good to call a commonsense witness, an expert on multiple personality, but not on the higher reaches of Wittgenstein. I mean Cornelia Wilbur. There have been many multobiographies since the 1973 story of her work with "Sybil." A recent one is *The Flock: The Autobiography of a Multiple Personality*.[25] It is not an autobiography but, like *Sybil*, a novelized true story told by a professional writer. Shortly before her death in 1992, Dr. Wilbur allowed the publishers to quote her for advertising purposes. *The Flock*, she told them, "states the disorder with understanding and gives a clear indication of what being a multiple is like."[26] Exactly so. There is no other way to know, and there is no special problem about knowing what it is like to be a multiple.

There is, however, a problem about treating human beings as specimens. If you look from the point of view of the doctor, the classroom, or the medical anthropologist, multiples seem distressingly similar to each other, all clustered around the prototype. Every one is different, though: each is filled with a unique history of shame and pain and confusion, but also aware of some good times, many hopes, and often lots of happy achievement. So I have to apologize for the impersonal, distanced way in which I refer to real people. An account of multiplicity can quickly turn into a freak show. Indeed P. T. Barnum probably did invite one seeming multiple to join the circus.[27] Multiples have done service for Geraldo Rivera and Oprah Winfrey. Those shows have an important role in modern American life, but they sensationalize, they stereotype, they are the circuses of our days. I have encountered many dismissive references to those shows in the writings, presentations, and lectures of multiple personality clinicians—and nary a good word for the talk shows, which revel in controversies that highlight the bizarre. I see things differently. Many of those shows are brilliant. They are a forum for a great spectrum of ordinary—and amazingly articulate—Americans to whom nobody else pays much attention. Multiples are among them: very ordinary persons who are suffering a great deal, and who probably have suffered even more. We are talking about how they cope and survive in a world that has too often been hostile. We are talking about failed love, about background cruelty, about family violence, about how to confront and overcome terror, evil, indifference. I apologize to all those individuals, anywhere, who see or feel their personality fragmented but who resent being treated as specimens. I am sorry about the extent to which I distance myself from their suffering. I shall occasionally be critical of, or even hold in contempt, this or that expert on multiple personality, whether skeptic or advocate. I am of course as cynical as anyone else about a few actresses who enjoy public wallowing in the trough of their early abuse and subsequent multiplicity. But for ordinary patients, appropriate emotions are empathy and respect, which is not to say that one should be permissive or indulgent.

Multiples have formed themselves into self-help groups. Early attempts tended to be unstable, for if one person switched into an aggressive alter during a meeting, everyone else felt threatened. Unless there is a nonmultiple facilitator present, more switching may occur, and pandemonium can break out. One group that has tried to get itself together is in Ashville, North Carolina, where the Highland Hospital has a Dissociative Disorders Unit. In January 1993, some of its clients formed a Multiple Personality Consortium, now legally incorporated as a nonprofit organization. It began with about 30 members; by the end of the year there were about 130. Debbie Davis, a businesswoman and a multiple, is a leader of the consortium. She is also chair of the Patient Liaison Committee of the International Society for the Study of Multiple Personality and Dissociation.[28] She hopes to change the name to the Client Liaison Committee. "We feel that is more empowering." She says that the consortium has a transition house in which clients of the hospital can prepare to move back into the world. It maintains a support group regularly attended by between 11 and 20 multiples. The consortium arranges trips—for example, to Six Flags over Georgia—and has regular peer-led meetings. Social get-togethers are particularly welcome, because they provide an opportunity for child alters to come out. One evening it is finger painting for four-year-olds; another it is the *Just So Stories*. It is clear that Davis and her group are unhappy with the very word "disorder" no matter how it is modified, whether as multiple personality disorder or as dissociative identity disorder.

Now whether or not Davis was telling the whole story about her consortium—such enterprises are of their nature bound to have disruptions—we have evidence here of another stage in the evolution of multiplicity. Could this cease to be a disorder and become a way of life? Some multiples feel threatened at the thought of being cured, of developing one and only one personality, for they lose companions who help them cope with difficult situations. Others feel they have found a community of like-minded people, each of whom dissociates into alters. Multiple self-help groups, which are found all over the continent, have until now developed and progressed in their own ways. Davis intends to bring them all into a communicating network. An electronic bulletin board for multiples was founded several years ago. These people hope to become more and more empowered. And so there may evolve subcultures of multiples, or even a larger, networked, continental subculture. Not everyone favors this development. Richard Kluft concluded an address to the November 1993 meeting of fellow professionals in Chicago by challenging what he called "the MPD subculture."

> Part of the socially prescribed role of being ill is working to recover and leave your illness behind. We are in a position where many of our MPD patients and some of us ourselves are not necessarily bearing this in mind. Instead we are giving license to a lot of MPD patients sitting around learning how to deal with an MPD environment, making MPD friends, talking MPD all day. . . . I think we're giving the implicit message to many MPD patients that MPD is forever. . . . The wish to be validated and not to be alone with one's illness is understandable. . . . We all understand the wonderful forces that group cohesion and group membership can bring. However, it is important to realize that one's commonality should not only be to have MPD, but to get rid of it as soon as possible and to go on with one's life.

I began this chapter talking about a feedback effect, the way in which classifications affect the people classified, and vice versa. In medicine, the authorities who know, the doctors, tend to dominate the known about, the patients. The known about come to behave in the ways that the knowers expect them to. But not always. Sometimes the known take matters into their own hands. The famous example is gay liberation. The word "homosexual," along with the medical and legal classification, emerged during the last half of the nineteenth century. For a time the classification was owned by medicine, by physicians and psychiatrists. The knowers determined, at least on the surface, what it was to be a homosexual. But then the known took charge. I do not suppose, even now, that multiples will do that. But I am well aware of how things change. In the fall of 1983 I said, "At the risk of giving offense, I suggest that the quickest way to see the contrast between making up multiple personalities and making up homosexuals is to try to imagine multiple-personality bars. Multiples, insofar as they are declared, are under care, and the syndrome, the form of behavior, is orchestrated by a team of experts. Whatever the medico-forensic experts tried to do with their categories, the homosexual person became autonomous of the labeling, but the multiple is not."[29] I may yet come to eat those words.

The Movement

WE HAVE BEEN FAMILIAR with psychological "movements" ever since madness was medicalized, and certainly since the advent of psychoanalysis. No one hesitates to speak of the movement founded and orchestrated by Sigmund Freud. Multiplicity has no founding and controlling parent, but if ever there was a movement, it is the multiple personality movement. It has a rather fresh, American quality to it. It appeals to down-home folks, who are much more at ease with the bizarre than city slickers are. Although the professional organization, the International Society for the Study of Multiple Personality and Dissociation, was established by psychiatrists (M.D.'s) and a few psychologists (Ph.D.'s), the movement has had an egalitarian look. Patients and doctors share platforms. At the May 1994 Fourth Annual Spring Conference of the ISSMP&D, the full registration fee for ISSMP&D members was $250, but there was a category for patients, "Multiple Attending Members," with a $25 reduction. From the beginning, when the leading figures were at the podium, it was Connie and Buddy and Rick and Cathy, not Dr. This and Dr. That. As for patients, some afflicted people find it a relief to be able to come out and manifest their multiplicity in public. Thus the movement has been able to draw both on the recent language of liberation—for example, gay liberation—and on older memories of fundamentalist revival meetings. No statistics exist, and perhaps none could exist, but many therapists who work with multiples say that they themselves have suffered from dissociative disorders, and add that they recovered memories of childhood abuse during their own therapy.

In the coarse measure of decades, the multiple movement germinated in the sixties, emerged in the seventies, matured in the eighties, and is adapting itself to new environments in the nineties. If my talk of a movement seems a little sardonic, consider that when I subscribed to *Dissociation*, "The Official Journal of the International Society for the Study of Multiple Personality and Dissociation," and became an Affiliate of the Society, I received a document designed to look just like a medical school diploma. An accompanying flyer enjoined me as follows: "Display your professionalism. Be proud of your commitment to the field of multiple personality and dissociative disorders. Display your certificate in a handsome membership plaque ($18.00 including shipping/handling)." Successful movements require accidents, essentials, and institutions. They begin in corridors, in chance encounters of like minds, in late-night conversations, in small but vigorous meetings. Both hard work and some charisma are needed. But a movement will "take" only if there is a larger social setting that will receive it. The essential ingredient for the multiple movement has been the American obsession with child abuse, a mix of fascination, revulsion, anger, and fear. I shall describe some of that in the next chapter, and I conclude this one with a few words about institutions. First I will describe three isolated initiating events each of which has left its stamp on the movement. Before there were any thoughts of institutionalizing multiple personality, the achievements of three people stand out: Cornelia Wilbur (1908–1992), Henri Ellenberger (1905–1992), and, in the next generation, Ralph Allison.

Wilbur was a psychiatrist and psychoanalyst, but her impact came largely through the novel about her patient Sybil. There has always been a popular face to the idea of multiple personality. The romantic fiction and poetry of the nineteenth century positively reeks of duality. *Dr. Jekyll and Mr. Hyde* is the best known, Dostoyevsky's Mr. Golyadkin of *The Double* is the greatest artistic creation, and James Hogg's *The Private Memoirs and Confessions of a Justified Sinner* is the one that scares me the most. There is a host of lesser works. Stories, rather than medicine, entrenched the idea of the double in European consciousness. The modern movement has thrived not on fiction but on a new genre, the multobiography. This is the book-length story of a multiple, usually packaged as an "as-told-to," and often turned into a movie or TV special.

The Three Faces of Eve set the pace.[1] Surprisingly many people have heard of this 1957 work, even though they cannot remember ever having read the book or seen the movie. Perhaps it is the brilliant title that we remember. *Eve* was the work of two psychiatrists who treated Chris Costner Sizemore. In 1954 they wrote her up for an academic journal.[2] Their popularized book of the case became a best-seller, and the movie did well. But *Eve* did not begin the modern movement. No one who writes in movement literature has a good word to say for the book, and many critics voice harsh judgment of her psychiatrists. In order for multiple personality to take off, it needed a larger cultural framework within which it could be explained and located. That framework was child abuse. *Eve* happened before child abuse had become an American obsession. Written in an age of innocence, the book did nothing to make multiplicity intelligible.

There are specific reasons why *Eve* is light-years away from more recent multiplicity. The doctors in charge elicited only three personalities. The patient took over the story and wrote three books giving very different visions of her life—these books, in retrospect, are the three faces of Eve. First, using a pseudonym, and with the support of her doctors, she published her own version of their story, *The Final Faces of Eve*.[3] Those faces were not final, for she later went public, granting a scoop to the *Washington Post* on 25 May 1975. She reneged on her doctors, upon whom she poured scorn in her next book, *I'm Eve*.[4] She found more than twenty personalities and her own hidden history of abuse. She did not so much join the movement as serve as a perfect exemplar of the new vision of multiplicity that emerged in the 1970s—including misdiagnosis or maltreatment by an earlier generation of doctors. She went on the lecture circuit denouncing her former therapists, although movement psychiatrists gave the impression of keeping their distance from her. Does one ever trust a double agent? Sizemore was not yet finished. In 1989 she gave us *A Mind of My Own*.[5] It turns out that her first alters had been with her from birth. That's because they are past-life alters.

Eve's original psychiatrists were later to condemn the profligacy and propagandizing of the multiple movement. They accused it of finding vastly too many multiples.[6] 'Eve,' they implied, had been correctly treated, even if she later fell into bad company. A clinician might at best see one or two genuine cases of multiple personality in a lifetime. The epidemic that surged in the late 1970s was, they said, largely composed of unhappy people who cultivated symptoms that made them feel important, and was fostered by uncritical medicine.

So the multiple movement was introduced not by *The Three Faces of Eve* but by a very different multobiography: *Sybil*, published in 1973.[7] It too became a movie, a very long one. I recently watched the film in the company of a mixed bag of undergraduates. Even they found it pretty horrifying, these young people who have lived their whole lives in a media world that made them sharply aware of family violence. The book is a fictionalized "as told to" story. Cornelia Wilbur began treating Sybil in Nebraska; it happened that when Wilbur moved to New York to begin psychoanalytic training, Sybil also moved there to enter graduate school, and resumed treatment. Wilbur began to uncover Sybil's personalities. The process continued even when Wilbur moved on to a medical school position in Lexington, Kentucky.[8]

Wilbur's professional accounts of the case were routinely rejected by scholarly and medical journals, apparently on the grounds that no one could take multiple personality seriously. One crushing insult followed upon a paper she read at the annual meeting of the American Academy of Psychoanalysis. Wilbur believed that the academy published all the papers that were read, but she was telephoned and told there were "space problems." Since Sybil's story would not be received by the experts, it had to be told for the public. It was written up by a journalist, Flora Rheta Schreiber. Schreiber insisted that Sybil be cured before she began work.[9] A book without a happy ending would not sell. When Sybil was cured, Schreiber came to live in what had virtually become the Wilbur-Sybil ménage, and wrote the book. Wilbur had at least six other multiples under her care during that period, one of whom was Jonah, whom I mentioned in the previous chapter.[10]

Wilbur's work broke new ground because she actively sought out childhood traumas. She traced Sybil's multiplicity to perverse, vindictive, and usually sexually oriented assaults by Sybil's mother. Wilbur was no orthodox Freudian. She worked on Sybil's memories with both hypnosis (anathema to Freud) and Amytal.[11] She did not believe in the ritualized distancing between patient and analyst demanded by American psychoanalysis. The two women became friends, went for long rides in the country, and lived for a while in the same house. Sybil's treatment involved 2,534 office hours. It took so long, Wilbur was to tell people, only because in the 1960s there was simply no knowledge about multiple personality.[12]

A doctrinaire Freudian would work with Sybil's memories of abuse in order to help the patient understand what they meant to her in the present. It would be of little moment whether these were true memories or fantasies. But the growing bond, in popular awareness, between child abuse and perverse family sex was a perfect fit for the mistreatment of Sybil by her mother. That involved not just cruelty but a barely concealed sexual fetishism—constant punishment by cold water enemas, with the anus tied so as to prevent expulsion. Her mother stuck sharp objects into her anus and vagina. There was what has since become a dreary litany of sex-associated cruelty. Wilbur went on to confirm, as best she could, that the events Sybil painfully came to remember really had happened. She went to the family home and saw at least the instruments of torture, the enema bag, the tool for lacing boots that had been stuck into Sybil's orifices. The passive father did not contradict the stories. Of course the existence of the objects of torture—which were also, in those days, common household furnishings—did not prove that they had been perverted for sadistic uses. But Wilbur believed Sybil, and by the time of the book and above all the film, no one could doubt the reality.

Sybil became a prototype for what was to count as a multiple. She was an intelligent young woman, with a promising career, who experienced substantial periods of lost time. She had fugue episodes; she would recover herself in a strange place with no idea how she got there. But other features are more important. Patients in the past had tended to have two or three or even four alters. Sybil had sixteen. There were child alters. There were two alters of the opposite sex. Some alters knew about others. They argued, fought, tried to help or destroy each other. This idea of dynamic relationships between different personalities had been glimpsed before, but it was the reports of Sybil that made them prominent. Above all, the etiology of her disorder was writ large. She really had been abused as a child. "Sybil," the main presenting personality, had no memory of those sorry events. But her alters did remember. Indeed they had been created in order to cope with horror. They would be dissociated from the main personality, so that Sybil, herself, did not need to be conscious of those scars. She did not need to hate her mother, who had done those things to her. She could even love her mother, while some of the alters were full of hate. Other alters lived out a life that Sybil would like to have lived, had she not been so assaulted when she was growing up.

In only one way did Sybil differ from the subsequent prototype of the multiple. She had been abused by her mother, not her father or another male. Sexual abuse and incest did not fully reach public consciousness until 1975, two years after *Sybil*'s publication. In the years after 1975, sexual abuse was primarily abuse by men in the extended family. The story of Sybil did not fit that mold. Her father was passive, at best a facilitator. The evil figure was the sadistic mother.

Sybil set the stage. A very large book of a very different type provided a magnificent backdrop for the revival of multiple personality and dissociation. Henri Ellenberger's *The Discovery of the Unconscious* dwarfs most other contributions to the history of psychiatry.[13] It will long remain the most richly textured study of thinking about the unconscious before Freud, and of the relationships between that thinking and later

43

dynamic psychiatry. The book is the work of an extraordinary amateur, in the best sense of that word, one who deeply loved his subject and devoted his life to it, while earning his living as a psychiatrist and teacher.[14] Ellenberger recovered a good deal of the history of multiple personality in the nineteenth century. He brought to life the greatest theorist of the subject, the man who invented the very word *dissociation* in its present psychiatric sense—Pierre Janet, who had once been an influential French theorist and investigator. Psychoanalysis has been opposed to multiple personality as an independent diagnosis and may be responsible for the waning of multiplicity during the first half of the twentieth century. But one thing is certain. Freud personally saw Janet as a threat and a rival, and was at pains to emphasize the originality of his own ideas and the triviality of Janet's. Janet was a victim of Freud's self-aware management of the psychoanalytic movement. Janet was a scholar; Freud, by comparison, was an entrepreneur who annihilated Janet's reputation. Unfortunately, Janet's repeated remarks about Freud's success read so much like childish spite that the reader's sympathy for the loser is undermined.[15]

When Janet died in 1947 he was almost completely forgotten. But not by Ellenberger, who had known Janet, and who deeply admired his achievements. Ellenberger saw Freud as one in a long line of contributors, and as one who owed much to Janet. Janet himself came to maturity in the heyday of French multiple personalities. He personally studied a number of the most celebrated French multiples. He formulated a theory of multiplicity, and its dynamics, a model suggested by his choice of French words such as *dissociation* and *désagrégation*. The word "dissociation" entered English in 1890 thanks to William James, who was fascinated by French psychology, and who was deeply impressed by Janet as a person. Morton Prince, the great American pioneer of multiple personality who came to lead the Boston school of psychology, also used the word in print in 1890, after his visit to France, and it was he who cemented it into English.[16] Janet, in contrast, dropped the word after his philosophy thesis of 1889, *Psychological Automatism*. I shall point out, in chapter 9 below, that he even ceased to take multiple personality seriously. He decided it was a special case of what is today called bipolar disorder. That is, he came to think that multiples are manic-depressives. But Ellenberger said virtually nothing about Janet's later work. Hence the legend has accumulated around Janet that he was the great founder of the theory of dissociation.

Ellenberger had nothing to do with the multiple personality movement. But the publication of his book made plain that multiple personality had once been an important part of psychiatric thinking. It showed that there was a nonpsychoanalytic but dynamic model of the mind that had been buried by the analysts. The book helped to legitimate multiple personality. Ellenberger unwittingly made it possible for Janet to become the patriarch of dissociation. Fledgling movements tend to have a Manichaean view of the world; they are the Forces of Good fighting real Evil. It helps to have mythic figures to represent the conflict. Once Ellenberger had brought Janet back to life, one could see Janet as Hero, a sort of Anti-Freud.

Ellenberger had another effect that was pure accident. He inspired Richard Kluft, a founding member of the ISSMP&D and the editor of its journal *Dissociation*. Kluft may have treated more multiples than anyone else; he has the most impressive success rates in therapy leading to integration; he probably has had more patients referred to him for assessment than any other therapist.[17] Kluft became fascinated by multiples as a young psychiatrist "who first encountered MPD phenomena in 1970." He could get no advice. When *Sybil* appeared, a professor told him it was a fake and he did not read it. Ralph Allison, whom I next describe, was out west and had not published yet. Where did Kluft get his multiple lore? "I hold in high esteem a man whom I consider my teacher, Antoine Despine, M.D., a French general practitioner of high repute, and a student of magnetism (hypnosis), [who] appears to be the first to have effected a non-exorcistic cure of MPD, in his treatment of 'Estelle.'"[18] Despine was a fashionable spa doctor; Estelle was an eleven-year-old girl. Despine treated her in 1836 and wrote her up in 1838. I shall say more about Estelle in chapter 10. "Despine was indeed my teacher," Kluft repeats, yet he did not read Despine. "I read about Despine, over and over, in Ellenberger." Ellenberger wrote a two-page summary of the case of Estelle, just the right length to read over and over again.[19] Ellenberger knew about Despine because for a short time in midcareer Janet referred often to the case and even discovered that his early star patient, Léonie, had probably been trained by a previous handler to pattern her behavior after Estelle's.[20] Here then is a typical accident in the history of science. Ellenberger's uncritical account of a book published 130 years earlier served by chance as a model for an ambitious young man trying to carve out a new way in psychiatry.

Ralph Allison created his own model. In 1980 George Greaves stated that "there are conservatively some fifty cases of multiple personality that have been identified during the past decade," i.e., between 1970 and 1979.[21] His tally of 50 was remarkable, for he had located only 14 cases between 1944 and 1969, seven of which were patients of Cornelia Wilbur. Twenty of the 50 new cases had been described, with some overlap, by a total of 28 clinicians, *excluding* Ralph Allison. Allison was cited in connection with 36 of the 50 cases.[22] He also knew "a psychiatrist in Honolulu who has seen 50 cases, and one in Phoenix who has seen 30." The latter was Milton Erickson, the greatest of hypnotherapists, who told Allison that the thirty patients were incurable.[23]

Allison's writing reveals a man of vast enthusiasms, deeply caring for his patients, and charmingly romantic. In his 1980 autobiography *Minds in Many Pieces* he described not only his rediscovery of multiple personality but also a good deal of pain. He was honest almost to the point of masochism in confessing two failures, one patient who killed herself, and a client who participated in the gang rape of a woman and then murdered her.[24] He was sensitive to the harms done to children, but he was able to see that sexual cruelty and exploitation were only one feature of a configuration. In 1974, writing for the new Californian periodical *Family Therapy*, he published "A Guide to Parents: How to Raise Your Daughter to Have Multiple Personality."[25] Using three of his patients as examples, he offered seven rules for a parent who would like to have a multiple daughter. In the first place, don't want your child. Let mother and father be at loggerheads, with at most one of them serving as a model for your child, the other despised. The preferred parent should leave home before your child is six years old. Encourage rivalry with her brothers and sisters. Be ashamed of her older relatives and family tree. Ensure that her first sex experience is disgusting, rape at thirteen, say. Make home life so miserable that she will want to leave and marry as soon as possible—setting up house with a mate who perpetuates this tradition of repulsive family life.

Many recent publications about multiples are tricked out with the apparatus of statistics—and with fashionable scientific metaphors, parallel distributed processing, state dependent learning, or whatever. Allison's writings are from another world and another time. He practiced in Santa Cruz, California, in the late 1960s. In trying to understand the self, he suggested that Theosophy provides the best model. "There is one life in all beings." The task of every human being is to come to be aware of one's Inner Self, tranquil and understanding, a self that shares in that one world-life. "To be truly in touch with one's Inner Self," he wrote, "is the key to mental and spiritual health. Patients with multiple personality provide a striking example of persons who have lost touch with that inner part of them which is creative, non neurotic, problem-solving and everything else that is needed to survive and grow in the world as it is." The doctor needs this sensibility, for "the therapist must be in touch with his own Inner Self, since his Inner Self is in constant communication with the patient's Inner Self."

The last thing that an emergent science wants is intimations of Madame Blavatsky, so Allison has been slightly marginalized. In retrospect he is honored as the pioneer of the first protocol for treating multiple personality disorder, a suitably scientific-sounding achievement.[26] But it was his proselytizing that fired up the movement. During the late 1970s it was he, above all others, who was organizing workshops on multiplicity at the annual meetings of the American Psychiatric Association, and even presenting papers in the main program.[27] He circulated copies of two manuals about the psychotherapy of multiple personality.[28] His idea of the Inner Self Helper was cautiously accepted, at least in the early days, by some mainstream psychiatrists. In his conception, the Helper is not at all like alters as envisaged by modern multiple theory. It is not created in childhood to cope with trauma. It "has no date of origin as an alter personality. The ISH is not 'born' to handle a patient's unexpressed anger or violent trauma." It "is present from birth and is present in a normal person as well as in a multiple, although in a multiple personality, the ISH appears as a separate individual." Helpers are incapable of hate; they feel only love and express both awareness of and belief in God. "They serve as a conduit for God's healing power and love." They are ungendered, unemotional. They communicate "in the manner of a computer repeating programmed information."[29] That sounds all too like the benevolent computer Hal, in Stanley Kubrick's 1968 movie, *2001: A Space Odyssey*. Allison's Helpers seem to have voices like Hal's: calm, measured, knowing, slightly awe-inspiring. Clinicians have written about the effect on some patients of reading *Sybil*, but multiples, as I have suggested, reflect or distort a far wider spectrum of current culture than that, and Kubrick's film loomed large in the popular imagination of the day.

Allison wrote that the Inner Self Helper "is really the conscience."[30] He would work with the Helper to find out more about the patient. "There is no human to human relationship with which to compare this partnership. It is so unique a relationship that it has to be experienced to be believed."[31] "Inner Self Helper" is naturally parsed as Inner Self-Helper, i.e., something internal that helps the self. Allison meant the Helper from the Inner-Self, the Self that has always been there. When

Allison published his autobiography in 1980, he pictured Helpers as transcending individuals. "There may be more than one ISH, each ranked in a hierarchy, and the highest ISH often speaks of being next to God. I have found it difficult to summon this type of ISH; it seems almost as though the therapist is not worthy of such contact." Allison asks, "Do I believe this?" He answers, "I have no other explanation."

Putnam discussed uses of the Internal Self Helper in his textbook, but he omitted the theosophical background. The idea was secularized; perhaps even the switch from "Inner" to "Internal" Self Helper signals this (and moves us from Inner-Self Helper to Internal Self-Helper).[32] Other workers took a less than benign view. The personality structure of multiples is full of plots and subplots, threats and counterthreats, and Helpers are not immune. David Caul said that

> the therapist must not be afraid to "horse trade" with the ISH, who will always be protective of the personalities and will see to it that therapy is provided and that the personalities will get the best deal possible. . . . The ISH will almost never play all of his cards at once.[33]

Multiple personality has long had close links with spiritism and reincarnation. Some alters, it has been thought, may be spirits who find a home in a multiple; mediums may be multiples who are hosts to spirits. The scientific version of this idea goes back to the 1870s; much of the best turn-of-the-century English-language research on multiple personality was published in the journals of the London- or Boston-based societies for psychical research. Allison has been sympathetic to this vein of ideas. He once found it necessary to exorcise an intruding evil spirit. One of his most important patients, Henry Hawksworth, had psychic powers and could perceive the auras of people he met. When he was cured, he used this ability in his job as a personnel officer, assessing actual and potential employees in part by their auras. Allison encouraged Hawksworth to write an auto-multobiography, *The Five of Me*.[34]

Hawksworth had been in trouble with the law, and the painful practice of forensic psychiatry became Allison's vocation. One client was condemned to death for a brutal rape-murder. He had first been directed to Allison as an arsonist. Mark (it turned out) set fires in an alter state. There had been a grisly incident in his youth; he was gang-raped by teenagers. Later his mother was decapitated in a car crash for which the man wrongly blamed himself. After much work Allison elicited "an enraged monster," Carl, and then a rescuer alter. Mark, qua Carl, married another of Allison's patients, Lila; she, in her personality of Esther, was another violent being. Switching took place even during the wedding, and the marriage was doomed. Carl subsequently murdered a homosexual lover. Later on, Mark, or whoever, in the company of a pal, raped a woman chosen at random for her good looks; then Carl murdered her. Allison does not exonerate Mark. He makes plain that all of Mark's alters knew about these murders, even the rescuer personality whom Allison regarded as an Inner Self Helper. Allison learned a powerful lesson from this horrible sequence of events. Contrary to his view that an Inner Helper would never allow a person to do profound wrong, the rescuer knew about the murders. Mark, wrote Allison, had no conscience.

Allison has continued working with criminals. But even he reached a point of partial burnout, arguing in 1994 that it is impossible to treat multiple personality successfully within the prison system.[35] The cruelties of other prisoners, the needs of the patients, but above all the behavior of the authorities themselves invalidate any psychiatric process.

As a pioneer in the field, Allison was an expert witness in the trial of the famous Hillside Strangler, a man who had terrified Los Angeles in the late 1970s. A rapist in Columbus, Ohio, was diagnosed in 1977 as suffering from multiple personality, and the man was found not guilty by reason of insanity.[36] Kenneth Bianchi entered the same plea for the murders in Los Angeles and Washington State. He plea-bargained but the proceedings seemed to turn into a trial not of disgusting serial killings but of hypnosis and psychiatric diagnosis.[37] Allison himself concluded at the end of it all that the defendant was not a multiple but did dissociate during psychiatric interviews.

We should not think of these trials as something new. As soon as the new wave of double personality appeared in France in 1876, the doctor of the first and most famous patient raised the forensic question. "To what extent," he asked, "would such a person be responsible for committing a crime or misdemeanor?" He consulted a number of Bordeaux magistrates and legal experts. They argued that the multiple would be responsible for the actions of an alter, but "eminent psychiatrists think otherwise." Little has changed in the intervening hundred years; the division of professional opinion still exists. "The courts," the doctor concluded, "have not hitherto had to deal with such a situation, but it could happen tomorrow."[38] How right he was. The Hillside Strangler case, with its battery of competing expert witnesses, recapitulated a French trial that took place in Nice in 1892. The events were less gruesome but included two attempted murders, the victims were women, and the accused pleaded (using the terminology of the day) that an alter had committed the crime. The expert witnesses for the defense were the best, starting with Charcot. The three prosecution witnesses were almost equally distinguished.[39] The experts for the prosecution complained that the accused was schooled in his disorder and knew the medical facts all too well. They placed him under conditions of strict observation for three months, undoubtedly violating what we would now think of as his civil rights. The plea failed: the court declared the defendant guilty, but with diminished responsibility.

Allison has never sensationalized his patients. When it comes to multiple personality, students of jurisprudence and forensic psychology quite properly focus on questions of responsibility.[40] But we should not ignore the other side of that, the voyeurism captured in generations of gothic horror stories. My favorite plot is from Paul Lindau's *The Other*; it played on the Vienna stage in 1893. An investigative magistrate gradually finds that the crime he has been assigned to solve was committed by his second self.[41]

These stories continue to the present day, endlessly reinforcing a certain image of the multiple. In November 1992, a hundred years after *The Other* opened in Vienna, the soap *As the World Turns* hired Terry Lester to play a successful architect who had been abused as a child and acquired a number of alters, one of whom killed his sister. Viewers got courtroom scenes, acquittal, and therapy, but unfortunately the screenwriter died and the killer had to be cured in two posttrial therapy sessions. When the scenes were first aired, many multiples and some clinicians wrote in to say how faithful the story was to real life. When the plot collapsed, Lester "felt particularly bad for the 'multiples' I'd been hearing from because we appeared to trivialize the whole thing. I wrote them letters of apology on behalf of the show."[42]

There will be a steady diet of thrillers and potboilers telling the latest version of the theory of multiple personality.[43] In no other field of mental illness do fact, fiction, and fear play so relentlessly to each other. Serious clinicians deplore the sensationalism, but they cannot escape it. If real child abuse is the major key for the popular acceptance of the theme of multiple personality, then fantasy crime is its minor.

Successful movements, I said, require accidents, essentials, and institutions. Allison, Ellenberger, and Wilbur were fortuitous, accidental meteors in the night sky. During the late 1960s, the essential ingredient, child abuse, was maturing as a major item on the American political and social agenda, and would soon become an integral part of radical femi-

nist campaigns. And institutions were soon to take over multiple personality from a handful of isolated workers. Two years after the publication
of *Sybil* there was a symposium on multiple personality at the mental
health center in Athens, Ohio. By 1979, Allison was circulating a newsletter, *Memos in Multiplicity.* He and others were giving workshops at
the annual meetings of the American Psychiatric Association. The real
politicking came in the late seventies, when elaborate preparations were
made for the third edition of the *Diagnostic and Statistical Manual* of
the American Psychiatric Association, with results that we have seen in
chapter 1. With *DSM-III* the movement had legitimated itself. Regional
study groups were established; the first and most enduring may have
been in that bastion of conservative politics, Orange County, near Los
Angeles. These have proved to be stable organizations: in April 1995 the
Orange County Chapter of the ISSMP&D hosted the Eighth Annual
Western Clinical Conference of Trauma and Dissociation.

The year 1982 was something of a watershed for these developments,
for it was then that the late David Caul organized a steering committee
for forming a national organization. That was a matter of quiet and careful planning, but, as is so often the case with watersheds, *Time* magazine
marked this one in its own way. In the fall it ran "The Twenty-Seven
Faces of 'Charles,'" about a twenty-nine-year-old Texan picked up at
Daytona Beach, Florida. He would speak in two voices, "the infantile
rhythms of 'young Eric,' a dim and frightened child, and the measured
tones of 'older Eric,' who told a tale of terror and child abuse." In therapy there appeared the religious mystic Cye, forty-eight-year-old house-
wife Maria, Michael the jock, Mark the enforcer, the German-speaking
librarian Max, Spanish-speaking Pete, litigious Philip, lesbian Rachel,
prostitute Tina, and more, for a total of twenty-seven alters. Multiples
were on the move and *Time* had it exactly right. By the end of the decade the large number of alters, and the age and gender switches, would
be commonplace. Incidents of child abuse would be regarded as a standard part of the causation of multiple personality. Maybe *Time* was too
prescient, for it reported that Eric's memories of abuse were fantasies.[44]
Hypnosis was used extensively in treatment. Just before *Time* published,
it was reported elsewhere that "most of the personalities have been
purged, although there are three or four being treated, officials say. It
was the real personality that signed the consent form that allowed [his
psychologist] to comment on the case."[45]

Meanwhile, all during 1982, institutions were quietly coalescing. According to movement folklore, the die was cast on Saturday, 30 April

1983, during a historic supper at Mama Leone's restaurant in New York.[46] Boor, Braun, Caul, Jane Dubrow, Kluft, Putnam, and Sachs resolved to found the International Society for the Study of Multiple Personality and Dissociation. The first of many annual conferences met in Chicago in December. Until 1995 the conferences were under the aegis of Braun and Sachs and Rush-Presbyterian-St. Luke's hospital in that city, but are cosponsored by the American Society for Experimental and Clinical Hypnosis. In 1983, 325 people came. In 1983–1984 four major professional journals devoted entire issues to the topic.[47] In October 1985, one active multiple established a newsletter, "Speaking for Ourselves." Specialized clinics began. In Atlanta, the Ridgeview Institute inaugurated a full program on 2 June 1987. On 31 July of that year Sachs and Braun created the first hospital unit dedicated solely to inpatient treatment—the Dissociative Disorders Unit at Rush-Presbyterian-St. Luke's. The publication of *DSM-III-R* in that year confirmed the place of multiple personality among the official diagnoses. "I love victory," wrote Greaves, president of the ISSMP&D, in the July 1987 newsletter.[48] The only item missing was a professional journal. *Dissociation: Progress in the Dissociative Disorders* commenced publication in March 1988, edited, and legally owned, by Richard Kluft.[49]

The first meeting of the ISSMP&D challenged orthodoxy. The ninth meeting, in 1992, had health insurance as its theme. A keynote address was given by the vice president of Aetna, a large insurance provider that has found its health insurance products extremely lucrative. On the same platform, from Canada, which has long had completely comprehensive provincial health insurance, George Fraser lectured on the cost-effectiveness of multiple therapy, as evidenced by his clinic at the Royal Ottawa Hospital. When a maverick brand of psychotherapy starts addressing issues such as cost containment for the benefit of insurance carriers, we know that it has established itself. But danger lurks. Has the movement come to mirror Orwell's *Animal Farm?* Has the once-radical leadership become complacent about its original concerns—worried about accounting, not patients? I have been speaking of a multiple movement. No one ever challenged that phrase until the fall of 1994, when an old-timer asked me whether there still was, or is going to be, *one* movement.

I have quoted Spiegel and Kluft: Spiegel working hard to change the name of the disorder, and Kluft inveighing about a multiple subculture. These men are as central to the movement as could be. They are doing what has to be done, when institutions evolve: reestablishing the structure of their discipline, and declaring it a science to be governed by a body of selectmen. The grass roots know what is happening; class differences declare themselves. Putnam has expressed grave worries about the populist base of the multiple movement, observing that "the North American MPD literature, which is very uneven in quality, reflects the heterogeneity of clinical and therapeutic perspectives brought to bear on this syndrome." He worries about the training of therapists. Much of it is cavalierly dispensed as a cash-and-carry service. In Putnam's careful phrasing:

> At present, MPD therapist education is largely conducted through a recently instituted educational system, designed to provide therapists with the updated information necessary for them to retain their professional licensure. This system, known as Continuing Medical Education (CME), is largely unregulated and caters to popular interests in order to attract paying participants. CME courses and workshops are short, usually only one or two days in length, and typically offer no clinical supervision or direct patient contact.[50]

Who will finally own the illness: highly qualified clinicians with years of training, or a populist alliance of patients and therapists who welcome a culture of multiples and who cultivate personalities? The movement is perfectly capable of splitting. Stakes are high. Whatever health plan the American people settle for, coverage will be more universal. Who will pay for what? Psychiatric disorders divide into two types—those that respond reasonably well to medication available at a given time, and those that do not. Drugs, no matter how expensive, are much cheaper than long-term psychotherapy. Insurers prefer drug treatment. There is no belief, on the part of anyone in the field, that dissociative identity disorder will respond in a specific way to drugs in the foreseeable future, although of course nonspecific drugs will be used to change behavior, mood, and attitude. Dissociation doctors must capture as much non-drug coverage for dissociative disorders as they can. That will be a top item on the agenda for the medical wing of multiple personality. It will also make dissociation an important player for the wide range of therapies that do not use drugs, and that hope for a share of public health funding. There will certainly be no public funding for the motley assembly of therapies that Putnam alludes to. So the economic interests of the grassroots therapists fundamentally diverge, for the first time, from those of the leading psychiatrists and psychologists in the field.

The name change, from multiple personality disorder to dissociative identity disorder, does matter. A few years ago professionals were advising that one should never, in therapy, eliminate a single alter personality, for that would be akin to murder. Now the message is, get rid of the personalities altogether. Dissociation has become the name of the game, of the disorder, of the journal, and of the organization. If the upper echelon of the movement has its way, multiple personality (literally understood) will disappear. Yet at a deeper level the dissociation game is the same old game as multiple personality, namely, the memory game. For the fundamental shared conviction that may stop schism is that lost memories are the keys to whatever illness this is. The best possible thing to happen to the multiple personality movement has been the appearance of an antimemory movement, the False Memory Foundation. There is nothing like a common enemy to heal splits.

Child Abuse

CHILD ABUSE made sense of multiplicity. Most multiples, according to recent theorizing, dissociated when they were little children. That was their way to cope with early terror and pain, usually in the form of or accompanied by sexual abuse. Before we see how this etiology became an item of faith, amply confirmed by clinical experience, we should consider the trajectory of the very idea of child abuse itself. For it is not a transparent idea that we all understand as soon as we think about it, notice examples of it, or recall having experienced it. You might think that the experiences speak for themselves, at least for the victims. Yes— and yet events, no matter how painful or terrifying, have been experienced or recalled *as child abuse* only after consciousness-raising. That requires inventing new descriptions, providing new ways to see old acts—and a great deal of social agitation. As Judith Herman observes in her powerful book *Trauma and Recovery*, every time we have taken trauma seriously, it has been "in affiliation with a political movement."[1]

That said, we must insist that child abuse has been with us always. If we restrict ourselves only to the industrial or industrializing world after 1800, we have endless documentation of horrible things done to children—things that were at the time perceived as dreadful and that the children obviously hated. Certainly other things were done to children that we now think of as bad, and which children now would hate, but which may not have been so clearly perceived as bad by anyone long ago. But that is beside the main point: cruelty and exploitation, loathed by everyone, have been omnipresent. Focus on any specific type of vile behavior directed at children, and you can quickly document its occurrence in our recent and not so recent past. I hesitate to project this statement into European culture of too early an epoch, for the idea of child abuse takes for granted the idea of the child. There is enough plausibility in Philippe Ariès's famous thesis about the invention of childhood to make one pause. Ariès argued that the social roles of children that we take for granted are, at the earliest, of eighteenth-century origin. But he also urged the more radical thesis that the very idea of a child, with all that it implies, is quite recent.[2] The thought of child sexual abuse is very closely tied to the notion that children develop through successive stages, each with its own canon of "appropriate" sexual behavior. The concept of child development came into its own only during the nineteenth century.[3] Yet even that was not enough to give us our present notion of child abuse. The phrase "child abuse"—that exact phrase—is seldom found before 1960; its predecessor was "cruelty to children." More important, the concept of child abuse, our concept, even when given a name, underwent a number of fairly radical mutations during the 1970s. I have written at length about these transitions elsewhere; a few highlights will suffice here.[4]

"Cruelty to children" of Victorian times seems so similar to our "child abuse" that I have to explain their differences. They differ in respect of class, evil, sex, and medicine. The Victorian movement against cruelty to children itself had plenty of predecessors, such as the agitation producing numerous Factory Acts that limited working hours for children. The first children's aid society was founded in New York in 1853 and was much imitated elsewhere. But *cruelty to children*, as a quite specific concept, bearing that name, came expressly to the fore as late as 1874. Cruelty to children was targeted after a sensational incident—a pattern since repeated over and over again for child abuse. A girl who had been brutally beaten and degraded by her stepmother became the symbol of hidden horror. In response, the New York Society for the Prevention of Cruelty to Children was established. It was an offshoot of an organization hitherto dedicated to preventing cruelty to animals, the American Humane Society. It was as if there had been no place for this concept, cruelty to children, so that concern had first to be fostered in an existing organization that looked after animals. The idea spread quickly in the United States and immediately crossed the ocean to Liverpool and then to London. Note the date, 1874 and after: that was the time of the first great wave of multiple personality, beginning in 1876. Yet cruelty to children and multiple personality seem never to have been connected in those days.

Cruelty to children had a riveting place in the overall portfolio of Victorian moral causes. Antislavery had been the first cause. There was the agitation over working hours for children, which conceptually linked children and slavery. Temperance, extending suffrage, opposition to vivisection and cruelty to animals, and above all women's rights became an interconnected net that functioned powerfully to raise the moral sensibilities of the industrial world and to improve the lot of diverse victims. The campaigns were couched in similar terms. Support came from the same social subclasses and often from the same individuals.

These movements took different forms in different parts of the industrialized world. Standard social legislation covering health, workman's compensation, and pensions originates in Prussia and then the German Empire, with its collectivist, rather than individualist, conception of the relationships between the state and its people. Many educational reforms, kindergartens, and even the idea of sending slum children to the country for their moral and physical health all originate in German language communities. In the more atomistic and individualistic Western nations such as France, Britain, and the United States, private philanthropy was the norm. The Victorian agitations were driven by a genteel mix of passionate concern, charity, and self-interest, but by and large the activists were not running scared. If they were frightened, they were prompted by the laboring and criminal classes, and by threats of revolution.

This leads to my first difference between child abuse and cruelty to children. As I shall elaborate below, child abuse, especially in America, was supposed to be classless. It was supposed to occur in constant proportion, more or less, in every social class. Poverty was not an issue. This was an American political exigency, for legislation could succeed—and succeed it did, with a vengeance—only if it were not perceived as predominantly liberal social reform. Hence class differences were explicitly excluded. Cruelty to children, in contrast, was presented primarily as a vice of the lower classes, prosperous examples notwithstanding. One potent force behind the modern child abuse movement has been fear about the rot in the American family, an internal fear, as opposed to fear of the smoldering poor. Fear for the family forms the conservative pole of child abuse activism, matched by the radical pole of feminism and its belief that child abuse is part of the patriarchal system. Child abuse agitation drew on an unusual coalition of those who challenged the traditional family and those who feared its dissolution. Class warfare, of the sort that drove part of the philanthropic cruelty to children movement, was excluded, as far as possible, in order to create a common front for child abuse activists.

My next difference between cruelty to children and child abuse has to do with evil. Cruelty to children was a very bad thing. It was wicked, depraved, despicable, wrong—in a word, cruel. But it was not absurd to locate the first anticruelty organization within the Humane Society, founded to look after animals. Cruelty to children was one among many cruelties, especially bad because innocence suffered and often grew up to become a danger to the state by entering the criminal classes.

57

Contrast this with the outlook of recent times, when child abuse, especially when it has sexual content or overtones, seems to be the greatest evil in private life. It was not felt as the outstanding evil in the nineteenth century. Cruelty to children was bad; child abuse is an ultimate evil.

This is connected to my third difference, sex. Child abuse agitation began in 1961, when battered baby syndrome was presented to the American Medical Association. Active feminists soon placed an emphasis on sexual abuse. As familial sex abuse became incorporated into the very meaning of child abuse, abuse acquired connotations of incest. Incest produces peculiar feelings of horror in a great many societies. Explanations of this horror are unsatisfactory; they sound more like the edicts of famous psychologists or anthropologists than genuine explanations. But no matter why incest produces such widespread feelings of revulsion, it is a fact that it does, and that revulsion spread to child abuse in general. Moreover, child abuse became associated with a collection of acts that most people find monstrous for reasons having nothing to do with classical incest. Three-year-olds are sodomized by a male relative. Some of us find this not only repugnant, but also absolutely unintelligible, in the way that only rank evil can be unintelligible. Such acts have, for many, become the very prototype of child abuse. They were never central to cruelty to children. Victorians were amply aware of what we call sexual abuse of children and minors, and many cases went to court. But such vices were not grouped together, in general, with cruelty to children. When they were, it was only under a larger class umbrella, of the several iniquities of *les misérables*, or, occasionally, of the debauched rich. Cruelty to children did not collect, conceptually, anything like the same set of evils spanned by the idea of child abuse.

Social class, evil, and sex may seem enough to differentiate child abuse from cruelty to children—the three of them cover most of sociology. But there is one more factor, medicalization. Doctors put child abuse and neglect on the political agenda in the early 1960s. They declared that abusers are sick. Medicine has by no means kept uniform control of the administration of child abuse, but whoever aims at control must treat child abuse within some science. Contrast Victorian cruelty. The medicalization and, more generally, scientization of deviancy during the nineteenth century has become a cliché of intellectual history. Yet cruelty to children was not seriously incorporated in the medical, psychological, or even sociostatistical lore of the Victorian era. Some social control of families was exercised by physicians and through medical theories, but efforts to restrain cruelty followed another route. People did not try to control cruelty by means of a special kind of knowledge about the cruel. Some of the most vigilant agitators were medical men, but they campaigned as philanthropists, and as men of standing who happened to be doctors. They never made out that the cruel parent was a definite kind of human being, in the way in which a child abuser is now a kind of person. The man who beat or raped his daughter may have been called a beast, but there was no expert knowledge to help, cure, or manage that type of individual. He was a wretch to be punished. The mother who callously neglected her children or threw them to the floor in a drunken rage had to be separated from her flock because she harmed them, but not because she was of the child-harming species.

Medicalization is much less interesting than sex, class, or evil, yet from one perspective it is the hallmark of the concept of child abuse. There are supposed to be certain kinds of person, such as the child abuser, or the abused child, about whom scientific knowledge is possible. If the knowledge is sound, then there will be numerous different kinds of abuse, of abuser, and of abused, subject to various types of medical, psychiatric, and statistical laws. These laws will tell how to intervene and prevent or ameliorate child abuse. Multiple personality has recently thrived on child abuse *as an object of knowledge*. Cruelty to children was a bad thing, but it could not of its very nature have caused a mental illness. Individual acts of cruelty might drive a person mad— what else are gothic tales of horror all about? But those acts were not of the madness-causing kind about which doctors, as opposed to novelists, wrote books. Clinically, the first great treatise on hysteria, published in 1859 by Paul Briquet, makes perfectly clear that many cases of female hysteria are the product of family violence, even in childhood.[5] But he never proposed that the violence itself, and its causes, should become an object of scientific knowledge.

Causes are objects of knowledge, and child abuse could be the cause of an illness only if it was something like what is called a natural kind, a kind of event found in nature and hooked up to other events by laws of nature. Medical knowledge about child abuse would be knowledge of those kinds of event and of the laws that connect them. During the late-Victorian heyday of cruelty to children, cruelty was never in the running to be such an object, such a kind, such a topic for information, control, and medical intervention.

The crusade against cruelty to children faded from notice by 1910. In the half-century 1910–1960 there were plenty of problems concerning children and adolescents. While cruelty had dropped out of the agenda, infant mortality and then juvenile delinquency rose to prominence. Then, in 1961, came child abuse. The immediate stimulus was a group of pediatricians in Denver led by C. H. Kempe. Using X rays as the objective proof, they drew attention to repeated injuries to small children. Children were found to have healed fractures in legs or arms, and similar signs of unrecorded, unreported injury. This had been widely known at least since 1945, but no one had dared to say that the scarred bones were caused by parents who had beaten up their babies. Once the Denver group had published the battered child syndrome in 1962, newspapers, television, and the mass weeklies announced this new scourge.

A new body of knowledge was abroad. It was often peculiarly a priori. "Often parents may be repeating the type of child care practiced on them in childhood."[6] This observation comes from the first paper about battered babies. It is cautious enough, with its "often" and "may," but it was gearing up for removing the qualifications and reversing the direction of implication: "Abused as a child, abusive as a parent." The latter became virtually an axiom believed by the vast majority of clinicians and social service workers, and an item of general knowledge among lay people. The technical literature on the "inheritance" of child abuse was nevertheless quite mixed, with firm believers ranged against skeptics who asked for some evidence. The believers held the field, for two reasons. First, the claim sounds right: that is, it fits in with twentieth-century beliefs that childhood experience forms the adult. Second, it is now a foregone conclusion that an abusive parent will profess having been abused as a child: that explains and thereby mitigates the behavior. So there is plenty of confirming evidence. The doctrine has been completely absorbed by the multiple personality movement: recall Braun's striking statement to the ISSMP&D congress of 1993 that child abuse all too often "metastasizes across families and generations."[7]

Surely there is a fact of the matter? Either most abusers were abused as children, or not? A thorough survey article of 1993 quotes, as an example, a statement made in a classic study of 1973: "The most constant fact [concerning child abusers] is that parents themselves were nearly always abused or battered or neglected as children." And again from 1976: "We see an unbroken line in the repetition of parental abuse from childhood into the adult years." In 1993, however: "More than 15 years after these comments were made, there are few in the scientific community who would embrace such remarks."[8] Notice that it is the "scientific community" who count. What is the problem for this community?

"Most scholars are all too aware of the inherent limitations of the available database." Usually when people complain about the database, they mean that there are too few data. That is hardly the problem here, for this review article alone cites about ninety statistical studies, many of large samples, bearing on "the etiology of child maltreatment." I do not want to criticize the methodology of these seemingly endless studies. All this work assumes that there is knowledge to be had. That may be a mistake. There may be no true general answers to the question "Why do parents X-abuse their children?" where X is a defined type of child abuse. Moreover, there is the looping effect of human kinds that I have mentioned already. The concept of child abuse may itself be so made and molded by attempts at knowledge and intervention, and social reaction to these studies, that there is no stable object, child abuse, to have knowledge about.

The thesis that abusers were once abused was not the only principle laid down in the early days of child abuse agitation. There was also, for example, the practical injunction to separate babies from their parents or caretakers: "Physicians should not be satisfied to return the child to an environment where even a moderate risk of repetition exists."[9] And it was explicitly declared that the entire topic was one for medical expertise: "It is the responsibility of the medical profession to assume leadership in this field."[10] The popular press was faithful, speaking of "sick adults who commit such crimes." To talk about the etiology of child abuse is already to grant the authority of a medical model. "Etiology" is medicine's word for cause. It may beg the question. The question "Why do people abuse their children?" may have no general medical answer at all.

In the beginning we had battered child syndrome. It applied to babies three years old and under. The Denver pediatricians said later that they had made the deliberate decision not to go public with physical abuse as a general label for what was happening in many American families. They feared that a conservative audience of colleagues would not acknowledge anything more than what could be proved by X rays. But once searing photographs of damaged innocents were in place—injured not only with sticks and stones but by straps, nails, cigarette butts, scalding water—it would quickly be acknowledged that babies are not the only victims. It had helped, as a point of political tactics, to begin with infants. To do so enabled doctors to evade the issue of the supposed right of parents to mete out severe physical punishment to their children. No one argued that parents had a right to punish mere babies.

Once the cry was raised, battered babies would be seen as only a sub-class of a central classification, the abused child. Physical abuse and the less sensational but far more pervasive neglect remained the focus. Sex was peripheral or absent. The pioneers of 1962 said later that they were well aware of sexual abuse and had it on the list of future targets. Police officers, social workers, psychotherapists, schoolteachers, and ministers of religion were certainly not unaware that sexual abuse and physical abuse often occur in the same households. But public attention was deferred. Perhaps the first great outcry occurred in a speech by Florence Rush to the New York Radical Feminist Conference, 17 April 1971. This ferment reached a more general public in 1975: "Sexual Molestation of Children: The Last Frontier in Child Abuse."[11]

In the old days sex molesters were supposed to be strangers. If molester and victim were acquainted, the former would be a household servant molesting the children of the employer—or the master molesting the children of the servants. It was allowed that perpetrators could be caretakers, foster parents, wicked stepfathers, perverted schoolteachers, and priests. Molestation occurred across class boundaries and outside the ties of blood. But babies were battered *in* the family! What about molesting within the family? The two ideas, intrafamilial abuse and sexual molestation, began to be fused. Sexual molestation within the family means incest. By May 1977, when *Ms.* magazine's lead story was "Incest: Child Abuse Begins at Home," this agitation furiously burst into the open. A welter of otherwise discordant statistics confirmed that men abuse girls in their families far more often than anyone abuses boys.[12]

The traditional prohibition on incest applies to sexual intercourse. As soon as incest and child abuse came together, the concept was radically extended. Fondling and touching became incest just as much as intercourse.[13] Cornelia Wilbur went a step further: "Chronic exposure to sexual displays and sexual acts during infancy and early childhood is abusive. This occurs when parents insist that a child sleep in the parental bedroom until eight or nine years of age."[14] Child abuse was molded to take in a range of acts that had never before been put together as one single kind of behavior. On the one hand, incest came to mean any type of sexually oriented activity involving an adult and a child in the same family. Or even, by an implicit slide of meanings, in the American extended family, which includes baby-sitters and day-care centers. On the other hand, the concept of child abuse picked up a whole range of behavior, all of which became colored by the horror of incest.

These events were extraordinarily liberating. They made it possible for many women, and increasingly many men, to bring into the open their degrading experiences at the hands (usually) of male relatives by blood, marriage, or convenience. Fathers, uncles, grandfathers, cousins, stepfathers, boyfriends, companions, paramours, priests. There were also memories of forced sex with mothers and aunts. Telling the stories was cathartic. The suffering lay not just in the immediate assault, and fear of the next one, but in an ongoing destruction of personality, a growing inability to trust anyone, to establish loving and confident relations with any human being. There was not only a twisting of sexual responses but also a distortion of any affectionate response. Not battered babies but battered lives. This is exactly what multiple personality clinicians began to uncover: the sad lives that they tried to put back together had experienced terrible childhoods.

There is a further item of knowledge. We might consider whether sexual experiences involving a child and an adult inevitably harm the child. In 1953, Kinsey, already made famous by his studies of male sexuality, found that 24 percent of his female informants had experienced the sexual attentions of adults while they were still girls. Kinsey seems to have thought that this might even be good for a girl, but that was before the appearance of child abuse as a concept ranging from battering to incest.[15] No one seems to have been much worried by Kinsey's finding, then. In 1979, after the rich concept of child abuse had been molded, the most influential scientific expert on child sexual abuse was David Finkelhor. He concluded, almost without qualification, that the sexual attentions of adults harm the subsequent development of children.[16] There has since been a prodigious number of studies of the *sequelae* of child abuse—once again note the medical language. Hence it is worth repeating a more recent remark by Finkelhor and a colleague: child abuse would be wicked and evil even if it had no significant effect on the person's growth into an adult.

> There is an unfortunate tendency in interpreting the effects of sexual abuse (as well as in other studies of childhood trauma) to overemphasize long-term impact as the ultimate criterion. Effects seem to be considered less "serious" if their impact is transient and disappears in the course of development. However this tendency to stress everything in terms of its long-term effect betrays an "adulto-centric" bias. Adult traumas such as rape are not assessed in terms of whether they will have an impact on old age. They are acknowledged to be painful and alarming events, whether

their impact lasts 1 year or 10. Similarly childhood traumas should not be dismissed because no "long-term effects" can be demonstrated. Child sexual abuse needs to be recognized as a serious problem of childhood, if only for the immediate pain, confusion, and upset that can ensue.[17]

This is absolutely right. But there is a subtext. Knowledge about the bad effects of child abuse is in a surprisingly poor state. A 1993 review by Finkelhor and his associates observes that "since 1985 . . . there has been an explosion in the number of studies that have concentrated specifically on sexually abused children." The results, however, are not satisfying. "The role of disturbance to self-esteem and of a child's prior dispositions or vulnerabilities has not been well substantiated." Clinicians are warned that "there are too many sexually abused children who are apparently asymptomatic." The authors complain that despite the explosion in empirical studies, there is no "theoretical underpinning." There is great concern about "the effects of sexual abuse but disappointingly little concern about why the effects occur." So where are we? We apparently know that sexually abused children "are more symptomatic than their nonabused counterparts." But the sexually abused children under study had already been selected because of their symptoms. When we compare sexually abused children and "other clinical nonabused children" (i.e., children getting psychiatric treatment for something else), the sexually abused children are *less* symptomatic in general, except for being more highly "sexualized."[18] It is obvious to everyone that sexual abuse must have bad consequences for the development of a child—yet once again, the search for scientific proof is not doing very well.

There is a comparable number of studies on the long-term effects of physical abuse and neglect.[19] Any given study seems to prove a lot, but put together, they are so at odds with each other that the net effect is inconclusive. All these studies, of sexual or physical abuse, are amazingly indifferent to social class. In a classic contribution to political science, Barbara Nelson analyzed the way in which physical abuse and neglect of children entered the American political arena.[20] From the outset it was essential to separate the problem of injured children from any social issues. "This is a political problem, not a poverty problem," insisted Senator and then Vice President Mondale, who led the drive for national legislation. That approach ensured unanimity. Liberals and conservatives could agree, and social issues should not arise, because child abuse is an illness. Mondale's words hover over most subsequent American research: "not a poverty problem." And yet there is a "highly replicated finding that poverty and low income are related to both child abuse and neglect"; ten studies are cited in this 1993 paper.[21] Writers outside the United States tend to express themselves more vigorously. "For all its horror, child sexual abuse (or physical battering) harms, indeed kills, far fewer children, either in [Great Britain] or the United States, than simple, miserable and unremitting poverty. Why, when poverty has been intensifying and welfare programmes run down, has our attention been drawn to sexual or other abuse?"[22] In the author's view part of the answer is that child abuse and especially sexual abuse offer scapegoats. It is clear that the children who die from maltreatment are the poor ones.[23] In the United States the availability of public funds for poor families with small children decreased substantially every year during the 1980s, while every year there was more and more talk about the horrors of child abuse. In 1990 a presidential panel announced that child abuse was a "national emergency."[24] The first task was to "alert the nation to the existence of the problem." Then what? "We want a system in which it is as easy for a family member to get help as it is to report a neighbor for suspected abuse." But the panel's focus elided unpleasant topics like filth, danger, the stench of urine in the halls, broken elevators, smashed glass, curtailed food programs, guns.

One piece of knowledge about child abuse, especially child sexual abuse, would be particularly relevant to multiple personality. Most multiples are adult women. Their illness, it is claimed, is due to childhood abuse commonly involving sexual abuse. Is this a special case? Does child abuse produce psychiatric illnesses later in life? Many clinicians are certain that it does. Can epidemiology and statistics produce confirmation of this? Anyone who reviews the literature will be extremely cautious. The claim that early abuse causes adult dysfunction is far closer to an act of faith than an item of knowledge. It seems so obviously true— yet even when there are statistical connections, they seem to be more local than might be thought. Thus a longitudinal study in New Zealand (where the universal health coverage applies to psychiatric care) found that psychiatric problems of adult women correlated less well with abuse than with straightforward poverty.[25]

To repeat Finkelhor's admonition: even if it is hard to correlate child abuse and subsequent psychiatric problems, child abuse remains an evil in itself. Moral philosophers distinguish, on the one hand, utilitarian or consequentialist ethics and, on the other, deontological ethics. Consequentialism assesses whether an act is good or bad in terms of its consequences. Deontology urges that there may be categorical imperatives to do, or refrain from, certain acts, regardless of their consequences. Many child abuse activists who ought (in my opinion) to be deontologists, attending to the absolute evil of child abuse, are in practice consequentialists, trying to discover bad results of such acts. The multiple personality movement has been helped by the ruthless utilitarian thrust of American sociology. Sociology is never content to say that something is just plain bad. To be bad, an act has to have bad consequences. If we had been content to intervene in child abuse just because it is bad, we would not have our present set of beliefs about the consequences of child abuse. Absent those, the multiple personality movement would not have been able to have a causal theory of the origin of splitting on which to flourish.

I have been belaboring a curious fact. On the one hand, there is an immense amount of confident general knowledge about child abuse. Much of that knowledge sprang full-blown, a priori, as the concept of child abuse was formed. On the other hand, the innumerable empirical studies do not add up. Sometimes they put in question what has always been taken for granted. What remains? First, faith. Second, purely empirical experience of particular situations and individuals that confirm the faith. And the conviction stands that there must be knowledge to be had, if only we could get it. Perhaps that is what is wrong: an assumption about the possibility of knowledge and the kind of knowledge that it must be.

There are endless studies but people are affected by them, so that the very phenomenon being investigated may be changed by the inquiry itself. It is as if there were a principle of human indeterminacy at work. Nowhere is this more clear than in the exoneration effect, as when violent people discover in their past a history of their abuse because they know that explains, excuses, and perhaps even causes their violence. I am not referring to the fact that some abusers will lie in order to avoid judicial sanctions. I mean that they may comprehend their own past differently, and now honestly see themselves as having been abused. This is not an effect to be avoided. It is inherent in the concept of child abuse. Is the concept then "simply subjective"? Not in the least, but the concept does have its own internal dynamics.

I never tire of saying that the child abuse movement is the most important piece of consciousness-raising of the past three decades or so. It has not only made us aware: it has also changed our sensibilities and our values. It has wiped out a little of our humanity—no man in his right mind today would help a strange child in a park trying to reach the water fountain. It has provided leverage for some litigious souls and it has given rise to some crazy panics. There have been some victims of false accusation—but nothing like the number of unsung victims of a less self-conscious age. There have also been some appalling miscarriages of justice. At a time of radical moral change, we have to sort these issues out case by case. But the net effect of the consciousness-raising has been overwhelmingly positive.

It is particularly necessary for me to say this here, for some readers may feel I am too distanced from the topic. Indeed a previous essay of mine has been called a "brilliant and disturbing deconstruction of child abuse."[26] I do not find this as complimentary as intended, for deconstruction so often implies irony, mockery, a lack of respect for what is being "deconstructed." I analyze, but I never intend to deconstruct. I take a distanced view of child abuse, here, because I am preoccupied by the way in which it has become an object of knowledge, and has, in turn, become an object of causal knowledge for the new science of multiple personality.

There has been a great deal of talk, recently, about the social construction of this or that. Sometimes this is exciting, as when we read about the social construction of the present basic building blocks of physics: the social construction of quarks.[27] I respect someone who can argue that quarks are socially constructed: this is a daring and provocative thesis that makes us think. I feel a certain guarded admiration when a fact whose discovery was rewarded with a Nobel Prize for medicine is described as the social construction of a scientific fact; anyone who shares my respect and admiration for fundamental science has to sit up and take notice.[28] I do not find it similarly thrilling to read about the social construction of events that could occur only historically, only in the context of a society. It can hardly be of interest that the concept of child abuse is a social construct (if "social construct" means anything at all). What will be of interest is the successive stages in which this concept has been made and molded, and how it has interacted with children, with adults, with moral sensibilities, and with a larger sense of what it is to be a human being.

At least one published paper has the title "The Social Construction of Child Abuse."[29] The example of child abuse can be a useful beacon to help us steer clear of the more tedious questions about social construction. Some of the more strident social constructionists say (without noticing the switch) that child abuse is no social construction; it is a real evil that the family and the state have so often covered up. They are right and wrong. It *is* a real evil, and it was so before the concept was constructed. It was nevertheless constructed. Neither reality nor construction should be in question.

Yet there is a quite different type of construction, familiar in philosophy from the time of Rousseau and Kant. Those thinkers wrote about how we construct ourselves and our sense of moral worth. But they did not think of wholly new moral concepts coming into circulation. When new moral concepts emerge or when old ones acquire new connotations, then our sense of who we are is affected. The effect is more pervasive when the moral concept is also taken to be a causal one. Child abuse is both an ultimate evil and causally powerful. We may have little conventional proof that child abuse has terrible sequelae in adult life, but those supposed sequelae are part of the common ground of psychiatrists, scientists, social workers, and lay people. That knowledge affects the way in which individual human beings come to conceive of themselves.

Child abuse, and repressed memories of child abuse, are supposed to have powerful effects on the developing adult. What interests me is less the truth or falsehood of that proposition than the way in which assuming it leads people to describe their own past anew. Individuals explain their behavior differently and feel differently about themselves. Each of us becomes a new person as we redescribe the past. I find the so-called social construction of child abuse a topic of limited interest. But I shall constantly return to the question of how that constructed knowledge loops in upon people's moral lives, changes their sense of self-worth, reorganizes and reevaluates the soul.

Gender

NINE OUT OF TEN patients who have been diagnosed with multiple personality disorder are women. The same proportion is observed in old cases of double consciousness or alternating personality. I do not claim the latter as a statistical fact, because it depends whom you count. One survey finds a larger proportion of males among old reports than I do.[1] But whatever proportion one fixes on, the majority of multiples are female. Why?

There is another question about gender and multiple personality. Multiples now develop a large number of alter personalities or personality fragments, some of whom are of the opposite sex, or promiscuous, or bisexual, or homosexual, or some combination of these gendered traits not found in the host personality. Are these instabilities in sexuality a superficial phenomenon, or is sexual ambivalence integral to the disorder and its causes?

Nine out of ten diagnosed multiples are female. That sounds as if there were some well-established piece of knowledge, a Fact of Epidemiology. There is no such thing; there are only a few data and a good deal of anecdotal experience. We have a consistent impression that the vast majority of patients have been women.[2] This may result from a mix of only loosely connected causes. For example, throughout most of the nineteenth century and even into our own, multiples were also said to have hysterical symptoms. In the great French wave of multiples, all multiples were, first and foremost, florid hysterics. Whatever else may be true of hysteria, it is a thoroughly gender-laden diagnosis, description, or discourse. Questions about multiplicity yield to the overarching question about the gender role of hysteria in French clinical practice. I shall touch on some of those questions later, but for the present we should examine only recent information.

In 1986 Frank Putnam and his colleagues published the results of their now-famous survey. Questionnaires were sent to clinicians, and, as I understand it, the sample was constituted by the first 100 patients recorded in replies that fit the protocols of the survey; 92 of the 100 patients reported were women.[3] Three years later Colin Ross and his associates published a larger series, again based on a mailed questionnaire. It was sent to two populations of clinicians, members of the ISSMP&D, and Canadian psychiatrists selected by Ross. Of 236 cases reported, 207—that is, just shy of 90 percent—were women.[4]

Why the imbalance? The earliest and still the most common explanation may show more about attitudes to gender than about multiplicity. There are, it is suggested, a great number of male multiples out there but we are not diagnosing them. It is as if the fact that most of the people who suffer from a certain mental illness are women produces a feeling of guilt, of political incorrectness even. Perhaps this is partly because a female complaint has less cachet than a male one—just another instance of the powerlessness of women. At any rate, the drive to find more male multiples has been a constant theme from 1970 to the present day. When gender is discussed, the most common question asked is "Where are the men?" Contrast people with other problems. Most alcoholics are men. We do not hear ringing cries of "Where are the female alcoholics?" A few epidemiologists do ask why schizophrenia is more common among men than women, but no one imagines that we have to search through new populations in order to find more female schizophrenics.

Where are the male multiples? Cornelia Wilbur proposed that they are to be found in the criminal justice system rather than the mental health system.[5] Hence the aphorism "Most males with MPD are in jail." There is a slightly less loaded way to understand the suggestion. Perhaps these gigantic unsystematic "systems" of health and justice play an important part in channeling and organizing symptoms and their display. Not only do people of different sex get caught by different systems, but also the functionaries and people with little pieces of authority within these systems work on those whom they catch in order to train them to fit in with expectations. And of course once you are caught by justice or mental health, the easiest thing to do is to behave as you are supposed to— violently or weakly, as the case may be. It becomes second nature. That is a traditional suggestion of labeling theory: people adapt their natures to the labels assigned to them by authority.

Wilbur suspected from early on that there was a missing mass of male multiples. She may have felt vindicated when she worked as a consultant in the case of Billy Milligan, the Columbia rapist who pleaded that his crimes had been committed by alters. In contrast, Ralph Allison did at first believe that male multiples had to be rare, because so few men suffered as much extreme youthful trauma as his female patients. But then he realized that the "trigger" need not be sexual abuse but only "trauma so severe that the child had to flee inside his head, creating a new personality to take his place."[6] Moreover, violent behavior, albeit the work of vicious alters, was all too socially permissible. That was why so few male multiples showed up for help. One of his most important patients, Henry Hawksworth, was a gentle man who would get drunk and have fabulous barroom fights of which Henry had no memory. A judge thought the fighting exploits were so stupendous that he let Hawksworth off with a caution and told him not to drink so much and to quit watching cowboy shows on television. Yet in Allison's therapy, it was one of Henry's alters who decided to get drunk, or, when drunk, got into brawls. On the other hand, when the behavior went over the edge, it really went over the edge. I have already described Allison's patient who in an alter state set fires and later raped and murdered a woman.

The deep-felt need on the part of some clinicians to find more multiple males virtually guarantees that in the short run an increasing proportion of males will be diagnosed with dissociative identity disorder. Ross thinks that "the clinical ratio will probably drop over the next decade as MPD is diagnosed in prisons and other settings." He argues that hypnotizability is strongly correlated with multiple personality disorder, and asserts: "Given that men and women are equally hypnotizable and do not appear to differ in dissociative experiences in the general population, the sex ratio of MPD ought to be about the same as the ratio for abuse (somewhere between 1:1 and 9:1)."[7] There is something chilling about Ross's deterministic prediction that once we have got the latent multiple males to behave properly, that is, as overt multiples, the sex ratio of multiples will be identical to that of children who are both abused and hypnotizable.

The male multiples will come from a variety of sources. The quest has already prompted a research interest in prison populations. There is also the class of patients treated in the U.S. Veterans Administration hospitals. Post-traumatic stress disorder has become a common diagnosis. Clinicians who treat it are increasingly open to a diagnosis of multiple personality. In another direction, the interest in child and adolescent multiples may produce numerous males because disturbed boys are more of a nuisance than their female counterparts and come more readily to the attention of psychiatrists.[8]

The factor of males abused in childhood by their mothers may also become increasingly pertinent as this concept is applied to the treatment of men in unsatisfactory marriages who are given to drink and womanizing.[9] A recent study reports twenty-two men who have never been arrested or behaved in a way to warrant felonious arrest. These cases confirm the pattern that male multiples do not seek psychiatric help except in connection with other difficulties such as alcohol, temper, or marital discord.[10]

Although the net for men has been cast wide, and although its mesh is tight, crime and violence continue to provide the majority of public accounts of male multiples. We must not discount the interaction between fact and fiction here. At first glance, fact and fiction are completely mismatched. The fictional multiples are men, the diagnosed real ones women.[11] But when we look again, the match is perfect, because the stories are almost all stories of violence or crime. Among the greatest tales, only Mr. Golyadkin in Dostoyevsky's terrifying *The Double* is wily rather than violent; the terror results from ambiguity rather than sadism. The prototype of the double in romantic fiction was furnished by E.T.W. Hoffmann, James Hogg, and Robert Louis Stevenson, all of whom wrote about men, but all of whom were also well acquainted with the relevant medical literature and with experts who knew that women, not men, were the doubles.[12]

Only one great female double was imagined during the nineteenth century, and she was an Amazon. Heinrich von Kleist's *Penthesilea* of 1808 is a searing play in which the heroine acts almost exactly according to the prototype of doubling then current. In one state she is "sweet as a nightingale"; in the other she is so ferocious that she horrifies her closest companions. She passes between states by an intervening trance. She has two-way amnesia between alters, except for a slight, dreamlike recollection, in her gentle state, of what happened in her fierce state. Finally, in her fierce state she not only kills Achilles—a man whom she loves and who loves her—but attacks him with mastiffs after she has driven an arrow through his neck. Then she leaps off her horse and, on her knees in the company of her dogs, helps tear Achilles limb from limb and devours his flesh. Before she kills herself, in her gentle state, she kisses the remains.

> A kiss, a bite—how cheek by jowl
> They are, and when you love straight from the heart
> The greedy mouth so easily mistakes
> One for the other.[13]

After that, every subsequent story about a double seems tepid. Nevertheless, she is the only woman on the roster; all the rest of the better-known gothic tales of doubling are about men.

I regularly turn, in this book, from the clinic to works of the imagination, because clinician and storyteller so obviously reinforce each other. The earnest search for male multiples follows the trail laid by the novelist. It also distracts from more pressing questions of gender. Why is it that women come to be diagnosed as multiples far more often than men? Four explanations have been canvassed, all heavily influenced by background opinions about multiple personality. They are by no means mutually exclusive.

First, there is the crime hypothesis I have been discussing. Men with latent multiple personalities are violent and fall into the hands of police rather than doctors. Moreover, the anger of female multiples tends to be self-directed, with self-mutilation being quite common.

Second, it is suggested that multiples make an implicit choice that fits in with their cultural milieu. At any time, people suffering severe psychological distress that is not of organic or other biological origin "choose" from socially available and clinically reinforced modes. Dissociative behavior is a language of distress preferred by women. It may even be a means of escape; some alters may express socially inadmissible aspects of personality that the woman wants to own but is not allowed to. Thus in the nineteenth century, some women may have found in their alter a way to be uninhibited; in the twentieth century, some women may have found ways to be lesbian.[14] Men choose other ways of expressing distress, such as alcohol or violence.

Third is the causal explanation. Multiplicity is strongly associated with early and repeated child abuse, especially sexual abuse. Far more girls are thought to be subject to this sort of abuse than boys. A feminist tradition in the past has expected this ratio to be about 9:1. These considerations provide a standard explanation of the 9:1 sex ratio among diagnosed multiples.

Fourth, the element of suggestion is emphasized. Troubled North American women in a therapeutic or clinical setting, even one that rigorously tries to avoid a stereotypical power structure, may cooperate more readily with therapeutic expectations than do men experiencing comparable distress. The men aggressively refuse to cooperate, and hence resist suggestion, while women, who are the cooperators in our society, accept it.

All four of these proposed explanations of the disproportion of female multiples may be correct and may work together. There is remarkably little serious discussion of the gender question in multiplicity. The very first workshop on gender held at an ISSMP&D conference took place in

1992.[15] Numerous participants reported having seen more than one male multiple in therapy. One of the three facilitators, Richard Loewenstein, emphasized that at present "there are no data," but there is little doubt about what data are expected to be forthcoming: more men. Unfortunately, the workshop quickly turned from questions about the gender of patients to questions about sexual relations between clinician and patient, a topic that seemed to fascinate many a participant.

If ever there was a field that needed some caustic feminist analysis, it is multiple personality. The most immediate feminist reaction to multiple personality, before any analysis, has rightly emphasized child abuse. But that is only the beginning of the story. Although child abuse, and the suffering of individual patients, must be resolved immediately, and in personal terms, there are larger issues in the background. Child abuse is not an isolated aspect of present North American society that can be removed by economic and psychological palliatives, preventives, and controls. Just as multiple personality is one indicator of child abuse, so child abuse is just one expression of the violence inherent in our existing patriarchal power structure. That has been a theme in powerful writings ever since the child abuse movement got under way.[16] We now self-righteously condemn the sexually abusive male. Feminist critics find a lot of hypocrisy in this stance. It allows us to conceal from ourselves that the man's behavior is only an extreme form of a more commonplace aggression toward women and children that is condoned and even encouraged, both in popular media and within the economic power structure.

The most detailed analysis of this sort specifically worked out in the context of multiple personality is by Margo Rivera.[17] She is a clinical psychologist, a feminist theoretician, and extremely active in seeking public support for patients with abusive backgrounds. She does take trauma and violence against women as a basis from which to start but may regard multiplicity more metaphorically than do most other clinicians. Traumas, she writes, "are sequestered in disaggregate self-states called alters."[18] What is important for her is what people say about themselves. If they come to talk in multiple language, and in the personae of alters, then that is their way of expressing their problems. She regards detailed recollections of abuse as problematic. One aim of her therapy is "the strategic reworking of the history of experiences of trauma" leading to nondissociative coping skills.

She also encourages some patients, those who are healthy enough, to gain a larger and more political awareness of their plight. Hence she can address, in therapy, issues that many others ignore. Why are *these* your alters? Why are so many of them big men, or little children? Who in the real world do you think your alters resemble? Are the forms of your dissociation both personal and a reaction to the society that you find around you?

Rivera has an approach based on a well-developed political sensibility. She is deeply involved in the women's movement but steers clear of what might be called scapegoat feminism—a feminism that, though often presented as the exact opposite of traditional religious principles and practices, in fact mirrors them closely. Recollection of trauma inflicted by father or another patriarch is very much like a Protestant conversion experience. It begins with the watchword "denial": Peter-like, one thrice denies past abuse. Then comes therapy as conversion, confession, and the restructuring of remembrances of one's past. But informing this familiar pattern there is an almighty twist. Accusation. Your confession is not to *your* sins, but to your father's sins. We do not have Christ the Son taking on the sins of the world. The father takes on the sins that have destroyed your life, for he committed those very sins. We are not concerned with Jesus, the Sacrificial Lamb, but with an old goat, a literal scapegoat, the father, the Sacrificial Ram. This is an incredibly powerful mystique, for it draws on millennia of accumulated meanings. One of the great values of Rivera's analysis is that it does not find scapegoats but proceeds by social critique.

Emphasis on abuse is usually presented as empowering, but it may be the very opposite. This is suggested by Ruth Leys, a rare feminist scholar who addresses multiple personality head on. She criticizes the majority feminist perspective represented by Judith Herman's *Trauma and Recovery* and, in more general terms, by Catharine MacKinnon.[19] Women, in the majority view, are abused. Children are abused. Females are far more frequently abused than are men. Repeated early abuse is the primary occasioning cause of MPD. Hence far more women than men are multiples. Leys speaks for a minority feminist view, which draws on the analyses of Jacqueline Rose. She urges a rethinking of the role and meaning of violence. She writes that Rose poses a challenge to "Catharine MacKinnon, Jeffrey Masson and others who, rejecting the notion of unconscious conflict, embrace instead a rigid dichotomy between the internal and the external such that violence is imagined as coming to the subject entirely from the outside—a point of view that inevitably reinforces a politically retrograde stereotype of the female as a purely passive victim." She holds that discourse like MacKinnon's "in effect denies the female subject of all possibility of agency."[20]

Leys's intentions have nothing in common with the merely skeptical opinion that multiplicity is the consequence of the power of suggestion on women. She implies instead that the great preponderance of female multiples is due to a covert alliance between clinicians and the patients. The alliance is intended to be supportive of women, but in fact it continues the old system of disempowerment. Leys offers a genuinely radical critique of current theories and practices connected with multiple personality. It does not dispute the prevalence of family violence or question its societal foundations. It does not deny that past abuse can, in a cultural and clinical milieu, lead to symptomatology of a florid sort. It does question the complacency of a theory that purports to take the part of the patient. It conjectures that the theory, practice, and underlying assumptions reinforce the patient's self-image as a passive victim. Taken to one possible conclusion, this type of analysis might suggest that current theories of abuse, trauma, and dissociation are part of another cycle of oppression of women, all the more dangerous because the theorists and clinicians represent themselves as being so entirely on the side of the "victim"—whom they thereby construct as helpless, rather than as an autonomous human being.

These reflections lead on to yet another question about gender and multiple personality, one that is specifically about the illness itself. There are three constant features of the phenomenology of multiple personality, from the end of the eighteenth century to the present. One is that most diagnosed patients are women. The second is that it is very common for one alter to be younger than the host, often a child. The third is ambivalence about sexuality. Why is that so common among prototypical multiples?

Virtually every female patient, of whom there is much reporting, is said to have a second personality that is more lively than the personality regarded as the host. Words used are "vivacious," "mischievous," "naughty," and, as reporting becomes less inhibited, "promiscuous." As early as the 1820s a Scottish woman servant had sex with a man who had "taken advantage" of her second state.[21] Félida X., the most famous French multiple, topic of chapter 11, conceived and gave birth in her second state, while denying pregnancy in her first state. Variations on this sequence of events are well known.[22] According to Leys, there is ample evidence that the main alter of Prince's 1906 Miss Beauchamp behaved in a way that would now be described as bisexual. Indeed Saul Rosenzweig suggested not only that Miss Beauchamp was bisexual, but that Breuer's Anna O., described by many as being a multiple, was similar to Prince's patient in many respects, including bisexuality.[23] Gender ambivalence continued in the occasional cases reported later in the century.[24] Nevertheless, there is much truth in the following statement about Wilbur's patient Sybil: "The uniqueness which, before, was based on Sybil's having developed more alternating selves than had any other known multiple personality, was now founded as well on her being the only multiple personality to have crossed the borders of sexual difference to develop personalities of the opposite sex."[25]

After *Sybil* the floodgates were opened for transsexual alters. There is a close correlation between the emergence of theoretical perspectives and the emergence of different types of cross-sex alters. Thus in the late 1970s "imaginary playmates" were widely canvassed as an origin of multiplicity—many children have imaginary playmates, and it was thought that in some, the imagined figure coalesces and develops into a personality that uses the body of the host. One such male alter of a female patient was described in 1980.[26] A second source of the male alters was explained as male self-fantasies of the growing female child herself—Sybil's two male alters were prepubertal boy-Sybils who never quite grew up. Also around 1980 there was a notable stylization of the range of alters, such that one would find one or more persecutor alters, and one or more protector alters. Females developed male protector alters who were strong, heavyset, reliable—cowboys or truckers, for example. Throughout this period, the sexuality of cross-sex alters was not discussed in published reports.

As the number of reported alters increased from a typical three or four to an average of sixteen or more, the number of cases with disclosed opposite sex alters radically increased. So did the number of alters who contrasted with the host in other ways. The alters were often stereotypes of the worst sort: racial, ethnic, even stereotypes of old age.[27] Notice that if a patient is to have a large number of alters, there is some difficulty in recognizing who is who. Differences that in our society are taken to be definite, immutable, and central to identity help to shore up the distinctions between multiples. In American culture the cardinal differences between people are gender, age, race, and, to a much lesser degree, income, job, ethnicity, language, or dialect. It is not surprising that when a host of type X (middle-class white American woman aged thirty-nine, say) develops distinct alters, many should be distinctly non-X, that is, of different gender, race, age, social status, or dialect.

The results of Ross's questionnaire, based on 236 cases, showed that 62 percent of reported cases had alters of the opposite sex. But the survey only began to look into switches in gendered attributes. The combinations and permutations of gender identity have become enormous in scope. The nineteenth-century contrast, inhibited/vivacious, remains a commonplace. But now the menu of contrasts has been greatly expanded. Each alter can now be characterized by choices made from each of the following options: same sex/opposite sex, heterosexual/bisexual/homosexual, infantile/prepubertal/adolescent/mature/senile. Mixing and matching these could give sixty alter states distinguished on gender grounds alone.

That may prompt a cynical functionalist insight into the variety of gender roles: it helps to keep the alters distinct. There are, however, many deeper functions to be served by alters of different sexes. One is that, given the standard sex roles, male alters can be a way for an oppressed woman to assume power. Where in the nineteenth century the alter was naughty, mischievous, or promiscuous, in the late twentieth century she can be a man. Margo Rivera has observed:

> In my experience of working with women who experience multiple personalities, it is very common for their vulnerable child personalities and their seductive and/or compliant personalities to be female and their aggressive protector personalities to be male, and other therapists with a wider range of experience than I have confirmed my clinical impression (Kluft, 1987, personal communication), though there has not been any research done so far that would document it. The experience of these alter personalities as they fight with each other for status, power and influence over the individual is powerfully illustrative of the social construction of masculinity and femininity in our society.[28]

This subtle analysis is combined with another one, namely, of the woman who is socially constrained to be heterosexual, but who finds in some of her alters ways of evading this social demand.[29] There is a striking resonance in this insight with a very different attitude to multiple personality. Michael Kenny's *The Passion of Ansel Bourne* argued that nineteenth-century female American multiples used their multiplicity to escape the confines of Protestant duty and submission. Kenny is a debunker, unsympathetic to radical feminisms, and is comfortable with those who say that therapists induce false memories. Yet there is, in both his very negative attitude to multiple personality and Rivera's very positive one, a recognition that multiple personality is one possible response to the roles assigned to women. One way to stop being a sex object is to adopt an alternative gender role.

This idea can be further enriched. One may break out of compulsory gendering, and in particular compulsory heterosexism, by adopting other roles. Initially multiples in therapy are ill; they do not choose roles self-consciously. But suppose they acquire sufficient maturity to see that they have options open to them, and aim not so much at integration as at finding the kind of person they want to be. Then a formerly pathological gender could become the chosen way to be a person. This must be treated as a sophisticated idea. We should not think that the patient discovers some "true" underlying self but that she has broken through to the freedom to choose, create, and construct her own identity. Rather than being a pawn in a deterministic game, she has become an autonomous person. That would be the precise opposite of what, in my concluding chapter, I call false consciousness.

It would be a counsel of perfection to hope that therapy could usually have such results. It is plain, however, that multiple personality needs more gender inquiry beyond Ross's deterministic claim, which amounts to this: the more girls outnumber boys as victims of abuse, the more women will outnumber men as multiples. Ross calls Rivera's analysis "the feminist analysis," instead of calling it one of many feminist analyses of multiple personality. After two paragraphs favoring a political approach to multiple personality, he abruptly switches and states that Rivera's work "is based on linear or nonsystemic thinking," and that it "founders" on the facts that he and his colleagues have discovered about similarities between male and female dissociative experiences.[30] I have no idea what nonsystemic thinking is, but if Rivera provides an example of it, it is more valuable than simplistic deterministic thinking.

We do badly need further feminist analysis of multiple personality disorder. It need not necessarily go the way of the multiple movement. I discussed novels earlier in this chapter and will end by quoting an old-time feminist freedom fighter, Doris Lessing. I can think of very few authors less given to cant. Faye is a relatively minor character in an unnerving book published in 1985, *The Good Terrorist*. Faye, a revolutionary, does her best to stay clear of mental health authorities. She is English, in the early 1980s: hence there is no way, in real life, that she could have been diagnosed as a multiple by the British psychiatric establishment. But Lessing presents her very clearly as multiple, kindly sparing us the jargon. A few deft phrases and brief episodes do the work. Faye is lesbian, usually coy and Cockney, with hair in ringlets, the seductive and gentle member of a couple. But she can switch to being harsh, cruel, scary, with an upper-class accent. "Her face seemed to crumple up out of itself, suggesting some other Faye, a pale, awful, violent Faye, the unwilling prisoner of the pretty Cockney."[31] On the next page Lessing writes of "this outburst from Faye's other self. Or selves?" In a later episode, a pathetic mother and infant are at the door of the house occupied by squatters. Alice, the novel's protagonist,

> turned to see Faye standing on the landing, looking down. There was something about her that held Alice's attention, some deadliness of purpose, or mood. The pretty, wispy, frail creature, Faye, had again disappeared; in her place was a white faced malevolent woman, with punishing cold eyes, who came in a swift rush down the stairs.[32]

Faye has attempted suicide before the novel begins, cuts her wrists in the middle of it, and apparently chooses to have herself blown up at the end. In case we have any doubts about her being a multiple, her lover, Roberta, says to Alice "in a low, quick vibrant voice, 'If you knew about her childhood, if you knew what had happened to her . . .'"

> "I don't care about her fucking childhood," remarked Alice.
> "No, I've got to tell you, for her sake, for Faye's. She was a battered baby, you see . . ."
> "I don't care," Alice shouted suddenly, "you don't understand. I've had all the bloody unhappy childhoods I am going to listen to. People go on and on. . . . As far as I am concerned, unhappy childhoods are the great con, the great alibi."
> Shocked, Roberta said, "A battered *baby*—and battered babies grow up to become adults." She was back in her place, sitting, leaning forward, her eyes on Alice's determined to make Alice respond.
> "I know one thing," Alice said. "Communes. Squats. If you don't take care, that's what they become—people sitting around discussing their shitty childhoods. Never again. We're not here for that. Or is that what you want? A sort of permanent encounter group. Everything turns into that, if you let it."[33]

Lessing's character Alice is not just saying that unhappy childhoods are the great con. She is implying that specialist knowledge of memory, sciences of memory that tell us what our souls are really like, are a great con. Lessing, in other work, has taught us about the power of memory, but she has never resorted to esoteric expertise about its nature in order to use memory as a powerful means of rebellion or liberation.

Cause

"NEVER in the history of psychiatry have we ever come to know so well the specific etiology of a major illness, its natural course, its treatment." This remarkable statement was made in 1989 by Richard Loewenstein, when he was president of the ISSMP&D.[1] In the course of twenty years an illness had passed from being virtually unknown to being better understood than any other mental malady.

Etiology is defined as that branch of medicine which deals with the causes or origins of disease. Causation matters to the practitioner because the most effective treatment of a disease usually relies on a knowledge of its causes. Knowledge of causes helps us prevent illness. But causation also matters to theory. When we know the causes we feel confident that we have identified a disease entity, something more than a cluster of symptoms. How did the knowledge of the cause of multiple personality come into being? It was not a matter of simple discovery. Since so few people worked in the field in the early days, we can watch the development of this central piece of knowledge about multiplicity.

There are different types of causal knowledge. We know the causes of *individual* events, and we know *general* laws of causation. To be totally simplistic, when historians discuss the causes of a historical event— they seldom do—they invoke other individual events. (Parody: the shot at Sarajevo caused the outbreak of the Great War.) When physicists speak of causation—they seldom do—they are usually concerned with causal laws that hold universally or with a definite degree of probability. The simplest statements of an individual cause will be of the form "This event or condition A caused or produced that event or condition B." Such causal questions interest clinicians and patients: I want to know what made *me* ill. Philosophers argue that statements of individual causes are warranted only when there is a general causal statement in the background.[2] Such a general statement might be nothing more than "Events or conditions like A tend to produce events or conditions like B."

When we speak of etiology, we mean something more than a clinical judgment that on a certain occasion event A caused event B. Etiology has to do with warranted judgments of causality, and so it demands generality. We ought, however, to be very tolerant about the logical form of such generalizations. Causal generalizations lie between extremes. At one end is the *strictly universal*: Whenever there is an event or condition of kind K, then there results an event or condition of kind J. Old-fashioned physics preferred laws like that. At the other end are truly modest statements of *fairly necessary conditions*: Without events or conditions of kind K, events or conditions of kind J are unlikely to occur. In between we have probabilities and tendencies.

"Never in the history of psychiatry," said Loewenstein, "have we ever come to know so well the specific etiology of a major illness." His assertion demands that some general causal statement about this major illness be in the background. But it does not demand anything as stringent as strict universality. A fairly necessary condition is sufficient. That is surely what Loewenstein meant. His fairly necessary condition might be this: "Without severe and repeated childhood trauma, typically of a sexual sort, multiple personality is not likely to appear." The specific etiology of which Loewenstein speaks never goes beyond fairly-necessary-conditions. No one should demand more of psychology. We should, however, be put on our guard against rhetoric. "Specific etiology" sounds very impressive. It sounds as if we are getting to the other extreme of causal statements, to strictly universal statements. Not at all. Loewenstein's specific etiology is the weakest imaginable etiology.

The fairly-necessary-condition evolved together with the characterization of multiple personality. Consider a careful statement by Cornelia Wilbur and Richard Kluft. "MPD is most parsimoniously understood as a posttraumatic dissociative disorder of childhood onset."[3] Here the childhood onset and the presence of trauma are not parts of an empirical generalization or a statistically checkable fairly-necessary-condition. They are part of the authors' understanding of multiple personality disorder, part of what they mean by "MPD." There is nothing methodologically or scientifically wrong with this. I warn only against having it both ways. There is a tendency (a) to define the concept "MPD" (or dissociative identity disorder) in terms of early childhood trauma, and (b) to state, as if it were a discovery, that multiple personality is caused (in the sense of fairly-necessary-condition) by childhood trauma. We should not delude ourselves into thinking that we first defined the disorder and then discovered its cause.

I have just spoken of definitions. That is not quite right. Very seldom is definition the right concept in psychiatry. The linguists' idea of a prototype is more serviceable. Child sexual abuse became part of the proto-type of multiple personality. That is, if you were giving a best example of a multiple, you would include child abuse as one feature of the example. It is easy to confirm the impression that when clinicians of multiples give an example of a client and cite a causal event, they regularly mention child sexual abuse. People are most revealing when they are very slightly off guard—for instance, when they are not formally discussing causes but mention causes in passing. The way in which a prototype comes into play is striking when an authority is not trying to be scientific, but just lets the common understanding slip out. Here are two examples, chosen from two experts who are not doctrinaire. Both remarks date from 1993, and not from the years of early enthusiasms, the mid-eighties.

A psychologist mentions, in an aside, a thirty-eight-year-old woman who, while in his office, switches into a thirteen-year-old boy who is in her uncle's house. She then reenacts an anal rape. Or a psychiatrist, de-scribing research on post-traumatic stress disorder in connection with the San Francisco Bay area earthquake of 1991, lets out, as an anecdote, that at the time of the earthquake he was treating a heavy woman. She switched into a six-year-old, thinking the rumble of the quake was the stumbling drunken footsteps of her childhood molesters. He had to get her out of the building, which, in her alter state, was no mean task.[4] My two examples are not intended to establish current scientific teaching about multiplicity and abuse. They show how the ideas are associated in the talk of serious contributors to the field. Just as people, at least those who live in Atlanta or the Bay area, do not say "ostrich" when wanting to mention an example of a bird, so it seems that clinicians do not casu-ally give nonabused patients as examples of multiples. Of course os-triches are birds, and known to be so, and there are nonabused multi-ples, but they are not prototypical.

The connection between abuse and multiplicity became stronger and stronger during the 1970s, just when the meaning of "child abuse" moved from the prototype of battered babies through the full range of physical abuse and gradually centered on sexual abuse. As a point of logic it is useful to see how concepts are used to lift themselves up by their own bootstraps. That sounds highly figurative, but consider this. In a 1986 essay Wilbur wrote, "In discussing the psychoanalysis of MPD, Marmer (1980) pointed out that childhood trauma is central and causal."[5] In fact Steven Marmer had ended his prizewinning essay by posing some questions. He said that in recent *previous* reports of multi-plicity "childhood trauma is central and causal." He did not "point out" that trauma is, as a sort of law of nature, central and causal; he said that it appeared in previous cases. He proposed as a topic for future research the question of whether this was generally true. And what were the recent cases to which he referred? Wilbur was a primary reference.[6] I am not now questioning whether childhood trauma is central and causal. I am making an observation about the use of evidence in the firming up of a conceptual connection. How does it happen? In part, by circular self-support.

Marmer's psychoanalysis of a multiple is beautifully and simply described. It may also be something of a cautionary tale. His patient was a gifted and artistic Los Angeles woman from a culturally endowed New York family. She saw both of her parents as having two sides to their characters. She was forty-one and had been in therapy when she was much younger, but was now experiencing familial and other crises. Three distinct personalities did emerge in the course of a year or so of intense analysis. The analysis unfolded in a rather classic way, making rich use of dreams, and complete with a primal scene in which the young child interrupts her parents making love. Marmer was careful to enter a caveat that he was not committed to the "historical 'truth'" of this event. Those are his quotation marks around "truth."

The central crisis of his patient's young life was the death of her father when she was eight. At one stage in the analysis she acquired a belief that she had been raped by strange teenagers in the hours after this event. Marmer listened and let the memories work themselves out. As the analysis proceeded, these recollections dissolved into a fantasy that had briefly and conveniently covered over what the woman later came to believe had happened. Immediately after the death she had been forced to be alone in a room with her teddy bear; she had gone out and run through an underground tunnel to an open space. Part of her had been desperately denying her father's death. She had run screaming up to a stranger in a raincoat, crying, "You're my daddy, you're all right, aren't you," and had been brusquely turned away. These events—the death of her father, her anguish, loneliness, and temporary abandonment—formed that aspect of her life with which she left analysis.

Marmer's description is far richer than my summary and naturally involves the child's ambivalent love for her parents, their two sides, the primal scene, and so forth. But the father's death, followed by her abandonment for three hours, was the central trauma. According to Marmer there never was a rape or literal sexual abuse. Why should we believe a Freudian, given Freud's infamous denial of his own 1893 theory on the cause of hysteria, namely, sexual assault in childhood? We don't have to believe him: Wilbur cited this case report with apparent approval. Marmer made no assumption about the historical truth of the memories; quite the contrary. Yet his case became part of the evidence that actual historical sexual trauma causes multiple personality.[7]

The connection between multiple personality and real, not fantasized, child abuse was cemented in clinical journals throughout the 1980s. By 1982 there were vivid musterings of data about the relationship between incest and multiple personality.[8] Philip Coons had stated the connection cautiously in a paper of 1980; in his classic 1984 essay on differential diagnosis of multiple personality, he wrote that "the onset of multiple personality is early in childhood, and is often associated with physical and sexual abuse."[9] At that time no child multiples were known—none. But the hunt was on. The first in what is now a long series of books of contributed papers about multiple personality had a fitting title: *Childhood Antecedents of Multiple Personality*.[10] Theory preceded observation. There is nothing wrong with that; indeed, in one of the most influential philosophies of science created during the twentieth century, Karl Popper vigorously insisted that the work of the theoretician always precedes that of the experimenter. The Popperian question must be this: Could anything have falsified the conjecture that there exist children with multiple personality disorder?

At this point it is worth reading the text, line by line, of Frank Putnam's exemplary clinical textbook of 1989, *Diagnosis and Treatment of Multiple Personality Disorder*. Line-by-line readings of any text inevitably make one ask, What did the author mean here? I do not intend to be querulous. This book is universally acknowledged as the best in the field. Putnam begins his chapter on etiology with the words "MPD appears to be a psychobiological response to a relatively specific set of experiences occurring within a circumscribed developmental window."[11] Psychobiological? Thus far, no biological concomitants specific to multiple personality have been sustained. Putnam's sentence is intended to get at two distinct propositions. First, there is a systematic connection between multiplicity and childhood trauma. But why is that psycho*biological*?

The answer lies in a second proposition from the traumatic stress literature. Something is known about the brain chemistry of terrified animals. Rats subjected to inescapable electric shocks are paralyzed by fear, and this reaction is correlated with the depletion of important brain chemicals. Moreover, the behavior of the rats is said to resemble that of war veterans diagnosed with post-traumatic stress disorder. From a study of "the psychobiology of the trauma response," Putnam quotes the assertion that "the symptoms of hyper-reactivity (i.e. startle responses, explosive outbursts, nightmares, and intrusive recollections) in humans resemble those produced by chronic nonadenergic hypersensitivity following transient catecholamine depletion after acute trauma in animals."[12] It is a reasonable research guess that human hyperreactivity (psychological) is paralleled by chemical changes in traumatized rats. But it is not knowledge.

Putnam did not develop the psychobiology theme in his book. He mentioned a fascinating research program and then turned to clinical experience. "The linkage between childhood trauma and MPD," he writes, "has slowly emerged in the clinical literature over the last 100 years, although this association is obvious to any clinician who has worked with several cases." The first part of that statement needs clarification.

The connection between psychological trauma and hysteria had certainly been in place for a century when Putnam wrote his book—almost exactly a century. We find it in the work of Pierre Janet, more famously in Breuer and Freud, and in forgotten predecessors whom I discuss in chapter 13. The linkage of trauma and hysteria became firmly established about 1889. But Putnam was not speaking of that time. Rather, he had in mind the way in which, very occasionally, painful life experiences—such as parental death—occur in some early-twentieth-century reports of multiple personality. Traumatic abuse seems absent until, as Putnam notes, H. H. Goddard's 1921 patient Bernice R. That young woman had no problem with repressed memories; she spoke directly about incest with her father. But Goddard thought his patient was imagining things, and used hypnotic suggestion to convince her that no such thing had ever happened.[13] During the 1920s no one of any influence took actual sexual abuse very seriously, and so it did not figure in the multiple personality case literature. *We* see sexual trauma in the history of Bernice, but her psychologist did not. Putnam continues, "It was not until the 1970s that the first reports clearly connecting MPD to childhood trauma began to appear in single case histories." That is, the connection followed in the wake of consciousness-raising about child abuse. The linkage between childhood trauma and multiple personality did not emerge slowly over one hundred years. It came into being almost suddenly, in the 1970s.

After that time multiple personality became very firmly associated with childhood trauma, but association is not causation. Putnam offers "a developmental model of multiple personality." Models are to be welcomed: often, in the natural sciences, it is in simplified models of reality that we get the clearest grasp of causal laws.[14] Perhaps the very word "model" implicitly carries the cachet, if not of models in physics and cosmology, at least of statistical or economic models. But Putnam's model is not like physics or economics. It is a story. It is a story in a time-honored tradition, a story that explains by telling how things originated. Like Genesis, the first book of the Bible.

"The evidence suggests" to Putnam "that we are all born with the potential for multiple personalities and over the course of normal development we more or less succeed in consolidating an integrated sense of self." What evidence? Putnam refers to one important school of "infant-consciousness researchers [who] have evolved an agreed-upon taxonomy of newborn infant behavioral states." He finds that the ways in which infants change states exhibit "psychophysiological properties" that resemble those which occur when alters switch personalities.[15] Psychophysiology is more directly observable than the psychobiology alluded to earlier. It means change in facial expression, demeanor, muscle tension, and the like.

Putnam has an eminently plausible story of growing up. The baby, then the child, manages to "consolidate self and identity." Multiple personality is proposed as failure at this "developmental task." Putnam then turns to a "second normative process"—the first one, presumably, being the process of consolidating self. The word "normative" is not used in the dictionary meaning, "Of, relating to, or *prescribing* a norm or standard." Since Putnam uses the word in contrast to "pathological" he must mean not "normative," but "normal," viz. "conforming with, adhering to, or constituting a norm, standard, pattern, level or type; typical."[16] What Putnam calls the second normative process is the "propensity of the child to enter into a specific kind of state of consciousness, the dissociative state." He is saying that this is normal, ordinary, but can become pathological. Such states are characterized by "significant alterations in the integrative functions of memory for thoughts, feelings or actions, and significant alterations in the sense of self." Thus far they are ordinary and healthy (not pathological, anyway). Adults who spontaneously dissociate tend to have a capacity "to enter voluntary hypnotic states." Children are more readily hypnotized than adults and are most hypnotizable around nine or ten years of age. Hence if children make use of ordinary and commonplace dissociation to cope with stress, they may do it best at that time in their lives.

The third "normative development substrate" is the ability of children to fantasize. Some children invent imaginary playmates or companions (most recently immortalized in the comic strip *Calvin and Hobbes*). In the early eighties the imaginary playmate who stayed on was proposed as a source of an alter personality. The suggestion seems to have been too benign to account for the horror in the lives of multiples, and this conjecture has been largely discarded. Putnam still had to discuss it when he was writing his textbook, published in 1989, where he calls the idea "tantalizing but ambiguous."

With this story of development in place, we have room for a relation between multiple personality and overwhelming trauma. A child copes by heightening the separation between behavioral states "in order to compartmentalize overwhelming affects and memories generated by the trauma." Children may in a sense deliberately enter into dissociative states. In addition, parents and caretakers play an active role in helping their child "enter and sustain appropriate behavioral states." The child abuse that is prototypically associated with multiples comes from people who ought to have been caring for the child, and ought to be deserving of trust. "It is easy to speculate that the bad parenting accompanying abuse fails to aid the child in learning to modulate behavioral states." Finally, the dissociated states get firmed up and take on their own characters. "One can easily conceive of these dissociated states, each imbued with a specific sense of self, being elaborated over time as a child repeatedly re-enters a given state to escape from trauma." This may be the only way in which the child can carry on; it may be "life-saving," says Putnam. "It becomes maladaptive, however, in an adult world that stresses continuity of memory, behavior, and sense of self."

Putnam has carefully hedged his discussion with such qualifiers as "it is easy to speculate," "one can easily conceive of," and "one can postulate." Yet the reader tends to discard these phrases and the innumerable "may"s and "possibly"s. This is how it is—without qualification. This is how the child dissociates. This is the causal effect of trauma. In a book published the next year Denis Donovan and Deborah McIntyre quote and paraphrase Putnam's discussion at length, but manage to omit every single qualifier. Within one year speculation and postulation had come to be cited as fact.[17]

Thus Loewenstein's "specific etiology" is a self-sustaining and self-confirming etiology. A certain picture of origins is imparted to disturbed and unhappy people, who then use it to reorder or reorganize their conception of their past. It becomes their past. I am not saying that their past is directly created by doctors. I am saying that this picture becomes disseminated as a way of thinking of what it was like to be a child and to grow up. There is no canonical way to think of our own past. In the endless quest for order and structure, we grasp at whatever picture is floating by and put our past into its frame.

There is an abbreviated version of this account of development and the past, Kluft's Four-Factor Model of Multiple Personality Disorder. Instead of one fairly necessary causal condition, we get four. According to Kluft, multiple personality "begins in childhood and occurs when (1) a child able to dissociate is exposed to overwhelming stimuli; (2) these cannot be managed by less drastic defenses; (3) dissociated contents become linked to underlying substrates for personality organization; and (4) there are no restorative influences, or there are too many 'double-binds.'"[18]

We should notice the phrase "a child able to dissociate." There are many suggestions, in the literature, that degrees of this ability are innate, inherited. There are two parts to this suggestion. The first is that dissociation comes in degrees, as if everyone could be arranged in a line, with the most dissociation-prone at one end, and the least dissociation-prone at the other. This proposition is defended by work on the measurement of dissociation. I discuss that in the next chapter, and show how measurement and causation support each other. Once the assumption is made that dissociation is linear, a matter of more or less, there appears the second part of the suggestion, that these degrees can be inherited. That is interesting, but such genetically oriented claims are extraordinarily difficult to substantiate. We must be very careful about spurious correlations. For example, one might find that multiple personality runs in families. But the explanation might be that members of a family go to the same group of therapists who specialize in multiples.

What evidence might bear on the models of Putnam or Kluft? One kind would be very general. Childhood trauma, and particularly repeated sexual abuse, might be shown to have specific psychiatric sequelae in adulthood. There is an immense amount of folklore on this issue, but my survey in chapter 4 suggests that there is very little agreed stable and specific knowledge about such effects. The most promising venue is current research on post-traumatic stress disorder. This approach was favored by David Spiegel from the beginning, and it is not at all clear that it leads us in the direction of understanding multiple personality. It is no accident that Spiegel himself helped rename multiple personality, or that he discounts the idea of fully rounded alters. He sees the problem as one of integrating a person who has broken down; the breakdown is connected with a terrible early life. That may well be the future of multiple personality. But whereas the florid multiple personality of the 1980s seemed to demand something like the models of Kluft or Putnam, Spiegel's potential future for the disorder may not need anything of the sort.

A second type of evidence for models like those of Putnam and Kluft is based on clinical experience. Clinicians find it absolutely compelling. As Putnam wrote, "this association is obvious to any clinician who has worked with several cases." Patients themselves come, in therapy, to describe their dissociation in ways that conform to these pictures. A therapist can hardly resist such evidence, and yet there is reason to worry that the process of therapy and healing concretizes a story into a fact.

A third type of evidence would come from examining multiple personality as it develops in children. If multiple personality has its onset in childhood, then it should be possible to elicit it at that time. Treatment should be easier, and adult disintegration could be precluded. It becomes an obligation—indeed a therapeutic imperative—for therapists to seek multiplicity in children, where the alters or personality fragments will not be so entrenched. There is also a great theoretical incentive for finding child multiples, for they would confirm the models of how multiple personality originates. The hunt was on for child multiples. One leader in this field has been Gary Peterson, who proposed the first diagnostic guidelines.[19] Peterson is chair of the ISSMP&D committee on child multiple personality disorder and is leading the campaign to have the disorder introduced into the next *Diagnostic and Statistical Manual*, *DSM-V*. The campaign failed for *DSM-IV*, although that volume does contain a passing acknowledgment of the possibility of such a condition.

A skeptic will observe that throughout the twentieth century, child multiple personality disorder was absolutely unknown until a certain account of multiple personality emerged in the 1980s. Such a skeptic could well be picking up the wrong end of the stick. The physical sciences abound with examples of phenomena that no one noticed until there was a theory to make one look. It could be one of the strengths of Putnam's account that it makes us examine disturbed children more closely, to see if they are nascent multiples.

So let us look at children to determine whether they have alters. Jane was nine.[20] Her parents were appalled by her grossly aggressive behavior and took her to a therapist. She had awful food allergies and would not eat; Jane appeared to have been starved. Yet when she was sent for treatment away from home her eating problems and allergies seemed to vanish. Her school reported she was not a "behavior" problem at all; her problem was that she was too isolated and withdrawn. The family environment was not a happy one, with a deserting father, a stepfather, and plenty of indifference and cruelty. Her therapist asked Jane if she had been abused. No. But she played knowingly with anatomically correct dolls. She came to speak of a Bad Sister who did bad things. Then Jane spoke in the voice of the Bad Sister: yes, she had indeed had sex and enjoyed it thoroughly. The therapist read stories about a girl who had developed another personality to deal with bad things. Jane listened attentively. At the next session she said that was right. That was *her*. Soon she was able to eat, laugh, and get along with other children at school.

Jane's therapist deliberately encouraged splitting and the embodiment of the character Bad Sister. Now consider another approach. Twelve-year-old "Sally Brown" was viciously aggressive and exhibited uncontrollable switching and other dissociative behavior. She was adopted by the Browns from a foster home, where she had been placed because her mother, father, and mother's boyfriends abused her both physically and sexually. For well over a year an enormous sum had been spent on testing, hospitalization, and treatment. She was repeatedly diagnosed with multiple personality disorder. Because she did not respond to any type of therapy, the Browns called a number of experts on multiple personality. They were eventually referred to Donovan and McIntyre, a psychiatrist and a psychotherapist.

Donovan and McIntyre hold that the usual process of confirming a diagnosis of child multiple personality strongly reinforces dissociation. They do not attempt to elicit any kind of pathological behavior. Instead they try, as they put it, "to mobilize learning, growth, adaptation, health, and change." Whenever Sally answered a question with "I don't know" when they were taking her history, Donovan or McIntyre replied, "You're kidding!" As a result Sally cheerfully answered most of the questions and displayed none of her usual abrupt changes in consciousness. When Mrs. Brown discussed Sally's life in school, she said, "We're not doing too well in that area," Donovan and McIntyre made fun of the "we" because it muddles how many people there are, and who. When Mrs. Brown referred to herself as "Mommy" in the third person, as if that were another person, they pointed out the equation this suggested: Mrs. Brown = Mommy = Sally's biological mother (far away, who had beaten Sally). Mrs. Brown thereby invited Sally to punish

Mrs. Brown for the biological mother's behavior. When Mrs. Brown spoke of "the real mother," one of the therapists remarked, in Sally's presence, that real mothers protect their children. In short, Donovan and McIntyre redefined Sally's relations to her adoptive mother and blocked dissociative behavior.

It is a general strategy of Donovan and McIntyre's *Healing the Hurt Child* to use straight talk. When Mrs. Brown said to Sally, "Can you tell them . . ." (suggesting that maybe Sally could not tell them), the two clinicians insisted on "Tell them. . . ." It was made plain that Sally's previous therapies did not have to be accepted, and that she could carry on in the new straightforward way outside the office, at home. This made it increasingly hard for Sally to forget, space out, or blur boundaries within or between persons.

Donovan and McIntyre use their sense of how a child, not an adult, thinks, finds out, and behaves; they rely on what they call the normal "childhood capacity for adaptive-integrative-transformative change." This approach is altogether different from identifying, meeting, and negotiating with child alters, or bargaining with them to get along with each other. After a second two-hour session on the first afternoon, Sally found it hard to dissociate. By the end of the final hour-and-a-half session the next day, she could no longer dissociate. Donovan and McIntyre argue that their child-centered approach allows them to start healing during the very first encounter. Their refusal to support any type of dissociation very often at once reduces the number and intensity of symptoms.[21]

Donovan and McIntyre have not taken a public position on the causes of adult multiple personality. In practice they say that children should not be treated as if they were miniature adult multiples enduring classical therapy for their disorder. Hence Donovan and McIntyre have to be critical of, for example, Jane's therapy. They will need to know much more about the case than I have gleaned from the report, and they will be dubious about the way that her therapist elicited and cemented distinct alters. But that is a difference over treatment styles for children, not a difference about the causes of adult multiple personality.

From the point of view of the theory of trauma and multiplicity, there are at least two ways to react to stories like that of Sally. One is to say that childhood multiplicity can be treated very easily. It becomes pathological in adulthood precisely when it has gone underground. Childhood and adult multiple personality are nevertheless one and the same illness. But there is a very different inference to draw from the case of

Sally Brown: Childhood and adult multiplicity and dissociation are different kinds of things. One cannot use observed multiplicity in some children, given certain types of therapy, to conclude that one is watching, in miniature, the very same illness as troubles adults. Hence child multiplicity, such as it is, is not evidence that childhood trauma causes adult multiple personality.

Clinicians committed to the diagnosis and treatment of multiple personality do see a continuum connecting child, adolescent, and adult multiple personality. This continuum is not merely clinical. It furnishes part of the basis for the current etiology of multiple personality. The same dissociative phenomena are said to be at work with nine-year-olds as we find in thirty-nine-year-olds. It is asserted that the dissociation in the woman of thirty-nine began when she was nine, or three. There is an implied contrary-to-fact conditional here; if the nine-year-old had not been treated, then even if she were to mature into a relatively stable adult, we would expect manifestations of multiple personality to emerge later. Bad Sister would become an alter, perhaps forever locked into the age of nine. Conversely, if we find a patient who has Bad Sister as an alter, then that alter was formed when the patient was nine, and had the patient had the good fortune to enter into therapy at nine, then she would have behaved like Jane.

But suppose we take another route. Suppose that multiple personality in childhood, if there is such a thing, is not a childhood version of the adult syndrome. That would radically undermine the entire causal story that I have been discussing. For the specific etiology of multiple personality—the discovery trumpeted by Loewenstein—is that splitting occurred during childhood, as a coping response. But what we find in children is something else. Hence we are led to a quite different version of multiple personality. The disorder becomes a way of seeing childhood and its terrors. It is not that one split early in life in order to cope. Rather, in therapy, one begins to see oneself as having split at that time in order to cope.

It is easy to be misconstrued here. Some people still say that the terrors of awful childhood do not occur in the lives of many children. That is not only ludicrous but vile, exculpatory. I suggest something entirely different. It is far more complex, and at odds with our ordinary sense of causation. I want to express the paradoxical idea in terms most favorable to the recent styles of diagnosis and treatment of multiple personality. Contrary to Loewenstein, I suggest that we have not found any ordinary etiology of this illness. We should not think of multiplicity as being strictly caused by child abuse. It is rather that the multiple finds or sees the cause of her condition in what she comes to remember about her childhood, and is thereby helped. This is passed off as a specific etiology, but what is happening is more extraordinary than that. It is a way of explaining oneself, not by recovering the past, but by redescribing it, rethinking it, refeeling it.

It is tempting to say that a new past comes into being once events are recalled and described within a new structure of causation and explanation. It need not be a false past, in the sense that it is at odds with, inconsistent with, what would have been recorded if everything had been overseen by a great camcorder in the sky. But the permanent videotape thus imagined gives pictures of events, not descriptions of them. The past becomes rewritten in memory, with new kinds of descriptions, new words, new ways of feeling, such as those grouped under the general heading of child abuse. The events as described, which the multiple in therapy comes to feel as the cause of her illness, did not produce her present state. Instead, redescriptions of the past are caused by the present. Nevertheless, the patient feels that events as newly described *do* produce her present state. She feels that way because of the kinds of knowledge about memory that are current. She may not be healthy enough or educated enough to use words such as "etiology," but this causal story has become part of the conceptual space in which she lives, thinks, feels, and talks.

In this chapter I have described how the causation of multiple personality became an item of knowledge. Psychiatry did not discover that early and repeated child abuse causes multiple personality. It forged that connection, in the way that a blacksmith turns formless molten metal into tempered steel. I have traced the lines of development, using the best textbook in the field in conjunction with the standard research papers. A disturbed type of behavior has been joined to events in early childhood that may surface in memory. Cynics about the multiple movement argue that both the behavior and the memories are cultivated by therapists. That is not my argument. I am pursuing a far more profound concern, namely, the way in which the very idea of the cause was forged. Once we have that idea, we have a very powerful tool for making up people, or, indeed, for making up ourselves. The soul that we are constantly constructing we construct according to an explanatory model of how we came to be the way we are.

It follows that this chapter has not been concerned with an empirical question: Does early and repeated child abuse cause, under the right conditions, adult multiple personality? I have been discussing a reformulation of how we can come to be the way we are, and of how we come to view our own nature. A seemingly innocent theory on causation (which might as a matter of empirical fact be true or false) becomes formative and regulatory. And of course multiple personality is only a tiny microcosm used to illustrate this phenomenon. The theory of multiple personality has the virtue, for exposition and study, of being incredibly simple. I hope it is obvious by now that the recent theory of multiple personality, as opposed to clinical practice, is the most elementary psychological theory that has ever existed.

Multiple personality disorder illustrates, in a heightened way, a completely general phenomenon about memory, description, the past, and the soul. Such difficult matters are the topics of my last two chapters. I believe that the causal theory about dissociative disorders cannot be understood on its own. For we must come to see how it became obvious, inevitable, the sort of thing that nobody even asks about. It did so because memory became the way to have knowledge of the soul. I shall presently turn to that, but first we should examine another way in which knowledge about multiple personality became objective. The measurement of dissociation supports the simple theory of multiple personality because it became an item of knowledge that all people dissociate to some degree. There is just one kind of thing, "dissociation," and we all dissociate. There are two parts to the causal theory of multiplicity. There is the occasioning cause, child abuse. And there is the innate tendency of some children to dissociate to a great degree and thereby have a special way of coping with trauma. We know about these degrees of dissociation because we can measure them. I shall now describe how this knowledge came into being.

Measure

AN ILLNESS becomes an object of knowledge when it is identified, as its causes are discovered, and as methods of prevention, treatment, or cure are developed. Measurement is a second route to knowledge, and the two routes cross. For example, the causal story about multiple personality is bolstered by measurements used to establish that dissociation comes in degrees, so that children with a strong innate predisposition to dissociate may use that as a device to cope with trauma. Thus Putnam writes that "central to the concept of the adaptive function(s) of dissociation is the idea that dissociative phenomena exist on a continuum."[1]

Why does he think that there is a continuum? He cites two sources of evidence. First, hypnotizability in the general population forms a continuum from those who are highly resistant to those who are hypnotized at the wave of a hand. It is postulated that there is an analogy between susceptibility to hypnotism and tendency to dissociate. *"The second line of evidence supporting the concept of a continuum of dissociative experiences . . . comes from surveys using the Dissociative Experiences Scale."*[2] That scale was the first objective measure of dissociative experiences.

The continuum of dissociative experiences has become something of an accepted fact within the multiple personality movement. It has been criticized from outside. Fred Frankel, a psychiatrist who is an expert on clinical and experimental uses of hypnotism, cautions against equating hypnotizability scores with dissociative capacity, and warns against the ready assumption that hypnotizability itself is a single phenomenon, so that everyone is simply more or less hypnotizable. Thus he doubts Putnam's first line of evidence.[3] He also queries the second line for reasons that I will soon mention. Unlike Frankel I am less concerned to question Putnam's continuum hypothesis than to show how creating systems of measurement, such as the Dissociative Experiences Scale, can bring a fact—the fact of a dissociative continuum—into being.

The past ten years have seen rapid development of quantitative measures of dissociation and multiplicity. That makes the study of the disorder more and more like other branches of empirical psychology. To avoid getting lost in statistical details, I shall focus on two related items: Putnam's continuum hypothesis and the very first method of measuring dissociation, the Dissociative Experiences Scale ("DES") published by Putnam and Eve Bernstein Carlson in 1986. These two authors used their scale to test their hypothesis that "the number and frequency of experiences and symptoms attributable to dissociation lie along a continuum."[4]

I approach matters this way for several reasons. First, it allows us to focus on the logical nature of the concept "dissociation." Is it well represented by a linear continuum? Second, the continuum hypothesis, established by the use of objective questionnaires, leads on to the objective theory of causation. A third reason for my approach is that testing hypotheses has cachet in itself: thanks to Karl Popper's influential philosophy of science, testing hypotheses is widely regarded as the sine qua non of objective science. Bernstein and Putnam stated two hypotheses they "sought to test," one of which was the continuum hypothesis. Their work thereby acquired the tone of Popper's hard-nosed science, yet these authors did not, in fact, test their hypotheses at all. Finally, Colin Ross asserted in 1994 that "over the past ten years, the MPD literature has evolved from prescientific to scientific status."[5] By studying the DES and related statistical tests we shall be able to form a just appreciation of this scientific status.

Empirical psychology has created its own genre of objectivity, the questionnaire subjected to standardized scoring and statistical comparisons.[6] Best known to most of us are IQ tests. Nothing could seem much further from multiple personality than the intelligence quotient. Yet by what ought to be the sheerest coincidence, the early histories of the two are intertwined. Alfred Binet is usually regarded as the founder of intelligence testing; descendants of the Stanford-Binet tests are still in use. Early in his career, before he turned to intelligence, Binet was writing about multiple personality.[7] He studied hypnotism intensively and discussed its ability to produce alter states. He was up to his neck in one of the zanier types of research, metallotherapy, in which hysterical symptoms were relieved by the application of different metals to different parts of the body. The very first truly multiple personality, the subject of chapter 12 below, was made multiple by metallotherapy.

Morton Prince, the great American pioneer of multiplicity, during a visit to France where his mother was to be treated for neurasthenia, took the opportunity to study under Binet. H. H. Goddard, whose 1921 patient Bernice was among the last of the first American wave of multiples (and whom I use as an example in my final chapter) also began his career under Binet. He returned to America to develop the low end of intelligence testing and invented the word "moron." Goddard's measures of feeblemindedness showed that nearly all immigrants from central and southern Europe were unintelligent. It was surely Binet$_2$, measurer of intelligence, and not Binet$_1$, student of multiple personality, who left his mark on the larger history of psychology, yet Binet$_1$ would surely be delighted at the way in which testing, which Binet$_2$ fostered, has now found a niche in what Binet$_1$ called "alterations of the personality."

Psychologists often refer to tests and questionnaires as instruments. That makes us think of the material apparatus of chemistry or physics. The analogy usefully points to one of the central methodological practices of the natural sciences, what the philosopher of science Nicholas Jardine has called calibration.[8] When a new kind of instrument is introduced for purposes of measurement, it has to be calibrated against old measurements or judgments. The atomic clock may supersede astronomical clocks, but it must also give very much the same readings of time as previous instruments. And we should be able to explain how it differs and show why its revised measurements of time are to be preferred.

The expression used in psychology is not *calibration* but *validation*. A key phrase is "construct validity"; I shall avoid that language, for although it is standard in experimental psychology, its usage is largely restricted to that field. Psychologists talk of instruments and call the Dissociative Experiences Scale an instrument. What we do as we begin to use ordinary instruments—such as physical science apparatus—is to calibrate, not to validate. No one ever talked about validating the atomic clock. Of course "validity" is a value word: a validated instrument or construct is *all right*. But when we look at how the Dissociative Experience Scale is said to be validated, we see something very ordinary, unproblematic, and untechnical.[9] We see that it is checked and calibrated against prior expert judgments and diagnoses, just as the atomic clock was calibrated to prior astronomical judgments of time. We check, for example, to see that people diagnosed as multiples score highly on the DES, and that scores do not correlate with traits thought to be irrelevant to dissociation.

The history of intelligence testing has been a history of calibration of instruments. Binet was immured in a world dense with scholastic examinations. None was more uniform and interpersonal than those administered by the French educational bureaucracy. Binet had qualms about the system, especially in regard to less gifted children, but he did not flaunt his doubts. His measures of "intelligence" had to agree, generally, with preexisting judgments and then be adapted at the margins. Had he declared that many children who could not cope with French elementary education were intelligent, he would have been mocked. Had he said that the better students at the lycées were stupid, he would have been reviled. He had perhaps measured something, generous people might have said, but not intelligence. (Compare: if the atomic clock did not calibrate with sun time, it might measure something, but not what we call time.) Binet's great innovation, the testing of intelligence, made sense only against a background of shared judgments about intelligence, and it had to agree with them by and large, and also to explain when it disagreed. Who shared the judgments? Those who matter, namely, the educators, other civil servants, and Binet's peers in the middle classes of society.

Despite the sometimes unattractive features of the history of intelligence testing, there was seldom a deep problem about calibration. This was because, at any time, there was a body of agreed judgments and discriminations of intelligence to which the IQ tests were calibrated. Sometimes prior judgments were modified in the light of test results, and sometimes tests were revised as a result of calibration failure.[10] Most of the sciences work that way, although each has its own traditions and terminology. One result of calibration is that prior judgments became both sharpened and objectified. What were once discriminations made by suitably educated or trained individuals were turned into impartial, distant, nonsubjective measures of intelligence. Intelligence became an object, independent of any human opinions. Empirical psychology has regularly achieved objectivity by following this route. The pattern for the objectification of multiple personality by measurement had been established for decades when Putnam and Bernstein introduced the DES.

Two types of questionnaires are used for multiple personality. One type is self-administered. A subject answers some printed questions and is scored accordingly. The DES was the first example of this type of test; two additional ones are now being studied.[11] These tests are said to be intended for screening only, and not for diagnosis. A more searching type of probe is based on a set of questions printed in a manual; an interviewer puts the questions to the subject and records responses, which are then scored. It is proposed that such questionnaires can be used for tentative diagnosis.

These questionnaires are research tools for studying dissociation. They may also be used to select and screen subjects who will be examined further. They can be used for surveys of chosen populations—psychiatric inpatients, college students, or randomly selected city-dwellers—in order to discover the incidence or distribution of dissociative experiences. The questionnaires are sometimes presented as instruments for routine screening or tentative diagnosing in a hospital or outpatient clinic. There is no information on the extent to which they are so used, outside of research settings. Their day-to-day (nonresearch) use is encouraged less in clinics than at some of the small workshops for therapists that take place all over the continent. As Putnam himself has regretfully noted, such workshops often do not involve actual clinical work or follow-up training.[12] That is one way in which the questionnaires objectify and legitimate multiple personality—the therapist is made to feel that she is using a scientific tool. An anthropologist observing the practices of designing and testing questionnaires might suggest that the primary function served is not to provide a working tool for the hospital admissions department or for the clinic. It is rather to establish the objectivity of knowledge about dissociative disorders.

Dissociation questionnaires are checked and calibrated through a comparison between scores and diagnoses made by qualified personnel. There are incidental but necessary checks. Do subjects held to be normal respond roughly in the same way when asked to fill in the questionnaire a second time, a few months later? As successive questionnaires in the field are developed, each is calibrated with previous questionnaires and further clinical judgments. Hence a network of mutually consistent and self-confirming testing devices is set in place. For example, the results of an interview questionnaire are compared to those of a self-administered questionnaire, and both are compared to expert clinical judgment.

There is a superficial but grave problem about the calibration of dissociation questionnaires. To what agreed judgments should they be calibrated? In the field of dissociative disorders there is no body of agreed judgment. Many leading psychiatrists say there is no such field. What we are observing is not the calibration of dissociative scales to judgments shared by students of the human mind and its pathologies. Instead, the scales are calibrated to the judgments of a movement within psychiatry. They are presented as objective, scientific results like any other. Formally, the procedures of calibration are no different from those used in other branches of psychology and clinical medicine. The problem is that they are not calibrated to an independent standard.

The issue of independence is seldom addressed squarely. Responses to the DES made by psychiatric patients in seven different establishments in North America were compared, in part to check on independence. At each of these seven centers, patients were selected, tested on the scale, and independently diagnosed. According to the authors of the study, "We can safely say that the DES data collected in this study were unrelated to the diagnostic process." The paper was written by Eve Bernstein Carlson, statistician, six psychiatrists from six of the seven centers, and an expert on testing from the seventh center. I have more to say about the seventh center later in this chapter. The six psychiatrists are six leading researchers on multiple personality, mostly past or future presidents of the ISSMP&D, each running a clinic or research center studying or treating multiple personality.[13] "The Dissociative Experiences Scale items do not measure the diagnostic criteria for multiple personality, and Dissociative Experiences Scale data collected in this study were unrelated to the diagnostic process." But the conclusion cannot be drawn that the diagnoses and the scale were in any ordinary sense independent. This was a calibration of an in-house scale against in-house diagnoses—in places where multiple personality behavior was acknowledged, elicited, encouraged, and even fostered. At many other centers one would have had zero diagnoses of multiple personality.

Calibrating the atomic clock involves going to the experts, the astronomers, so why not have experts on multiple personality calibrate the dissociation scale? The comparison fails. There is no viable body of astronomers—let alone a majority—who disagree with standard solar and astronomical time measurements. An unkind skeptic might compare calibration based on the judgments of multiple personality experts to calibrating a clock on the basis of the judgments of sophisticated flat-earthers who hold that the regularity of solar time is an illusion. Their time has no regular connection with solar time, or even with lunar time. An internal consistency might be established between their new clock and their "time," but so what?

Internal consistency does have a power of its own. Once we have enough internally consistent tests, once we apply a routine battery of statistical comparisons, once we produce a sufficient number of charts and graphs, then, so long as we use the mantra of statistical degrees of significance, the entire structure does seem to become objective. Let's see how this happens in practice.

Bernstein Carlson and Putnam published their initial results in 1986. Their slightly revised questionnaire of 1993 begins with the following instructions.[14]

> This questionnaire consists of 28 questions about experiences that you may have in your daily life. We are interested in how often you have these experiences. It is important, however, that your answers show how often these experiences happen to you when you *are not* under the influence of alcohol or drugs. To answer the questions, please determine to what degree the experience described in the question applies to you and circle the number to show what percentage of the time you have the experience.

Then the subject is given a choice of percentages, 0 percent, 10 percent, 20 percent, etc. Some of the questions involve what we often call daydreaming, absentmindedness, or being caught up in a story. How often do you find you can't recall whether or not you mailed the letter you intended to post? How often do you have the experience, when taking a trip in a car, bus, subway, or whatever, of suddenly realizing that you don't remember part or all of the trip? How often, when watching TV or a movie, do you lose track of what is going on around you?

Some questions involve classic aspects of prototypical multiple personality: Being accused of lying, when you don't think you lied. Finding unfamiliar things among your belongings. Discovering evidence that you've done something you can't recall doing. Having no memory of an important event in your life, such as a wedding or graduation. Being approached by people you don't know who call you by name. Failing to recognize friends or family members.

Other questions involve what is called depersonalization or derealization. Depersonalization is listed in both *DSM-III* and *DSM-IV* as a dissociative disorder, but this diagnosis has a complex history. It appears with other types of disorder, and is held by some theorists of dissociation not to be a dissociative disorder at all. The issues, both historical and diagnostic, lead in so many directions that I decided not to discuss them in this book. In the dissociation questionnaire, depersonalization or derealization is broached by questions about whether one has the feeling that other people or objects are not real—or that one is not real oneself. Do you feel your body is not your own? Do you look in the mirror and not recognize yourself? Do you sometimes have the feeling that you are standing next to yourself, or watching yourself, as if you were another person?

One of the odd things about such questionnaires is that they cannot be taken literally. Even the directions that I just quoted are puzzling. The investigators want to know "how often" you have certain experiences, but two sentences later they ask "to what degree" you have these experiences. These are two materially different questions, yet you have only one "percentage" to answer with.[15] The ambiguity poses no practical problem, though: no one has any trouble completing the questionnaire. The test determines the responses to 28 printed sentences. And it is very clear, in a nonliteral way, what the questions are getting at.

The very directness of the questions unfortunately means that anyone who catches on and who wants to reply as if ill, pretend to be well, or otherwise play the fool can easily do so. This was confirmed in an experiment in which one group of student nurses was asked to answer straightforwardly, a second group to answer as if they had problems ("to fake bad"), and a third group to answer as if they were supernormal ("to fake good"). Nurses in a final group were asked "to fake MPD." Without further instruction, the nurses produced the profiles requested.[16] It is not only experimental subjects who behave like this. There is a feedback effect from the questionnaire to potential multiple personality patients. Richard Kluft has remarked whimsically that "many 'well-travelled' dissociative disorder patients have become overly familiar with the DES, and may enter the clinician's office with a copy of their last DES as one of the many exhibits in their bulging files."[17]

It is hardly the fault of Bernstein and Putnam that their questionnaire has had an effect on patient symptomatology. Their initial research was purely scientific in intention. Their first experiment used 34 normal adults, 31 college undergraduates aged 18–22, 14 alcoholics, 24 phobic-anxious patients, 29 agoraphobics, 10 post-traumatic stress disorder patients, 20 schizophrenics, and 20 patients with multiple personality disorder. The patients had been diagnosed by authorized clinics, hospitals, or research groups.

Scores on the 28 questions are averaged for a final score out of 100. Normal adults and alcoholics scored about 4, phobics about 6, college students about 14, and schizophrenics about 20. Post-traumatic stress disorder patients scored 31.35 and multiples scored 57.06. Thus the test seems to sort diagnosed multiples from diagnosed schizophrenics, although, as we shall see in chapter 9, the borders between schizophrenia and multiplicity are contested.

It was no miracle that diagnosed multiples scored so highly. Numerous questions on the test correspond to the 1980s prototype for multiplicity. Moreover, these questions specifically draw attention to aspects

103

of multiplicity that are emphasized in clinical treatment for the illness, so that the diagnosed patients know when to score themselves highly. The authors themselves note such learning effects.[18] But there is nothing illicit about choosing such questions. The point of the test design is to include questions on which multiples score highly.

Some of the results may nevertheless have nothing to do with dissociation. Thus the college students score far more highly than normal adults, and are not so far short of schizophrenics. A number of other studies find a high degree of dissociation among college students. Does this show that students are abnormally dissociative? Or does it show that young people, especially those pursuing university education, daydream, are imaginative, can become absorbed in what they are doing? I dread the thought of teaching a class with an average score on the DES of less than 15.[19]

Bernstein and Putnam obtained fascinating data. Karl Popper taught that there is a difference between mere data collection and the testing of hypotheses. He counted only hypothesis testing as scientific. Bernstein and Putnam would seem to have honored his precept, for they "sought to test two general hypotheses." The first is the hypothesis "that the number and frequency of experiences attributable to dissociation lie along a continuum." The idea is easy to understand: almost everyone dissociates from time to time, some people dissociate quite a lot, and multiples dissociate more than anyone else. It is not so easy to turn that into a testable hypothesis.

What would be a precise version of the continuum hypothesis? One is that dissociative tendencies are what logicians call *well-ordered*. That is, we can say of any two people that they are equally dissociative, or that one is more dissociative than the other. Anyone who completes all 28 questions gets a score between 0 and 100. The scores of different people automatically "lie along a continuum." That is a result of the test design. Hence the well-ordering version of the continuum hypothesis was not tested.

Under the assumption—by no means a negligible one—that dissociation is well-ordered, we can frame a second continuum hypothesis. There are no holes in the test results. That is, for any degree of dissociation, some people are dissociated to that degree. This *no-gap* hypothesis can be stated precisely.[20] It is part of what Bernstein and Putnam had in mind. It is a very weak hypothesis, tested by noting whether, for each segment between the lowest and highest score observed in a given population, at least one person has a score in that segment. Bernstein and

Putnam did not bother to test the no-gap hypothesis, probably because it is so uninteresting.

They were preoccupied by other questions. They noted that many authorities on dissociation assume that virtually everyone is a little bit dissociative. Under the assumption that dissociation is well-ordered, we can frame a *no-threshold* hypothesis. Groups of what psychiatrists classify as normal people have on average a nonzero dissociative score.[21] This was not, however, a test of the no-threshhold hypothesis because the result depended so heavily on the choice of questions. If they had used a suitable subset of the 28 questions, virtually all people called normal would score zero. How often do you look in the mirror and not recognize yourself? How often do you fail to recognize close family and friends, whom you've seen recently, and whom you meet again in ordinary circumstances? If the test had used only questions like that, there would have been a sharp threshold, with the normals on one side and some very disturbed people on the other. Instead the authors included questions bearing on absentmindedness, daydreaming, self-absorption, and fantasy. As Frankel noted, almost two-thirds of the items on the questionnaire "can be readily explained by the manner in which subjects recall memories, apply or redistribute attention, use their imagination, or direct or monitor control."[22] The no-threshold hypothesis was not tested because questions were included that would preclude a break between those who score zero and those who score positively.[23]

A fourth interpretation of the continuum hypothesis is that not only are there no gaps in degrees of dissociative experience, but there is also a smooth flow of dissociative experiences from those of normal people to those of multiples. Call this the *smooth* hypothesis. There are many ways to be smooth. Suppose we drew a bar graph of discriminable scores or groups of scores. Then the most natural way to understand the vague word "smooth" would be that the graph looks like a slope, up or down, or like a hill, or like a valley.[24] That gives four possible hypotheses; many people would expect a hill. The *hill* hypothesis for a chosen population is that a bar graph of dissociative scores forms a hill. Such hypotheses are tested on a random sample from the population. Bernstein and Putnam did not randomly sample any whole population but instead took volunteers from a number of specific populations, such as college students or phobics. Hence they did not test the hill hypothesis.

I have now distinguished four versions of the continuum hypothesis. Bernstein and Putnam did not test the *well-ordering* hypothesis because they designed a test that gave well-ordered results. They did not test the intrinsically uninteresting *no-gap* hypothesis—they could have done so, but they did not mention it. They did not test the *no-threshold* hypothesis because they included questions that prejudge the issue. They did not test the *smooth* hypothesis because they did not randomly sample any whole population. They said that they "sought to test" the continuum hypothesis, but they did not do so.

"Testing hypotheses" is one of the activities commonly supposed to make work count as scientific. Bernstein and Putnam head one section of their paper with the title "Hypotheses to be Tested," yet in this paper the authors did not report any tests of their hypotheses. An anthropologist observing psychological testing practices might go so far as to suggest that it is part of the way in which such papers are assessed and used that no one raises questions such as, did you test the hypothesis you said you tested? Once you have said you are testing a hypothesis, it is as if you have done it. The peer referees and the journal editor do not look to see if you have tested the hypothesis. They look to see if you have used various prescribed statistical procedures. No one asks about the meaning of those procedures.

This is even more apparent when we turn to the second of the two hypotheses that the authors "sought to test." "The second hypothesis is that the distribution of dissociative experiences in the population would not follow a Normal probability (Gaussian) curve but would exhibit a skewed distribution similar to that observed for the 'trait' of hypnotic susceptibility."[25] Normal distributions are the most commonly used probability distributions; they are often described as "bell shaped," but they are literally bell shaped—symmetrical—only when the mean is 0.5. Evidently Bernstein and Putnam expected the distribution of experiences to look like a hill, but not to be Gaussian. Their hypothesis is about a population. They do not say which one, but it might be the population of the United States, or the population of patients admitted to psychiatric care in Washington, D.C. Such hypotheses can only be tested on a random sample of the population. Bernstein and Putnam, who did not randomly sample any population, did not test this hypothesis.

Yet they say something very curious in this connection. They present a graph of scores for all subjects. It peaks at about 10 percent. The authors write, "Clearly this distribution is not normal."[26] By "this distribution" they mean the distribution of scores from their population of 34 normal nonstudent adults, 31 college students, 20 schizophrenics, 20 severe multiples, 14 alcoholics, 53 phobics, 20 multiples, and 10 people diagnosed with post-traumatic stress disorder. It makes no sense to talk about the probability distribution or sampling distribution of a population constituted in these proportions.[27]

Bernstein and Putnam's second hypothesis is testable, and so is the "hill" version of the continuum hypothesis. The first random sample of a population tested by the DES consisted of 1,055 citizens of Winnipeg, Manitoba, and did apparently result in a smooth hill-shaped curve.[28] It has not been determined whether the hill is Gaussian, although the authors do say that the curve qualitatively resembles curves for susceptibility to hypnotism, which are said not to be Gaussian. No one bothered to look into these matters, because *the hypothesis of a continuum of dissociative experiences had already become a fact.*

The DES inspired a welter of new instruments. There are several new self-report scales, and there are interview-type questionnaires. Thus Ross and his coworkers developed a Dissociative Disorders Interview Schedule tied to *DSM-III* diagnostic criteria.[29] They have asserted that this interview schedule is more reliable at detecting multiple personality disorder than are other questionnaire tests for other disorders.[30] Marlene Steinberg designed a schedule keyed to *DSM-III-R*, and then one for *DSM-IV*.[31] The most extended set of mutual calibrations has been conducted in the Netherlands.[32]

One standard statistical procedure is factor analysis. It is a technique to assess the extent to which the variability of a trait in a population can be attributed to a number of distinct causes. The factors are ranked according to their impact in producing variability. Not only has the DES been made the object of factor analysis, but different self-report scales have been studied to see how they elicit different factors. Carlson et al. identified three factors in a population of clinical and nonclinical subjects. "The first factor was thought to reflect amnesic dissociation," the second, "absorption and imaginative involvement," the third, "depersonalization and derealization."[33] With nonclinical subjects the chief factor identified is called "an absorption and changeability factor."

Ross's group found that dissociation scores in Winnipeg were produced by three factors that they called "absorptive-imaginative involvement," "activities of dissociated states," and "depersonalization-derealization."[34] Ray and colleagues found that scores on the DES could be attributed to seven factors ordered as follows: "(1) Fantasy/Absorption; (2) Segment Amnesia, (3) Depersonalization, (4) *In situ* Amnesia, (5) Different Selves, (6) Denial and (7) Critical Events." But scores on another self-report scale for dissociation could be attributed to six factors that they called "(1) Depersonalization, (2) Process Amnesia,

(3) Fantasy/Daydream, (4) Dissociated Body Behaviors, (5) Trance and (6) Imaginary Companions."[35]

It is familiar to statisticians that factor analysis is a remarkably useful tool when in safe hands, but that its use also demands a considerable amount of good sense.[36] This is a miscellaneous stew of "factors"—after duplication is eliminated, there appear to be at least eleven of them. If they mean anything at all, they seem to suggest that the original continuum hypothesis is false. This is because low scores on the DES may be attributable to factors quite distinct from the factors that account for high scores. Before these studies were published, Frankel wrote that a "distinct qualitative difference between subjects with high and low scores has not been ruled out."[37] Has that qualitative difference now been confirmed by factor analysis? No, because one doubts that these analyses, taken together, confirm anything.

Questionnaires about dissociation should help to answer a different kind of question. How common is pathological dissociation? A number of authors have suggested that a score above 30 is a sign of pathology or, more specifically, of multiple personality. Ross conjectured that the incidence of multiple personality in North America may be as high as 2 percent. He proposed that the incidence among college students may be as high as 5 percent; subsequently he and his colleagues have suggested that the rate may be even higher.[38] In a letter published in a British journal, Ross, writing from Canada, implied that 5 percent of "all individuals admitted to an acute care adult psychiatric in-patient unit in Britain or South Africa . . . [would] meet *DSM-III-R* criteria for MPD." A second Canadian doctor, Lal Fernando, replied in exasperation, "Considering the fact that the majority of psychiatrists on both sides of the Atlantic have never seen or diagnosed a case of MPD, I find these figures and predictions incredible."[39] This is a stark statement of the problem of calibration that I mentioned earlier. Fernando need not disagree with Ross's statistical analysis. He is questioning the calibration itself.

We can well imagine that if multiple practitioners trained by Ross were to take over a South African hospital, they would find that 5 percent of patients admitted were multiples. The problem for Fernando and many other doctors is that the DES is not calibrated against judgments made by a consensus in the psychiatric community, but against the judgments of psychiatrists who are advocates of multiple personality. The nearest we get to an outside opinion is the seven-center study mentioned above. The authors, as I noted, include six leading multiple personality researchers. What about the seventh center, McLean Hospital in Belmont, Massachusetts? It has a dissociative disorders unit directed by James Chu. Chu has published favorably on the diagnosis of multiple personality and has written about how difficult it is for some patients to face up to their multiplicity.[40] Thus he is not a skeptic, but he has warned against overdiagnosis. In the clinical approach to dissociation he recommends treating other disorders first and minimizing the expression of dissociative symptoms.[41] He insists strongly on patient responsibility. The coauthor for the seven-center study from McLean Hospital was a colleague of Chu's who had supervised the testing.[42]

The six centers other than McLean provided the study with 953 patients, 227 of whom were diagnosed with multiple personality disorder. McLean provided 98 patients, only one of whom was diagnosed with multiple personality, and that patient was excluded from the results. Patients with diagnoses of illnesses that are not widely regarded as "dissociative" consistently had *higher* DES scores at McLean than similarly diagnosed patients at the six other centers. On the other hand, patients at McLean with what are often urged to be dissociation-prone disorders— post-traumatic stress disorder, eating disorders—had *lower* DES scores than their counterparts at the other centers. Qualitatively speaking, these results from McLean are the *opposite* of those from the other six centers. But that hospital is not an environment hostile to multiple personality or dissociation. As soon as we edge even a very short distance away from absolute commitment to multiple personality, the scores and their relations to diagnoses begin to change radically.

Thus the very study intended to clinch the "validity of the dissociative experiences scale in screening for multiple personality disorder" reveals that there is a serious problem about calibration. A logic textbook has described one type of fallacy as the fallacy of the self-sealing argument. This is an argument whose only confirmation is provided by itself.[43] The "construct validity" of multiple personality is daringly close to being self-sealing. When the seal is torn only a little, to admit the patients from McLean Hospital, the problem is plain for all to see.

I shall conclude with one other aspect of measurement. The DES is proposed as a screening instrument, comparable to routine screening for an infectious disease using a blood sample. Suppose we are told that an instrument is right 99 percent of the time—in the following sense. Ninety-nine percent of diseased people who are tested show up as diseased; 99 percent of well people who are tested show up as well. On hearing that the screen picks me as diseased, I am mortally afraid. But if the disease is very rare in the whole population of which I am a member, and I am not a member of a more vulnerable subpopulation, my fear may be unjustified. For suppose only one person in 100,000 has the disease. Then after the instrument has surveyed a million people, it will have picked 99 percent of the sick people as sick (that is, 10 people) and 1 percent of the remaining 999,990 will also be picked as diseased. This means that in total about 9,999 healthy people are found to be ill. Hence in this extreme case, the screen picks about 10,009 as diseased, but only 10 of them actually are. Nearly all the picks are *false positives*. Exactly this argument was used against universal indiscriminate AIDS screening.[44]

When we want to understand a test result, the bottom line is *not* "the probability that the test picks a person as ill, when they are ill." Instead we want to know *the probability that a person is ill, given that the test says she is ill*. In symbols the bottom line is not

(1) *Probability (test says person is ill / person is really ill)*

but

(2) *Probability (person is really ill / test says person is ill)*.

To calculate (2) we need to know the "base rate" of the disease in a chosen population, that is, the rate with which the illness does occur in the population. In a famous series of papers Amos Tversky and Daniel Kahneman showed that one of the most common fallacies, in thinking about probabilities, was failing to take the base rate into account.[45]

When the DES is used as a screening instrument, a high enough score is taken to indicate multiple personality. Carlson et al. urge a cutoff point of 30: score over 30, and the DES says you are a multiple. How good a screen is this? We can work out (2) using an elementary rule of probability. It requires three items: (a) the population being screened, (b) the base rate of multiple personality in that population, and (c) the ability of the screen to pick a multiple as a multiple, and the ability to pick a nonmultiple as a nonmultiple—in effect (1) above.

Carlson and her colleagues present such a calculation. They do not actually state (a), the population for which they are doing the calculation, but since their study is about psychiatric patients, it must be the population at present in psychiatric treatment (say, in the United States). Their data tell them (c), because they applied the DES to patients who were independently diagnosed. They found that 80 percent of diagnosed multiples score over 30, and 80 percent of nonmultiples score below 30. So now we have (a) and (c), and lack only (b), the base rate in the population of psychiatric patients.

Carlson et al. use a base rate of 5 percent, which means that one in twenty psychiatric patients is a multiple. They do not state where this figure comes from. This is the figure Ross expected and Fernando found preposterous. On the basis of *this* figure the probability of a psychiatric patient's being a multiple, given a score above 30 on the DES, is 17 percent. The remaining 83 percent of patients picked as multiples are not multiples. This may not be troubling, since many of these false positives may have other dissociative problems such as post-traumatic stress disorder.

But where did this 5 percent figure come from?[46] The majority of psychiatrists would very much doubt that 5 percent of psychiatric patients have multiple personalities. At McLean one patient of the selected 98 had multiple personality, but many psychiatrists would doubt that even a rate of 1 in 98, or 1 percent, is typical. With a base rate of 1 percent, it would follow that 94 percent of psychiatric patients screened as multiples are "false positives." If we thought that the base rate for multiple personality were a good deal less than what is found at a hospital near Boston with a dissociative disorders unit, then we would expect almost all the people picked by the DES as multiples to be false positives.

My purpose has been only to show how the measurement of multiple personality legitimates multiple personality and turns it into an object of knowledge. It happens to have been easier than might be expected because of the way that statistics are so often used in psychology. We have long had a multitude of highly sophisticated statistical procedures. We now have many statistical software packages. Their power is incredible, but the pioneers of statistical inference would have mixed feelings, for they always insisted that people think before using a routine. In the old days routines took endless hours to apply, so one had to spend a lot of time thinking in order to justify using a routine. Now one enters data and presses a button. One result is that people seem to be cowed into not asking silly questions, such as: What hypothesis are you testing? What distribution is it that you say is not normal? What population are you talking about? Where did this base rate come from? Most important of all: Whose judgments do you use to calibrate scores on your questionnaires? Are those judgments generally agreed to by the qualified experts in the entire community?

The increasingly massive array of "instruments" for assessing multiple personality has a primary function that is seldom acknowledged. They make the field of multiple personality look like the rest of empirical psychology, and thereby turn the study of the disorder into an objective science. Many sociologists of science, and a few philosophers, have recently welcomed the idea that scientific knowledge is a social construction. They contend that science does not discover facts but constructs them. I am not arguing such a case in the present chapter. More traditional students of scientific method, variously called logical empiricists or scientific realists, hold that scientists aim at discovering facts, at finding out the truth. It is precisely these traditional thinkers who would be thunderstruck at the practices I have just described.

I have focused on the continuum hypothesis about dissociation because, as Putnam saw from the start, it is absolutely fundamental. Multiple personality may be an important object for psychiatric study almost no matter how rare it is. Even if the incidence rate among psychiatric inpatients were not 5 percent but .05 percent, it is still a striking phenomenon. The present theory invokes a cause, child abuse, and invokes a continuum of dissociative experiences. "Dissociation" is a technical word, put to use in psychology by Pierre Janet, and almost immediately dropped by him. It caught on. But there is not one definite thing that the word "dissociation" was invented to name. It is not as if Janet designated something, leaving us with the task of finding out what it is. On the contrary, we can use the word "dissociation" in any way that is useful. But a problem arises when it seems to many observers that "dissociative experiences" is used to refer to a great many experiences that have singularly little in common with each other. The whole machinery of the DES has been constructed—quite literally constructed—in order to make it appear to be an objective fact that there is a continuum of one and the same kind of experience, the dissociative experience. Once one dismantles that construction, it is not so clear that there is one kind of experience there to study. Until 1994 there was an International Society for the Study of Multiple Personality and Dissociation. It had something to study, namely, multiple personality. But now we have the International Society for the Study of Dissociation. It is less than clear that there is a distinct object, named "dissociation," there to be studied.

Truth in Memory

TOLSTOY famously observed that all happy families are more or less alike, but every unhappy family is unhappy in its own particular way. Today he might revise the second part of that judgment if he were to come across families torn by memories recovered in therapy, adults' memories of child abuse and incest perpetrated by now-aging parents, memories denied as false, impossible, incoherent, by the elders. Many of these families seem to be unhappy in almost exactly the same way. The families look and perhaps become alike because they learn a new language and a new set of emotions. Hence their stories come out sounding remarkably similar.

The media of every kind are full of these confrontations. I shall spare us the roster of court cases and media notables, and the litany of accusations and counteraccusations. I shall touch on them only because they illustrate the present-day politics of memory, and then only insofar as that comes out in connection with multiple personality. This is the saddest part of my story. At first the topic might seem titillating, at least to the voyeur in us all, but it quickly palls.

Some families have been badly hurt by ill-trained and ideologically motivated therapists. Some evils have been exposed, in some cases, by the same therapists. We hear on all sides the question, Who is right? There is no general statement about who is right. That issue must be fought out from case to case. New standards of licensing, training, and review of therapists will be developed and enforced. For those who can afford it, individual charges have to be settled in or out of court. Personally I have a strong prejudice in favor of the jury system, but the more I read of both convictions and acquittals, the less confident I am, in this or that case, that the jury decided wisely. We are left with only one sound rule of thumb. Any expert who is confident in these matters is thoroughly suspect.

Extraordinary accusations began flying everywhere when ritual and satanic child sexual abuse hit flash point in 1982. Because early trauma, especially child abuse, is the acknowledged cause of multiple personality, every event in child abuse very quickly transfers to multiplicity. The 1986 meeting of the ISSMP&D had one discussion paper on cult abuse on the program; the 1987 meeting had eleven. Sherrill Mulhern, of the

Laboratory for the Study of Rumors, Myths of the Future, and Sects, located in Paris, has summarized some of these unpublished presentations.[1] There was much talk of alters deliberately created by cults. They were programmed to interfere with therapy. When a patient was treated with medicine, one had to be sure that the right alter got it. A cult-induced alter would likely steal it.

Some practitioners of multiple therapy, who were also flooded by victims claiming abuse by satanic cults, could not believe their ears. George Ganaway, director of the Center for Dissociative Disorders at the Ridgeview Institute in Georgia—from which the journal *Dissociation* is distributed—was the first to sound the alarm in print. He wrote, in 1989, that almost half the patients in his clinic and many more elsewhere in North America "are reporting vividly detailed memories of cannibalistic revels, and extensive experiences such as being used by cults during adolescence as serial baby breeders for ritual sacrifices."[2]

Satan had become the star of American television talk shows. Geraldo Rivera gave major prominence to satanic rituals in 1988, and the TV tabloids reveled in them. Victims appeared on-screen, backed up by their therapists, to tell amazing tales. According to Ganaway, the Cult Crime Impact Network estimated that if the reports are correct, then a secret network of satanists spanning the United States is conducting fifty thousand ritual murders a year.

This ferment created a problem for the multiple movement. Multiple personality had thrived in a climate of consciousness-raising about child abuse and had been legitimated by the etiology that it suggested. In the early days, as claims to vicious abuse became increasingly credible, the multiple movement felt vindicated. When multiples recalled incest, their recollections were not only believed but encouraged. An eclectic therapy evolved, in which alters were elicited in order to remember and then work through childhood trauma. The traumas were taken to be historical fact, not reworked fantasy. Then, as the child abuse movement developed a ritual abuse wing, patients increasingly recalled terrifying tales of cults. The instinct of the therapist was to believe, for belief in shocking revelations had been the right strategy in the past. Yet the stories seemed to become increasingly impossible. The movement was threatened with polarization, even schism. One side, by and large the populist one, cried, "We told you to believe the children! Now you must believe the alters!" The other side retorted, "Stop—this stuff has to be fantasy!" Often religious difference lay near the surface of the argument. Believers tended to style themselves conservative Christians, that is, fundamentalist Protestants, while the skeptics tended to be secular in orientation.

The resultant level of rhetoric was pretty mind-numbing. Credulity about stories provided by alters was compared to a sort of reverse transference: the therapist was too emotionally committed to what an alter said, and had lost all critical faculties. On the other hand, those who believe in the stories about cults say that the disbelievers are afraid of hard truths. "MPD patients' descriptions of extraordinary sadistic and prolonged experiences of satanic ritual abuse would seem to be peculiarly vulnerable to therapists' self-protective incredulity."[3]

There was panic in the air. In an editorial in *Dissociation*, Richard Kluft pleaded for moderation, but he acknowledged that powerful emotions were at work. He also raised the stakes by printing a comparison that I find rather odious. He noted that one party refers to Nazis and the holocaust, asking, "Should he or she be silent, emulating the 'good Germans' who did not speak out about the atrocities in their midst, and by his or her silence become a facilitator?" The other side, disgusted by such rhetoric, countered with "mass hysteria," "present-day witch-hunt," and the like.[4] In an ISSMP&D newsletter, Catherine Fine, the president for 1991, wrote, "How we deal with the ritualistic abuse issue will be one of our tests. This issue has the ability to strengthen our organization as we negotiate the necessary steps to growth, but it also has the possibility of being a divisive—or even lethal element."[5] Lethal: I unkindly compare multiple personality to a parasite that needs a host; the host in recent times has been child abuse. A parasite can kill itself by feeding on a weak part of its host, killing the host, and thereby killing itself. Ganaway almost said as much. He thought that uncritical acceptance of memories of satanic abuse not only imperiled the credibility of multiple personality but put *research on child abuse in general at risk*:

> In the wake of the current wave of extensive, incredible, often unverifiable abuse accounts, however, therapists who continue to feel compelled to suspend their critical judgment in active support of the veridicality of all their patients' reconstructed traumatic memories may be placing the MPD field in particular and research on child abuse in general at risk. . . . Unless scientifically documented proof is forthcoming, patients and therapists who validate and publicly defend the unsubstantiated veracity of these reports may find themselves developing into a cult of their own, validating each others' beliefs while ignoring (and being ignored by) the scientific and psychotherapeutic community at large.[6]

Rumors were flying. Early in 1992 Frank Putnam asked the newly founded False Memory Syndrome Foundation to help him track down one of these. Readers of the *FMS Foundation Newsletter* were to report whether they had come across the following statement, and if so, where: "Dr Putnam of the NIMH has found that 20% to 50% of multiple personality disorder patients have histories of Satanic ritual abuse."[7] I understand that Putnam did not find that a high proportion even had memories (let alone true histories) of satanic ritual abuse. Hence we have to wonder about clinicians who did elicit such memories. Consider Ganaway himself, opposed to the historical truth of such memories though he may be. He stated in mid-1993 that he had treated about 350 patients for dissociative disorders, between 100 and 150 of whom had memories of satanic cult abuse.[8] Ganaway observed that other workers encounter a comparable proportion of stories of abduction by aliens, but no cult abuse survivors, whereas he meets no alien abductees. One possibility is that the cults are active in Georgia and the aliens in Massachusetts. Another is that the consulting clinician has a great deal to do with the form these memories take—even when that selfsame clinician is outspoken in denouncing those very memories.

The division within the multiple movement largely conformed to existing status divisions. The skeptics tended to be psychiatrists, while an astonishingly large, or at any rate vocal, proportion of the rank and file were believers. Two therapists from southern California assert: "Our own experience indicates that there may be a very high rate of ritual abuse among multiples. Of the population we are most familiar with, which includes our clients and those of our colleagues, two-thirds may have been involved in ritual abuse as children."[9] As soon as satanic abuse was out in the open there was the inevitable multobiography, *Suffer the Child*.[10] Here the multiple has more than four hundred personalities, and her illness was caused by horrendous cult abuse in which her mother played a major role. *The Exorcist* (1973) and *Exorcist II* (1977) were movies intended to scare you and doubtless had a significant role in the development of ritual abuse concerns, but they are just stagy compared to what happens to this supposedly real-life victim. Her husband was a strict fundamentalist Christian; she went to doctors secretly because he did not believe in them. But a meeting with Sizemore ("Eve") was what turned her around. It must not be thought that the radical Protestant denominations are necessarily uncritical. One autobiography of satanic abuse was withdrawn by its publisher after an exposé that won an award from the Evangelical Christian Press Association, although it was then reissued in Los Angeles by another publisher.[11]

Some psychiatrists did go along with the extreme stories and then changed their minds. Thus George Fraser published a paper about the

full gamut of baby-breeders and baby or fetal sacrifice. "The child is subjected to every sort of sexual perversion known to mankind" in the satanic churches of sedate Ottawa.[12] Fraser soon changed his mind and
very much regretted having published the paper. Another group of four
psychiatrists, including Roberta Sachs and Bennett Braun, described
thirty-seven patients who reported ritual abuse in childhood.[13] Their
paper certainly sounds as if they believed their patients, but upon challenge they said they were just reporting what their patients said.[14]
Among movement psychiatrists, Putnam made the most forthright
statement on the topic, calm, measured, and forceful. Speaking in 1992,
he referred to "allegations by some MPD patients that they are the victims of abuse involving sexual torture, human sacrifice and cannibalism
by international religious cults worshipping Satan." The allegations,
whether by multiples or others, are, he said, typically based on memories
recovered in therapy. "Despite almost a decade of sensational allegations, no independent evidence has emerged to corroborate these
claims."[15]

The ISSMP&D set up a task force, headed by Kluft, to negotiate
peace between cult-believers and cult-skeptics. Kluft may have decided
that peacemaking was impossible. At any rate he resigned without calling the working group together for a meeting. One astute move was
made during this period. Satanic ritual abuse had acquired an instant
acronym, SRA. Now satanism, in itself, is not illegal. In the United
States, it is probably protected by the guarantees of freedom of religion
in the Bill of Rights. Hence *satanic* ritual abuse was hardly a charge that
could be prosecuted in court. SRA turned into *sadistic* ritual abuse.[16]
The move to "sadistic abuse" may hint at a return to something more
old-fashioned. What is sadism here but plain old extreme cruelty, cruelty
inflicted with the deliberate intention of satisfying nonstandard desires?
Are we seeing a return to older roots, namely, cruelty to children?

Probably not. The English language has not yet been exhausted; we
now have "abuse within a malevolent context."[17] I do not foresee any
shortage of future material with such titles as *Other Altars: Roots and
Realities of Cultic and Satanic Ritual Abuse and Multiple Personality
Disorder*.[18] As for legal technicalities, works like this grant that "the
ritual aspect was not introduced in court, but was clearly indicated by
the account of the victims."[19] For the converted, this assertion means
that these things were "really" evidenced, even proved, in court. For the
skeptics, it means the opposite. The only systematic public inquiry on
these matters took place in Great Britain. The committee gathered

information over three years, and their findings were published in June 1994. The "defining characteristic" of satanic or satanistic rites that include torture, forced abortion, human sacrifice, cannibalism, and bestiality is that "the sexual and physical abuse of children is part of rites directed to magical or religious objectives." The committee investigated eighty-four cases in which such satanic abuse had been publicly claimed and found no evidence whatsoever. Yet they had no doubt that in many cases children had been abused in more mundane ways.[20]

Psychiatrists such as Putnam, and scholars such as Mulhern, are right to insist that no case of satanic ritual abuse has been proven. It is essential for therapists to listen to their patients, and to let them express their fears and thoughts. But it would be a grave mistake for any therapist to believe memories of such events without conclusive independent corroboration. It is wicked for a therapist to encourage a patient to believe such fears as fact until the facts can be independently established at the level of the judicial standard: beyond any reasonable doubt.

To fence-sit on such hot issues would be cowardice, but since my own opinion on the existence of satanic ritual abuse is not founded on hard work, I shall state it only in a personal note.[21] As for the fables of worldwide satanic conspiracy, they are, to speak strictly, incredible. That is, it is impossible to give them any credence on the basis of available evidence. The stories that were spreading like wildfire from place to place all sound the same. We are observing the powerful contagion of panicky rumors. The sociology of such rumors is a fascinating study with dreadful practical overtones. Nevertheless, I do not find the countercry of witch-hunt very helpful. Conspiracy and witch-hunt are mirror images, so far as explanations go. When it comes to rhetorical parrying, comparisons to witch-hunts are all too quickly neutralized, because people convinced that vicious cults and rituals are all around us produce abbreviated populist sketches of similar goings-on in the past.[22] Mulhern has drawn important parallels between the recent satanic scare and fifteenth-century mass panics about witches or demons.[23] Her analogies are useful because they are backed by a serious historical understanding. Casual invocation of witch-hunts by people who know nothing of the witch craze of the past is worthless.

One recent item of the satanism agenda is grotesque and should be discredited: programming. It has close ties to some models of multiple personality. The cult programs the child or adult to respond to triggers—a telephone call, a flashing light, a playing card, black clothing. These triggers make an alter come out. The alter is a cult member, cult slave, cult spy, or cult killer. A subdued bank teller suddenly becomes a cult member and works at plots that interest the cult. Or she reports back to the cult, telling when the psychiatrist is probing into the cult. The cult-alter lies or misleads, bullying the bank-teller host so that no secrets will be exposed. Malicious or persecuting alters are deliberate creations of the cult and are ready to be switched on for offensive or defensive action; they were probably preprogrammed when the victim was a child.

Programming is a weird brew of old and new. It draws on the old hypnotism threat of a century and more ago. There was a deep-seated fear that innocent people could be hypnotized into committing heinous crimes in response to a signal arranged by the hypnotist. This notion permeates the psychiatric journals as well as the popular press during the years 1870–1910. Then there is the Pavlovian theory of conditioned responses. Next is a 1962 cold war movie, *The Manchurian Candidate*, in which evil Chinese and worse Russians (from the Pavlov Institute in Moscow) use drugs and hypnotism to program an American sergeant captured in Korea to commit murder. Pauline Kael, who was for many years the *New Yorker*'s film critic, called the film daring, funny, far-out: "It may be the most sophisticated political satire ever made in Hollywood."[24] Outside the Big Apple they don't see things that way. The film is regularly mentioned in far-flung workshops for therapists. Even the standard reference to a playing card as a trigger for programming alters is taken straight from the Richard Condon novel on which the movie was based.[25] Then came the Moonies, unhappy and typically idealistic young people, lacking direction, lacking love, and often lacking powers of critical thinking, who fell under the influence of the Reverend Moon. Not so long ago it was the current wisdom that their families should employ professional "deprogrammers" to reclaim their children. This bundle of confused notions is then merged with the idea of computer programming to produce a smooth fantasy that has no resemblance to anything ever encountered in real life. It is comfortably accepted by all too many therapists. I'm not just saying that we have no evidence for cult programming—I'm saying that nothing resembling a systematic and reliable technology of programming has ever been witnessed in the history of the human race.

A brief account of programming lore may be useful. A two-day fee-charging workshop held in March 1994 was titled "Overcoming the Shadows of Ritual Abuse"; the facilitator was a regionally well-known therapist and expert in ritual abuse, herself a survivor; the participants consisted of thirty therapists, all women, and one observer.[26] The programming segment of the workshop began with the statement that children dissociate a lot. When they are abused, they dissociate more. Alters produced for coping can be adopted and manipulated by cult members. The *Manchurian Candidate* was invoked as an instructive video on the power of programming—but cults, it was stressed, are more insidious than communists. Triggers are built into early abuse, starting when babies are exposed to sounds, shapes, or colors during abuse. That is why such distinctly colored and shaped objects as playing cards can be so effective later. After infancy programming methods include sleep deprivation, induced confusion about time, drugs, hypnosis, degradation, electroshock. Programs include self-injury or self-mutilation, which is induced to stop confession during therapy. Self-harm may also take the form of anorexia or bulimia: eating disorders are programmed. A victim may be programmed to commit suicide if she begins to expose the cult to her therapist. An alter may be created with the specific role of reporting back to the cult about what other alters are doing or noticing. Another alter may be programmed to force the victim to check in and get reprogrammed. You may be programmed to have nightmares, to avoid people, to be silent, or even to tell the therapist that all this ritual abuse stuff is a bunch of silly rumors to prevent her probing deeper.

Notice the air of what, to abuse psychiatric terminology, might be called batty narcissistic paranoia. The therapists in the workshop were learning that the cults are out to get *them*, either indirectly, by interfering with therapy, or directly, by getting patients to harm therapists. Many more cautious members of the multiple movement have stated that bizarre memories elicited in therapy are not strictly true but are ways in which a patient can shield herself from the grim reality that it was her immediate family that abused her. The abuse was real, but cloaked in fantasy.[27] There is a halfway stage to that opinion among the cult-therapists, that many of the victims received cult abuse from members of their own families.

Ganaway was right. With so many bizarre events coming out of recovered memory therapies—and so many silly theories going into them— recovered memories in general were cast in doubt. Many therapists encouraged confrontation after a client came to recall abuse by family in childhood. By 1990 it became a fixed doctrine, in some quarters, that the client must break with the family. Many accused parents could not believe what was happening. The alleged memories were simply false, they said, developed in the course of therapy, just as dubious as alien abduction. And so after several months of intense activity the False Memory Syndrome Foundation was established in Philadelphia in March 1992.

The foundation is a banding together of parents whose adult children, during therapy, recall hideous scenes of familial child abuse. Its mission is to tell the world that patients in psychotherapy can be brought to seem to remember horrible events of childhood that never happened. Distressed thirty-somethings (and up) believe that they were abused by parents or relatives long ago. But, urges the foundation, many of the resulting accusations and subsequent family chaos result not from past evils but from false memories engendered by ideologically committed therapists.

The foundation first became known by word of mouth, along with a little reporting. It has now furnished feature stories for all the significant media in North America. By coincidence I encountered it early in its career; it may be useful to report how the rhetoric has gone from the start (it is still exactly the same today). The first major daily newspaper in North America to publicize the foundation at length was the *Toronto Star*, in mid-May 1992. The *Star* is a middlebrow daily with a substantial market between the relatively highbrow *Globe* and the tabloid *Sun*. The headline for the opening story was WHAT IF SEXUAL ABUSE MEMORIES ARE WRONG? The third day's heading was THERAPIST TURNED PATIENT'S WORLD UPSIDE DOWN. The series ran to about ninety column inches of text, plus ample headlining, some photographs, and a short item accompanying the second installment, printed in a pink box, PSYCHOTHERAPY UNREGULATED IN CANADA. A Philadelphia phone number was given, and about four hundred readers of the *Star* called at once.[28]

The effect of publicity like this is remarkable. The foundation's newsletter tabulates the number of calls it has received, and breaks down member "families" by region. In April 1992, it recorded 2 Ontario families. In June, after the story broke, the province of Ontario had more paid-up families (71) than any American state except the home base, Pennsylvania (97). The most populous state in the union, California, was way down (40). The next month Ontario rose to 84 subscribing families and stayed there for the rest of the year. After the *San Francisco Chronicle* broke the news in northern California, membership in that state jumped to 315. The January 1994 newsletter announced that 10,000 families had contacted the foundation, and 6,007 were members. California (928) had three times as many as the runner-up, Pennsylvania

(302). The big membership surges can be identified with daily news-papers rather than television shows on the topic.

Ten days after running its series, the *Star* gave equal prominence and fifty-two inches of text to a reply by Sylvia Fraser, whom the paper styled "noted author" and "incest survivor": "DESPERATELY WANTING *not* TO BELIEVE."[29] Fraser is a widely read novelist who has also written an auto-multobiography.[30] In the reply she summarized the effect of disbelief on incest victims. "*The truth can plunge them into a lonely chaos and terror.*" The second page featured a photo of a sad old man captioned "SIGMUND FREUD: Father of psychoanalysis likely was molested as a child." More than half of the text is given over to the story made famous by Jeffrey Masson, that in mid-1897 cowardly Freud abandoned his 1893 theory that hysteria was caused by what we now call childhood sexual abuse. In the newspaper Fraser drew not on Masson but on an earlier, and insightful, psychological study of Freud by Marianne Krüll, who argued that Freud gave up the seduction theory at his father's fu-neral, 25 October 1896, where he closed his father's eyes.[31] As Fraser has it (she refrains from mentioning that she is referring to a dream of Freud's, reported by Freud himself), "the last service Freud rendered his father was to close his [Sigmund's] eyes to Jacob [Freud]'s sexual abuse of him [Sigmund]."

The False Memory Syndrome Foundation makes two important rhe-torical moves. First, it distances itself from custody disputes between di-vorcing parents and says it is concerned only to heal families that have been torn apart by false memories. "Family" is a key word; indeed mem-bers of the foundation were first put in two classes, "families" and "pro-fessionals." Now there is an additional category: "retractors," people who in therapy denounced their families but now abjure the charges. Second, the experts on repressed memories of abuse, often called when a case goes to law, are trumped with the word "syndrome." False mem-ory itself is medicalized, thereby demanding a new type of expert. Sylvia Fraser, at least in a medium like the *Star*, cannot reply with the self-evident but subtle retort, "Who says this is a syndrome? Your use of the word 'syndrome' is a piece of rhetoric, not psychiatry."[32] The less ag-gressive British version of the foundation has called itself the False Mem-ory Society.

The American foundation was set up by Pamela Freyd. The Freyd family has had more than its share of problems; according to Freyd her-self, writing in her own newsletter, the December 1993 issue of *Phila-delphia* magazine ran a cover story about them titled "The Most Dysfunctional Family in America."[33] I avoid issues of personality, but I have to mention two pieces of writing. Pamela Freyd was driven to establish her foundation because her daughter Jenifer had broken with the parents after intensive therapy. Pamela Freyd circulated a highly personal description, initially published under the pseudonym Jane Doe, and in a later version printed anonymously in an anthology titled *Confabulations: Creating False Memories, Destroying Families.*[34] Jenifer Freyd is a professor of psychology at the University of Oregon. Her mother's anonymous account had circulated widely and (according to Jenifer) was sent to Jenifer's colleagues, employers, and in-laws, and to reporters for the Oregon newspapers. Jenifer Freyd then told her version of events in an appendix to a paper that she delivered at a conference in the summer of 1993.[35] When artists present us with the same events told from different vantage points—Marcel Proust's *Remembrance of Things Past*, Lawrence Durrell's *Alexandria Quartet*, Akira Kurosawa's 1951 film *Rashomon*—we come away enriched, improved, full of the complexity of life. The Freyd stories, read separately, are quite moving, but read consecutively in either order they leave the uncommitted bystander impoverished, unable to believe either party.

The FMS Foundation did not at once address multiple personality, but within months of the organization's establishment the multiple personality movement was running scared. The foundation was felt as a direct threat to multiple personality. A systematic challenge to repressed and hence forgotten "memories" of early child sexual abuse could undermine the etiology of multiple personality. There was talk of a Rich, Big, (and guilty) Man who was orchestrating the whole thing. When He was exposed, the foundation would collapse. During the next few months the main attempts at damage control were driven by fear of lawsuits. The fear was well justified. A former patient is bringing suit against Bennett G. Braun for finding three hundred of her personalities and encouraging her to recall satanic ritual abuse. This occurred at Rush-Presbyterian in Chicago—site of the first MPD clinic, and home to the annual ISSMP&D conference; Braun is the former ISSMP&D president. "There's always a good effect from attacks on professions or products," the lawyer defending Braun against malpractice is quoted as saying; "before product liability cases, manufacturers were not as stringent as they are today."[36] Well, perhaps she is right: we are discussing a product, not the healing arts.

The False Memory Syndrome Foundation established the "FMSF Scientific and Professional Advisory Board." This quickly attracted several avowed skeptics of multiple personality—distinguished psychiatrists such as Fred Frankel, Paul MacHugh, Harold Merskey, Martin Orne. Other board members are Elizabeth Loftus, the great critic of the idea of repressed memory of central life events; Richard Ofshe, the sociologist who has studied some of the more sensational court cases based on recovered memory; and Ernest Hilgard, his generation's most eminent investigator of hypnotism. There are also well-known debunkers like Martin Gardner, the longtime *Scientific American* columnist and parapsychology-basher, and James Randi, one of the great magicians of our time, who exposes the miraculous and the spooky as plain old prestidigitation. The board draws also on a wide spectrum of concerned people of international repute.

The antimultiple psychiatrists on the board, together with families that joined the foundation, drew the attention of the staff office to the relation between memories of abuse and multiple personalty. The first annual meeting of the foundation took place at Valley Forge, a symbolic choice, in April 1993. The invited speakers did make extremely critical allusions to multiple personality. This prompted a gracious letter to the *FMS Foundation Newsletter* from Philip Coons, a past president of the ISSMP&D, regretting these comments in an otherwise serious conference. He insisted that MPD was a legitimate *DSM* diagnosis, and suggested the FMSF speak at ISSMP&D conferences, and vice versa. But aside from printing this letter and Putnam's request for information about rumors, the newsletter made no mention of multiple personality for a year or more. There was a rebuttal of an offhand remark attributed to Kluft, but it did not mention multiple personality. Thereafter, however, it did launch out—with sharp thrusts to the jugular.

For example, Herbert Spiegel, an eminent elder psychiatrist from Columbia University, knew Sybil and was familiar with her treatment by Cornelia Wilbur in New York. The foundation newsletter drew upon an *Esquire* article in which Spiegel is quoted as saying that Sybil's personalities were artifacts of treatment.[37] That is powerful, given how central Wilbur is to the self-history of the multiple personality movement. For another example, the April 1994 newsletter includes a few paragraphs of a transcript of investigative reporting from a Canadian television program. It aired an hour on recovered memory, with a strong emphasis on Canadian multiple personality practitioners such as Colin Ross, Margo Rivera, and their trainees. The program includes several scenes involving Ross. In one we are shown a typescript with what looks like a title page headed "CIA MIND CONTROL"; the byline is "Colin Ross, M.D." On the show Ross said that as far back as the 1940s the CIA took people to "special training centers where these different techniques like sensory isolation, deprivation, flotation tanks, hypnosis, various memorization tanks, virtual reality goggles, hallucinogenic drugs and so on are used on them to try and deliberately create more alternate personalities that can hold information." Ross is recovering memories of CIA brain-meddling from his patients in therapy. The CIA knows this. That is how Ross explains the intense present criticism of the multiple movement—it is being orchestrated by the CIA.[38] At Canadian meetings of the False Memory Syndrome Foundation, members are told that they will be very lucky if Ross is called as an expert witness for the other side. He will be instantly discredited in front of any jury (the foundation speakers suggest) once his CIA conspiracy theories are made known.

These battles will continue to be fought out in the public arena for some time to come. The latest entrants to weigh in are two distinguished scholars, each of whom has enlisted the help of a professional writer to produce a rigorous but fiercely polemical book. Richard Ofshe is a social psychologist who has followed court cases in which an accused person has remembered bizarre and gruesome things that plainly never happened. He has studied other individuals who have not gone to court but have suffered grievously at the hands of therapists. He and his collaborator chose the title *Making Monsters: False Memories, Psychotherapy and Sexual Hysteria*.[39]

Elizabeth Loftus, a psychologist and expert on memory, has long upheld as a demonstrable fact of empirical psychology that the brain virtually never represses the memory of a profoundly important event and then reproduces it later, accurately. She and her collaborator chose the title *The Myth of Repressed Memories: False Memories and Allegations of Sexual Abuse*.[40] Her doctrine was already being undermined (for advocates of recovered memory) by Bessell van der Kolk, director of the Trauma Center at Harvard University. Loftus, he generously told the members of the ISSMP&D, was surely right about the sorts of things that she studies, memories of isolated facts, schoolbook learning, and propositional memory in general. But she knows nothing of another kind of memory, which expresses itself not in sentences but in scenes that come whole to a trauma victim, flashbacks constituted by feelings and images.[41]

If only we were able to leave the experts to fight it out. If only we could forget about the very ordinary and very unhappy individuals who are caught up in this memory maelstrom. If only we could ignore the searing pain and destruction caused on the one hand by early abuse, and on the other hand by false accusations. If we could leave all that aside, then this entire morass would verge on the ridiculous. We could treat the television confessionals, pro and con, like the game shows. Unfortunately, though, out there in the audience many people are being enlisted into shoddy causes by both sides.

How did we get here, to a land where forgetting becomes so central an issue for competing ideologies? The basic confrontations seem to have nothing to do with memory. They occur on other fronts. One is outright religious: fundamentalist, evangelical, or charismatic Protestant faiths provide a fertile ground for memories of ritual abuse; wise secularism is an equally fertile ground for outraged antagonism. But even more important are competing ideologies of the family. The anthropologist Jean Comaroff has stated that the resurgence of the incest taboo is to be expected when the family itself is being challenged.[42] There could hardly be a more potent alliance than incest and Satan. But why should the terrain of the confrontations be memory? The answer comes at two levels. At the lower and less inflamed level of discussion, memory is deployed because we want reasonable discourse about the family, no matter whether we want to preserve old structures or to destroy them. But since such discourse would involve us in values, and hence in what is supposed to be undebatable, "value judgments," we turn instead to science. The only sciences tailor-made to swim on top of the sea of morality and personal values are the sciences of memory. Hence each side presents knowledge about the very nature of memory, pure scientific knowledge. But there is a second level. That comes after everything has heated up and closed in on passionate concerns, but the escape route is the same. At that level we are scared of talking about what frightens us, incest and the devil. So we turn to science, and the only science available is about memory. This is a thesis about the role of the sciences of memory. I have to show, in later chapters, that the ground for these confrontations, in terms of memory, was set up long ago, when the sciences of memory were used as a way to master the soul.

Already I have illustrated on several occasions how fact and fiction play into each other to support multiple personality. Recovered memory, however, may seem to be on its own, free of the novelist, and driven by real-life revelations. It seems as if psychology and psychiatry, from the time of Freud to the present moment, have delivered to us the very idea of recovered memory. Not so. The most disturbing flashback scene of all must be the one that comes at the end of *Crime and Punishment*

(1866). There we read pages of wracking nightmare, indistinguishable from remembering. The feeling and tone of the successive scenes, rather than their literal content, overpower the dreamer. Is this the flashback of a victim, in this case a five-year-old girl? No. It is the molester's flash-back. It is the last event in the life of Svidrigaylov before he wakes at dawn, and walks toward the little Neva, and pulls the trigger.[43]

Dostoyevsky had planned the story twenty years earlier, for a novel he never completed. At that time there was to be less ambiguity than in the final version. It was to be an incident "in which a middle-aged man is lying in bed in an agreeable state between sleep and waking, when he is suddenly tormented by an indefinable feeling of mental discomfort; it proves to be the memory of a crime he had committed twenty years be-fore, when he had violated a little girl; this he had 'forgotten' until now, when it chose to emerge painfully from his unconscious mind."[44] Such scenes, which in less gifted hands served gothic romances, fueled the science of pathological psychology that would be the direct line to the soul.

Schizophrenia

IN THE NEXT PART of the book we move into the past, settling, for a while, in the period 1874–1886. That was when a wave of multiplicity swept over France, when the sciences of memory firmed up, and when the idea of trauma, previously used only for a bodily wound or lesion, came also to apply to psychic hurt. My aim will be to understand the underlying configuration of knowledge that simultaneously brought into being the sciences of memory, psychic trauma, and multiple personality. It will ease the transition to mention a few aspects of the period between then and now, a period when multiple personality languished, psychoanalysis flourished, and schizophrenia was the most baffling psychosis.

The prototype of multiple personality, as it matured in the time frame 1874–1886, was very different from the recent one that I have described. Here is a brilliant précis by Eugen Bleuler (1857–1939), best known as the man who, in the first decade of the twentieth century, created schizophrenia as a diagnostic category. He used early names for multiple personality, one English (double consciousness) and one French (alternating personality).

A special type of disturbance of personality is the *alternating personality*, also known as *double consciousness*. Let us consider a hysterical woman who until now has lived a mediocre existence. For some known or unknown reason she falls into a hysterical sleep, and on awakening she has forgotten her entire previous existence; she does not know who she is, where she has lived until now, and who the persons are whom she sees around her. Notwithstanding this change, the ordinary faculties of walking, speaking, eating, the use of clothes and other things are usually transferred to the new state (*état second*). Whatever the patient needs for her intercourse with other people, she learns very quickly. Her character, too, undergoes a change; formerly a serious-minded girl, she now becomes frivolous and pleasure-seeking. After some time, she again merges into a state of sleep, and on awakening the patient is back in her first state. She has no realization of the intervening time; all that she remembers is that she went to sleep, and has now awakened as usual. Such changed states may appear alternately for years. While in the first state the patient only remembers the former states and when in the second she always recalls only those of the second series. More frequently, however, it seems that in the second state the patient can recall the first (normal) series, but while in the first state she cannot recall the second (morbid) series. It may also happen that eventually the second state will become permanent and this way cause a *transformation of the personality*. In quite rare cases there may be an alternation of many such states, each with its very definite character and special memory group (personality); as many as twelve have been observed. As a matter of fact cases of pure dual personalities are very rare. Yet their theoretical significance is very great, for they show what marked changes can be brought about by a systematic elimination or intercalation of association paths.[1]

État second was Eugène Azam's name for the alter state of his patient Félida, the first of the French multiples to be studied after 1876. The phrase was standard; Breuer and Freud used it in more than half a dozen different places in *Studies in Hysteria*.[2]

During the 1980s, both Bleuler and Freud were seen by many members of the multiple movement as enemies. I will return to the question of why Freud is so loathed, but I begin with Bleuler. It has become an accepted fact that a thriving multiple movement in Boston, led by Morton Prince (1854–1929), was destroyed by a pincer attack mounted 1908–1926. On the left, the psychoanalysts practiced a type of dynamic psychology that had no place for the theories of Janet or Prince. And on the right, the more neurologically and biologically minded psychiatrists treated multiples as if they were schizophrenics. There is a wonderfully mythic quality to this account. Two forces of legendary evil, Freud and Bleuler, overpowered that precious and innocent stripling, multiple personality and dissociation. They won the battle, but perhaps not the war. Some multiple personality activists are now trying to reclaim lost territory from schizophrenia. I shall end by describing this irredentism, but first let us examine the historical story that, as in the case of every irredentism, is essential to legitimating the project.

The foundation for the official history is a single historical note published by Rosenbaum in 1980.[3] He observed that after 1926 the *Index Medicus* listed far more papers about schizophrenia than about multiple personality; between 1914 and 1926 the reverse had been the case. So schizophrenia overwhelmed multiplicity. Why? Putnam writes, "Rosenbaum notes that Bleuler included multiple personality in his category of schizophrenia."[4] Using the same source Greaves asserts that Bleuler "included at least some instances of [multiple personality disorder] in his global diagnosis of schizophrenia. Those remaining cases, which he deemed hysterical, he relegated (at least by implication) to the realm of hypnotic artifacts."[5] These statements are based on a misreading of three consecutive sentences of Bleuler's, which have been extracted, truncated without notice, and actually misquoted from a paragraph whose context is ignored. A libel against a scrupulous author by writers of another caliber is of no moment. But relations between multiplicity and schizophrenia may be hot in the future, so the record should be set straight.

Ellenberger offers an excellent brief summary of Bleuler's theory and practice, which, as he says, "has often been misunderstood."[6] Bleuler was director of the Burghölzli mental hospital, the university psychiatric clinic of Zurich. The crucial division among psychoses had been established by Emil Kraepelin (1856–1926). On the one hand there were manic-depressive illnesses. On the other was dementia praecox, so-called because of its frequent onset in adolescence—it was premature senility. In 1908 Bleuler published what he had been teaching to his assistants for some years. Kraepelin had been wrong to focus on early onset.[7] No existing label suited this baffling disease. Bleuler settled on split-brain-disease, in Greek: schizophrenia. He did not mean a splitting into personalities that would alternate in control of an individual, as in the prototype for double consciousness. He meant to indicate "the 'splitting' of psychic functions."[8] To oversimplify enormously, one kind of cleavage was between that part of a person who knew what was going on, and another who felt what was going on—a split between sense and sensibility.

Bleuler had little interest in alternating personality, but he insisted on differential diagnosis. In the literature he knew, one alter succeeds another in taking control, as in the prototype I quoted above. He was not acquainted with what Morton Prince was to call co-consciousness, in which two alters may be aware of each other—that was part of a later prototype of the disorder. Thus schizophrenia and alternating personality both involve splitting, but splitting of very different sorts. The schizophrenic simultaneously has irreconcilable attitudes, emotions, and behaviors, as well as terrible distortions of logic and sense of reality. The multiple has no logical or reality problems but fractures into successive fragments:

> Systematic splitting, with respect to personality, for example, may be found in many other psychotic conditions [in addition to the group of schizophrenias]; in hysteria (multiple personality) they are even more marked than in schizophrenia. Definite splitting, however, in the sense

that various personality fragments exist side by side in a state of clear orientation as to environment, will only be found in our disease [viz. schizophrenia].[9]

Had Bleuler known about co-consciousness he would have had to revise this discussion. But he did not. I have quoted his prototype of double consciousness. The three sentences that follow my previous quotation are these:

It is not alone in hysteria that one finds an arrangement of different per-sonalities one *succeeding* the other; through similar mechanisms schizo-phrenia produces different personalities existing *side by side*. As a matter of fact, there is no need of delving into these rare though most demonstrable hysterical cases; we can produce the very same phenomena, experimen-tally, through hypnotic suggestion, and we also know that in the ordinary hysterical twilight states the memory of former attacks, concerning which the patient shows an amnesia in her normal state, can be retained or can be aroused by suggestion.

The emphases are Bleuler's in the original German, and are preserved in the faithful English translation. Now, these very sentences are the basis of the claim by Rosenbaum and all subsequent movement writers that Bleuler included multiple personality under schizophrenia. These very sentences? Well, not exactly. Rosenbaum left out Bleuler's two empha-ses, "*succeeding*" and "*side by side*"; the emphasis was essential, for that was the basis of Bleuler's differential diagnosis. Instead Rosenbaum ital-icized quite different words. He also changed the punctuation and omit-ted the end of the last sentence. He did not mention the impeccable description of multiple personality that came earlier in the very same paragraph.

Bleuler has been so maligned that I should summarize his actual posi-tions. In his view, (1) multiples—alternating personalities—are rare; (2) they are "demonstrably existent"; and (3) they are to be understood in terms of dissociation—"systematic elimination or intercalation of as-sociation paths." Further, (4) dissociation ("similar mechanisms") also occurs in schizophrenia; there, however, it results not in alternation but in side-by-side fragmentation, which is not known in nineteenth-cen-tury reports of multiple personality. And, finally, (5) we can study the important phenomenon of dissociation experimentally, through hyp-notic suggestion, rather than seeking out rare spontaneous alternating personalities. In every respect Bleuler is faithful to the literature of mul-tiple personality, and in particular to Pierre Janet. For example, it was above all Janet who taught that multiple personality could be studied experimentally through hypnotism.

Bleuler did not, as Greaves puts it, imply that some alternating personalities were schizophrenic while the rest were hypnotic artifacts. There is a sad irony here. Greaves wonders why Bleuler was so effective at "conscripting" multiple personality into schizophrenia. He explains it by what he calls "inoculation theory: . . . Whoever relates information first—'whoever gets there firstest with the mostest'—is in a highly advantaged position."[10] How untrue! Bleuler, who is not read, got there first and is highly disadvantaged. It was Rosenbaum who inoculated people against reading Bleuler by misquoting three truncated sentences out of context.

After its gross misrepresentation of Bleuler, the official history of multiple personality goes as follows. Morton Prince learned of multiplicity from French doctors and diagnosed it in his Boston practice. His two famous cases, Sally Beauchamp and B.C.A., were landmarks.[11] A Boston school of psychiatry flourished in the first decade of this century, with a heavy emphasis on dissociation. In 1906, as he was finishing his treatment of Miss Beauchamp, Prince founded the *Journal of Abnormal Psychology*, which runs to this day, and which featured a good many cases of multiplicity. But within a few years, the diagnosis virtually disappeared. It was savaged by the two demons, psychoanalysis and schizophrenia. Since the multiple movement is American, its official history is American, and its problem is American, the movement asks why multiple personality disappeared in America. The more interesting question concerns France, the begetter of so many patients after 1876, and homeland of the legendary theorist Pierre Janet. The next few chapters will describe that French scene in some detail. No one (to my knowledge) has ever asked why multiple personality disappeared in France.

Psychoanalysis is not the answer. Psychoanalysis has had its own career in France. The work of Jacques Lacan has become famous outside his homeland, but previous events are less well known. Freud's French evangelist was the redoubtable Marie Bonaparte (1882–1962). She bankrolled the French wing of psychoanalysis; it was she for whom Lacan had the greatest contempt. She seems not to have even thought about Freud before she read the *Introductory Lectures on Psychoanalysis* in 1924—rather too late to have caused the suppression of multiple personality in France.[12] In fact the French wave of multiples had almost completely subsided by 1910.[13] There is a very easy explanation for this. French multiple personality was born under the sign of hysteria. All multiples were hysterics, usually with the extraordinary symptoms that Jean-Martin Charcot had made famous. In the period 1895–1910, hysteria ceased to be central to French psychiatry. A simple syllogism follows. Out went hysteria; all multiples were hysterics; so out went multiples.

Mark Micale has shown how the symptoms of hysteria, insofar as they persisted, dissipated into other diagnoses. Hysteria, Micale writes, "vanished into a hundred places in the medical textbooks." And, as he says, "the large majority of these changes took place during 1895–1910."[14] Freud's anxiety neurosis collected some bits of hysteria; so did Kraepelin's dementia praecox, the predecessor of schizophrenia; likewise Janet's diagnosis of psychasthenia—and many more that are today remembered chiefly by historians of medicine. The result? There was no medical space in which multiple personality could thrive.

Consider Janet himself, who in his first psychological papers, 1886–1887, was so fascinated by double personality. It is a major topic for his philosophy dissertation of 1889, *Psychological Automatism*. In 1894, in the second volume of *The Mental State of Hystericals*, a short but significant section was devoted to it. There is substantial attention to the phenomenon in his 1906 Harvard lectures, *The Major Symptoms of Hysteria*, addressed to an audience that, thanks to Morton Prince, could say it lived in the world capital of multiple personality. But in 1909 his book *The Neuroses* was rather dismissive of doubling.[15] Note the date: it coincides with Micale's dating of the demise of French hysteria. Janet was no more true to his youthful enthusiasm than anyone else. In his three-volume *Psychological Healing* of 1919, in many ways the accumulation of a life's experience, exactly one page out of 1,147 is dedicated to multiple personality, or rather double personality. There he discusses "a series of periodic transformations of activity and memory, which as I have shown elsewhere [*Les Névroses*] enable us to interpret in a simpler fashion the phenomena of double personality, which were so mysterious in the early days of pathological psychology."[16]

Skeptics about multiple personality will be astonished and delighted at what Janet wrote in the next paragraph. Double personality should be assimilated to a much more familiar condition of which it is a special and rare case. That is, patients with alternating periods of depression, mania, and stability: "*les circulaires*, as the early French alienists called them." In 1854 J.-P. Falret had coined the name *folie circulaire*, which is roughly coextensive with Kraepelin's manic-depression or the bipolar disorders of *DSM-IV*. Notice that Janet did not, in the end, file multiple personality with schizophrenia. Insofar as he used German classification (which on patriotic grounds he detested), he filed the condition with what for Kraepelin was the very opposite of dementia praecox, namely, manic-depressive illness. *Janet concluded that multiple personality was a special case of bipolar disorder.*

The disappearance of multiple personality in France is completely explicable within a medical history of hysteria. The fact that Janet himself gave it up is of merely anecdotal interest; by 1919, he was no longer influential. What of the United States? Morton Prince's Boston school did strongly advocate the diagnosis of multiple personality and the use of the concept of dissociation. It lost. Psychoanalysis was irrelevant to the disappearance of multiple personality in France, but it really did matter in America. There was a celebrated congress at Clark University in 1907, to which most of the world's luminaries in psychology were invited. Freud seems to have dominated the occasion. A gradual groundswell of support for analysis appeared, and for many years psychoanalysis was dominant in American medical schools of psychiatry. In private practice, the American versions of psychoanalysis boomed. There was no place for Prince. Freud's repression swamped Prince's dissociation as a cardinal tool of the trade. Nowadays there may be a casual and unreflective interlacing of the two, but once they were two models in confrontation, a situation best described in its own day by the British psychiatrist Bernard Hart (1879–1966).[17] The attitude of the analysts to Prince himself verged on contempt. Ernest Jones describes Prince "as a very thorough gentleman, a man of the world, and a very pleasant colleague. . . . But he had one serious failing. He was rather stupid, which to Freud was always the unpardonable sin."[18]

Thus psychoanalysis—one-half of the multiple movement's official explanation for the disappearance of multiple personality—is correct for the United States, although irrelevant for France. What of the other half of the explanation, the claim that the diagnosis of schizophrenia engulfed multiple personality? I have shown that Bleuler himself carefully distinguished the two diagnoses. Yet he did contribute indirectly to the disappearance of multiple personality, because he had a major hand in the dissipation of hysteria and hence helped destroy the home base of multiplicity. No one will dispute the increase in diagnosis, reporting, and discussion of schizophrenia during the 1920s. Rosenbaum looked at *Index Medicus*; we are now able to consult the bibliography collected by George Greaves and his colleagues.[19] We find that the incidence of papers on multiple personality published in English is remarkably flat for five-year periods between 1910 and 1970. Schizophrenia is going up and up, unmistakably, but reports of multiplicity do not vary significantly. What is true is that aside from the flurry of interest in "Eve" in the late 1950s, no one took the subject seriously. No longer was there a Morton Prince to fascinate the world. The number of published papers is a mere epiphenomenon. Since multiple personality was, for the French and for Prince, an unusual kind of hysteria, we should, if we are to count papers, count the publication rate for papers on hysteria. The results are summarized in a note.[20] Both hysteria and neurasthenia decline steadily from a high around 1905. In fact by 1917, hysteria without multiple personality has become no more common than multiple personality itself. These statistics should not, however, be taken to prove anything, because the types and volume of psychiatric publication themselves change so much during these years. They merely illustrate what we know on more theoretical ground: that hysteria was being phased out, and with it, multiple personality.

Even if psychoanalysis was the main direct threat, Prince knew full well that the decline of hysteria would be a disaster for multiple personality. One of the major figures in the termination of hysteria was Charcot's former favorite student, Joseph Babinski. In magnificent Oedipal fashion, Babinski "dynamited hysteria," to use the apt phrase of a French encyclopedia article. "There has developed," Prince wrote in 1919, "amongst French neurologists, under the teachings of Babinski, a reaction against the classical conception of hysteria of Charcot and his school."[21] Then followed a polite but heartfelt denunciation of Babinski. It came too late in the day to have any effect, and it was too out of touch with the demise of hysteria in Europe. Today's advocates of multiple personality want to explain the virtual disappearance of the diagnosis of multiple personality. They are asking the wrong question. A better one is: why did it hang on so long in the United States?

One element in the American and English fascination with multiplicity—one that encouraged a more enduring interest in the early years of this century than was found in France—has been underplayed. The disorder always needs a host, much in the way that a parasite needs hosts. In our day, as we have seen, the host has been child abuse. In France the hosts were Charcotian hysteria, hypnotism, and positivism. In New England in particular, and in both America and Britain more generally, an additional host was psychic research linked with spiritualism. One idea was that alters were departed spirits; mediumship and multiple personality grew close. This thought had occurred early in France. Charles Richet (who won the 1909 Nobel Prize for medicine) was the first investigator to apply statistical inference to extrasensory perception. After trying pure randomization, he turned to stellar performers such as Janet's very first multiple, Léonie, who had originally attracted Janet's interest because of her ability to be hypnotized at a distance. When Richet did his work on telepathy in 1884, he was virtually the first person to use randomized experimental design in any field of inquiry whatsoever.[22] It was, however, in England and the United States that the scientific pursuit of psychical research flourished, starting in 1882. The most careful summaries of the entire nineteenth-century multiple literature are to be found in the writings of F.W.H. Myers, a cofounder of the Society for Psychical Research in London—especially his magnum opus, subtitled *Survival of Bodily Death*, a work published in 1903 and still one of the richest collections of early reports of multiple personality.[23] The longest single case report of a multiple, or of any other case of apparent mental illness, is the 1,396-page study of Doris Fisher, by Walter Franklin Prince (no relation to Morton Prince). It was published in 1915–1916 in a magazine for psychical research.[24] Stephen Braude, whose philosophical views are discussed in chapter 16, remains true to these roots, having published books favorable to psychical research and to multiple personality disorder, and connecting the two in the trance states of mediums.[25] These themata will of course go on being updated. A 1994 paper confirms that belief in psychical phenomena—spooks, aliens, and the like—is well correlated with a history of childhood trauma.[26] But after thirty-odd years of high times around the turn of the century, mediumship, spiritism, and psychical research went into radical decline. Once again, a zone of deviancy that was hospitable to multiple personality severely contracted.

We have now said everything necessary to explain the virtual disappearance of multiple personality, as a diagnosis or as a serious research topic, in the years 1921–1970. But the relationships among multiple personality, schizophrenia, and psychoanalysis are not over yet. I should say a few words about the multiple movement and Freud, and then turn back to schizophrenia.

The loathing of the multiple movement for Freud is best expressed by Colin Ross: "Freud did to the unconscious mind with his theories what New York does to the ocean with its garbage."[27] Between 1971 and 1990 acknowledgments of Freud by advocates of multiplicity were stunningly brief, even in Cornelia Wilbur, the maverick psychoanalyst. Here is an almost unique example that alludes to Freud: "Freud (1938) contributed to the concept of the unconscious mind as potentially holding the entirety of memories of the life experience." The citation, "Freud (1938)," is to a generic pocket-book *Basic Writings* of Freud, to which the author gives no page references.[28] The index to Putnam's textbook refers us only once to Freud: "Even Sigmund Freud reported personal experiences with feelings of depersonalization."[29]

The fear and loathing of Freud is easy to understand. The feminist wing of the child abuse movement despised Freud; that wing was hospitable to multiple personality. Jeffrey Masson's brilliant attack on Freud for abandoning the so-called seduction theory made Freud the villain for anyone who cared about sexual abuse of children. There is the additional feeling of betrayal, in that Breuer's case of Anna O. is so easily read as a case of multiplicity: Breuer and Freud themselves said she had double consciousness.[30] Why did they not keep faith? Then there is a slightly guilty feeling of debt. The etiology of multiple personality is remarkably akin to early Freud, at the time of his collaboration with Breuer. The suffering from memories, the effect of trauma: everyone learned that from Freud, even if in fact Janet was saying much the same thing around 1890.

Perhaps there is even a nagging doubt on the part of a few reflective clinicians: How come we are stuck with the very earliest, simplest, kindergarten Freud, the stock-in-trade of those prewar black-and-white psychodramas shown on late-night television? How come we have not even gone so far as Freud had gone by 1899—how come we have not thought seriously about what Freud called screen memories? Why have we been so literalist, so mechanical, and imagined that an illness produced by trauma is produced at the time of the trauma, in early childhood? Why can't we at least discuss the idea that the experience of the original event, apparently kept in memory, is not what causes distress and dysfunction; why can't we ask whether the problem comes from the possibly repressed memory itself, much later in life, and the way in which the mind has worked on and recomposed that memory? But times are changing. The crises of recovered memory have made clinicians go back to Freud. Conversely, students of psychoanalysis have increasingly thought about multiple personality. Sometimes they use traditional Freudian concepts. Otto Rank, one of Freud's inner circle, wrote about the double as a type of narcissism,[31] an idea that has been revived by

Sheldon Bach.[32] The Menninger Clinic, long an important American center of psychoanalytic research, has just devoted a whole issue of its journal to multiple personality.

The relations between schizophrenia and multiple personality are also in flux, although all the action comes from the multiple side. It is urged that many patients now called schizophrenic should be recognized as multiples, and not just because of misdiagnosis, but because many of the classic symptoms of schizophrenia are actually symptoms of multiple personality instead. How can this be? In chapter 1, I urged that we keep multiple personality and schizophrenia completely apart. At the beginning I had to guard against semantic confusion through the misleading but natural equation: multiple personality = split personality = schizophrenia. To make sense of current speculation I now have to lower the barriers a bit. But not too far. There is a lot of good sense in the folksy distinction implied in the book *Sibyl*: "Dr. Wilbur had seen schizophrenics—psychotics—who had not been as ill as Sibyl. One might say they were running a psychotic temperature of 99 degrees, whereas Sibyl was running a psychoneurotic temperature of 105."[33] And Wilbur insisted that she had never encountered multiples with the flat affect or disordered thought patterns of schizophrenics.

I mentioned other differences between the two illnesses, but not what really matters. Schizophrenia is an absolutely dreadful condition. There are those who urge that it is the worst illness that is now rampant in the Western industrial world. You can think of schizophrenia, rather than cancer, say, as the worst disease of prosperity because it so often strikes at young people just as they are about to enter adult life. The impact on families is horrible. One of the worst things about severe episodes in the life of schizophrenics is that other people are terrified as they see good sense and order turned upside down, chains of ideas turned into threatening parodies of ordinary life. The withdrawal, the indifference, the fascinations; speech awry, glances blocked, feelings inverted—above all, strangeness. And then the opposite, now much alleviated by drugs for many patients, the catatonic state once so characteristic of insane asylums: people, or former people, who don't move, don't respond, who have gone. One of the important ideas in the antipsychiatry movement inspired by R. D. Laing was that the nonschizophrenics were a serious part of the problem.[34] One important residue of that movement has been the formation of Friends of Schizophrenics and similar support groups.

The outlook for schizophrenics is not entirely bleak. Bleuler thought schizophrenia could be helped by careful treatment, but that despite spontaneous remissions, patients never truly recover from it. However, the symptom profile and history have been evolving. A few have argued that "the disorder itself has undergone a benign metamorphosis such as has occurred with some infectious diseases."[35] The advent of antipsychotic drugs about 1957 has had an immense effect on the lives of many schizophrenics. These drugs are constantly under development, and one hopes that the undesirable effects on many patients will gradually be modulated.[36] For most dedicated psychiatrists the psychotropic drugs are a means, not the final treatment. They make it possible to do long-term therapeutic work, and to reintegrate a patient into the world of friends, family, and employment. It is true that desperate shortage of funds for psychiatric care often results in "warehousing" of patients not further helped by family or action groups to act as their advocates. But responsible medicine does not end treatment for schizophrenics with a package of tablets.

There is no agreement on the extent to which schizophrenia is genetic. There are regional variations in its incidence and manifestations. There is a series of claims for genes associated with schizophrenia, and a barrage of clues to specific biochemical causation. We know precious little about the underlying causes and nature of schizophrenia. The most frequently used word in clinical descriptions of schizophrenia is that it is a "heterogeneous" illness. There are three main approaches to the disease.[37] Possibly a majority of scientists think there is one fundamental cause, which has many manifestations. Some suggest that there are two fundamental types, one of which is genetic and associated with the traditional onset in late adolescence, and the other of which is biochemical.[38] Others think we are still further away from understanding, and that what we are faced with amounts only to several groups of symptom clusters. And finally, there is an iconoclastic group who deny that schizophrenia is a legitimate grouping at all.[39]

There has always been a tension between those who strive for an etiological definition of schizophrenia and those who, because of our ignorance, want a purely phenomenological set of diagnostic criteria. The behavior of schizophrenics changes over time. How can the clinician pick out a schizophrenic on interview? There was a search for what were called "prognomic" indicators. (That's prog-nomic, not pro-gnomic; prognomic indicators are behaviors that justify an expectation that other, more fundamental and lawlike, symptoms will reveal themselves.)

The diagnosis of schizophrenia has never been easy. In 1939 the psychiatrist Kurt Schneider proposed a list of eleven "first-rank" symptoms of the illness.[40] A patient showing any sizable number of these symptoms could be confidently diagnosed as schizophrenic. The patient

(1) hears voices speaking the patient's own thoughts out loud; (2) or is the subject about which voices are arguing; (3) or is the subject of a commentary by the voices, who comment on what the patient is doing or has done; (4) has normal perceptions followed by delusional versions of them; (5) is the passive recipient of body sensations coming from outside; (6) feels thoughts being extracted from the mind by external forces; (7) believes thoughts are broadcast to others; (8) or complains of thoughts being inserted into the mind from outside. Or has the sense that (9) feelings and affects, or (10) sudden impulses, or (11) motor activities, are controlled from outside the patient's own body.

Schneider thought that any one of these features could be used for a diagnosis of schizophrenia, but it is now generally agreed that Schneiderian first-rank symptoms are no guarantees of schizophrenia. It is here that multiple personality enters. These symptoms, or behaviors very reminiscent of them, are manifested by a great many patients now diagnosed as multiples. In a series of 30 patients whom he had diagnosed as multiples, Richard Kluft found an average of 4.4 Schneiderian first-order symptoms per patient.[41] In a larger series of 236 people diagnosed as multiples, Colin Ross and his associates found that the average number of Schneiderian symptoms per patient was 4.5. Ninety-six out of the 236 patients surveyed had a previous diagnosis of schizophrenia.[42] Ross infers that the symptoms proposed by Schneider well over fifty years ago as justifying a schizophrenia diagnosis actually are at least as likely to indicate multiple personality. Multiples can have "schizophreniform episodes." That means acting like a schizophrenic, but not for too long a time. *DSM-IV* insists that one should not diagnose schizophrenia definitively until the symptoms have been seen for at least six months. The World Health Organization guide, *ICD-10*, is satisfied with one month; *DSM-IV* leaves a door open for dissociative identity disorder diagnosis that would be shut by *ICD-10*. There is now a quite common distinction between positive and negative diagnostic criteria for schizophrenia. The Schneiderian first-rank symptoms are all positive; they are unusual things that schizophrenics and some others do, things that, in their strangeness, often seem scary and threatening to healthy people. Multiples can display many of the positive symptoms of hallucinations and the like. But they do not have the negative symptoms, the sheer absences, the profoundly flat affect, that are so often, in daily practice, the grounds for a diagnosis of schizophrenia. The traditional distinctions between schizophrenia and multiple personality, already insisted upon by Bleuler, still remain intact. But advocates of multiplicity do not limit themselves to claiming back patients diagnosed as schizophrenics because of first-rank symptoms; they want to claim as much of the field of psychiatric research as they can. Ross writes: "MPD is the most important and interesting disorder in psychiatry, which is why I study it. I believe it to be the key diagnosis in an impending paradigm shift in psychiatry. . . . Biological psychiatry might obtain more clinically meaningful results if it focused on the psychobiology of trauma and abandoned the search for causality in genes and endogenous chemical derangements."[43]

Fortunately the paradigm shift that Ross envisages will not take place. When T. S. Kuhn published *The Structure of Scientific Revolutions* in 1962, he truly knew not what he had wrought. "Paradigm shift" has become a war chant. I finish this chapter at the end of the year 1994. February 1995 will see an aggressive conference titled The First Annual Conference on Trauma, Loss, and Dissociation: The Foundations of Twenty-First Century Traumatology. Psychobiology will figure, to be sure, but one aim of the organizers is to move treatment of trauma away from multiple personality models. The preconference publicity quotes one of the speakers: "Advances in the field of traumatic stress research have led to exciting new paradigm shifts. The conference will break new ground for the 21st century."[44] Perhaps I may be allowed a dour Canadian joke. In 1900 the prime minister of Canada announced, "The Twentieth Century Belongs to Canada."

Before Memory

MULTIPLE PERSONALITY has been specifically Western, peculiar to the industrialized world, and consistently diagnosed in only this or that region and then only for a few decades at a time. It may nevertheless be a local manifestation of something universal: trance. People go into trance states in almost every society. We must be cautious about that, because "trance" is a Western word, a European concept used by anthropologists. From the Arctic Circle to the Cape of Good Hope, travelers encounter what seems to them to be similar behavior. Maybe "trance" is itself only a symptom of how Western eyes see the world. What trance "is," or whether there is indeed one human universal behavior or state to be classified as trance, is an entirely open question. On the other hand, perhaps it is not just a human but a mammalian trait. I. P. Pavlov's student F. A. Völgyesi seems to have hypnotized most of the mammals and has photographs to show it. Maybe trance goes further down the scale of evolution. Völgyesi has photographs of a hypnotized praying mantis, although one wonders if there was a touch of anthropomorphism there; he chose to hypnotize a *praying* insect.[1]

I suggest that "trance" may be as seen by Western eyes, but it may be more specific than that: as seen by speakers of English. The French medical name for trance was *extase*—which in that context did not strictly mean "ecstasy," as some translators of old medical texts have supposed. But of course it still connotes a more exalted state than the comparatively neutral English word "trance." Although French has an old word *transe*, it took over a word *trance* or *transe* from English, initially for the trance of mediums, who were in the first instance American or English. French anthropologists now tend to use this word for describing what Anglos call trance. German has taken on the word *Trance*, but the term used in medicine has often been, literally, deep unconsciousness. Trance, in short, may be a very parochial notion indeed.

Both *DSM-IV* and *ICD-10* have sections on trance. *ICD-10* of 1992 has "Trance and Possession Disorders." *DSM-IV* more cautiously has "Dissociative Trance Disorder" listed as a topic for further study but has not declared it to be "disorder." The definitions do not cover any trance whatsoever, but only trances not used in religious practices—as if "religious" were a clean cross-cultural concept. We see that cultural imperialism is not dead, even if it is now conducted by psychiatrists rather than missionaries. Anyone who thinks otherwise should reflect that *DSM-IV* and *ICD-10* were issued in 1994 and 1992 respectively, and have the imprimatur of Washington and Geneva. Instead of seeing Western dissociative disorders as a local and specific form of trance, they suggest that trance is a subtype of a Western illness, dissociative disorders. Worse, they turn central and meaningful parts of other civilizations into pathologies. This is not done innocently. David Spiegel, chair of the committee that recommended the dissociative disorders entries for *DSM-IV*, justified the addition of trance with the assertion that although we in the West have multiple personality, most of the rest of the world has trance.[2] This is true. But it is not a ground for making trance a disorder on a par with what has hitherto been a very unusual and peculiarly Western mental illness, dissociative disorders. The dissociative disorders were conceptualized as part of what, in chapter 15, I call memoro-politics. The concept of trance has nothing inherently to do with memory.

Hypnotism is one of the phenomena that Western culture tends to group under trance: the hypnotized person is said to be in a trance state. Hypnotism seems to be the one form of trance that can be subjected to experimental investigation. It is easy to hypnotize people, although some are more easily hypnotized than others. But hypnotism has usually been relegated to the status of a scientific "curiosity," if not a "marvel." Scientific curiosities are topics whose existence is acknowledged by scientists, but about which they can do nothing. The Brownian motion of molecules was a curiosity for a century. It was well known. When it was fashionable for nineteenth-century country houses to keep microscopes, one showed one's guests the latest insect from the Amazon—and the Brownian motion. The photoelectric effect was a more recherché curiosity for eighty years. These effects were scientific because they could be observed with a certain amount of instrumentation; they were curiosities because they were isolated phenomena that fit no vision of the world. Hypnotism is a curiosity, more often seen on the stage than in the psychology laboratory. To use an old but honest word, common in seventeenth-century science but not used today, hypnotism is something of a *marvel*.

One way to silence a topic of research is to treat it as a curiosity or turn it into a marvel. Science abhors a marvel, not because marvels are vacuous, empty of meaning, but because they are too full of meaning, of hints, of feeling. Marvels are meanings out of control. You can expel a topic from science by making it a marvel. Conversely, if you are forced to look a marvel in the face, the thing to do is to bring it into the laboratory. There it will languish and die until the laboratory itself is cast out of science. Then it will become a marvel again, but it has been somehow rendered less potent because it has been declined a laboratory niche. That has been the fate of psychical research, or parapsychology.

Philosophers like to talk about "the aims of science." Usually science has no self-conscious aims, but if ever there was a time that Science acted with concerted Aim, it was in the two commissions that worked in 1785 to determine the validity of animal magnetism, the predecessor of hypnotism. One commission was established by the Academy of Medicine in Paris, while the other was a royal commission over which Lavoisier presided, and which numbered Benjamin Franklin among its five commissioners. Mesmer had proposed a new theoretical entity, the magnetic fluid: he had laboratory practice; he had cures. He had all the trappings of science. But it was determined that there was no substance to his claims. Mesmerism was consigned to the level of popular marvel, where it played a significant role in underground antiestablishment movements leading up to 1789.[3]

By 1840 James Braid was trying to restore animal magnetism to science. He abandoned all talk of the fluid and renamed the practice neurhypnology or "scientific hypnotism."[4] But scientific it never became. It did briefly flourish in France at the time of Charcot and *la grande hystérie*, starting in 1878. By 1892 Pierre Janet was propounding a general therapeutics of hypnotism for restoring past memories and then resolving them. Freud first followed in Charcot's footsteps, but then renounced hypnotism and developed other techniques for getting in touch with memories. Psychoanalysis has remained true to Freud, particularly in France during the dominance of Lacan, where hypnotism was the greatest taboo of all. America, always more attuned to popular movements and ill-disposed to authority, has been much more eclectic about hypnotism. Yet remarkably little in the way of research funds from the overall budgets for research psychology is dedicated to hypnotism or trance.

Anthropologists are fascinated by the subject, but although they say a great deal about trance behavior and its social roles, their discipline does not have the tools for studying the physiology of trance. They can tell us what initiation procedures are used to encourage trance in suitable people. They can tell us which drugs or medicines may help. For example, the people of Mayotte, Malagasy-speakers who live on a small island in the Indian Ocean, are Muslims. Hence they cannot touch alcohol. Certain festivities connected with trance and "spirit possession" begin with the participants consuming lots of cheap French perfume—mostly alcohol.[5] Is the phenomenon of trance in Mayotte the same as shamanism in northern Canada? Anthropologists use the same word for both, and also for hypnotism; let us suppose they are right to do so. Under that supposition, the phenomenology of multiple personality has evolved within the general category of trance.

Western industrial society has no place for trance except in leisure or marginalized activities. We have psychic mediums. We have meditation. We have prayer, and we use music, both privately and en masse, to produce states that, when observed in other cultures, may be called trance. But these activities are not allowed to get in the way of the manufacturing and service industries. Perhaps on the old assembly lines workers did achieve a trance state, but the anthropologists don't call it that, and men were fired on account of it. In contrast, Haida weavers, in the Queen Charlotte Islands off the coast of British Columbia, regularly went into trance states in the course of their repetitive, rhythmic duties, and this was a much venerated condition, making the material woven acquire a certain blessed quality.

To get a sense of the range of trancelike states in the modern world, consider the fashionable attention deficit disorder of childhood. The summer camp section of the *New York Times Magazine* is full of advertisements for camps that specialize in children with ADD. Cynics, not denying that some children have real problems, suggest that many children who once were allowed to daydream and were treated with tolerant amusement are now shunted off to the therapist in winter and to camp in summer. Trancelike conditions continue to be further pathologized; the future for absentminded professors is grim. The one place in modern America that trance states are socially approved is in commuters driving to and from work. Eco-reformers inveigh about the wastage of gasoline as they see endless commuter highways clogged with steel. They cannot understand why people will not carpool or use public transport. One reason is clear: trancelike states, with a private program of your own type of music or chatter, can be very nice. Even the pathologizers mentioned in chapter 7, who prove by tests that car-driving-dissociation is at one end of a line that ends in multiple personality, allow that dissociation while commuting is benign.

Trance had been declared a potential disorder, alongside multiple personality. A reverse account is waiting to be given, one that sees multiple personality as one way to use or abuse the ability to go into a trance. Our ignorance about trance, and our wish to make it pathological, probably means that we colonize our own past, destroying traces of the original inhabitants. That is, we read multiple personality into other uses of trance, those that appeared in earlier European societies, and find it very hard to see them as they were seen then, not as precursors of multiple personality disorder, inadequately diagnosed, but as cultural uses of trance with their own integrity.

Why do we marginalize trance? It is not only because we demand constant attention to the wheels of industry. Our exclusion of trancelike behavior seems to have preceded industrialization, even if it was less rigid in earlier times. West European and American societies are by and large examples of what Mary Douglas has called enterprise cultures.[6] They are characterized by extremely high levels of individual responsibility and correspondingly great opportunities for individuals. You can succeed, but you can also fail and be abandoned by an enterprise society. That is very different from a hierarchical society, in which every person has a place. There you may become the lowest among people of your station, but there is no intelligible way of dropping out or being discarded, short of death.

Douglas applies her analysis to the Western idea of a person, using John Locke's theory of personal identity as an example. Locke thought that there were distinctions to be made because there are really two concepts of identity. He chose the word "person" for what he called a forensic concept, having to do with memory and responsibility. He chose the word "man" for a concept based in part on bodily continuity. Douglas argues, in a way that I find compelling, that Locke's notion of the person as forensic and as linked by chains of memory and responsibility is a characteristic of the enterprise culture. It involves a very different conception of selfhood than what she found in African communities with which she has worked. There people are happy to have four selves, and although trance is not a major part of their life, it has a respected role to play.

Locke's forensic person is a relatively new figure who arises from new practices of commerce, law, property, and trade. Yet he is not altogether new, for as Locke himself makes plain, the forensic person has a role in the divine plan, thereby harking back to an earlier Christian conception according to which our destiny is eternal bliss or damnation. There will be a resurrection of the body, so that the same *man* (that is, the same bodily man or woman) will be found in the hereafter. However, the reward or punishment is prepared for the same *person*.

This spiritual force of Locke's forensic concept of the person takes us at least as far back as the High Middle Ages, the late twelfth and thirteenth centuries. The French historian Alain Bourreau has recently argued that "sleepers" were a significant phenomenon during that period.[7] These appear to be individuals who went into some sort of trance state, analogous to what was later called somnambulism. The sleepers were significant not because they were plentiful (we do not know) but because they created an intellectual, metaphysical, and virtually theological problem. Sleepers perform acts, often violent or at least forbidden, that are different in character and style from what they do in their waking lives. When they come to, after a sleeping episode, they have at most a confused awareness of what they have done. Yet their actions looked just like intentional actions. Hence, in the metaphysics of the day, a soul must have been acting. But what soul?

Thomists firmly insisted that there was but one soul per body. In scholastic psychology, the soul was the "substantial form" of the person. There was, Bourreau informs us, an anti-Thomist minority which held that a person, such as a sleeper, might have two substantial forms, one for each state. This was important for responsibility. Although sleepers seem not to have been considered in the civil law, they did receive attention in the canon law. A text of 1313 states that if a sleeper kills a man, he cannot be barred (in his normal state) from priestly functions on the grounds that he has committed a crime. The minority lost. Thus sleepers were marginalized; they became pathological. Insisting on only one substantial form per person ensures a clear delineation of forensic responsibility, both before earthly tribunals and at the Last Judgment.

Once marginalized by Establishment philosophy, the idea of the sleeper was outside jurisprudence. Bourreau argues that the idea of the sleeper with a second substantial form reemerged at the beginning of the witch craze and served as part of its underpinnings. According to Bourreau the suspect behavior that allowed the accusation of sorcery was typically the behavior of a sleeper. Bourreau's analysis reminds us that large parts of Western culture have been suppressed, even in the West. The sleepers may have manifested a certain kind of trance state, but the meaning of that state can be understood only in its own context. It is altogether simplistic to conjecture that sleepers were multiples. It is slightly less simplistic to see late-twentieth-century multiples and late-twelfth-century sleepers as two different cultural manifestations of a more universal human potentiality for trance. To call them cultural manifestations is not to question their reality. Sleepers were real. Multiples are real. Trance is not more real than the conditions of multiple personality or "sleeping," because reality does not come in degrees. Trance is simply a more general concept, covering many more kinds of unusual behavior. And to repeat, it may not be a lasting concept, for we may decide that there simply is no commonality to what we generously call trance states.

When we pass from sleepers to more recent times, it is easy to see somnambulism as a precursor of multiple personality. I have myself described some somnambules from the eighteenth and nineteenth centuries, and shown how in the English-speaking world somnambulism merged into what was called double consciousness.[8] Nowadays somnambulism means sleepwalking, which of course is what it is, etymologically speaking. But most of us have a very limited view of sleepwalking. We have the comic-strip picture of the boy in his pajamas with his arms straight out and eyes closed, bumping into things, or not. We are more familiar with people who talk in their sleep. Somnambulism, in the old use of the term, covered any form of behavior that resembled waking behavior but was done while "asleep" or "in a trance." The entry "Somnambulisme" in Diderot's *Encyclopédie* (1765–1766) includes the statement that people who suffer from somnambulism are "plunged into a profound sleep, but walk, speak, write, and carry out different actions, as if they were wide awake, and sometimes with even more intelligence and precision."[9] Eugène Azam, who after 1875 was physician to the most famous French multiple, Félida, described her second state as "total somnambulism."[10] By that he meant that she had all her faculties, all her wits about her; she was walking, chatting, sewing, loving, quarreling. She was in an alter state that she had entered by going through a trancelike switch. Azam identified that alter state with the phenomenon of somnambulism.

Alan Gauld's truly encyclopedic *History of Hypnotism* rightly keeps animal magnetism distinct from hypnotism. He maintains the distinction even in his bibliography, which has about 850 items for animal magnetism and 1,250 for hypnotism.[11] He takes seriously the possibility that two different kinds of things, each with its own cultural meanings, are involved. Yet despite the break, effected in part by the work and teaching of James Braid, there was a common terminology, that of som-nambulism. Both the magnetized and the hypnotic states were called provoked or artificial somnambulism, as opposed to natural somnambu-lism. Gauld scrupulously considers whether provoked and natural som-nambulism can be regarded, from a physiological point of view, as the same type of state. He very much doubts it. Culturally and scientifically they were seen as the same, just as today we can group both as examples of what the anthropologists call trance states.

The pairing of somnambulism and hypnotism deeply affected the fu-ture course of multiple personality. Advocates of multiple personality are very nervous about any connections with hypnotism—and quite rightly, because hypnotism is a curiosity, a marvel, and hence marginalized. To make plain that I am not trying to slander multiplicity by tagging it with hypnotism, it will be useful to quote at length a perceptive historical observation by Adam Crabtree. He is a clinical psychologist, whose practice includes much work with multiplicity. His philosophical book *Multiple Man* was a pioneering and innovative work in the field. He is no foe of multiple personality. In his most recent book he writes that

> the discovery of magnetic sleep and the appearance of multiple personality are directly related. . . . In non-organic mental illness there are two ele-ments: the disturbance itself, and the phenomenological expression of that disturbance, the symptom language of the illness. . . . Until the emergence of the alternate consciousness paradigm the only category to express the inner experience of an alien consciousness was that of *posses-sion*, intrusion from the outside. With the rise of awareness of a second consciousness *intrinsic* to the human mind, a new symptom-language be-came possible. Now the victim could express (and society could under-stand) the experience in a new way. . . . This means that when Puységur discovered magnetic sleep, he contributed significantly to the *form* in which mental disturbance could manifest itself from then on.[12]

I would enter only one crucial caveat. Crabtree implies that there is one *experience* to be expressed, one that is expressed in a variety of symptom languages. That is, there is a sort of pure inner experience, prior to any description or social environment, that one just has. I cannot separate experience and expression as readily as Crabtree. His historical claim, as opposed to his ontological one, is along the right lines. In fact I would like to extend his idea of the symptom language. There were two symp-tom languages of precursors to multiple personality. One was primarily

Continental, the language of spontaneous somnambulism, and strongly connected with the language of artificial somnambulism. The other symptom language, primarily British and American, was the language of double consciousness, which was largely separated from animal magnetism and hypnotism. This is particularly important because there is virtually no interest in memory within the symptom language of double consciousness.

Thus I discourage the tendency among enthusiasts for multiple personality to run all examples together. They occur, after all, in entirely different social and medical traditions; they have not only different names but also different meanings for the various concerned parties—observers, reporters, readers, the general public of different social classes, and, I hazard, the afflicted people themselves. Just as Gauld did not automatically identify animal magnetism with hypnotism, or the somnambulism in provoked somnambulism with that in spontaneous somnambulism, I will use old names such as "double consciousness."

In 1816 Mary Reynolds was described as "a very extraordinary case of *double consciousness*, in a woman." She has become the best-known English-speaking multiple of the nineteenth century. The very name "double consciousness" is rich in implications. Double means two, so we do not expect more than two alternative states—certainly not the seventeen or a hundred personality fragments current today. But the word "consciousness" is even more powerful, because it is passive. There is no suggestion of action or interaction, no hint of a rounded personality. In fact Mary Reynolds did have two strikingly different personalities, however we understand that word. The first brief account of her was titled "A Double Consciousness, or a Duality of Person in the same Individual," but "duality of person" did not catch on.[13] Double consciousness did, and it became the diagnostic category, in English, for most of the nineteenth century. It is an essential part of what Crabtree calls the symptom language.

French writers had no such diagnostic category except ones framed in terms of somnambulism. They took over the English expression quite late in the century, rendering it in the French expression *double conscience* (*conscience* translates "consciousness," not the English "conscience"). They also moved on to new labels, such as alternating personality and doubling of the personality. Breuer and Freud famously asserted "that *the splitting of consciousness which is so striking in the classical cases under the form of* double conscience *is present to a rudimentary degree in every hysteria, and that a tendency to such a dissociation, and with it the emergence of abnormal states of consciousness (which we shall bring together under the term 'hypnoid') is the basic phenomenon of this neurosis."[14]*

Mary Reynolds is not the oldest candidate for the earliest modern multiple personality. Two are known from 1791: a European one was well described by Henri Ellenberger, an American one by Eric Carlson. Those two authors between them supply excellent sources for subsequent multiples, and Michael Kenny has provided remarkable biographies of American nineteenth-century multiples in their social settings.[15] Alan Gauld argues that although Ellenberger's 1791 example has now become canonical in the multiple literature, one finds very similar accounts, mostly in the German-speaking world, rather earlier.[16] I shall not repeat any of their findings, which have now been augmented by the major new books of Alan Gauld and Adam Crabtree. I wish instead briefly to indicate the prototype for double consciousness. I have in large measure done so already, by quoting Eugen Bleuler's description of alternating personality, in chapter 9.

There was just as great a variety of cases covered by the label double consciousness as one finds today covered by multiple personality. We have seen that the search is on today for male multiples and for children with multiple personality. In earlier times we have no problem. Men are reported. There is a girl of eleven and a half, Mary Porter, who was treated in 1836. Her physician observed that "the cases of double consciousness, hitherto published, have mostly occurred in young females in whom the uterine functions were disturbed or, if in the male sex, where the nervous system has been weakened by excesses, terror, or other cerebral excitement."[17] That certainly sounds like boys who have had traumatic experiences. Recently advocates of multiplicity have thought that eating disorders may be manifestations of multiple personality. The anorexic has a persecutor alter who prevents her from eating. The bulimic patient binge-eats only in an alter state. There is a clear report of a nineteenth-century bulimic boy in just such terms.[18] But just as there is an unmistakable prototype for the multiple during the 1980s, as presented in chapter 2 above, so there is a very distinct prototype for double consciousness. This is not the occasion to describe endless cases and distill a prototype. Instead two long quotations, separated by a quarter of a century, will do the job.

One comes from a physiology textbook by Herbert Mayo that was to become a standard reference for some decades.[19] Mayo was a magnetizer, author of *On the Truths Contained in Popular Superstitions with an Account of Mesmerism.* Mayo's young woman had an attractive feature not often noticed in reports of double consciousness or its successor disorders. She had a sense of humor.

> This young lady has two distinct states of existence: during the time that the fit is on her, which varies from a few hours to a few days, she is occasionally merry and in spirits, occasionally she appears in pain, and rolls about in uneasiness, but in general she seems so much herself that a stranger coming into the room would not remark anything extraordinary. She amuses herself with reading and working, sometimes plays on the piano better than at other times, knows everybody, and converses rationally, and makes very accurate observations on what she has seen and read. The fit leaves her suddenly and then she forgets everything that has passed during it and imagines that she has been asleep, and sometimes that she has dreamt of any circumstance that made a vivid impression on her. During one of these fits she was reading one of Miss Edgeworth's tales and had in the morning been reading one of them to her mother; she went for a few minutes to the window and suddenly exclaimed, "Mamma, I am quite well, my headache is gone": returning to the table she took up the open volume which she had been reading five minutes before, and said "what book is this," she turned over the leaves, looked at the frontispiece and replaced it on the table; seven or eight hours after, when the fit returned, she asked for the book, went on at the very paragraph where she had left off, and remembered every circumstance of the narrative; and so it is always, as she reads one set of books during one state and another during the other. She seems conscious of her state, for she said one day, "Mamma, this is a novel, but I may safely read it: it will not hurt my morals for when I am well I shall not remember a word of it."

This is very much the prototype of double consciousness. The literature is full of young women who switch from the docile to the daring, from the melancholy to the merry. Most of them come from the sedate parlor of a comfortable but not extravagant family. Notice that they do what they are supposed to be accomplished at better than in their normal state. For this young lady, that means the piano. Mary Reynolds had the same general features. Michael Kenny suggests that in general the young women implicitly switched in order to act out a rebellious life that they could not get away with in the normal course of events. This aspect of the disorder is not peculiar to women. Eric Carlson's case of 1791 has much the same form. A Mr. Miller was a young man in Springfield, Massachusetts, son of a military man, who switched and undertook high jinks. Just as women were better at "what they were supposed to be good at," so was Mr. Miller. In a man's case, virtuosity would not be expressed on a parlor piano. Male prowess was called for; he ought to become something of an athlete. And so he did—he had "more agility" in his somnambulistic state.[20]

My second example is from a discussion of personal identity by a well-known expert on mental illness, J. Crichton Browne. After reviewing many of the canonical cases from the literature he concluded with a new one taken from his father's casebook.

> J. H——, about two years ago, was affected with hysteria, previous to a great constitutional change. The symptoms noticed were of globus and spasmodic flexure of the fingers. The phenomena which now exist followed this state, and were not modified by the establishment of the constitutional change alluded to. For many hours each day the patient is in what may be called her normal condition; for nearly an equal number she is in an abnormal state. She has no recollection during the one what passes or what she has done, or acquired, or suffered, during the other. There is no tie or connection between the two periods. The somnambulic state is ushered in by a yawn, a sensation of globus, and the dropping of the eyelids, which remain half-closed during its continuance, but do not obstruct vision. It generally passes away by the ejection of a mouthful of phlegm. Between these two acts, the yawn and the eructation, the woman is vivacious, more mirthful than when *herself*, knits, reads, sings, converses with relatives and acquaintances, and is said to display greater shrewdness than at other times. Her letters are better in composition and penmanship than she can produce when awake or in her natural state. This may be called her state of clairvoyance. When aroused, she has no recollection whatever of anything that has taken place. She has forgotten the persons she has seen, the songs she has learned, the books she has read, and if she resumes reading it is at the place at which she stopped when in her natural condition. When she reads in her abnormal state the same thing happens. The development of the fit is generally sudden and unexpected, but occasionally it is determined by noise or the movement of articles in the room, such as the fall of a poker or an alteration in the position of the chair. Her bodily health is perfect; all her functions are regular and vigorous. She has lately complained of headache after the cessation of the somnambulism, and upon one occasion she described the pain as confined to one side of her head.[21]

I have deliberately chosen two quotations that say the woman "forgets," "has forgotten," or "has no recollection." The authors quite naturally use the language of forgetting. But it is of little significance, and other

153

authors use other terms, such as "has no awareness" or "does not know" what was done in the alter state. Memory was simply not problematic in the symptom language of double consciousness. There is a remarkable proof of this. These and other physicians tell us that the woman does not remember, in her normal state, what happened during her trance or somnambulistic state. But they do not inquire whether, in her abnormal state, she knows all about the normal one. In Mayo's case I infer that she does know about her normal state. She at least knows that when she comes out of her fit, she will not remember the novel she reads when under the influence of the fit.

Accounts of Mary Reynolds make plain that she has what the French were later to call "two-way amnesia." That is, neither state knew what happened in the other state. French authors contrasted this to their own prototypical cases, in which there was just one-way amnesia. The British and American writers were so indifferent to questions of memory that they did not even bother to say whether the forgetting went both ways, or only one way. What then were they interested in, aside from the sheer curiosity value of these cases? They were fascinated by the character switch. The following words are regularly used to describe the altered state: lively, vivacious, pert, gay, mirthful, impudent, mischievous, forward, passionate, and vindictive. Those words are at the core of the prototype of double consciousness.

Another concern of the British doctors was to show that alters did not have extraordinary sensory powers. The French literature of somnambulism, being so intimately linked to mesmerism and then on to the occult, had many stories of abnormal perception. It began innocently enough, with the observation that somnambules got around just fine in the dark. Then they were able to read and write in the dark, and in no time at all could see at a distance, or into the future. That is the origin of our word "clairvoyance" for psychic abilities to tell the future. The British physicians, mostly products of the Edinburgh medical school with its strong tradition of Scottish empirical and so-called commonsense philosophy, did not believe such ideas for a moment. Early in the century they were at pains to refute them. When Crichton Browne speaks of the "clairvoyant" state of J. H. he means simply her trance state, with no suggestion of heightened sensory powers. But there was a corresponding fascination, among the British doctors, with the increase in ability, at piano or agility, at Greek or penmanship, that their patients exhibited. There were further interests—for example, in the connection, if any, of double consciousness with the dual hemispheres of the brain.[22] These male physicians saw chiefly female cases of double consciousness and treated them in a gendered way. They described their patients in terms of hysteria, although not the florid, Charcotian hysteria I shall describe in the next chapter. They noticed that their young female patients lost their second consciousness when their menstrual periods began, and hence connected the illness with "uterine" disorder.[23]

Memory and forgetting were simply unimportant to what was known, in the English-speaking world, as double consciousness. This is an absolutely fundamental contrast with the French cases after 1875. The chief reason for this is that memory had not yet become an object of scientific knowledge. That is my radical thesis that will be increasingly confirmed in the following chapters. But there was also a parochial reason. British and American double consciousness was not, in general, connected with animal magnetism or hypnotism. It is true that Herbert Mayo, author of my first version of the prototype of double consciousness, was a magnetizer, but he does not appear to have hypnotized his patient on this occasion. Double consciousness fascinated foes of hypnotism. Thus the longtime editor of the British medical journal *The Lancet*, Thomas Wakley, was so antagonistic to hypnotism that its finest historian, Alan Gauld, in a rare display of irritation, calls him "the egregious Wakley." Yet in 1843 Wakley was making a plea for the study of double consciousness in order to reduce metaphysical dogmatism about personal identity.[24]

Unlike their British counterparts, Continental students of magnetism or hypnotism paid keener attention to memory. It had early been noted that subjects awakened from a hypnotic trance did not remember what had happened. The connection with spontaneous, or nervous, or hysterical, somnambulism (as doubling was variously called in France at the time) is particularly clear in a report published in 1823, by J.-F.-A. Bertrand. He described a prepubertal girl of thirteen or fourteen years of age. She had four states that he classified as follows: (1) magnetic somnambulism, (2) nocturnal somnambulism, viz. during ordinary sleep, (3) nervous or hysteric somnambulism, and (4) waking somnambulism. These were one-way amnesic in order, as listed; that is, (1) recalled all four states, while state (2) recalled states (2), (3), and (4). The waking state (4) knew nothing of the other three states.[25]

The French animal magnetizers did not have much to say about memory in general. Their theoretical project was to understand the magnetic fluid, not memory. But at least memory was present to them. The symptom language of spontaneous somnambulism included memory because of its connection with provoked somnambulism, otherwise known as animal magnetism. The symptom language of double consciousness made only passing reference to memory, perhaps because it was largely cut off from the literature of magnetism and hypnotism.

I shall not describe the French prototype for spontaneous somnambulism because it had relatively little effect on the French wave of multiple personality after 1875. Partly because hypnotism had been so discredited in medical circles before its revival by Charcot in 1878, earlier French prototypes were ignored, and French authors referred to British or American works, not those in their own language. I must mention one case, however, because it has recently assumed some prominence: Despine's Estelle, treated in 1836. As quoted in chapter 3, Kluft has stated that before he learned of other American workers in the field, Despine had been his teacher. Hence Despine is worth attending to today, as mentor of one of today's most influential students of multiple personality. Despine also serves as a fairly typical example of the doctors (whom he himself cites in abundance) who treated spontaneous somnambulism by the use of animal magnetism.

Estelle L'Hardy was eleven and a half years old when she came to the attention of C.H.A. Despine in 1836. By coincidence, she was an exact contemporary of the above-mentioned Mary Porter, treated in the same year in London. Both girls got better after they entered puberty. Mary's doctor thought that the problem was one of the onset of puberty, and although he describes his treatment, he makes no claims for its efficacy. Nature took its course. The story of Estelle is radically different, for her physician was a great magnetizer and the medical inspector at the fashionable spa in Aix-le-Savoie.[26] The spa was filled with a great many persons, mostly women, with remarkable ailments. Edward Shorter, the highly critical historian of psychosomatic illnesses, notes that Despine had already, in 1822, described a woman with six distinct states, one of which was "an incomplete magnetic state which gave the patient an interior feeling of second existence." Having examined the goings-on in such spas, Shorter writes that "the context of Estelle's multiple personality disorder was therefore the theater of florid magnetism and catalepsy then prevailing in Aix. Many of the other patients were producing bizarre symptoms; it must have seemed to an intelligent young girl rather the order of the day that she bring forth some of her own."[27]

Catherine Fine, past president of the ISSMP&D, sees things quite differently.[28] Despine, in her reading of his text, was a brilliant clinician, precursor of the modern understanding and treatment of multiple personality. The diary of Estelle's mother shows that the girl communicated with a heavenly host of angels—no shortage of alters there. At a more day-to-day level she went into trances; she had crises during sleep and terrible somatic symptoms of paraplegia, anesthesia, hyperesthesia, and more. She did alternate between her ordinary state and her crisis (*état de crise*). In crisis she was able to swim in ice water, whereas in her ordinary state she was paralyzed and complained constantly of cold, thanks to the hyperesthesia of her back. Under hypnosis she was fine.

Evidently theory determines not only how we see the world and disease today, but how we interpret old texts. Shorter, fierce skeptic about psychosomatic diseases, finds L'Hardy almost indistinguishable from innumerable other cases of the day that he has read. Fine, a psychologist in the forefront of research on multiple personality, reading a single text, thinks that Despine was a remarkable healer. Perhaps one could agree with Fine and yet still, after a careful reading of materials, see Estelle L'Hardy as a spoiled brat from Switzerland who loved publicity, manipulated the self-indulgent community of a French spa, and took advantage of the fashionable charlatan who was medical inspector there. She certainly had her minutes of fame in 1836 (crowds turned out to watch her, in paralysis or trance, being transported through the mountains in a basket on her way to the spa) or 1837 (she starred in the local newspapers when she went home). None of this means that she was not a multiple; plenty of multiples are show-offs.

No matter how we interpret this case, it was of almost no immediate importance to the history or symptom language of multiple personality. Estelle was quickly forgotten and remained almost unknown until rediscovered by Janet in the early 1890s. Yet she may have had a delayed effect. In 1919 Janet confided that "at the time I was studying complete somnambulism"—what Azam called total somnambulism—"I was not yet acquainted with Charles Despine's book, and did not read it until much later. . . . Although there was no direct influence exercised by Despine's record of Estelle, it is possible that Despine's book had an influence on my work, in an indirect way." This is because Janet's most famous early patient, who made his reputation, was one Léonie, who had been in the hands of magnetizers, off and on, for what seems like forever. She was under the care of a Dr. Perrier before she was brought, in 1885, to Le Havre for Janet to study. "Despine's book was certainly known to Perrier of Caen, who quotes it in his records. . . . It is likely enough that Perrier had induced such states [of complete somnambulism] in her, and had made them habitual to her."[29] Interestingly, what

157

Janet emphasized after his first reading of Despine was that his study of Estelle was "one of the first and most remarkable descriptions of the mental state of a hysterical."[30] He referred to her a total of eleven times in different parts of that work, always to illustrate the somatic accompaniments of hysteria (the so-called conversion symptoms). As we shall see, the most important feature of French multiples after 1875 was that they had florid hysterical symptoms. That was the historically important way in which Estelle is a precursor of French multiples, post-1875.

Doubling of the Personality

IT WAS "in the spring of 1875, in the course of a conversation on the *bizarreries* of memory," that Eugène Azam first told the story of the classic French double, Félida X. Somnambulism had been a topic for medical expertise and folklore for millennia. There had been trickles of interest in double consciousness and spontaneous somnambulism throughout the nineteenth century. But there was never any systematic study of multiple personality before Azam.[1]

> Allow me to make you acquainted with Félida. She is a very remarkable personage who has played a rather important part in the history of ideas. Do not forget that this humble person was the educator of Taine and Ribot. Her history was the great argument of which the positivist psychologists made use at the time of the heroic struggles against the spiritualistic dogmatism of Cousin's school. But for Félida, it is not certain that there would be a professorship at the Collège de France and that I should be here speaking to you of the mental state of hystericals. It is a physician of Bordeaux who has attached his name to the history of Félida: Azam reported this astonishing history first at the "Society of Surgery," then at the "Academy of Medicine" in January 1860. He entitled his communication "Note on Nervous Sleep or Hypnotism," and spoke of this case in connection with the discussion of the existence of an abnormal sleep in which it would be possible to operate without pain. And this communication, thus incidentally made, was to revolutionize psychology in fifty years.[2]

Those are the words of Pierre Janet, lecturing at Harvard in 1906. Janet held that chair of psychology at the Collège de France, the most prestigious academic site in France. There is only one thing wrong with this story. Azam did *not* tell the world about Félida's double personality in his 1860 paper. He mentioned the woman, but not by name, and one can make out that she spontaneously went into something like a hypnotic trance. He also stated that he would write more about Félida, but he never did, until 1876. In 1860 she simply did not fit into any possible discourse, except hypnotism. In the spring of 1875 she began to fit into

159

an entirely new discourse, the emerging sciences of memory. It was not until 1876 that this humble person burst upon the French world of psychology and psychiatry.

Eugène Azam (1822–1899) was a leading figure of the Bordeaux region, a dignified local booster, key to the establishment of a university in Bordeaux, and central in organizing the fight against the phylloxera that was annihilating the vineyards. He was a notable local archaeologist in one of the oldest inhabited regions of Europe, and a substantial collector of paintings. One has the impression that there was hardly a literary or scientific society in Bordeaux of which he was not sometime president. Yet he would barely be remembered in little volumes of local history today were it not for Félida. He was, perhaps, fated for the role, because he was one of the first French students of Braid's scientific hypnotism. That was what he reported in 1860, not multiplicity. But hypnotism, along with hysteria, was to become one of the essential ingredients for the French era of multiple personality.

Azam tried out almost every imaginable name for Félida's disorder; to take only titles from his papers about her, we have: *Névrose extraordinaire, doublement de la vie* (14 January 1876). *Amnésie périodique, ou dédoublement de la vie* (6 May 1876). *Amnésie périodique, ou doublement de la vie* (20 May 1876). *La double conscience* (23 August 1876). *Le dédoublement de la personnalité* (6 September 1876). We also have *La double personnalité* on 8 March 1879.[3] Azam's publisher encouraged him to use *double conscience*, the French translation of the English name. Azam did not much care for that. He preferred *dédoublement de la personnalité*. It can be translated as dividing, doubling, or splitting of the personality, and doubtless contributed to our expression "split personality," which gets confused with the split brain of *schizophrenia*. Notice that no longer is it consciousness, a rather passive thing, that is doubled. It is *life*, *personality*, all that is active in the human soul.

Azam took pride in being the first man to introduce scientific hypnotism to France. (There are at least two other claimants to that honor, but no matter.) His father had been a surgeon and alienist in Bordeaux. The son in due course became chief surgeon at the asylum for women. In June 1858 he was called in to care for "a young woman of the people." She was thought to be mad; she exhibited curious phenomena of spontaneous catalepsy, anesthesia, and hyperesthesia. "In addition she presented with an interesting lesion of the memory, to which I shall return." This was Félida, but Azam never did write the memoir he intended. He displayed the woman to numerous colleagues, some of whom thought that the morbid phenomena were a sham but others of whom encouraged him. His boss told him of an encyclopedia article in an English encyclopedia about sleep, in which it was reported that Braid could produce artificially the very phenomena which Azam noticed in Félida. Thus it was Félida who led Azam to hypnotism, not the other way about.

Braid's book at his side, it took Azam one minute to hypnotize Félida and create the symptoms that also occurred spontaneously. This did not prove hypnotism, because the symptoms occurred naturally. So he turned to another woman who happened to be living in the same house. This was a perfectly healthy twenty-two-year-old who worked for a jewelry manufacturer. Azam quickly produced all the phenomena of hypnotism that he had read about. He became convinced that although Braid exaggerated on many issues, and greatly overestimated the healing power of hypnotism, Braid was correct in his basic points. Azam was a friend of Broca, now remembered for the localization of language in what is called Broca's region of the right hemisphere of the brain. Azam told Broca about hypnotism during a visit to Paris in 1859, and Broca was intrigued. Would it anesthetize during surgery? The two men hypnotized a woman with a terrible abscess and lanced it, and she felt no pain. Broca at once informed *tout Paris*. Azam was briefly famous. But to most doctors, hypnotism meant magnetizers—charlatans. No matter how hard Azam tried to distance himself, he was tainted. Hypnotism was not reliable for anesthetic surgery, and chloroform was almost universally in use by 1860. After a brief fad the French medical world left hypnotism to the masses and the stage magnetizers. Only in 1878, after Azam's Félida had become celebrated for other reasons, was Charcot to give a "decisive demonstration of hypnotism" (to quote Babinski's authorized version of the events).[4] Azam was always rather peeved that he did not get full recognition for having introduced scientific hypnotism to France.

Notice that Félida, unlike Janet's Léonie and a host of others, did not develop her *dédoublement* only after she had been hypnotized. Azam did not even know about hypnotism when he met Félida; he experimented with her first because she spontaneously dissociated. As soon as he discovered that he could hypnotize her, he turned to a healthy woman to try his newfound skill. He continued his hypnotic experiments with other subjects precisely because Félida was already a spontaneous somnambule. He did continue to hypnotize Félida in the hope of curing her, but without success, and he eventually abandoned the project. She seemed to get somewhat better toward the end of 1859. Azam did not see her again for sixteen years.

Hypnotism was central to the new French wave of multiples, and that is one way in which they differ from British instances of double consciousness. I am not making the tired suggestion that the patients were made multiple by hypnotism. That is rubbish. We know that Félida had an alternative personality before her physician had even heard of Braid's scientific hypnotism. What is true is that all the individuals with doubling of the personality lived in a milieu that became fascinated by hypnotism, and where their behavior would be compared to that of hypnotized subjects.

There was an even more profound difference between double consciousness and the new era of Félida after 1875. Most cases of *dédoublement* had grotesque bodily ailments. The most dramatic of these were anesthesias over part of the body, hyperesthesia (oversensitivity), partial paralysis, spasms, tremors, and abnormalities of the senses, such as restrictions of the field of vision and loss of taste or smell. Often there was unexplained bleeding in the stomach or from the mouth, nose, or rectum; there were terrible headaches and vertigo. Tuberculosis was mimicked by pulmonary congestions. These complaints, which often were *awful*, had no known organic, physical, or neurological cause. We now call them conversion symptoms. I tend to avoid that expression, because it is too dismissive, too sanitized. It makes us forget the appalling pain that many of these patients experienced. I will presently describe Félida's own horrible suffering.

At the time of Félida, these symptoms were standardly associated with the diagnosis of hysteria. Every French case of *dédoublement* was described as hysteric. This does not immediately distinguish *dédoublement* from double consciousness, for cases of the latter—Crichton Browne's prototypical J. H., for example—were also tagged with hysteria. But hysteria itself had changed. I do not know when people first started calling hysteria *protean*, meaning that it could take indefinitely many forms; certainly Sauvages calls it protean in his classic 1768 *Nosologia Methodica*. The topic of hysteria in history serves many a book unto itself. I shall not touch on the marvelous studies of hysteria made by a generation of feminist historians.[5] The variety of gross things done to women diagnosed with hysteria is almost as loathsome as the burnings of their sisters during the witch craze. Here I wish only to emphasize how radically the prototype of hysteria changed in the course of European medicine.

Two psychiatrists have made a statistical survey of four hundred years of hysteria. These men state that until the middle of the nineteenth century, the emphasis in medical textbooks and reports was on depression (as that term is *now* used in clinical practice). Then came a radical increase in symptomatology. Their graph of the frequency of items mentioned in articles shows a high plateau in the "expansion of the overall concept" roughly 1850–1910. "No one wrote more about the hysterical personality than Janet. . . . Janet's items comprised the common features of depression, fearfulness, emotionality, lability and excitement, but also included exaggeration, suggestibility, deficient judgement, poor self-control, vivid imagination, erotic problems, self-destructive tendencies, regression, shame and diminution of the field of consciousness and dual personality."[6] These items were certainly used by doctors to describe their women patients. Yet the survey barely mentions all those anesthesias, hyperesthesias, spasms, paralyses, bleedings, and above all pains that were particularly prevalent in France in the era of Félida X.

Hypnotism and hysteria were two aspects of the matrix where the new French *dédoublement* was conceived. Philosophy also had an important role, and not only in the sense that throughout most of the nineteenth century psychology was a branch of philosophy. For much of that time, the dominant French style of philosophy was inspired by Victor Cousin (1792–1867). It was called eclectic spiritualism—or "spiritualist dogmatism" by people like Janet who did not like it. It was deeply entrenched in the school system. The hegemony of Cousin's ideas was seriously challenged only in the Third Republic, established after the 1870 war with Prussia.

Cousin argued that the spiritual substances—God, the soul, ideas—were real, objective, independent, and autonomous of what anyone thinks. Philosophy should proceed by what he called the "psychological method" of inspecting our immediate ideas: the truly French method of Descartes and Condillac. Cousin and his followers regarded their work as empirical and scientific, since it began with introspection of actual ideas. They rejected biological reduction of psychological data and resisted any type of determinism in matters of human thought or behavior. In short, they were in every way opposed to the positivist school founded by Auguste Comte (1798–1857). Positivism began to flourish in the Third Republic. One of the roots of multiple personality is republican positivism.

The connection is absolutely explicit. Hippolyte Taine (1828–1893), along with Renan, is commonly regarded as one of the two dominant intellectual figures of France during the last third of the nineteenth century. Both were positivists, advocating a scientific worldview. Taine's one major philosophical work was *De l'intelligence* (1870). Taine was no

163

routine, fact-gathering, antitheory, anticausation positivist of the sort that played an important role in parts of French medicine. His was a positivism modulated by an immersion in Hegel. I cannot here say what he was *for*, but can note one thing that he was against. He was against the autonomous, freestanding self or soul of the eclectic spiritualists, against the "*I* or *me*, unique, persisting, always the same [and which] is something distinct from my sensations, memories, images, ideas, perceptions, conceptions, which are diverse and transient."[7] The *I*, the *me*, together with the faculties or powers that they are supposed to possess, "are metaphysical beings, pure phantasms, engendered by words, which vanish when one examines scrupulously the means of the words." He was against the Kantian solution of the problem of free will, where the "I" is a noumenal self not subject to the causal laws of the phenomenal world. He thought of the self as a Hegelian being with a history; he thought of the self as a Lockean person constituted by a complex of consciousness, sensation, and memory. Hence he was delighted when doubled personality hit the headlines in 1876. In the next edition of his book, 1878, he cited these cases with intense fascination.[8] For here were two selves alternating in one body, each defined (thought Taine) by its awareness and chains of memories. There was no transcendental soul here, no noumenal self. Instead there were two distinct selves, and the self was made by its memories.

Taine's lesson of 1870 was not lost on his readers. The great French lexicographer Emile Littré had founded the *Revue de philosophie positive* in 1867 and edited it almost until his death. Early in 1875 he used it to publish a small piece on double consciousness, grouping together what we now count as distinct phenomena. There were references back to the British students of double consciousness—hence the title of his essay, "La double conscience." He was more interested in the sensation of being doubled, hearing oneself speak, observing oneself act, or feeling that one is literally not oneself. Littré cited fourteen chiefly German variants of what we would tend nowadays to call depersonalization rather than dissociation. He concluded that the person is far from being "a primordial principle from which the other psychic properties flow." Consciousness and self-identity result from a complex of experiences recorded in the brain, in "cerebral modifications." Despite his title he was inclined to discuss "personality" rather than "consciousness" as the key idea. He denounced eclectic spiritualism and its ilk. "Theology by revelation and metaphysics by intuition" attribute personality "to a soul which uses the brain like an instrument."[9] He thought that double consciousness should provide an elegant rebuttal of the one, original, transcendental consciousness. But the cases available to Littré were old anecdotes, or marginal recent cases of personality disorders. What was wanted was a good live multiple. Enter Félida. Within six years Théodule Ribot—Janet's predecessor as professor of psychology at the Collège de France—had published a book about diseases of the memory, subtitled *An Essay in the Positive Psychology*. There he had written about "the detailed and instructive observations of Dr. Azam."[10]

How did nonpositivists see things? Pierre Janet was not a positivist. He did not have the doctrinaire panache of Taine or Ribot, yet for a time he became caught up in *dédoublement*. His uncle Paul Janet was an influential philosopher, altogether opposed to positivism. Paul was nevertheless active in the creation of Ribot's chair, first at the Sorbonne and then at the Collège de France. The Collège, an ancient and autonomous institution, the highest in the land, has just so many chairs but can determine, at each appointment, the subject for a given chair. The chair of natural and international law was turned into the chair of experimental and comparative psychology. Paul Janet rationalized this radical move, devoting a substantial part of an essay in the leading intellectual review of the day to Azam's Félida and other cases of doubling. "Those," he concluded, "are the principal facts with which psychological science is occupied."[11]

Thus *dédoublement* played a powerful role in the philosophy of the era. But it involved more than a battle between the old school and the new school, the eclectic spiritualists and the positivists. The positivists were ranged on the anticlerical, republican side of the new Third Republic. They were part of a larger politics, a battle for the character of France itself, for a France that had just been disgraced in war, for a France that was obsessed by the problem of degeneration, for a France that saw its science in visible decline before the vigor of the German- and English-speaking worlds. That humble woman, Félida, was part of the republican armory.

Azam despised the magnetizers and hence the murky French tradition of spontaneous somnambulism. He did not at first know the British material, although he soon found it out. In need of a symptom language for Félida, he had an immediate model. Among the *bizarreries de la mémoire* being discussed during that fateful spring of 1875 were those of Louise Lateau. She was called the stigmatic of Bois-d'Haine (a small Belgian village near the French border). She was famous all across Roman Catholic Europe for the miraculous stigmata that appeared on her side, hands, and feet every Friday. She was also famous for her devotional trance, and for the fact that she had eaten no food for years. Secular medicine tried to ignore her, but finally the Belgian medical academy established a commission to study her. The report, written by Evariste Warlomont, appeared early in 1875. For some time this was the only work to which Azam referred.[12]

> In the first months of 1875 the Belgian academy of medicine, gripped by the question of *Louise Lateau*, charged Mr. Warlomont to make a report on this subject. This work, excellently done, insisted on the reality of *doublement de la vie*, double consciousness, *condition seconde*, states that can be produced spontaneously or artificially. . . . I recognized in these facts analogues to my observation in 1858. Although I had appreciated their importance ever since that time, I had not published them, thinking them to be too isolated in science, and too distant from the surgery that I practiced in Bordeaux. I thus sought out Félida X*** and found her again, presenting the same phenomena as before, but worse.[13]

He took some of Warlomont's terminology. Even his first tryout for the name of Félida's illness—*doublement de la vie*—was taken straight from Warlomont. Azam spoke of Félida's alters as her first and second states, using for the latter the terms *état second* and *condition seconde*. I remarked that most readers would have encountered the expression "double consciousness" only as it was going out of use, in Breuer and Freud's *Studies in Hysteria*. The same is true of *condition seconde* and *état second*, the names taken over by Azam. They became standard in French psychiatry for another two decades. Thus this other humble person, Louise Lateau, left her mark on psychiatry.

Félida was always a very sick woman. I find it remarkable that she got on with her life. She may have been the great teacher of Taine and Ribot, but psychology and psychiatry did not help her at all. Born in 1843, she became a seamstress at an early age. The family was poor; her father, a seaman, had drowned. When Azam saw her at the age of fifteen, she was, in her normal state, intelligent, sad, morose; she spoke little, worked hard, and seemed to have little emotional life. She was an extreme hysteric. In her normal state she had no sensations of taste. She had the *globus*, the lump experienced in the throat before a hysterical attack. Many parts of her body were anesthetic. Her visual field was restricted. After the least emotion she had convulsions in which she did not completely lose consciousness. She bled from the mouth when she was asleep. Azam declined to go on listing symptoms that "are so well known. Suffice to say that with Félida the [diagnosis of] hysteria is certain, and that the singular features that she presents depend on this overall illness." Félida set the pace. Every French multiple was a florid hysteric.

When Azam first encountered Félida, she would experience fierce pain in the temples and fall into a state of extreme fatigue, almost like sleep. This lasted ten minutes. She would then appear to wake up and would enter her *condition seconde*. This lasted a few hours, when she would again have a brief trance and return to her ordinary state. This happened every five or six days. In her second state she greeted people around her, smiled, exuded gaiety; she would say a few words and continue, for example, with her sewing, humming as she did so. She would do household chores, go shopping, pay visits, and she had the good cheer of a healthy young woman of her age. After her second brief trance, she woke up in her normal state and had no memory of what had happened, or of anything she had learned in her second state. Her family had to bring her up to date. During this early period the attacks became more and more frequent, and the second state lasted longer and longer.

She had a sweetheart. She was made pregnant in her second state, and in that state she enjoyed being pregnant. But in her first state she denied her pregnancy until a neighbor rudely insisted on it; she then had terrible seizures that lasted several hours. But her confinement went well. She married the young man and seemed to get somewhat better. That was in 1859. The child, a boy, grew up fairly healthy but with considerable minor psychopathology.

Azam lost sight of Félida for sixteen years. During that period she had ten additional pregnancies or miscarriages, with one more child surviving. Azam relied on her husband for accounts of what happened during that time. By 1875 she would spend as much as three months in her second, cheerful, state, which gradually became her normal state. In middle age she generally settled into the second state. In fact Azam's reporting became quite confusing. Initially the morose condition had been the first state, while the gadabout was in *condition seconde*. In due course the second state became the usual one, and the one previously called normal became increasingly unusual. As she grew older, that original state may almost have disappeared, but it also became unbearable. When she was in that state, she fell into despair. She would avoid people because she had no idea what had been going on for months and months. She believed that she was incurable. Her pains, bleedings, and paralyses became ever more intense.

Unfortunately the so-called second, but increasingly dominant, state was no longer one of irrepressible gaiety. She grew morose and began to acquire somatic symptoms. Parts of her body would become painful and inflamed. She had pulmonary hemorrhages and interminable nosebleeds. She would vomit blood. On one occasion blood oozed from her forehead "reproducing, without the least miracle, the bloody stigmata over which the ignorant make so much fuss."[14] At one time she became convinced that her husband had a mistress, a woman with whom, in her first state, she remained on good terms. In her *condition seconde* she hanged herself, but she botched it; she was rescued and woke up in the same condition.

Pursuing her livelihood as a seamstress, Félida took in sewing. In mature years, when she felt an attack coming she would scribble a quick note to her other self about the stage she had reached in her work, so that after a brief spell of discomfort she could continue without loss of time. But at that time the normal condition into which she switched was not so much that of a mature woman as that of a child of fourteen. She did not talk much; her memory was not looked into carefully, but she was sad and juvenile. Azam did not think of this as a third personality, but simply as a version of her normal state. Some clinicians today would wonder if this were not a child alter. There was yet another state, a terrible fourth condition of extreme terror. Azam described this as "accessory" to her *condition seconde*. She would begin to cry, "I am afraid, I am afraid. . . ." She had terrifying hallucinations, especially in the dark or when she shut her eyes. Azam said that "she was close to madness." Some would now call these attacks schizophreniform episodes. Other clinicians might suspect that a persecutor alter was at work. And there seems even to have been a fifth state. Victor Egger wrote that Azam had told him of one entirely different from anything in Azam's many articles—and then declined to say what this state was.[15] Something altogether improper? It is perfectly possible to imagine that Félida manifested at least three fragmentary alters in addition to her normal and second states. But Azam's model was of doubling: there could be no third personality to see. *Multiple* personality did not yet exist.

How did Azam think of Félida? To use the vogue word that is now current, he thought that her disorder was "psychobiological." He believed that all the phenomena—material, intellectual, or mixed—had the same cause and should be studied by the same science. He called this physiology, but a physiology enlarged by incorporating its relatives, metaphysics and psychology. "Today, although these are arbitrarily separated, they lean upon each other; tomorrow there will be an intimate fusion, and later the absorption will be complete."[16] Azam's conjectured explanations ran along physiological lines. Like so many others he was much taken with the relationship between the two hemispheres of the brain and the two states. He conjectured that an attack involved an impediment to the flow of blood to one hemisphere, causing inaccessibility of memories stored there.

Far from breaking with the tradition of somnambulism, Azam became more and more convinced that it was the right idea. The *condition seconde* of every double was a state of "total somnambulism." He stated this in one of his early papers, withdrew from it for a while, but returned to it in 1890 with renewed firmness.[17] Today's clinicians may find Azam's stance attractive. For he apparently believed that adult "total somnambulism" would, if one looked into it closely enough, have a precursor in childhood.

As soon as Azam published in Paris, a veritable torrent of doubles followed. On 15 July 1876 we have this from Paul Janet: "When I read [Azam], I seemed to recognize the history of one of my own former clients." And directly after Azam's memoir had been read to the Academy of Moral and Political Science, Bouchut, who later contributed other multiples, said, "I have observed two similar cases. . . ."[18] The cases go on, and on. In August 1887, when he was taking the waters in the Pyrenees, Azam encountered a spectacular case of a teenage boy. The characteristic features of the prototype established by Azam are clear. A woman. Early onset. Bad times in childhood. One-way amnesia. Subsidiary quasi-states additional to the *condition seconde*. Highly suggestible. Hypnotism reproduces second states. Second state is like (or is) total somnambulism. Above all: the prototypical case of *dédoublement* suffers from florid hysteria, and she is overwhelmed by bodily crises.

The connection between hysteria and *dédoublement* became so strong that someone who merely split had to be made to have hysterical symptoms. Take, for example, a young Swiss woman described by P. L. Ladame, a pioneer of Charcotian hypnotism in Geneva. The woman was as close to good old-fashioned British double consciousness as could be. As a child she had been terrified by a fire, and she developed a second state when she thought she had started a fire by overturning a lamp. In one state she was gentle, in the other aggressive. All the adjectives applied to this Swiss girl had been applied in the English-speaking world for a century. Aside from a certain paleness and indifference to grooming, "she presented no morbid symptom, and none of the marks of hysteria." But conceptually, from the point of view of her physician, she had to be a hysteric. Horrible bodily symptoms were produced by hypnosis, which also cured her.[19]

Félida was a confusing prototype. She had so much wrong with her, so much pain. Types of suffering needed to be sorted. So she, as proto-type, led to new models—two, as it happened. Wouldn't you know it? Both models were furnished by male patients. One was the first *multiple* personality in history, that is, the first person to have a substantial num-ber of what were perceived as distinct personalities. I describe that re-markable man in the next chapter. The other model was provided by another citizen of Bordeaux, who was treated by a medical student there; that student later became an associate of Azam's, not in medicine, but in archaeology. The patient, Albert, traveled compulsively, with lit-tle sense of who he was. He inaugurated psychogenic or dissociative fugue. Philippe Tissié described him in a thesis published in 1887, but Tissié was upstaged by Charcot a year later. Charcot's diagnosis of *am-bulatory automatism* was, for twenty years, an important part of French psychiatry.[20] An extraordinary battle was waged. Charcot had made pop-ular the diagnosis of male hysteria, but he denied that the *fugueurs* were hysterics; they were epileptics. His foes rallied to a diagnosis of hysteria. Several things are transparent in the debate. Some doctors described the *fugueurs* as having doubled personality, but these doctors could only do so when they came out against Charcot and held that the men had hys-teria. That is evidence for the intimate bond between hysteria and multi-ple personality. Hysteria disappeared from the French scene by 1910. So did fugue. A second feature of fugue is that we have an easy answer to the gender problem. In the 1980s it was suggested that the male multi-ples were in jail. We know much more about the late 1880s and early 1890s. In those days the male multiples took trips.

The relations between multiple personality and hysteria, or fugue, were fleeting. Something else became permanent. In the century before 1875, double consciousness, and even spontaneous somnambulism, had only an incidental relation to memory and forgetting. Félida came to life during a conversation about memory in 1875, and for the rest of the century double or multiple personality was unthinkable except with one-way or two-way amnesia. This was not an empirical fact but a conceptual one. It was part of the nature of a doubled personality to be a hysteric. It was part of her nature to be hypnotizable. And it was part of her na-ture to have a *maladie de la mémoire*.

The Very First Multiple Personality

MULTIPLE means more than two. Neither double consciousness nor *dédoublement* was multiple personality. Advocates of the diagnosis of multiple personality will want to say that Félida had more than two alters; we have intimations of as many as five. Under a different type of treatment all might have flourished; they might have been clues to Félida's underlying distress. But if we ask about what was, rather than what might have been, Félida had exactly two alternating personalities. That was how she was thought of, described, talked about, treated by her family, and regarded by her neighbors. That was how she felt about herself; that was how she experienced herself. In terms of symptom language, there were no actually multiple personalities when Félida became famous. Whatever might have been, had patients been treated differently, there were in fact only doubles. When did multiple personality come into being? Late in the afternoon of the 27th of July, 1885.

On that afternoon Jules Voisin, a student of Charcot's and a leading physician at Bicêtre, the Paris asylum for men, described a patient who had been under his care from August 1883 until 2 January 1885. His name was Louis Vivet. He was presented as a case of *grande hystérie chez l'homme avec dédoublement de la personnalité*. Voisin noticed some differences from Félida, but he still found it convenient to "use the terminology of Dr. Azam," namely, first and second states. Louis Vivet had *dédoublement*. By 1885 that was not especially interesting. Voisin was nevertheless fascinated by the man as a perfect, prototypical hysteric. He had all the extreme symptoms of hysteria that, in Charcot's ward, were commonplace among females. "In the long bibliography of male hysteria, one mostly encounters cases of hysteria that only roughly fit the prototype."[1] Vivet was marvelous because he had the whole gamut of symptoms familiar to doctors trained under Charcot at the Salpêtrière.

By what may have been a coincidence, one Dr. Hippolyte Bourru (1840–1914) was in the audience. Vivet had escaped from Bicêtre on 2 January 1885 but soon afterward came under the care of Bourru and his colleague, P. Burot. Bourru had a new story to tell. Louis Vivet had not

171

been long at large. At the end of February 1885 he was consigned to the military hospital in Rochefort and was there attended by Bourru and Burot. By July 1885 Bourru could report an entirely new phenomenon in the annals of psychiatry. Vivet had eight distinct personality states.[2] The meeting broke up at 6:30 P.M. The discourse of multiple personality had just been put in place. Our phrase "multiple personality" appeared in print in England within a year, explicitly to describe Louis Vivet.[3]

To understand what happened we have to enter one of the zanier reaches of our topic. First there was metallotherapy: it seemed that hysterical anesthesias, contractures (muscular spasms producing an enduring shortening of a limb), and paralyses could be removed if the appropriate part of the body were touched with magnets or various metals. In 1877 the Societé de Biologie established a commission to report on the method. The commissioners included Charcot and J. B. Luys (1828–1892). They observed more than they seem to have expected. Many bodily symptoms of hysteria such as paralysis, anesthesia, or contracture occurred on one side of the body. A left arm or leg might be affected; there was also left hemiplegia (paralysis of most or all of the left side of the body). Charcot, Luys, and their fellow commissioners found that symptoms could be transferred from one side of the body to another if they touched the first side with a magnet, or another piece of metal, and then applied the metal to the other side of the body. The symptoms obligingly moved with the metal. The most systematic experiments were made by Alfred Binet (1857–1911) and his colleague Charles Féré.[4] Charcot's great critic from Nancy, Hippolyte Bernheim (1840–1919), argued that if there was anything to these phenomena, they were solely the consequence of what he called *suggestion*. Binet's startling reply was that to deny the action of the magnet on an organism was to deny the action of electricity.[5] Soon afterward Binet was to write an enthusiastic tract about objective experiments confirming *double conscience*, stating firmly that the topic had now passed from the realm of pioneering exploration to science.

The young neurologist Joseph Babinski (1857–1932), a student of Charcot's, made a further discovery. We remember him for the Babinski reflex, but Babinski also discovered that you could use a magnet to transfer symptoms not just from one part of the body to another, but also from one person to another. You separated two somnambules (artificial or spontaneous) by a screen. Mrs. A's right arm, say, was paralyzed. You applied a magnet to Miss C's right arm. Mrs. A's right arm became mobile again, while Miss C's became paralyzed.[6]

Luys built on these results to develop an amazing method of therapy. He would transfer the real symptoms of a hysteric patient to a hypnotized patient by drawing a magnet along a limb of the ill person and on to the corresponding limb of the healthy but hypnotized one. The latter would assume not only the symptoms but also the personality of the hysteric. Then the somnambule would be awakened, the symptoms would vanish from everyone, and the hysteric would assume her own personality, without the paralysis or whatever else afflicted her.[7]

Bourru and Burot took this one step further. They put various liquids in tiny flasks and wrapped solids in paper. Often these were drugs, including alcohol. They would hold a drug or other substance behind a patient's head. After a short time, the patient would fall ill or get better as if he had actually swallowed the stuff. Louis Vivet was one of the two prime exhibits (another was a woman in Charcot's ward). Luys then put all these techniques together, achieving even more remarkable phenomena. Finally the Académie de Médecine got into the act and was unable to reproduce any of these phenomena at all. So much for background: it matters because Vivet's many states were induced by the application of magnets, metals, and metallic compounds such as gold bromide, and because he was used as a prime exhibit of the action at a distance of numerous metals and medications.

Cynics have decried multiple personality as *folie à deux*, a madness resulting from a strange if unwitting collaboration between patient and therapist. I have not made that accusation, nor will I in the future. But I have no doubt that the case of Louis Vivet involves what we might call *folie à combien?* I do not know how many people participated for long periods of time, but there were at least five, namely, Vivet, Bourru and Burot, a colleague of theirs, Mabille, and Jules Voisin. I have the names of some twenty physicians who worked with or witnessed Vivet's curious conditions. Charcot certainly saw him. Vivet was personally observed by at least as many topflight clinicians as have ever examined anyone.

In his faithful and admiring *History of Hypnotism* Alan Gauld can scarcely restrain his impatience with characters such as Luys who brought hypnotism into disrepute. We find expressions such as "positively crazy" and "still crazier" when Gauld turns to the "associated extravagances" of metallotherapy, including those of Bourru and Burot.[8] Why not leave it at that? Partly because there is a difference of opinion. Adam Crabtree writes that the book about Louis Vivet which Bourru and Burot issued in 1888 "ranks as the most important study of a single case of multiple personality to be published in the nineteenth century and contains significant advances in understanding the genesis and therapy of that condition."[9] As science and medicine the work of Bourru and Burot is, in my opinion, rubbish. It is nevertheless important not only because it presents the very first multiple, but because, in Crabtree's words, "the connection between specific personalities and specific memories was acknowledged."

This work inaugurated a new language of genuinely multiple personality. I am not here calling in question the truth of the descriptions furnished by Bourru and Burot. And of course the fact that his doctors were engaged in "positively crazy" research does not mean that Louis Vivet was a deliberate fraud. He was a very sick man. As usual, I am not concerned with what Vivet "really had." I am concerned with what was said about him, how he was treated, and how the discourse and the symptom language of multiple personality came into being.

I shall sketch some salient points in the life of Louis Vivet but I will not dwell on his bodily ailments. Aside from conditions that explicitly require female reproductive organs, Vivet displayed virtually every type of bodily distress known to the language of hysteria in the late nineteenth century. That was why Voisin presented the case to the Société Médico-psychologique. Every kind of pain, paralysis, anesthesia, contracture, muscular spasm, hyperesthesia, mutism, rash, bleeding, coughing, vomiting, convulsing; every kind of epileptic seizure, catatonia, somnambulism, Saint Vitus' dance (chorea), *arc de cercle* (in which the patient lies horizontal, face up, with a totally arched back), language impairment, animalization (the patient becomes a dog), machinization (the patient becomes a steam locomotive), delusions of persecution, kleptomania, loss of sight in this eye or that eye, restricted vision, taste, or smell, visual hallucinations, voices; every type of pseudotubercular lung congestion, headache, stomachache, constipation, anorexia, bulimia, alcoholism, debility, or trance that I have ever read about in the literature of hysteria—I can find all these in the reports of Louis Vivet. Yet a common thread among Vivet's innumerable maladies issued from the hands of his doctors, and it is that which held the medical imagination, for a while.

Louis Vivet's starting point in life is all too familiar, both then and now. Born in Paris in February 1863, he was the son of an alcoholic prostitute who beat and neglected him. By age eight, when his mother was working near Chartres, he became a runaway. From early childhood he had hysterical crises, as they were called, including spitting blood and brief paralyses. In October 1871, when he was not yet nine years old, he was convicted for stealing clothes and sent to a reformatory for children.

After almost two years he was moved to a prison farm in northwest France (Haut-Marne). He stayed there for some nine years, but in mid-term, March 1877, he was scared silly by the sight of an adder (in later accounts the viper wrapped itself around his arm). That night was followed by convulsions, after which his legs were completely paralyzed. He behaved just like a paraplegic, but with no spinal cord damage at all.

After three years of idleness at the prison farm, he was transferred to an insane asylum about twenty miles south of his mother's home in Chartres. The doctor in charge, Camuset, found him to be a delightful lad, simple but full of regret for his juvenile crimes. He was taught to be a tailor, a trade he could pursue while paraplegic. He was an apt student except that after two months he had an attack of convulsions lasting fifty hours. He woke up with no paralysis and believing he was still at the prison farm. He knew nothing of the insane asylum, paraplegia, the snake, or his new skills. He was violent, quarrelsome, and greedy; previously abstemious, he now pilfered wine. He then stole quite a lot of money (sixty francs) and the personal effects of an attendant, and escaped. He sold the clothes he was wearing, bought new ones, and was about to buy a train ticket to Paris, when he was captured, kicking and biting. During the rest of the time at the asylum he had various convulsive attacks, periods of local anesthesias, and contractures. But he got better and was released in the summer of 1881, aged eighteen. Camuset wrote him up as a case of *dédoublement de la personnalité*.[10]

Thus far, that is pretty much what he was. There were two characters, one of whom knew nothing of the other. The gentle personage was paraplegic, the violent one not. The criminal type had no memory of the events at the prison farm, the adder, and the subsequent paralysis. The only way in which Vivet failed to fit the prototype is that the extravagant violent character would count as the "normal state," while the *condition seconde* was docile, pious, and dull—quite the opposite of all the standard cases, where the normal state is the inhibited one.

After being released by Camuset, Louis Vivet went home to his mother and then was off to Burgundy to work on a large estate that grew grapes. He soon fell ill, spent a month in the hospital, and was transferred to another asylum twenty-five miles away. His history was unknown to the doctor in charge. Vivet had ample crises of every conceivable sort, from complete paralysis to imbecility. He was strongly aware of a moral code, and if he did something impulsively would slyly cover it up by acting crazy.[11] In spring 1883 he was declared improved. He was discharged and given some money to get home, but he did not quite make it. He spent three days in jail for a trifling theft, about forty miles from Chartres. We catch sight of him in a number of asylums; he spoke of Vaucluse and the Salpêtrière, of being treated by well-known doctors such as Lasègue and being hypnotized by Beurmann. He talked of roaming Paris in the company of a mate from one of his asylums.

He was again arrested for stealing clothes and other personal effects. Judged to be mentally retarded and epileptic, he ended up at Bicêtre, where he came under the care of Voisin. He had attacks of practically everything. Voisin attempted to transfer his symptoms by the use of magnets. The magnet had no effect at first, but later when Vivet realized the importance of the magnet to Voisin, the very sight of a magnet would make him switch states. Gold coins placed on afflicted parts caused him excruciating pain. Voisin put him into states of provoked somnambulism and conducted the usual tests of suggestion, getting the boy to taste numerous exotic wines and liquors, always from an empty glass; of course he got drunk. He was made to vomit. When it was suggested that he had gonorrhea, he at once picked up a chamber pot and tried to urinate, screaming in pain, cursing the woman from whom he had caught the disease. As Voisin aptly observed, "all of the usual arsenal of suggestions and provoked hallucinations was thus brought into play."[12]

It is not quite clear when Voisin recognized that he had Camuset's doubled personality in his care. I do infer from the texts that Vivet learned from Voisin of Camuset's having made him famous for *dédouble-ment*. At any rate Vivet would sometimes be his quarrelsome violent self, knowing nothing of the adder, and sometimes he would be his docile self, paralyzed from the waist down. But these states were modulated by innumerable hysterical crises. One was what we would call schizophreniform, and endured for two months. Voisin used Azam's terminology of a first and second state, but noticed some differences from Félida. The first state was the violent one, the second docile. But there were different versions of the docile state; for example, in one Vivet was previper and had no knowledge of the paralysis. But what most impressed Voisin was that Vivet's periods in the second state coincided exactly with a severe contracture (but not paraplegia). Moreover, when hypnotized, but only when hypnotized, Vivet would assume "some sort of third state" in which he was sixteen and a half years old and knew of his life at the prison farm only before he had seen the adder. But Voisin did not conclude that this was a third personality, or even properly a third state to compare to states 1 and 2—for it was not spontaneous, but the result of hypnotism.

Vivet was subjected to a strange variety of treatments, including morphine, injections of pilocarpine (a botanical alkaloid; in Vivet it produced transfers of contractures), oil of ipecac to induce vomiting, and magnets on numerous parts of the body; but the only treatment that could halt an attack was pressure on the Achilles tendon or the rotulian tendon below the kneecap. He was repeatedly hypnotized. After a hypnotism session on 2 January 1885 he had a crisis and, once again, stole an attendant's money and clothing—and escaped.

At the end of January 1885 Vivet enlisted as a soldier in the French navy, apparently with the intention of going to fight in Vietnam.[13] He was posted to Rochefort, a longtime naval base on the Bay of Biscay, about a hundred miles north of Bordeaux. He was caught stealing clothes (why always clothing?). He was court-martialed but found not responsible and sent to the military hospital, where he fell into the hands of Bourru and Burot.

These two were fascinated by the transfer of hysterical symptoms by the use of magnets, metals, and drugs. They went to town on Vivet and quickly discovered they could move him from one state to another by the application of specific materials. Moreover, he was wonderfully responsive to drugs acting at a distance. Behind the head of Louis Vivet you hold a drug, and suddenly he begins to act as if he has taken that drug internally. This was indeed the topic of their first book in which Vivet was the major figure—not a study of multiple personality but a work subtitled *The Action at a Distance of Toxic Substances and Medications.*[14]

When Bourru and Burot first encountered Vivet, they said that the very first thing to do was to see the effect of metals and magnets on their patient.[15] They experimented vigorously and obtained extraordinary results. The application of a substance would produce a new paralysis and/or anesthesia in a new part of the body. One of the possibilities was paraplegia, namely, Vivet's state at the prison farm after he saw the adder. This was reinduced through the application of a magnet to the nape of the neck. Recall that in Camuset's asylum, the loss of paraplegia was associated with amnesia for the viper; Vivet was docile and learned tailoring. When a magnet was applied to the nape of his neck in Rochefort, he not only became paraplegic but also recalled the adder.

Then comes the remarkable part. Various substances produced other hysterical somatic symptoms. It was as if to satisfy the suggestions of his doctors, Vivet had to respond to the metals, and, in addition, in his clouded or entranced mind, each new paralysis had to be associated with some part of his life, some set of memories and mode of behavior. Thus each metallic compound produced a new state consisting of a distinct somatic symptom and a character with memories of a distinct life-segment. Following Azam, Voisin had spoken of Vivet's first and second states. In their first communication of 1885, Bourru and Burot spoke of states 1 through 8. In their book of 1888 they cut this down to six fully developed states, plus a large number of fragmentary ones. They had Vivet pose for photographs in ten of his abnormal physical states— "nervous states." Each of these corresponded to a manner of behavior, general knowledge, and memories of a segment of life.

Thus plate 2 in the book is captioned "The Bicêtre state; complete paralysis of the left side of the body (face and limbs), 2 January 1884; twenty-one years old." Now this is just a little misleading. The photograph was not taken on 2 January 1884. It is a photograph, probably taken in 1885, of Vivet in the physical state that symbolized 2 January 1884. This state was produced through the placement of magnetized steel on Vivet's right arm, so the paralysis and anesthesia vacated to the left. A dynamometer was a usual test of the extent of a paralysis; in this state the strength in Vivet's right arm was measured as 36 kg, and 0 in the left. He acted as if he were in Bicêtre; he had seen Voisin yesterday. He had no memories later than 2 January 1884 and none before Bicêtre except a fleeting glimpse of Sainte-Anne's, which at that time served as the Paris general admission asylum. The magnet had transformed him from his first state, that of an arrogant, aggressive man paralyzed on the right side, to a gentle man paralyzed on the left. He spoke better, was polite, never used the "tu" form as he had just been doing, could read well and clearly, and preferred milk to wine. "This was not the same person (*personage*) as before."[16]

There are ten such photographs in the book, all taken, I imagine, during the course of a couple of days. Bourru and Burot had discovered that every mental state was associated with a state of nervous paralysis and anesthesia, and that they could induce each such physical condition by placing a substance on some part of the body of Louis Vivet. Transitions usually began, after induction, with deep breathing and spasms or convulsions. I should say that the sixth state (as counted in 1888; eighth as counted in 1885) was somewhat different from the others. It began with hours of tumult, convulsions, hallucinations. It was induced by soft iron applied to either thigh. The resultant personality remembered all of Vivet's life except the paraplegic episodes. He had no paralysis, but his left side was hypersensitive.

I may be thought to exaggerate Bourru and Burot's emphasis on the essential interaction of three ingredients: metallic substance applied to a specific part of the body, type of paralysis, and segment of life remembered. My point is that his doctors created conceptual space for the idea of multiplicity. There were many more fragments than the ten that were photographed. One day Louis Vivet went through what I suspect is the most elaborate spontaneous memory regression that took place during the nineteenth century. So far as I know, no one has recently paid any attention to it, but once it is noticed again it may become yet another part of the iconography of age regression therapists. So I had better set out what happened.

Louis Vivet was presented with a flask of gold bromide. He then fell asleep, and woke up over and over again, cycling through the following states:

(a) He wakes at age five in Chartres, living with his mother. His speech is childish, but sufficient for his age. He trails his right leg when he walks.

(b) He reawakens at age six and a half in Lève near Chartres. He manifests contracture of the left side; his right leg is extended, his arm bent, fingers clenched.

(c) He reawakens at age seven in Luysan, also near Chartres. He has contractures of the right side of the face, which hinders speech, and of the leg. His mother beats him. He begs for bread in an infantile voice.

(d) He reawakens in Chartres, aged eight. Here he is treated by a Dr. Salmon for eight months. He has contracture of the left arm, and of the right leg extended.

(e) He reawakens at the prison farm, aged thirteen, before he has seen the snake. He has not worked for six months because he fell ill on leaving a bath, and he has various contractures. There is a photograph of Vivet in this condition. He recalls that before the prison farm he was with a Mr. Bonjean near Evreux.

Bourru and Burot call this "a beautifully clear example of the spontaneous *déroulement* of several personality states, most of them unknown and which could be added to the states previously described." They say these states were induced specifically by gold bromide. Do we have, here, the first detailed example of spontaneous age regression on the part of a multiple? Unfortunately, age regression was a standard trick of stage hypnotists from the middle of the nineteenth century.[17] We cannot doubt that the practice was familiar to Bourru, Burot, and Mabille, intensely involved in avant-garde hypnotism as they were. And Vivet certainly got around; he should equally well have known of age regression from his asylums and from popular shows. I am not saying that he was deliberately faking. I say only that we can have every confidence that this way to be a somnambule was very well known to both Vivet and his audience.

What was up with Louis Vivet? Retroactive diagnosis would be preposterous. Anyone stating with confidence what was wrong with the man would thereby be playing the fool. We can at best read this complex and painful history in numerous ways. We can easily see him, for example, as a well-developed *DSM-III* multiple personality who dissociated early in life to cope with appalling conditions. My own take on this horrible life history is consistent with that but has a very different emphasis. As I see it, Vivet was in effect trained to make the correspondence between personality state and somatic symptom. In the first instance the reemergence of paraplegia and the docile second state was spontaneous. He was rewarded for that. Trivially, he stopped having to work and was in the end moved out of the prison farm, no mean achievement. More important, he was rewarded because he became famous, the subject of a much-discussed article by his doctor, Camuset. He fell into the hands of doctors fascinated with transfer of hysterical somatic symptoms by the use of magnets and metals. What better way to conform to their expectations, and hope for further reward, than to have the paralyses move, and with each movement to assume a different life-segment, mimicking what happened spontaneously in Camuset's asylum? Vivet desperately wanted to please, to be loved, to be rewarded. I am not saying that Vivet worked this out. I say only that the environment in which he found himself was conducive to this sort of learning. Others will read the events differently.

Bourru and Burot completely subscribed to the connection between personality and memory. "The comparison of previous states of consciousness with present states is the relation that unites a former psychic life with the present one. That is the *foundation of personality*. A consciousness that compares itself with a former one is a true personality."[18] That had become a commonplace, already urged by the entire school of positivist psychology, although no one, I think, took quite such a simplistic view as Bourru and Burot. They cited Théodule Ribot on the memory. The belief that memory was the foundation of personality gave weight to the idea that we did not just see some six or eight or ten states of Louis Vivet, but at least six personalities and some personality fragments. Truly multiple personality, as I have said, had entered the language of psychiatry.

Bourru and Burot stated that their results should prove rich in practical applications. Vivet was transferred from the military hospital to the asylum at La Rochelle, twenty miles up the coast. Daily care was left to colleagues such as Mabille and Ramadier. Voison had been able to prevent or diminish attacks by pressure on a tendon. Mabille and Ramadier were more draconian. When Vivet was in a state of major crisis, they found it easy to recognize the approach of an attack by the sensitivity of the body part with hysterical somatic symptoms. They found that they could prevent the attack by tightly squeezing the man's testicles. Then they induced somnambulism by pressing on the eyes, opening the eyelids, and rubbing the crown of the head. "To this extent, suggestion allowed his normal personality to return, and, as if by enchantment, to make the crisis and the majority of the symptoms disappear."

Thus far, we do not notice any use of memory in the day-to-day treatment of Louis Vivet. But the correlation between life-segment and paralysis was used. Ramadier and Mabille used it to catch Vivet when he was cycling through his states. They could tell what mental state he was in by his paralysis. When he was in a physical state corresponding to his most "normal" personality, one would intervene and stop him there, like a clock. We are not told how the doctors intervened, but presumably as before, by testicular shock and hypnotic devices.[19]

Mabille and Ramadier were confident that they had established the intimate relation between personality states and nervous crises, that is, the various attacks of somatic hysterical symptoms. In the case of Vivet, at least, they never encountered a change in personality without the crises or preliminary somatic modifications. That was the big discovery: hysterical paralyses match memory segments.

Our authors also state that subjects such as Vivet "are unhappy because of lacunae that crop up unexpectedly in their memories after a crisis; we believe that it will be possible to revive these numb memories." Today that may sound like recovering dissociated or repressed memories. It may sound as if our doctors foreshadowed the cathartic therapy of Janet, Breuer, and Freud. Absolutely not. No dynamic psychiatry was in view. The patients were, in an ordinary way, unhappy because of big gaps in their memories. Bourru and Burot thought they could locate, by noting the somatic correlates, a relatively normal state, corresponding to a fairly continuous life-segment; then, perhaps using magnets and metals, or perhaps using the more brutal technique of Mabille and Ramadier, they could wake the patient up in the relatively normal state.

After what is, in contrast to my own account, a mercifully brief description of what his doctors did to Louis Vivet, Alan Gauld concludes by noting that "despite this meddling he left [their hospital] in

1887 much improved." How do we know? F.W.H. Myers wrote that "in 1887 . . . Dr Burot informed me that [Vivet's] health had much improved, and that his peculiarities had in great part disappeared."[20] Since the symptoms had remitted twice before, and since Vivet had twice before been discharged from asylums as relatively cured, Burot's statement may be taken at face value. If the doctors really did make a grab for his private parts every time an attack was in the offing, you can see why he may have wanted out, fast. I have no idea what happened to Louis Vivet. Probably he went back to stealing clothes. My guess is that the next time he was caught he preferred the criminal justice system to the mental health system.

Azam briefly discussed Louis Vivet. "I remain convinced," wrote Azam in a sentence so tortuous that I suspect he did not want to write it, "that if this patient, rightly held to be ill with hystero-epilepsy, had been studied from the point of view of sleep, it would have been found that in his childhood, troubled by misery and vagrancy as it was, he was a somnambule, and that his second states were only exaggerations of his attack of somnambulism." Note the plural: Azam grudgingly went halfway to the position that there was more than one alter, but no further. On his view there is still, first, the normal state, and then second states that are all somnambulic, going back, it now appears, to childhood. Oddly, Azam found the present-day thesis of childhood origin a natural one, but he was disinclined to think that there were more than two personalities.

As Crabtree said, Bourru and Burot brought out the connection between specific personalities and specific memories. This was a further tightening of the connection between multiplicity and memory. But notice that only when we have *multiple* personalities does this connection become so critical. If there are only two personalities, the other personality is simply the other. But if there are several, then you need a way to tell which is which. Bourru, Burot, and Louis Vivet provided a beautiful way to identify personalities. Each personality had its three-part signature: a memory segment, a metallic compound, and a characteristic bodily infirmity.

Trauma

TRAUMATIC EVENTS, traumatic experiences—we know what they are: psychological blows, wounds to the spirit. Severe trauma early in life may irrevocably damage the development of a child. Trauma is psychic hurt. The word has become a metaphor for almost anything unpleasant: "That was really traumatic!" Previously "trauma" had been a surgeons' word. It referred to a wound on the body, most often the result of battle. It still has that old meaning. A trauma center deals with the immediate effects of accidents. It tries to stanch the flow of blood, attend to smashed bones or brains; its hope is to patch people up and put them together again. But few of us, in everyday conversation, even think of trauma in that sense. Trauma took the leap from body to mind just over a century ago, exactly when multiple personality emerged in France, and during the time when the sciences of memory were coming into being.

I shall single out only a single strand from a complex story, the connection between trauma and memory. It covers only part of what Esther Fischer-Homberg, in her definitive historical study of traumatic neurosis, calls the "psychologization" of trauma.[1] She had in mind the *complete* psychologization wrought by Freud and his school after 1897. After that year Freud allowed that purely psychic events, fantasies of childhood sex, could produce neuroses. Mark Micale speaks instead of "the progressive psychologization of the trauma concept in the late nineteenth century."[2] Trauma was already well psychologized in Freud's theory of 1893–1897, that hysteria was caused by buried memories of seduction or sexual assault in infancy. The trauma was the seduction, an event that left no physical scar or wound, and whose consequences were entirely psychological. But Freud did not originate this idea of psychological trauma. It was already in circulation in 1885, sometimes under the name of moral trauma—*traumatisme morale*—when Freud arrived in Paris to study under Charcot.

Where did the idea of moral trauma come from? In retrospect we can quite easily construct a chain of ideas that takes us from brain damage—straightforward physical and neurological trauma—to the idea of psychological trauma that produces hysterical symptoms and is to be relieved through recollection of lost memories. Start with the fact that head injuries can produce amnesia and other disabilities such as paralysis. One shock to one head, with manifest external or neurological damage, produces memory loss and other symptoms such as partial paralysis or insensitivity of the skin. Another shock to another head, with no detectable damage, can also produce loss of memory and other symptoms. In the case of a third shock to a third head, which resulted in amnesia, autopsy reveals no discernible damage to the brain or spinal cord. Hence a shock to the head can produce amnesia without detectable physical trauma.

Next step: hysteria is often accompanied by amnesia—double consciousness is an extreme form of hysterical amnesia. Could a shock to the head, which does not damage the brain, produce hysterical amnesia? If the amnesia and other symptoms are signs of a state of mind, then the causal links leading to amnesia might be mental rather than physical. The idea or memory of the shock, rather than the actual physical shock, could produce the effects. Thus a painful idea or psychological shock could cause hysteria.

Next: damage to the body requires physiological repair. How should we help a damaged mind? When physical shock produces amnesia, the patient often does not remember the physical shock. Hence the psychological shock that produces hysteria may not be remembered by a hysterical patient. Amnesia can be studied experimentally, by hypnosis. Memories of what happened or of what the subject did in the hypnotic trance can be restored by hypnotism. So, if we continue this chain of analogies, try hypnotizing hysterics to recover lost memories of psychological shocks. Paralyses or other symptoms disappear as memories are restored.

Thus by a chain of ideas we have been catapulted from amnesia and other neurological symptoms caused by accidental head injury to Janet's discovery that work on memories of psychological trauma can serve to treat hysteria. The essential ingredients for this free-floating sequence of associations are trauma, shock, amnesia, hysteria, multiple personality, and hypnosis. They provide a scaffolding upon which to hang an understanding of a very complex story.

Ideas do not associate by themselves. The context for these associations is a rich mix of elements from medical and social history. One way to tell the history is to begin with the railroad, the most potent instrument of the nineteenth-century industrializing world. It was a symbol, for some, of progress and good; for others it meant moral disaster. The network of railways came later to France than to England, but there it produced the most striking literary representation of all. As Gilles Deleuze says of Emile Zola's *La Bête humaine*, "the locomotive is not an object but evidently an epic symbol," such as is always to be found in Zola, "reflecting all the themes and situations of the book," including the disasters that stalk the machine-mad hero.[3] The railroad is also an epic symbol of the psychologization of trauma. Where Zola had made physical catastrophes stand for moral ones, the railroad itself transformed physical traumas into psychological lesions. Fischer-Homberg suggests that the official history of traumatic neuroses, which traces them back to railway accidents, is itself something of a metamyth about the power of the railroad to change the nineteenth-century vision of both the material world and the life of the mind.[4]

The railroad created the accident. Cuttings caved in, boilers exploded, and trains went off the rails. There was not just a wholly new kind of accident, the railway accident. The railroad fixed the very idea of an accident with its modern meaning. The word has always meant, among other things, something that happens by chance or is uncaused. In medieval philosophy, accidents were properties of a thing that were not necessarily contained in the essence of that thing. But our present specific meaning—something sudden, *bad*, harmful, and destructive— derives almost entirely from the railway accident. Nearly all the tort law of accident and liability was developed in connection with the railroads. People have had "accidents" forever, but they did not call them that until the industrial era: mining accidents, railroad accidents. There was a British Royal Commission on accidents in 1840. The more quickly a nation developed new technologies, the earlier its concern with accidents, with laws of negligence and liability, and with new types of injuries that were experienced.[5]

Some injuries were manifest: broken bones, pierced cheeks, torn flesh; in short, old-fashioned physical trauma. Yet something else happened. Some passengers walked away unscathed only to complain of terrible pain, in the back, say, a few days later. Today we talk of whiplash injury. Sometimes a physical problem could be readily recognized by the physiology and neurology of the day. But sometimes the symptoms did not seem to correspond to any discernible physical injury. In 1866 a distinguished London physician, John Eric Erichsen (1818–1896) lectured on this condition.[6] His was one of three studies of injuries from railway accidents published that year in England; remarkably, these simultaneous works were the first to address the topic in print. Erichsen referred to *railway spine*, a phrase he surely did not invent, but which he made famous. Head injury, together with what he called "spinal concussion," was at the heart of the problem; the damage was not peculiar to railways, but they had made it prevalent.

Victims of railway spine had no lesions, that is, no apparent trauma. In that respect they were like hysterics. Erichsen did not care for that comparison. A man of forty-five who is hit by a "sudden and overwhelming calamity" shall not be said to "become suddenly 'hysterical,' like a lovesick girl."[7] Erichsen was on the side of plaintiffs suing railway companies. To compare a psychologically injured man to a hysterical woman would be to guarantee that he collected almost nothing in damages. Hence a new disorder was required. But medically, as opposed to legally, the comparison remained. Three years after Erichsen's lectures, Russell Reynolds, another influential London physician, took up the theme. His object "was to show that some of the most serious disorders of the nervous system, such as paralysis, spasm, and other altered sensations, may depend on the morbid condition of idea, or of idea and emotion together."[8] He suggested that the "idea" or psychological origin might arise in many ways, although the memory or emotion connected with a railway accident was foremost in discussions of the day.

In the discussion following his paper, Reynolds made potent comparisons with hysteria. But he insisted that paralysis "produced by Idea" was not madness. The mind of typical patients was, aside from the symptoms, perfectly sound. His treatment still looks good today. He called it hope. First, "a real earnest dealing with the case, as one of grave character, although not of the kind supposed." The patient should be encouraged to walk, assisted, every day. Small electrical stimulations should be given to the muscle, "partly as a moral and mental agent, partly as a physical occasion of muscular contraction." And some massage should be applied.[9] Reynolds's paper produced a good discussion. Other instances of the efficacy of the hope treatment were described; "a stronger case could not be mentioned of the power of mind over bodily disability." One doctor thought that "hysteria" was not a useful term; it needed better definition. The president of the British Medical Association thought that in assimilating the effects of railway accidents "to the class of hysterical women, [Reynolds] had hit on the right idea." Another doctor brought up the vexed question of fraud. He mentioned a case of railway compensation in which all the symptoms had disappeared the moment the paralyzed man received a check for two thousand pounds.

The railways paid out millions of pounds. The lawyers were active, and these legal battles form another story.[10] The physicians who were expert witnesses for plaintiffs against the railways could hardly say that railway spine was a hysterical complaint, analogous to the maladies of women. But railway spine, and especially Reynolds's brief discussion of it in

1869, was a gift to Charcot, not because it feminized males, but because it made hysteria potentially masculine.[11] During the period 1872–1878 Charcot had become the world expert on florid hysteria. Yet a great turf war continued, because gynecologists and obstetricians, masters of the womb, claimed hysteria as their territory. Charcot's central theme was that hysteria was a neurological disorder. It was hereditary—that is, only those so disposed by ancestry could develop it. The best way to wrest hysteria from the gynecologists was to declare it to be a disease of both sexes.[12] Male hysteria had always been acknowledged, but usually with a connotation of effeminacy. Charcot found his male hysterics among brawny laborers; there was nothing effeminate about them.[13] Hysteria still had to be inherited—a thesis to which Charcot stood firm until his dying day. But it could be produced by trauma such as occurred in accidents, and it could also be induced by toxic substances, ranging from industrial chemicals to alcohol. Conversely, in one of his classic demonstrations, Charcot began with the symptoms described by Russell Reynolds, and showed how they could all be produced in a suitable male subject by hypnosis.[14] Thus memory, hysteria, hypnosis, and physical trauma were tightly interwoven in Charcot's lectures.

Charcot was the great master of the use of the case, especially of an ideal type exemplifying a disorder in a heightened state. From Charcot we learn cases, but no statistics. One of his acolytes in Bordeaux summarized a series of one hundred patients analyzed according to Charcotian precepts.[15] Hysteria was less florid in Bordeaux than in Charcot's ward: "The hysteria of the hôpital Saint-André is, in general, in relation to the *grande hystérie* of the Salpêtrière, *une petite hystérie*."[16] In this table, of a series of patients observed about 1885, I use the French names as a reminder that trauma means physical damage, and that the intoxications include both industrial poisoning and alcohol.

The Occasioning Causes of Hysteria

	MEN	WOMEN	TOTAL
Emotions morales	8	54	62
Traumatismes	12	4	16
Intoxications	9	0	9
Unknown	2	11	13
	31	69	100

Our modern theory of multiple personality requires that a multiple have an innate ability to dissociate in childhood plus repeated childhood trauma. This continues Charcot's doctrine that hysteria requires an inherited predisposition plus an occasioning cause. One of Charcot's students wrote a thesis titled *Les agents provocateurs de l'hystérie*. This phrase was picked up even by Freud—but increasingly critically—to mean the occasioning causes that brought out a hereditary disposition to neurosis.[17] We see from the table that for a good Charcotian most female hysteria is provoked by a psychological state, while most male hysteria is provoked by physical trauma or poisoning.

Charcot, one thinks, could have taken a further step by the decade's end: the step to psychological shock as a cause of hysteria in men as well as women. Some scholars have argued that he did, but that seems wishful thinking.[18] Charcot was a neurologist, who held that hysteria was a hereditary disorder of the nervous system. It was brought to life, particularly in the case of men, by physical trauma and poisoning, not by psychological events, even though one could mimic the effects of trauma by hypnosis.

But far more was happening beyond the precincts of Charcot's wards and his famous lectures. France had undergone a disastrous war; Paris had briefly and violently been communist. Quite aside from real brain injury, there was a great deal of psychological shock around. The phenomenon of "being in shock," and what *DSM-IV* calls acute stress disorder, are human universals. Post-traumatic stress disorder, as a resultant of combat, has been newly named, but Herodotus left us a fine example, as he did of most other features of the human condition. Studies of shell shock (Britain) and traumatic neurosis (Germany) became critical during the 1914–1918 war, but of course such effects were well known before then. After the war with Prussia French statisticians prepared reports on the psychological effects of 1870–1871. A thick volume of 1874, *On the Influence of Great Commotions on the Development of Mental Illness*, presented 386 civilians who experienced long-term distress from some wartime event.[19] The original meaning of a commotion, in French medical parlance, was "the shock experienced by certain parts of the body on the occasion of falls or when being struck."[20] Like trauma, commotions were psychologized. In the statistical report of 1874 the commotion did not involve literal physical harm, although in most cases the victim was terrified or did something that horrified him. Hence we have an extraordinary catalog of mental illness produced by emotional shock.

Here are four examples in which terror or revulsion produced amnesia as well as other symptoms.[21] In 1871 a rich farmer aged forty killed three people out of patriotic fervor. He subsequently suffered delusions of grandeur, visual hallucinations, and feelings of persecution. In 1874 he had no memory of the murders he had committed three years earlier. A man of fifty-five lost his business during the invasion. Later he suffered from insomnia, general delirium, and loss of memory. In 1873 he was in dementia. A former policeman, aged forty, was captured by the Communards and threatened with being shot. In 1873 he was suffering from severe depression, anxiety, and complete amnesia from the moment of his capture. A woman on a small family farm was terrified by a battle that took place a few yards from her house. She experienced very great memory loss and could respond to the simplest questions only with difficulty. She did not know her name or the number of her children. But she left the asylum cured at the end of February 1871. I call these cases of psychological trauma producing mental illness. I am not being anachronistic. Each of these cases was described, in a Paris medical thesis of 1885, as an example of amnesia produced by "moral trauma."[22]

So we have a great tangle of ideas. Charcot was teaching that hysteria can be produced by physical trauma. There were examples of moral trauma producing amnesia and other symptoms. A far greater focus of study was amnesia caused by straightforward physical trauma, namely, head injury. Since head injuries have undoubtedly produced amnesias as long as there have been human beings, it is remarkable that the systematic study of amnesia began only after 1870 or so. This again is not an anachronistic perception. Doctors of the day said that they were, to their own surprise, inaugurating a new field of study. We might have suspected as much from fiction. Amnesia produced by a blow on the head became a generic plot for bad novels and plays in the late 1870s. Amnesia produced by charms and drugs is as old as the hills, but amnesia produced by shock was a new theme for penny dreadfuls. An intermediary case is perhaps found in the first and finest English detective novel, Wilkie Collins's *The Moonstone* (1868). It was published just when memory was about to become the object of science. There are a number of references throughout the novel to leading authorities on the topic. But the amnesia on which the plot turns was induced by opium, a problem familiar to Collins himself, who was an addict. The character recovered memory by reenacting the intoxication. Fictional amnesia produced by a fall or a blow followed soon after Collins's novel, in the wake of the new medical enthusiasm for the topic.

The most massive French survey of amnesia and its causes was published in 1885. It was not the work of an established clinician but that of a medical student, A.-M.-P. Rouillard. He was well aware that "the question of amnesia is a large, a very large, question. It touches on the higher and very delicate issues of general pathology, on mental pathology, on philosophy, and even sociology. Such a subject, to be treated thoroughly, demands white hairs, experience, and erudition and talent that are scarcely to be found in a man of my age."[23] He surveyed all relevant literature, as seen from his point of view, in his enormous dissertation—enormous by the standards of its day: *thèse volumineux*, remarked a reviewer in 1886.[24] Rouillard said at the start that the study of amnesia *pur et simple* (as opposed to aphasia, or loss of memory for words) had begun only recently. Aside from a remarkable article by Falret in the *Encyclopedia of Medical Science*, there was nothing much on amnesia until the past few years. And who are the authors whom he cites? There was Legrand du Saulle, who had just published a synoptic study of amnesia in the *Gazette des Hôpitaux* for 1883. Otherwise Rouillard looked to Azam, the central figure of chapter 11 above, and Ribot, the central figure of chapter 14.

It is hardly surprising that Azam should figure, both because he was a surgeon in a mental asylum seeing brain-damaged patients, and because doubling and multiplicity were maladies of the memory. In 1881, while his observations on Félida were continuing, he presented a catalog of fifty-nine cases of head injury that produced various types of *troubles intellectuelles*.[25] As a study of head injury this work is unimportant; there had been a vast literature on the topic already. But Azam's focus was amnesia, which was rather new. Twenty of the cases displayed striking amnesias, and there were lesser memory deficits in most of the others. Azam made clear that there are two basic types of amnesia. His new terminology was widely adopted.[26] *Anterograde* amnesia involves forgetting the events at the time of the accident and following it. *Retrograde* amnesia involves forgetting events before the accident. Among Azam's clearest cases, fourteen were retrograde, four anterograde.

Azam's account strikes a present-day clinician who works with head injuries as subtle, accurate, and thorough. But for us the interest lies in the fact that, by 1881, amnesia had become a full-fledged object of study. In the next chapter I shall distinguish "depth" from "surface" knowledge, where the depth knowledge involves the kinds of objects that can be investigated, the types of questions that can be addressed, the sorts of propositions that may be either-true-or-false, the sorts of distinctions that make sense. Azam's distinction between two types of amnesia is, in this terminology, surface knowledge that indicates an underlying network of ideas about memory and forgetting.

Azam was three years older than Charcot, so that in 1881 he was already fifty-eight. He was an enterprising provincial, conservative and respectful of Paris. It was not for a man of his years and station to psychologize the concept of trauma. Today, when we read his cases, we can wonder if some of the amnesias and intellectual troubles that he describes might have been psychogenic rather than neurological in nature. But that was not for him to see. What was required to break on through to the full psychologization of trauma? The idea of moral trauma as a cause of amnesia was in place. The remaining essential ingredient was a psychologist not wedded to the neurological theory of hysteria but familiar with hysteria, amnesia, doubling of the personality, and hypnotism. Pierre Janet filled the bill. He had trained first as a philosopher, which allowed him to cover pathological and experimental psychology. His doctoral dissertation, *Psychological Automatism*, is the first systematic work to study the traumatic causes of hysteria. His brother Jules used hypnosis to study one of Charcot's own famous patients—Blanche Wittman—and shared Pierre's view of psychological trauma as the cause of hysteria, and of its role in treatment.[27] Freud and Breuer acknowledged that "the Janets" were ahead of them, although they express a note of skepticism about the Janets' work with hysterical anesthesias.[28]

Jules Janet went on to become a distinguished urologist while Pierre made psychological trauma the cornerstone of his clinical practice. At the end of his life he conscientiously had his innumerable case records destroyed. Hence we must judge his enthusiasm for trauma from his published work alone. In *Psychological Automatism* (1889) he described 19 cases, in 10 of which trauma played a dominant role. In *Neuroses and Fixed Ideas* (1892), trauma figured in 73 out of 199 cases. In *The Mental State of Hystericals* (1893–1894) it was in 26 out of 48. And in *Obsessions and Psychesthenia* (1903), trauma was central to 148 out of 325 case reports.[29] But what traumas? Freud and Janet make an interesting contrast. During the 1890s each man was fascinated by trauma, but the traumas they chose to emphasize were profoundly different in character.

Janet castigated Freud for emphasizing sex, and insisted that a great many of his own hysterical patients were afflicted by nonsexual trauma. Yet what I consider the crucial difference between the two men has little directly to do with sex. Janet's early examples of traumatic experiences include being immersed in freezing water at the time of menstruating, or sleeping beside a child with a gross skin disease of the face. The trauma itself is not a human action. It is not somebody doing something, to you or to another. It is an event, or a state. Of course the young woman got into the tub of freezing water; the girl was made to sleep beside a sick child. But the actual trauma was the cold water, or the skin of an infected face. Human action, what philosophers call action under a description, enters Janet's tales of trauma extraordinarily infrequently. Freud's traumas almost always involved somebody doing something, an intentional action. People and their deeds were central to Freud's traumas; the world at large was the stuff of Janet's. It was as if Janet painted Dutch landscapes of trauma, in which people appear at most on the horizon, while Freud painted Dutch interiors filled with people in action, bickering, bartering, seducing.

Because Janet's traumas were impersonal they did not invite reinterpretation, especially when it came to memory work. Because Freud's traumas involved human actions they invited reinterpretation in memory. I argue in chapter 17 that the possibility of redescribing human action, of making it an action under a new description, is central to our problems about memory today. They were automatically present to Freud, and excluded from Janet's studies, by the very choice of the traumas to be remembered.

Freud himself passed from loyal apprenticeship to recalcitrant independence. When he wrote an account of hysteria for an 1888 German medical handbook he was Charcot's apprentice.[30] When he added footnotes to his 1892 translation of Charcot's lectures he had become the journeyman—an Oedipal one at that, if you agree with Toby Gelfand and see Charcot as a father figure for Freud.[31] Much later Freud said that in his footnotes to Charcot he "really did infringe the rights of property that apply to publications."[32] This is a characteristic Freudian self-misdescription and/or deep insight. Freud did not infringe the rights of property (unless we playfully take hysteria to be Charcot's wife and Freud's mother). He contradicted his master outright, but secretively, in the footnotes to a translation.

In 1888 Freud wrote that a disposition to hysteria is inherited. The illness lacks a clear definition and can be characterized only in terms of its symptoms. The ideal type of hysteria is Charcot's *grande hystérie*. What causes hysteria? Sex does have a role—primarily for females, "on account of the high psychical significance of this function especially in the female sex." Physical trauma is a frequent cause of hysteria, "first, by a hitherto unobserved hysterical disposition being aroused by a powerful physical trauma, which is accompanied by fright and loss of consciousness, and secondly by the trauma becoming the seat of a local hysteria." Conditions brought about by general trauma and "known as 'railway spine' and 'railway brain' are regarded as hysteria by Charcot, with which the American writers, whose authority on this question is not to be disputed, are in agreement." Only at the end of the 1888 article did Freud give a hint of what was to come in his own work. Symptoms can be relieved by hypnotic suggestion. This is "even more effective if we adopt a method first practiced by Josef Breuer in Vienna and lead the patient under hypnosis to the psychical prehistory on which the disorder in question originated." Such sentences must be read in context. We are still much at the level of, to use the word of Russell Reynolds, physical symptoms produced by "Idea"—the idea of the physical trauma. By hypnosis (in 1888) we lead the patient back to the psychical surroundings of the physical trauma. That was one of many ways to use mental tricks to remove hysterical symptoms. In the very next sentence we learn that you can get a paralyzed person to start moving a limb by instilling a very great need to box someone on the ears.

In 1888 Janet had already published cases of hysteria produced by past but forgotten psychological trauma, and had already described healing by recollection induced in hypnosis. Freud was still working his way toward those ideas. He had arrived by the time he finished translating Charcot's lectures in 1892. His footnotes present his own "independent view of hysterical attacks."

> The core of a hysterical attack, in whatever form it may appear, is a *memory*, the hallucinatory reliving of a scene which is significant for the onset of the illness. . . . the *content of the memory* is as a rule a psychical *trauma* which is qualified by its intensity to provoke the outbreak of hysteria in the patient or is the event which, owing to its occurrence at a particular moment, has become a trauma.[33]

The upshot, from 1893 through the seduction theory and its abandonment in 1897, is well known. At present many readers of Freud pay less attention to what most interested Freud as theoretician, namely, causation. In 1888 hysteria and other neuroses could be defined only in terms of their symptoms. Half a dozen years later Freud thought he could define the distinct neuroses by their specific etiologies. That was the vogue in German medicine, including psychiatry, thanks to the stunning success of the germ theory of disease. Many diseases that had previously been defined only by their symptoms could now be defined by the microbes that caused them—literal, not metaphorical, agents provocateurs. Freud's doctrine of the unconscious and of hidden, invisible specific causes is in part an analogy with the most successful part of the medicine of the day. Psychoanalysis was to be the microscopy of the psyche.[34] There has recently been a somewhat idle debate as to how Freud should be seen: as primarily a scientist constantly generating bold conjectures, usually false, or as one who gently extended traditional psychological explanations into new areas, such as the unconscious and dream work. Both positions seem to be correct. Freud's etiologies of hysteria, the anxiety neuroses, and neurasthenia were intended to limn a sharp distinction between these types of illness, and to provide a specific cause—and by implication, a specific treatment—for each. His etiologies were brilliant leaps in the dark, and in his correspondence we see him reveling in what he thought were his great discoveries.

Freud's lunge toward specific causes of each neurosis can be read even in his 1892 footnotes. He contradicted Charcot's assertion that a phobia had a hereditary base; the more frequent cause "lies not in heredity but in abnormalities of sexual life. It is even possible to specify the form of abuse of the sexual function involved."[35] Most readers rightly see *sex*; I also see *specify*. In a series of papers (1895–1896) Freud addressed the question "Is it possible to establish a constant aetiological relation between a particular cause and a particular neurotic effect, in such a way that each of the major neuroses can be attributed to a specific aetiology?" His answer was a ringing *Yes!* Neurasthenia was caused by immoderate masturbation or spontaneous emission. The anxiety neuroses are caused by coitus interruptus and related frustrations. Hysteria in females and obsession in males are caused by sexual traumas that "*must have occurred in early childhood (before puberty), and their content must consist of an actual irritation of the genitals (or processes resembling copulation).*"[36] That is the so-called seduction theory of hysteria, which is part, and only part, of a general theory about the neuroses. Freud felt overwhelmed in 1897 not because he had to abandon the seduction theory but because he had to surrender what was to be his greatest contribution to modern psychological science, comparable to the germ theory of disease.

Jeffrey Masson's well-known and well-aimed assault on Freud is titled *The Assault on Truth*. Masson meant that Freud had assaulted truth by abandoning a true theory, the seduction theory of hysteria. Moreover, Freud thereby denied the truth that child sexual abuse was rampant in bourgeois Vienna (and everywhere else). I have little quarrel with Masson's version of events, but it is only one version. It passes by Freud the theoretician, the scientist, the man who, in Patricia Kitcher's vision of Freud, wanted a grand unified theory of everything.[37] *That* Freud simply did not care about the incidence of sexual abuse in his community. The seduction theory was not part of a critique of Western morals, as the latter-day child abuse movement has been. It was part of a systematic etiology of the neuroses. Freud cared at most incidentally about abused children. He cared about Truth and its partner, Causation, not about truths and little children.

I see Freud as driven by a terrible Will to Truth, illustrated by a second contrast with Janet. Ellenberger writes that the values of Freud were those of the romantic era; Janet was an Enlightenment rationalist. That insight is partial at best. Janet was flexible and pragmatic, while it was Freud who was the dedicated and rather rigid theoretician in the spirit of the Enlightenment. His early theory on the specific etiologies of the neuroses would have delighted seventeenth-century intellects; Leibniz would have loved it. Freud aspired after such theories all his life and, like many a dedicated theoretician, probably fudged the evidence in favor of theory. Freud had a passionate commitment to Truth, deep underlying Truth, as a value. That ideological commitment is fully compatible with—may even demand—lying through one's teeth. The emotionally felt aim is to get at the Truth by whatever means.

Janet had no such Will to Truth. He was an honorable man, and (we might say *hence*) he had no inflated sense of the Truth. He dealt with traumatically caused neuroses by convincing the patient that the trauma had never happened. He would do this by suggestion and hypnosis whenever he could. Take, for example, his early patient who at the age of six had been made to sleep beside a girl terribly suffering from impetigo on one side of the face. His patient would break out in hysterical marks, and would experience loss of sensibility, even blindness, on that side of her face. So Janet used hypnosis to suggest to his patient that she was caressing the soft beautiful face of the girl she had lain beside at age six. All symptoms, including the partial blindness, disappeared. Janet cured his patient by telling her a lie, and getting her to believe it. He did this over and over again with his patients—got them to believe what he himself knew was a lie.

Janet's admirers in the multiple and traumatic disorder movements make plain his deep commitment to the traumatic origins of most hysterias. They have euphemisms for lying, such as "substitute positive images": "if recovering the trauma and telling the accompanying details was impossible, or did not provide relief, Janet, like Milton Erickson, used hypnosis to substitute neutral or positive images for traumatic memories. For example, he asked the woman with hysterical blindness in her left eye to imagine that she was sleeping in the same bed with a 'very nice child who was not sick.'"[38]

Freud was the exact opposite of Janet. His patients had to face up to the truth—as he saw it. We can have no doubt, in retrospect, that Freud very often deluded himself, thanks to his resolute dedication to theory. Half a century of Freud scholarship has taught that Freud got patients to believe things about themselves that were false, things that were often so bizarre that only the most devout theorizer could propose them in the first place. But there is no evidence that Freud systematically, as a method of therapy, got his patients to believe what he himself knew to be lies. Janet fooled his patients; Freud fooled himself.

Thus we have a strange paradox. Janet was not, as Ellenberger asserted, an Enlightenment man. He was an honorable man of the Third Republic, hewing to what Anglos call Victorian virtues. There is no reason to think that he lied to his peers, fellow honorable men in the professions. He found it the most natural thing in the world to help his patients, often female and poor, by getting them to believe lies. Abstract Truth was not important to Janet, nor was it important that his patients know the truths about themselves. He was a physician, a healer, and by all accounts an excellent healer. The hysterically blind woman who had come to a public clinic was apparently cured. She was lucky, we may think, that she was not Viennese and wealthy enough to consult Freud.

We reach an unsettling conclusion. The doctrine of psychological trauma, recovered memory, and abreaction created a crisis of truth. Freud and Janet, the two most memorable individuals to pioneer the doctrine, faced the crisis in opposite ways. Janet had no compunction about lying to his patients, and creating false memories through which they could deal with their distress. Truth was not, for him, an absolute value. For Freud, it was. That is to say, he aimed at the true Theory to which all else had to be subservient, and he believed that his patients should confront the truths about themselves. When he came to doubt whether the memories elicited in analysis were true, he developed a theory that worked just as well when they were taken to be fantasies. He may have made completely the wrong decision. He may have deluded himself about his reasons for abandoning the seduction theory. Maybe he did so because he was terrified. But at another level Freud's motivation was the ideal of truth, not truth about the life of this or that patient, not truth about family life in turn-of-the-century Vienna, but a higher theoretical Truth about the psyche. He had an Enlightenment vision of what Kitcher calls "a complete interdisciplinary science of mind." And in his practice he firmly believed that it was the obligation of the analyst to lead each patient to a self-knowledge that squared with theory.

Does it matter whether a patient comes to have self-knowledge? Why not follow Janet, and hypnotize the patient into self-deception? I think true self-knowledge does matter, but the issues that arise are difficult. I state my own view in the final chapter of this book. One thing is, however, plain. In the matter of lost and recovered memories, we are the heirs of Freud and Janet. One lived for Truth, and quite possibly deluded himself a good deal of the time and even knew he was being deluded. The other, a far more honorable man, helped his patients by lying to them, and did not fool himself that he was doing anything else. The truth-in-memory debates that plague us at the end of the twentieth century may seem, by comparison with Freud's agony and Janet's complacency, like unrewarding recapitulations of bygone battles. The reason that we repeat ourselves may be that we are locked in to an underlying structure created in those twelve years, 1874–1886, when knowledge about memory became a surrogate for spiritual understanding of the soul. The psychologization of trauma is an essential part of that structure, because the spiritual travail of the soul, which so long served a previous ontology, could now become hidden psychological pain, not the result of sin that seduces us within, but caused by the sinner outside who seduced us. Trauma was a pivot upon which this revolution turned.

Trauma had been made psychological when Janet published his first insights into psychological trauma in the *Revue philosophique* of 1887. In that very year, in a different part of Europe, a very different kind of man was completing *On the Genealogy of Morals*. You can usually count on Nietzsche to be a prescient observer and analyst:

> "Psychological pain" does not by itself seem to me to be a definite fact, but on the contrary only an interpretation—a causal interpretation—of a collection of phenomena that cannot be exactly formulated—it is really only a fat word standing in place of a skinny question mark.[39]

Was not Nietzsche in another world, culturally, linguistically, intellectually, morally, from those who toiled in Paris on the lowly fields of memory? Not at all. He may well have read Janet's essays, which were published in Ribot's journal, *Revue philosophique*. He certainly had read Ribot himself, for he paraphrased, almost word for word, chunks of Ribot's *Les maladies de la mémoire* in the Genealogy of Morals.[40]

The Sciences of Memory

I NOW WISH to advance four theses. They are difficult in themselves; their interconnections are yet more difficult. Here and in the next chapter I propose a way in which to understand the events I have been describing, both old and recent. Here are the theses, in capsule form.

1. The sciences of memory were new in the latter part of the nineteenth century, and with them came new kinds of truths-or-falsehoods, new kinds of facts, new objects of knowledge.

2. Memory, already regarded as a criterion of personal identity, became a scientific key to the soul, so that by investigating memory (to find out its facts) one would conquer the spiritual domain of the soul and replace it by a surrogate, knowledge about memory.

3. The facts that are discovered in this or that science of memory are a surface knowledge; beneath them is the depth knowledge, that there are facts about memory to be found out.

4. Subsequently, what would previously have been debates on the moral and spiritual plane took place at the level of factual knowledge. These political debates all presuppose and are made possible by this depth knowledge.

The idea of surface and depth knowledge is patterned after what Michel Foucault called *connaissance* and *savoir*. Foucault defined *savoir* as "a group of elements that would have to be formed by a discursive practice if a scientific discourse was to be constituted, specified not only by its form and rigor, but also by the objects with which it deals, the types of enunciation [roughly, statement] that it uses, the concepts that it manipulates, and the strategies that it employs." As an example, he wrote that the *savoir* of psychiatry in the nineteenth century is not the sum of what was thought to be true, but "the whole set of practices, singularities, and deviations of which one could speak in psychiatric discourse."[1] Depth knowledge may not be known to anyone; it is more like a grammar, an underlying set of rules that determine, in this case, not what is grammatical, but what is up for grabs as true-or-false. Particular items counted as true, or as false, are *connaissance*, or what I call surface knowledge. My adjective "surface" is not intended to demean all our ordinary knowledge by implying that it is only on the surface, while there is something deeper that we ought to know. I pattern the terminology on Chomsky's depth and surface grammar. Surface grammar is, for example, the grammar of English, which, you might say, is what matters. Some critics of Chomsky would say there is no such thing as depth grammar, and some critics of Foucault would say there is no such thing as his *savoir*. I use surface knowledge as an analytical idea, not to make a value judgment about kinds of knowledge.

This is not the place to substantiate my four theses for all the sciences of memory. There is a complex tale to tell about each one. Despite our deep programmatic commitment to the unity of science, there is not very much practical overlap between the sciences of memory. Think of (a) the neurological studies of the location of different types of memory; (b) experimental studies of recall; and (c) what might be called the psychodynamics of memory, which even Freud-haters can never entirely separate from Freud's work. The word "dynamic" in psychology and psychiatry has had a checkered history.[2] I mean the study of memory in terms of observed or conjectured psychological processes and forces.

All three of these sciences of memory are creatures of the nineteenth century. Only neurology has been deeply affected by high-technology advances in the twentieth century: we really can do things to brains of which nineteenth-century neurologists could only dream. To the three old sciences of memory we should add two twentieth-century branches of science. First, there is (d), work at the level of cell biology, transmission across potassium channels and the like. The ambition is certainly to join this together with (a), to provide an account, at the level of the cell and smaller, of the storage and transmission of information in different parts of the brain. Finally, we might add (e), computer modeling of memory in artificial intelligence, parallel distributive processing, and other branches of cognitive science.

These five kinds of science are *connaissance*, surface knowledge, that take for granted the objects they investigate. To call them surface is in no way to demean them. They matter in different ways. Some, whose present ratio of practical application to theoretical knowledge or speculation approaches one to infinity, may in the future change our daily lives. Funding agencies act on such hopes: there is nothing like a paragraph about Alzheimer's disease to increase the probability that your application for a cell biology research grant on ion channels will succeed. Nevertheless, the psychodynamics of memory is the only knowledge, of the three old sciences of memory that I have mentioned, that has profoundly influenced Western culture. Laboratory work on recall continues in a thousand departments of experimental psychology today. It has given us certain phrases of common speech—who does not know of short- and long-term memory? Yet its chief function, from a larger point of view, may be to shore up the depth knowledge, the conviction we do not state, that there is a body of facts about memory to be known.

I shall argue my four theses only in connection with (c), the psychodynamic approach to memory, which is, of course, a central aspect of therapy for multiple personality. But I would not want to fixate only on the ephemeral political battles of the moment, the brouhaha over false memory, for example. Memory has always had political or ideological overtones, but each epoch has found its own meaning in memory. Sometimes we can be quite nonplussed at what our predecessors have said. Let us take an example from my critical twelve years, 1874–1886. How could a lecture on memory perfectly enshrine the social pecking order of its day? On 12 July 1879 a talk to the Société de Biologie in Paris did exactly that.[3] A Dr. Delannay told his audience that:

— People from the inferior races of modern times have better memories than those from the superior races. Blacks, Chinese, Italians, and Russians have a remarkable talent for learning languages (presumably, for learning French or English).

— The adult woman has a better memory than the man. Actresses learn their lines better and more quickly than actors. In undergraduate studies, female students do better than men.

— Adolescents have a better memory than adults. Memory is at its greatest powers at thirteen years of age and diminishes thereafter.

— The weak have a better memory than the strong. Memory is better among the less intelligent than the more intelligent. Children who get prizes for reciting from memory are less intelligent than others.

— The students at the Ecole Normale or at Val-de-Grâce—the school for military doctors—who have the best memories are not the most intelligent.

— Provincials have better memories than Parisians. Peasants have better memories than city-dwellers.

— Lawyers have better memories than doctors. Clerics have better memories than lay people.

— Musicians have better memories than other artists. One has better memory before eating than after. Education diminishes memory, in the sense that the illiterate have better memories than those who know how to write. One has a better memory in the morning than in the evening, in summer than in winter, in the south than in the north.

That pretty well covers the waterfront. Memory is an objective indicator of inferiority. An anticlerical physician has put priests and attorneys in their place, suitably ranked along with all the rest of humanity.

Delannay's statement cheerfully combined the new sciences of memory and of anthropometry. Anthropometry—the name is due to Francis Galton (1822–1911)—was the measured and statistical part of anthropology. Anthropology was much occupied with comparisons between the different races of humankind, between subgroups within a region, and between the characteristics of the sexes. It generated measures of intelligence. Anthropology, sociology, and psychology were on the march, and part of the terrain they had to traverse was memory. This was the period when the sciences of memory came into being. The ideological bent of the nascent human sciences has been well chronicled, particularly in connection with racism and sexism. The political connotations of memory studies have not, however, been much noticed. But before we turn to these we should pause to confirm that the sciences of memory (a)–(c) were, in fact, new and not part of an old tradition.

One contrast between them and their predecessors is that between science and art, or between knowing that and knowing how. The new sciences of memory provided new knowledge *that*, as opposed to the art of memory, which taught us *how* to remember. No art was more carefully studied, or esteemed, from Plato until the Enlightenment, than the art of memory. Or perhaps we had better say the art of memorizing. This art was a collection of techniques or technologies of memory, variously called *De arte memorativa, memoria technica*, mnemonics.[4] Plato and Aristotle refer often to one part of this art, particularly to a form of it that is translated as "placing." A more helpful name is supplied by Mary Carruthers: architectural mnemonics.[5] In the mind one forms the image of a three-dimensional space, a well-furnished house or even an entire city. Do you wish to remember that printing was invented in 1436? Then place a book in the thirty-sixth memory place in the fourth room of the first house in town. Cicero thought that such techniques, which survived long after the invention of printing, were of the highest importance, above all to the orator. Memory was also conceived of as essential to the formation of moral character; memory was highly ethical. The art of memory did languish until what are called the High Middle Ages. The greatest schoolmen, such as Thomas Aquinas, were marvels of memory. Carruthers argues for a complex relationship between books and memory; in many cases books were not the final, objective authorities that they later became, but mere adjuncts to the art of memory. The architectural mnemonic demanded rigorous discipline and regimens. One had to practice the building of houses and cities in the head, and learn how best to arrange things so that one could always be sure of where one had placed each object to be remembered. Texts were remembered in this way. Any competent scholar had an immense database stored in architectural mnemonics. Usually he could not go off to the library to check a citation or saying, but he had no need to do so. It was in his head.

Three things will be noticed. First, the art of memory had a central role in the ancient world, the High Middle Ages, and the Renaissance. Expertise in this art conferred great stature; it was a political asset. In the time of Cicero, it was an art for the orator, most esteemed of men. In the time of Aquinas, it was for the scholar. Carruthers makes a telling suggestion: "*Memoria* can be considered as one of the modalities of medieval culture (chivalry might be another)."[6] It was, like chivalry, only for some, and its applications are limited to the highest pursuits. The ideological potential of "memory" was hardly an invention of 1879—only its content changed. Memory was for the elite, and yet, like chivalry, it permeated the world. *Memoria*, Carruthers continues, "is also a value in itself, identified with the virtue of prudence. As modalities, values enable certain behavior, and also give greater privilege to some behavior over others."

Second, the art of memory was truly a *techne*, a knowing how, and not a knowing that. It was not a science that delivered knowledge about some object of study, "the memory." Third, the art of memory is outer-directed. It is at most incidentally concerned with remembering one's own experiences. The whole point is to provide instant recall of any body of desired facts, things, or texts. One arranges external material in a vivid picture in one's mind, to which one has direct access. Perhaps what we call computer memory, with its numerous technologies, is the lineal descendant of the art of memory. There is something linguistically adventitious about this. Every language carves the memory ideas into different groupings of words. In German neither *Erinerrung* nor *Gedächtnis* would serve at all for the memory of a computer, so the word is simply *Speicher*, storehouse. Medievals commonly used the metaphor of the storehouse for memory.

The art of memory waned during the Enlightenment, but it was not replaced by another art or science. Mnemonics were still taught yet were not invested with any moral authority or stature. Of course people did not lose interest in memory. One of the most moving statements about memory and its recovery—flashbacks, even—was penned by a most unlikely author, John Locke:

> The Mind very often sets it self on work in search of some hidden *Idea*, and turns, as it were, the Eye of the Soul upon it; though sometimes too they start up in our Minds of their own accord, and offer themselves to the Understanding; and very often are rouzed and tumbled out of their dark Cells into open Day-light, by some turbulent and tempestuous Passion; our affections bringing *Ideas* to our Memory, which had otherwise lain quiet and unregarded.[7]

In Locke's day there was no systematic attempt to uncover facts about memory. That began only late in the nineteenth century. Of course for every predecessor there is a predecessor. The localization project of neurology derives in part from phrenology, which located mental faculties and abilities by means of bumps on the skull. But only in 1861 did an anatomist open up a brain and identify a lesion with the loss of a mental faculty. That was Paul Broca (1824–1880). "We have every reason to believe that, in this case, the lesion of the frontal lobe was the cause of the loss of language."[8] (It will be recalled from chapter 11 that three years earlier Broca had enthusiastically tried out Azam's hypnotism in an actual surgical operation on an abscess.) Broca continued his work on localization until his death, but he was also enormously active in French anthropology, which was, in the first instance, very much a study of race and races. We remember him for Broca's region, the motor speech center of the brain. Broca successfully began the great neurological program, still with us, of locating different faculties in different parts of the brain. Broca's discovery generated enthusiastic research. Historians find the next landmark in Carl Wernicke's identification of another region in which words (or word images) are stored. This could be regarded as the first delineation of a part of the brain that serves as a specific type of memory bank. If a single essay pulled all this together, it was Ludwig Lichtheim's 1885 study of aphasia.[9] I should emphasize that this is an anatomical, physiological program, which we call neurological because the part of the body that is examined is the brain.

Now let us turn to the second science of memory, namely, recall. In 1879 Hermann Ebbinghaus (1850–1909) established a new paradigm for psychological research. It was far from the first experimental psychology. For example, Gustav Fechner's psychophysics transformed the experimental investigation of the relationship between body and mind. Fechner (1801–1887) discovered empirical laws about the least differences in pairs of weights that could be discerned by an experimental subject. There was experimentation in Germany before Fechner, and a great deal after. Nevertheless, Kurt Danziger plausibly takes Ebbinghaus to have inaugurated psychology as a laboratory science of measurement. "All the fundamental features of the measurement of psychological capacity were first manifested in Hermann Ebbinghaus's classical work on memory."[10] Ebbinghaus's research became public in 1885 with a major book, *On Memory*.[11]

Ebbinghaus wanted to study memory in its pure form, uncontaminated by other kinds of knowledge. So he experimented on the recall of nonsense syllables. Why is this so important? David Murray asserts that G. E. Müller (1850–1934) was far more influential, because he pioneered the interference theory of forgetting, and because Ebbinghaus himself was so entirely empirical, not speculating on the mechanisms of memory.[12] Why then has Danziger singled out Ebbinghaus as a "first," comparable to Broca? Aside from the great revolutionaries in the sciences, "firsts" are picked not so much for the importance of their contribution as for the way that they conveniently mark, for us, a new departure. The critical feature of Ebbinghaus's work was that he instituted statistical treatment of data. Memory was to be investigated in the context of the subject's ability to recall a series of nonsense syllables. Then one was to construct a statistical analysis of the ability to recall. Ebbinghaus began work on himself, a typical human being, but his behavior was to be understood only through statistical scrutiny. His approach became standard, integrated with learning theory. Whole cohorts of research psychologists have devoted their entire careers to continuing in the footsteps of Ebbinghaus. Few journals of experimental psychology will even consider refereeing a research paper that does not include a battery of statistical tests. Here, then, we have a remarkable conjunction: the first sustained study of recall and the first sustained use of statistical analysis in psychology.[13] If Broca conveniently marks the start of the anatomical science of memory, Ebbinghaus conveniently marks the start of the statistical science of memory.

For my purposes, the anatomical and statistical studies of memory are only asides, which is why I hang them on standard historical pegs like Broca and Ebbinghaus. In contrast, we have been immersed in psychodynamics from the start, and as soon as you go into detail there are no firsts. Instead I shall choose a figure who serves as an ideal type—one of many who well displays the third new science of memory. In 1879 Théodule Ribot, in Paris, gave a set of lectures on the diseases of memory. They were published in 1881, the first of a trio of books on diseases—of memory, of the will (1883), and of the personality (1885).[14] Coincidences abound: Ribot began lecturing on the topics that formed this sequence in Paris, in 1879, the year that Ebbinghaus, in Leipzig, began his memory experiments. He completed the trio in 1885, the year that Ebbinghaus published his results, and the year that Lichtheim brought together the state of the art on localization of brain function, including memory of words. Annual coincidences mean nothing in themselves, but we may begin to get a picture of three relatively unconnected sciences of memory driving on at about the same time, and at about the same pace.

The sciences take different courses in different institutional settings, and in different cultural or national environments. The development of psychology in France was very different from that in Germany or America. The French route was medical and pathological.[15] As a result the Parisian study of memory was the study of forgetting. Michael Roth has written elegantly about deeper French cultural meanings in the medical fascination with forgetting and nostalgia.[16] He notes that although most of Ribot's book is about forgetting, it concludes with a curious chapter on hypermnesia, too much memory, which was thought to be pathological. So he sees Ribot's text as almost a moral tract, intent to define the amount of memory that is just right.

Roth's analysis of the book's subtext is insightful, but more mundane facts of institutional history should also be taken into account. Danziger opens his book with a striking insight: In Germany and America experimental psychology patterned itself on experimental physiology; it was even called "physiological psychology."[17] The situation was entirely different in France. Psychiatry had always been a major feature of French medicine, ever since Pinel "liberated the asylums" at the end of the eighteenth century. The charismatic influence of the neurologist Charcot, from early in the 1870s until his death in 1893, made the connections between mind, brain, and mental illness central to scientific study.

Hence when one took up the psychological study of memory in Paris, in the 1870s, one could hardly fail to start with its pathologies, with forgetting and amnesia.

The effect was not entirely confined to France. The United States was in those days eclectically open to all new scientific ideas from anywhere in Europe. The article "Memory" in Baldwin's classic *Dictionary of Philosophy and Psychology* (1901) is only half as long as the article "Memory, defects of." The latter chiefly focuses on amnesia. The word "amnesia," or rather *amnésie*, was used in French in 1771, in the translation from the Latin of Sauvages's immensely influential nosology, or classification, of all diseases.[18] From the beginning the word named a medical disorder, a potential object of knowledge. But it was not an important research field until the 1870s. Then it became central to the new French science of memory.

As my "ideal type" for this new science I wanted to choose a figure who was not a pathologist or neurologist, and I wanted someone who was prepared not only to state facts but also to discuss method. That is why I chose Ribot, by training a philosopher. Since I single him out, I must make plain that his positive views about memory (as opposed to forgetting) were trite. He was a loyal disciple of British associationist psychology, acknowledging his debt to Scottish authors on the first page of his book.[19] He usefully insisted that we should not be talking about memory, as if there were just one faculty, but about "memories" (*mémoires*). But this is only a deduction from the claims that different types of acquired abilities, skills, and knowledge are stored in different parts of the brain. On the relations between mind and brain, Ribot was no more, and no less, programmatic than most other positivist or scientistic writers of the day. "Memory," he wrote, "is essentially a biological fact, accidentally a psychological fact."[20] He took the unconscious (*l'inconscient*) very seriously, and in ways very different from Eduard von Hartmann's massive and massively romantic *Philosophy of the Unconscious* of 1869.[21] But he did so only as part of his purely speculative neurophysiology. Consciousness comprised certain events in the nervous system (especially "discharges," in the parlance of the day) that endured more than a certain finite time. Events of the same type, but briefer, were unconscious. "The brain is like a laboratory full of movement, where thousands of tasks are performed at once. Unconscious cerebration, not being subject to the condition of time, takes place, so to speak, only in space, and may act in several places at once. Consciousness is the narrow gate through which a very small part of this work appears to us."[22] Such talk of the unconscious was so common in his day that it would be foolish to see Ribot as anticipating Janet's idea of the subconscious, or Janet's word *sous-conscience*. Janet himself used the word *inconscient* in the psychological essays preceding his *Psychological Automatism* of 1889. At that point he coined the name "subconscious" to separate himself from the tradition of Hartmann that still persisted in Germany.

Ribot held the chair of experimental and comparative psychology at the Collège de France. Recall how Pierre Janet, Ribot's successor in this chair, said (with some exaggeration), "But for Félida, it is not certain that there would be a professorship at the Collège de France and that I should be here speaking to you of the mental state of hystericals." In chapter 11 I said a little about French positivism, as argued by powerful cultural leaders such as Hippolyte Taine and Emile Littré. Theirs was the 1870s model, popular as a response to inglorious defeat by Prussia; it was republican and secular. Ribot was forthright in subscribing to their school of thought. He subtitled his 1881 book on memory *An Essay in the Positive Psychology*. In that book he discussed "the detailed and instructive observations of Dr. Azam." After describing work on *dédoublement*, he wrote:

> Let us first reject the idea of a *moi* conceived as an entity distinct from states of consciousness. That is a useless and contradictory hypothesis; it is an explanation worthy of a psychology in its infancy, which takes as simple that which appears simple, and which postulates instead of explaining. I join in the opinion of contemporaries who see the conscious person as a compound, a resultant of very complex states.[23]

Ribot went on to explain that there are two ways to consider the *moi*. As the *moi* appears to itself, it is a collection of present states of consciousness and may be compared to a present visual field. But "this *moi* of each moment, this present perpetually renewed is in large part fed by memory. . . . In a word, the *moi* can be considered in two ways: either in its actual form, and then it is the sum of actual states of consciousness; or in its continuity with its past, and then it is formed by memory."[24]

Ribot began his next book but one, on diseases of the personality, by saying, "It is but natural that the representatives of the old school, slightly bewildered at the situation [in psychology], should accuse the adherents of the new school of 'stealing their *moi*.'"[25] The "old school" was, as explained in chapter 11, the so-called eclectic spiritualism of Victor Cousin. The strategy of Ribot and his positivist colleagues was not to attack religious or philosophical ideas of the soul, but to provide a surrogate for the one aspect of a human being that seemed resistant to science. Instead of studying a unitary *moi*, we should study memory. But how do we know that there is no unitary self? The cases of *dédoublement*, Félida and her successors, seemed splendid for showing that a person was not constituted by a single transcendental, metaphysical or spiritual self or ego. For in those individuals, there was not one single self. Those individuals had two personalities, each connected by a continuous or normal chain of memories, aside from amnesic gaps. At least one personality was ignorant of the other. Hence (it seemed) there were two persons, two souls in one body.

The use of doubles to refute the idea of a transcendental ego was more rhetorical than logical. The rhetoric succeeded by changing the ground on which to think about the soul. The soul was the last bastion of thought free of scientific scrutiny. To be sure, there had long been mechanical models of the human being, including such as that presented in La Mettrie's scandalous book published in Holland in 1747, *Man a Machine*. The French positivists undoubtedly believed that all psychology would in the end have a neurological foundation. That was a commonplace, shared, for example, by Freud and by many of his German-speaking predecessors. The importance of Ribot and his peers was not that they had a program but that they offered knowledge. It was new knowledge, scientific knowledge about memory. Real knowledge, scientific laws about memory, even what is still called "Ribot's law." This law is a perfect example of surface knowledge, a statement about how the memory faculties decay, presupposing that those faculties are objects of a certain sort. His own name for the law was the law of regression or reversion. "The progressive destruction of the memory," owing to whatever pathology, "follows a logical order, a law. *It advances progressively from the unstable to the stable.*" Memories and skills acquired early are the stable ones, while the more recent are more unstable. His evidence was taken from various types of amnesia, including traumatic amnesia and dementia in senility. He held his law to be universal, to be applicable to any type of memory loss. His law seemed to him "to follow from facts, and to demand recognition as an objective truth."[26] I consign his own statement of the law to a note.[27] Our concern is the kind of law that it purports to be. It is an objective truth. It follows from facts. The facts in question are from pathological psychiatry. It is a law about loss of memory, about forgetting. Finally, the law covers, in a uniform way, both forgetting caused by physical lesions, and forgetting caused by psychic shock. Thus it covers trauma in the old sense of the word, and trauma in the about-to-be (this is 1881) sense of the word. When you stand back, ignoring the content of Ribot's law and looking only at its form, you see that it foreshadows the form of almost all subsequent dynamic psychiatry.

I am not saying that Ribot is a precursor of Freud, the modern multiple movement, or whatever. I am saying that he is an early instance of a man whose surface knowledge is worked out within the rules of that underlying depth knowledge which remains the depth knowledge to this very day. One feature of the modern sensibility is dazzling in its implausibility: the idea that what has been forgotten is what forms our character, our personality, our soul. Where did we get that idea? To grasp this we need to reflect on how knowledge about memory became possible late in the nineteenth century. What were the new sciences of memory trying to do? Find out, of course, and more power to them. But although I have argued the case for only one of the new sciences, I suggest that they all emerged as surrogate sciences of the soul, empirical sciences, positive sciences that would provide new kinds of knowledge in terms of which to cure, help, and control the one aspect of human beings that had hitherto been outside science. If we address only the surface facts about memory, the politicization of memory will seem only a curious accident. But if we think of how the very idea of such facts came into being, the battles may seem almost inevitable.

Memoro-Politics

IT HAS BECOME commonplace to speak of a politics of this or that or almost anything. Such generous usage strips the word of much meaning. But talk of a politics of memory is no metaphor. The confrontations between the False Memory Syndrome Foundation and various schools of recovered memory therapy are plainly political. The annual "drumming out child abuse" in Washington, at the Eastern Meeting of the ISSMP&D, is a political manifesto. Conference attendees are urged to bring drums, and, of a spring evening, demonstrate in order to influence lawmakers. The professed target of this event is child abuse, but its direct object is more along the lines of the "Believe the Children" bumper stickers. Memories, especially memories elicited during work with therapists, are to be believed. There are many more political demonstrations. For example, the organization Crimes against Children held a major lobbying event in Washington on 17 September 1993. It grimly warned of an unnamed menace: the conference "has received much adverse publicity from obvious individuals and organizations who do not want an aggressive agenda on crimes against children." The event was to be led by U.S. attorney general of the previous administration, Edwin Meese.

There are perhaps two kinds of politics of memory, the personal and the communal. A large photograph of a holocaust monument is captioned "Horror Unforgotten: The Politics of Memory." Communal memory has always played a major role in group identity. Almost any identifiable people has tales of origin. There is the genesis of the universe, and after that, the birth of *the* people. Many names that the West translates as the name of an ethnic stock are better translated simply as "people"—Bantu, for example. Or literally "People of people," the Khoikhoi whom Europeans called "Bushmen" or "Hottentots." Each such people has its own communal memory, its own chronicles, its own heroic odes. Group memory helps define the group. It becomes encoded in ritual. At a solemn moment in every Jewish wedding, a glass is broken in remembrance of the destruction of the Temple. "Do this in memory of me," Christ instructed his disciples at the Last Supper, reenacted at every subsequent Mass or Holy Communion.

It is possible, but by no means certain, that there is a distinct type of politics of remembering associated with what used to be called Peoples of the Book, that is, peoples, ethnic or cultural, who in part identify themselves through a sacred text. This includes adherents of the religions that arose in the Fertile Crescent: Judaism, the faith of Mani, Christianity, Islam. The sacred text, in each case, is solidified memory, and each text is further enshrined in endless commentary. Peoples of the Book keep on adding supplementary documents of memory. That is one distanced way to regard the rich flow of memories of the camps: even when they are memories of personal suffering, they are situated within an almost timeless communal practice of remembering, of preserving the story of the people.

Holocaust memories are unusual in that they are directed both inward and outward. Inward, to the group whose memory of suffering it is, and outward, to Gentiles, especially Westerners who must never forget that their culture (my culture) must take responsibility for the genocide. Yet despite the fact that the memory of every people has its own character, we shall not be misled if, briefly, we think in anthropological terms, and hold group memories to be among the ways in which group identity and difference are cemented. From that perspective, the holocaust politics of memory is an instance of an age-old human practice. The politics of personal memories is, in contrast, relatively new. My discussion of the politics of memory will be one-sided, because I am preoccupied by the question of how the politics of personal memory came into being. In no way do I deny that there are interconnections between group memory and personal memory. One obvious link is trauma. The science of traumatic stress teaches that individual concentration camp survivors, and by extension their progeny, suffer from the psychological effects of trauma very much as the victims of child abuse do. But this seems to be a one-way projection. That is, holocaust memories would have become part of group memory, and there would be an associated politics, even if traumatology never existed, and even if there had never arisen, late in the nineteenth century, the sciences of memory. But the politics of personal memory, I contend, could not have arisen without those sciences. Hence although there is much to be learned from the interactions between group and personal memory, it is the latter that we have to examine.

The politics of personal memory is a politics of a certain type. It is a power struggle built around knowledge, or claims to knowledge. It takes for granted that a certain sort of knowledge is possible. Individual factual claims are batted back and forth, claims about this patient, that therapist, combined with larger views about vice and virtue. Underlying these competing claims to surface knowledge there is a depth knowledge; that is, a knowledge that there are facts out there about memory, truth-or-falsehoods to get a fix on. There would not be politics of this sort if there were not that assumption of knowledge about memory, known to science. Power struggles are fought out on the basis of surface knowledge, where opponents take the depth knowledge as common ground. Each side opposes the other, claiming it has better, more exact, surface knowledge, drawing on superior evidence and methodology. That is exactly the form of the confrontations between those who recover memory of trauma and those who question it.

Could one see things in reverse, as politics making prominent what would otherwise be items from obscure sciences of memory? Judith Herman appears to do so in her book, *Trauma and Recovery*. She is explicit about the role of politics: "Three times over the past century, a particular form of psychological trauma has surfaced into public consciousness. Each time the investigation of that trauma has flourished in affiliation with a political movement."[1] Her three examples are hysteria, shell shock, and sexual and domestic violence. She rightly states that the study of sensational hysteria, whose epitome is Charcot's *grande hystérie*, was associated with the "republican, anticlerical political movement of the nineteenth century in France." In fact she says that it "grew out of" that movement, possibly an overstatement. She sees the development of shell shock into post-traumatic stress disorder in the "political context of the collapse of a cult of war and the growth of an antiwar movement." Finally, the political context for awareness of sexual and domestic violence is feminism.

Herman's linkages are plain to see; it is up to historians to round out and nuance each of these three complex stories. What underlies all three of these is memory, memory of trauma, although the relationship to remembered trauma is different in each case. Freud famously came to the opinion that hysterical patients suffer from reminiscences. Post-traumatic stress disorder has been entirely incorporated into the science of memory. There is, in contrast, a great deal of sexual and domestic violence that needs no memory: it is going on right now, and its evidence is bruises, blood, swollen lips, broken bones, and the stalking patterns of jilted husbands or lovers. Nevertheless, when we turn to Herman's side of that violence, namely, trauma, it is trauma remembered or forgotten that is central.

Herman's three political movements—French republicanism, antiwar, and feminism—are prominent features in the history of Western Europe and America. Each could have come into being and left its permanent marks without ever having had recourse to memory. My question is: why did questions of memory become so central to those aspects of all three of Herman's examples? I argue that each of the three made use of a politics of memory deeply embedded in the new sciences of memory that emerged a century or more ago. They were able to do so precisely because of the way in which those sciences proposed to wrest the soul from religion and turn it over to science. Moral confrontations could thus be made scientific, objective, impersonal—or so it seemed. My thesis is altogether consistent with what Herman writes, but it reverses the direction of her inquiry. She sees the study of trauma, especially forgotten trauma, as arising within three political movements. I see the way in which those movements latched on to trauma as part of a politics of memory legitimated by, indeed made possible by, the new sciences of memory. Although the sciences and the politics mutually interact, it is the underlying depth knowledge—that there are certain sorts of truths about memory and forgetting—that makes the politics possible.

The politicization of memory can be analyzed at many different levels. I do not claim that depth knowledge is the only story. I do claim that it has served as an essential backdrop to other events. It is to be expected that a full understanding of the phenomena must also involve more specific and local events than the sciences of memory. Many interests are in play, and the casual observer can distinguish many centers of power or subversion that seem central. Many wings of feminism, with their emphasis on survivors of incest and other forms of family violence, find in the recall of past evil a critical source of empowerment. Sects of Protestant fundamentalism impressed by tales of satanic ritual abuse, and of programming by diabolical cults, rely on the restoration of buried memory. Many people are hostile to both of these important social groupings. Almost no one is attracted by both militant feminism and militant fundamentalism, for these two have entirely different class allegiances and geographical distributions. Yet their differences should not conceal what their adherents take for granted. They all suppose that there is knowledge of memory to be had.

Why is it that the battles so often take place over what has been forgotten, in particular, over the terrain of forgotten pain? Forgetting, rather than ordinary remembering, is the present locus of memoro-politics. But I must clarify. First, we are not concerned with what we may think of as the erosion of memory, which we experience as events slip away into the past. Even "erosion" is a loaded metaphor, because it suggests a lump of material that gradually gets worn away by time and indifference. Memory in this sense has to do not with a thing but with an ability to recall, and without rehearsal we tend to become less and less able to recall the detail or even the order of older events. We also, without rehearsal, begin to falter over all those poems we learned when we first went courting or were forced to memorize in school. That is the erosion of ability, and not a topic of memoro-politics at all. Memoro-politics is above all a politics of the secret, of the forgotten event that can be turned, if only by strange flashbacks, into something monumental. It is a forgotten event that, when it is brought to light, can be memorialized in a narrative of pain. We are concerned less with losing information than with hiding it. The background for memoro-politics is pathological forgetting—literally pathological, referring to the nineteenth-century pathologies so familiar to Théodule Ribot and his contemporaries.

I have coined the term memoro-politics, but readers of Michel Foucault's *History of Sexuality* will know that I pattern it on his anatomo-politics and bio-politics. These were his names for "two poles of development linked together by a whole intermediary cluster of relations," two forms of power over life that (he claimed) came into existence in the seventeenth century.

> One of these poles—the first to be formed, it seems,—centered on the body as a machine: its disciplining, the optimization of its capabilities, the extortion of its forces . . . , all this was ensured by the procedures of power that characterized the *disciplines*: an *anatomo-politics of the human body*. The second, formed somewhat later, focused on the species body, the body imbued with the mechanics of life and serving as the basis of the biological processes: propagation. . . . Their supervision was effected through an entire series of interventions and *regulatory controls: a bio-politics of the population*.[2]

Foucault wrote of "an explosion of numerous and diverse techniques for achieving the subjugation of bodies and the control of populations, marking the beginning of an era of 'bio-power.'" When Foucault speaks of power he does not mean power exercised from above. The power of which Foucault wanted to speak runs through our lives; you and I are part of its exercise.

Each of Foucault's two pairs of power and politics had its own surface knowledges. For bio-power, there was biology and knowledge of the

population and the species, which in turn engendered the specific technologies of statistics. For anatamo-power, there was anatomy and
knowledge of the body. Thus each pole has three aspects: power, politics, and science. What about the sciences of memory? Using the results
of the previous chapter, we can say that the program of localization of
brain function, marked by Broca's identification of motor control of
speech, was a late appearance at the anatamo-pole. Experimental psychology may have begun in the physiology laboratory, once again part
of anatamo-knowledge, but with Ebbinghaus, when it became a statistical science, it no longer concerned itself with individual events or beings
but with averages and deviations. It was part of the generalized bio-pole
(a generalization that makes free with Foucault's own use of the "bio,"
but which in fact captures the essence of his "regulatory controls").

I propose to augment Foucault's two poles, anatamo- and bio-. What
is missing is pretty obvious. It is the mind, the psyche, the soul. Foucault
spoke of "two poles of development linked together by a whole cluster
of relations." On the next page he mentioned two initially distinct directions for the development of bio-power during the eighteenth century,
discipline and demography. The metaphor of poles and intermediary relations hardly gets at the complexities, yet I have found it useful to adapt
it. What I call memoro-politics is a third extreme point from which (to
continue the metaphor of mapping and surveying) we can triangulate
recent knowledge. But I cannot talk about three poles (the globe, after
all, has only two) unless I make a gross pun. I grow my runner beans—
pole beans—on a tripod made of three poles. The lush growth at the
top, as the beans planted around each pole tangle with the others, is the
richest image of Foucault's "cluster of intermediary relations."

Anatomo-politics *of the human body*; bio-politics *of the population*,
wrote Foucault. What is memoro-politics a politics of? Of the self, the
"subject" or the human mind? Or of those substantivized personal pronouns, *ego, moi*? I prefer to say a memoro-politics of the human soul, an
idea that invokes character, reflective choice, and self-understanding,
among much else. The idea of the soul—whether understood in my secular way or in others—is by no means a human universal. Ideas of soul,
earthly or spiritual, do permeate the European background in which
memoro-politics emerged. Other peoples don't have anything like the
historically situated notion of the soul that I have inherited from my
culture. Good for them. Other peoples don't have memoro-politics or
multiple personality disorder either.

It has been protested that European ideas of the soul are part of an oppressive, perhaps even patriarchal system.[3] I am sure there is much truth in that. Within various bits and pieces of the Western tradition, conceptions of the soul have been used to maintain a great many hierarchies and have had a central role in power plays. The soul has been a way of internalizing the social order, of putting into myself those very virtues and cruelties that enabled a society to endure. That is a thoroughly functionalist view of the soul, in the sense of the sociologists. That is, it is suggested that the idea of the soul serves a function in the society, even though those who want or accept the idea do not self-consciously know what the function is. The idea of the soul persists because it helps to maintain public order. That is its unintended function. A further factor is important to functionalist explanations: feedback.[4] When life seems parlous and a Western society is about to fall apart, there is a great talk of reviving the soul in its various manifestations, and if not the soul, then the values of the family. I agree with this sketch of a functionalist analysis, to some extent, but I am not unnerved. To expose a function is not to undermine a value, but to enrich understanding. And now, when family values are supposed to be in crisis, we hear talk not of the soul explicitly, but of its scientific stand-in, memory.

The centrality of the soul in the Western tradition is well illustrated by the fact that one can so quickly place it by allusions to either Plato or Aristotle. Most of our other ideas and sentiments—both in and on either side of what is now called modernity—ride more cheerfully with one camp or the other, but the soul mingles gladly with Platonists and Aristotelians, with sophists and Sapphists, with Ryle and Sartre. The soul undoubtedly makes us think of religion, but Western intellectuals have become more Athenian than Christian. We certainly are not overtly Cartesian; we do not profess a principled and ultimate distinction between soul and body. But we are a bit too prim and self-satisfied about that. I have always liked to annoy people by pointing out similarities between sayings of Descartes and Wittgenstein.[5] Those similarities exist in part because the soul has been so enduring in the Western vision of human beings and their place in nature.

What discipline aims at knowledge of the soul? We would expect it to be psychology, the science of mind, of the psyche. A cynic, doubting that psychology has taught us much, might still inquire: What has psychology done to the soul? Perhaps it invented an object on which it could experiment, instead of having to be a science of the soul. That is a theme of Danziger's history of psychology, of which I have made use already. His ambitious title, *Constructing the Subject*, implies a story about constructing the human subject as an object of study, and above all, as an object with attributes that can be measured. The book is not, however, a history of what everyone means by "psychology." Instead he tells us about what our university departments of psychology teach as psychology, and above all, the experimental psychology of measurement. That science quickly spread far beyond scholarly research; its measures of skill, intelligence, personal relationships, or child-parent bonding are the stock-in-trade of corporate personnel departments, prisons, schools, and maternity wards. Measurements of those quantities began in the psychology laboratory. They have a valid field of application in the larger world because they determine what is to be measured and counted as knowledge about the larger world. Danziger brought to the fore the institutional setting for the origins of German (and hence the world's) experimental psychology. Psychology patterned itself on physiology, on the study of the body. Its domain and its model, in terms of Foucault's poles, was the body. If the psychology laboratory had remained an adjunct or imitator of the old physiology laboratories, then, in terms of Foucault's poles, we would have been able to file it toward the anatomy side. But never is there more plainly an intermediary cluster of relations. It is certainly true that a great many studies connected with the mind are in fact directed at the body. Behaviorism, neurology, localized brain function, neurophilosophy, mood-altering drugs, or biochemical theories of mental maladies could all be regarded as sciences of the body. They lead to the exercise of anatomo-power, seen at its most extreme when disorderly minds are to be controlled by electroshock or chemicals. Of course we get *at* the soul this way, but we do so through knowledges of the body, through physiology and anatomy.

The second point for triangulating the soul is located at the level not of the body but of the population, the collection, the classification and enumeration of kinds of people. Here we have the politics of the species, of the human race as species to be categorized into its varieties—I use the word as did the horticulturists, seedsmen, and stockbreeders of old. The census takers and counters of every sort flood our panorama of humanity with new kinds of person.[6] The applied science that is the engine of bio-power is statistics. Experimental psychology may have begun by modeling itself on the physiology laboratory, but that was only the beginning, because it became a statistical science. This transition toward modern experimental psychology was set up in the memory laboratory of Ebbinghaus. It was precisely in the study of memory that laboratory psychology was transferred from the body to populations, from anatomo- to bio-, from the individual event to statistics. If we restrict the field of studies of the mind to Foucault's two poles, then at the foot of the anatomo-pole stands Broca, and at the foot of the bio-pole stands Ebbinghaus.

But are we not looking in the wrong place for a memoro-power? Should we not turn to biography? From Locke's exceptional point of view, the person is constituted not by a biography but by a remembered biography. We have had told "lives"—as in Plutarch's *Lives*, the lives of the saints, Aubrey's *Brief Lives*—for as long as we have had a written-down past. But those have been the lives of the exceptional. The typical life of a typical saint enjoins us against enthusiasm; the tale is told "more for our admiration than our emulation." Then there is the public confession. Augustine, Petrarch, Rousseau: might not each of us have confessed to such a life? No. Those are not ordinary folk. Where shall we locate the idea that everyone has a biography, even, or especially, the lowest of the low?

The image of biography is everywhere. A human life becomes conceived of as a story. A nation is thought of as its history. A species becomes an evolutionary object. A soul is a pilgrimage through life. A planet is thought of as Gaea. There are well-known suggestions about how the biography, the dossier, the medical or legal record became the life of the deviant, the lawbreaker, the mad person. If we are to look for the beginning of these dossiers, they and their role are described with surprising precision by their inventors. For example, in nineteenth-century England Thomas Plint said, in so many words, that once the criminals had been identified by their biographies, society would finally be able to protect itself.[7] Needless to say, identification—the hooking of a narrative onto a person in the dock—had in the end to be done by new technologies of anatomy, first ear-prints (standardized photographs of ears held in every police station in France) and then fingerprints—back to the body. We're still there, with DNA.

Likewise medical case histories, although used in the great eighteenth-century classificatory schemes of disease, did not flourish until the mid-nineteenth century. Part of the project, as Jan Goodstein puts it in the title of her book, was *To Console and Classify*.[8] But it was also to provide the life story of the patient. At first, what the patient said was no more to be trusted than what the criminal said. But even in 1859, not long after Plint had been telling London how to write the life stories of criminals, Paul Briquet in Paris was telling how to write the life stories of hysterical women.[9] Sometimes he indicated that these women had experienced terrible things early in life, even from their own fathers. Briquet's textbook on hysteria was the classic midcentury work. In retrospect we can go back to it and see a doctor horrified by what his female patients were telling him about their past.

Did memoro-politics emerge in the nineteenth century because of the systematic recording of the lives of utterly boring nonentities begun at midcentury? Those lives were written down only because they were a nuisance. Is memoro-politics a derivation from the recording in large ledgers of the lives of criminals, lives of men who usually lied about their past? Is that it, along with the simultaneous telling of the lives of disturbed women? Are these biographies of the unhappy, the ill, the deviant, the feared part of what so transformed modern mores, our present conception of who we are and what made us? Certainly such events are not irrelevant, but they are not central either. For example, whatever we find in Briquet's book, it was not, and I think could not have been, read in our way, in terms of child abuse, during his lifetime. Moreover, there was no question of forgetting. Briquet's patients knew all too well what had happened to them. Plint's criminals may have lied, but it was never suggested that they forgot. Forgetting may have been set up by new genres of biography, the medical case and the criminal record, and the recording of memories of deviant people. But something else was required to put forgetting in place: the sciences of memory, as they emerged and matured late in the nineteenth century.

I do not mean that we began to think about memory only late in the nineteenth century. The previous chapter dipped into the art of memory and listened to Locke's moving observation that episodes from the past "very often are roused and tumbled out of their dark cells into open daylight, by turbulent and tempestuous passions; our affections bringing ideas to our memories, which had otherwise lain quiet and unregarded." But there was little conception of a knowledge about memory before the nineteenth century. A century is a long period of time; so I have ruthlessly narrowed it down to a dozen years and called it 1874–1886. Certainly the generation that lived through that time had direct intellectual and practical predecessors. But that is when the depth knowledge, the knowledge that there are facts about memory, came into being. Why did it come into being then? Because the sciences of memory could serve as the public forum for something of which science could not openly speak. There could be no science of the soul. So there came to be a science of memory.

Our present power struggles about memory are formed within a space

of possibilities established in the nineteenth century. If one metaphorically speaks of the structure of the possible knowledges that we can have,
and which serve as the battlefield of our politics, they were put in place
at that time. Today, when we wish to have a moral dispute about spiritual matters, we democratically abjure subjective opinion. We move to
objective facts, science. The science is memory, a science crafted in my
chosen span of time, 1874–1886. We do not examine, any more,
whether incest is evil. To do so would be to talk about subjective values.
Instead we move to science and ask who remembers incest. About memory there can be objective scientific knowledge—or so we have been
schooled.

Mind and Body

DOES multiple personality matter to metaphysics? I do not think so. Metaphysics asks: What is a person, a soul, a self? It does not ask who I am, but what I am. What constitutes me as a person? One answer is well known to English empirical philosophy, for it is at least as old as John Locke. It is almost part of the general culture today: a person is constituted by consciousness and memory. Here is how it crops up in a popular science magazine: "The ability to retrieve a memory decays exponentially, and after only a month more than 85% of our experiences will have slipped beyond reach, unless boosted by artificial aids such as diaries and photographs. *Given that our memories are our identities*, this is a terrifying rate of loss."[1] It is easy enough to make fun of this. What? I'm losing my identity by the minute? Now that is terrifying! Or perhaps we should reach the opposite conclusion. Our memories are not (all there is to) our identities.

When did it first strike someone that multiple personality might be relevant to philosophical issues? The earliest example I have found is in a pithy editorial by Thomas Wakley, longtime editor of the British medical journal *The Lancet*. He began the issue of Saturday, 25 March 1843 by dismissing the philosophers addicted to pure reason and ignorant of matters of fact:

From the fact that the philosophy of the human mind has been almost wholly uncultivated by those who are best fitted for its pursuit, the study has received a wrong direction, and become a subtle exercise for lawyers and casuists, and abstract reasoners, rather than a useful field of scientific observation. Accordingly, we find the views, even of the most able and clear-headed metaphysicians, coming into frequent collision with the known facts of physiology and pathology. For example, that "consciousness is *single*" is an axiom among the mental philosophers, and the proof of *personal identity* is made by those gentlemen to rest chiefly on the supposed universality or certainty of that allegation. But what would they say to the case of a somnambulist who evinced what is regarded as double consciousness—the operation of the mind being perfectly distinct in the state of somnambulism from its developments in the wakeful condition?

> With reference to such an individual, the proof of *his* personal identity
> must rest with others, not with himself, for his memory in one state takes
> not the smallest cognisance of what he thought, felt, perceived, said, or
> did, in the other.[2]

Wakley refers to the Lockean tradition, but curiously, Locke himself
would be unmoved. For on his clearly stated criteria, we have one and
the same "man" (that is, woman), and two distinct persons. Now maybe
that is a preposterous conclusion, but it is what Locke would consistently have maintained. Locke himself was a physician who might well
have illustrated his theory of personal identity by the phenomenon of
double consciousness—but no doubles were reported in 1693. Somnambulism was familiar to Locke, but the person in the somnambulistic
state had not yet acquired the ability to conduct two distinct exis-
tences—or the physicians of the day had not yet discovered the ability to
cultivate such phenomena.

Was Wakley correct? Does double consciousness or multiple personality show anything about what it is to be a person, or about the human
mind, or about the nature of the self, or about the subject? I do not
think so, or at any rate, what it shows is only oblique. At most the progress of multiple personality in Western history teaches something about
what ordinary people or experts are prepared to say, and how they are
willing to interact with people of unsound mind. We do not find nature's illustrations of different possible conditions of the human mind,
illustrations to which every philosopher of mind should attend. What we
find are facts about communities whose central figures are the experts
and their patients, but whose circle quickly expands to families, law and
order, employers. Thanks to media exposure, the circle has expanded to
"everyone" in North America, for everyone knows about multiples now.
Television will not put the truly mad on display. Gone are the days when
the cruel show at Bedlam was fun. No, we want to feast our eyes on the
oddly dysfunctional, not on the crazed or catatonic. Only people with
bizarre but manageable mental disorders are broadcast to the world. If
multiple personality is a natural experiment, I contend, it is an experiment on the community.

I must make a distinction. Multiple personality shows nothing *direct*
about the mind. That is, it does not furnish any evidence for any sub-
stantive philosophical thesis about mind (or self, etc.). The phenomena
may certainly illustrate some claim about the mind that is held for reasons quite independent of the phenomena. If so, would not the phe-

nomena be supporting evidence for the philosophical claim? No. I maintain that they furnish no evidence at all. They add nothing but color. The sheer fact that there is a real-life illustration often seems like evidence, but the doctrines that are illustrated are rooted in principles unrelated to multiple personality, and unsupported by its existence. I shall argue my case by citing three very different contemporary philosophers. They have paid very close attention to medical literature or phenomena of multiple personality. They can hardly be subject to Wakley's strictures. One of them, Stephen Braude, has been intimately involved in the circles of patients and experts around the ISSMP&D. Another, Daniel Dennett and his collaborator Nicholas Humphrey have conducted almost an ethnography of the multiple movement. A third, Kathleen Wilkes, has immersed herself in older literature; whereas Braude and Dennett are American, with plenty of multiples and their clinicians available to talk with, she is English and her knowledge of multiplicity, at least at home, must be gleaned from books.

But first let us turn to two classics, two of the most powerful philosophical minds at work a century ago: William James and Alfred North Whitehead. James's *Principles of Psychology* includes an incisive review of the literature of what he called *alternating personality*.[3] He knew the French literature intimately. He also personally interviewed the famous American case of fugue, namely, Ansel Bourne.[4] Finally, he was always close to the Boston investigators of psychic phenomena, who had a lot to do with the upsurge and persistence of interest in multiple personality in New England. James's discussion is at the end of the chapter titled "The Consciousness of Self"—this follows the more famous chapter 11, "The Stream of Thought." "This long chapter" on consciousness of self concludes with three types of what he calls "mutations of self": losses of memory or false memories, alternating personality, and mediums. Following Ribot, he took alternating personality to be above all a disturbance of memory, since one personality knows nothing of another personality expressed by the same body at earlier times. James was willing to write that "the anaesthetic and 'amnesic' hysteric is one person." She becomes a different person when "you restore her inhibited sensibilities and memories by plunging her into the hypnotic trance—in other words when you rescue them from their 'dissociated' and split-off condition and make them rejoin the other sensibilities and memories."[5] But he lays no great or philosophical weight on the word "person" here, no more than when we commonly say that someone is a different person after a couple of drinks. Indeed William James is a model for all philosophers who would address the mind. He records alternating personality as a phenomenon that leads on to "questions which cannot now be answered."[6] James drew no philosophical inferences whatsoever from alternating personality.

The late philosophy of Alfred North Whitehead reads very differently from that of William James. It demands long periods of absorbed study. I ask absolution from his admirers for making a few superficial remarks about the way that Whitehead used multiplicity in his book *Process and Reality*. In his view each thing that we commonly think of as an entity is a society. An electron is a society of electron occasions. "Our epoch is to be considered a society of electron occasions."[7] It follows that any organism is a society. But people are special:

> In the case of the higher animals there is central direction, which suggests that in their case each animal body harbors a living person, or living persons. Our own self consciousness is direct awareness of such persons. There are limits to such unified control, which is indicated by dissociation of personality, multiple personalities in successive alternations, and even multiple personalities in joint possession.[8]

From Whitehead's perspective, multiple personalities are come by all too easily. For, as he continued, "*what needs to be explained is not dissociation of personality but unifying control*, by reason of which we not only have unified behavior, which can be observed for others, but also consciousness of a unified experience."[9] Whitehead's use of multiplicity is impeccable. He used it to illustrate a thesis, not to argue it. No phenomena known to Whitehead—certainly not those he had learned in Boston from Morton Prince or psychical research—constitute evidence for Whitehead's cosmology. This, in my opinion, is a desirable relationship between the philosophy of mind and multiple personality. Whitehead's philosophy has a ready-made slot for the multiple personality but can gain no support from it. His cosmology neither predicts nor explains any detail of the phenomena. Conversely, the clinical structure of multiple personality disorder is totally independent of Whitehead's cosmology.

More recent philosophers have tried to use multiple personality as evidence. One of these is Daniel Dennett, author of *Consciousness Explained*, one of the most widely read recent books of philosophy of mind. Nicholas Humphrey is, among other things, a practicing psychiatrist. The two men explored the multiple community of clinicians and clients, and their joint work led to a deeply argued essay, "Speaking for Ourselves." They observe how a termite colony can appear to act as if with a single purpose, even though each termite is doing its own thing. Their point is that what seems like collective agency does not need a master supervisor. "Most systems on earth that appear to have central controllers (and are usefully described as having them) do not."[10] Humphrey and Dennett use this fact as a partial model of what it is to be a person—a being with many subsystems. But how to characterize the sheer personhood? They offer an analogy, none other than the United States. We can speak of America's characteristics, its brashness, its Vietnam memories, its fantasy of being forever young. But there is no controlling entity that embodies these qualities. "There is no such thing as Mr. American Self, but as a matter of fact there is in every country on earth a Head of State." The American president is expected to inculcate and represent national values, and to be "the spokesman when it comes to dealing with other nation states." A nation, our authors conjecture, needs a head to get on reasonably well as a nation.

By curious coincidence, Whitehead had used almost the same analogy. Noting that we need unifying control in order to be persons, he wrote, "It is obvious that we must not demand another mentality presiding over these other actualities (a kind of Uncle Sam, over and above all the U.S. citizens)."[11] In the same spirit, Humphrey and Dennett's president is importantly not Uncle Sam but just another citizen, temporary head citizen.

What we think of as a person is, according to Humphrey and Dennett, many subsystems. It is nevertheless possible to have one subsystem that is crucially important in various ways, including the ways in which it has relationships with other people. According to the presidential analogy it is a chief representative for the public view of the collection of subsystems. The analogy suggests a neat way to think about multiple personality. There are several functioning, or malfunctioning, subsystems that take turns as the representative, as the president, particularly in dealing with distinct aspects of the system of subsystems. For the background philosophy we must turn to Dennett's best-known book, *Consciousness Explained*, where personality disorder is described as one "of the terrible experiments that nature conducts."[12]

What do such experiments teach? Dennett's skepticism about the very idea of the self is now quite well known. His theory of consciousness discredits the attitude to the self that he satirizes as "All or Nothing and One to a Customer."[13] He offers multiple personality as a good illustration of the way that his own theory challenges that attitude. On the same page he mentions a tale of forty-year-old twins who are never apart, who continue each other's sentences and perform acts jointly. One person with two bodies—fractional personality disorder! The power of "FPD" as an illustration in no way depends on whether the report of such twins is true or false. Dennett's view of the person allows such a description to make sense. Multiple personality is no more a surprise to Dennett than it was to Whitehead. He is astonished not at multiplicity but at the horrendous conditions in which some children grow up, and which, according to some clinicians, lead children to dissociate.

> These children have often been kept in such extraordinarily terrifying and confusing circumstances that I am more amazed that they survive psychologically at all than I am that they manage to preserve themselves by desperate redrawing of their boundaries. What they do, when confronted with overwhelming conflict and pain, is this: They "leave." They create a boundary so that the horror doesn't happen to them: it either happens to no one, or to some other self, better able to sustain its organization under such an onslaught—at least that's what they *say* they did, as best they recall.[14]

Is this the result of what Dennett calls "a terrible experiment of nature"? He was not the first to think of multiple personality as an experiment of nature; multiple personality has often seemed to furnish a great experiment for the study of the human mind. In 1944 the authors of a classic early survey of multiple personality ended by citing Francis Bacon, and saying that "cases of multiple personality are natural *experimentum lucifera*."[15] Ernest Hilgard, the great student of hypnotism, wrote in the same vein, "Overt multiple personalities of the kinds [that the dissociation theorists] studied appear to be rather rare experiments of nature."[16]

In his *Remarks on the Foundations of Mathematics*, Wittgenstein observed that if a picture of an experiment is compelling, then the picture is not functioning as an experiment at all.[17] He was making a point about the use of pictures in mathematical proofs, but what he said is true in general. It is not as experiments that cases of multiple personality do anything for Dennett's philosophy of mind. They serve only as illustrations. But what do they illustrate? Patients have been diagnosed with double consciousness or multiple personality for two centuries now. But they began to talk the way they do now—using the symptom language noticed by Dennett—only very recently. Today they all say such things, or at least suspect that they ought to say them. That is how they learn to describe themselves in therapy. They do not recall themselves dissociating so much as recall various bits of horror in the personae of a number of alters who experience it. What patients say about themselves has changed radically in the past two decades.

Dennett speaks of the terrible experiments that nature conducts. What exactly are these experiments? It is not as if nature produces for us adults on desert islands who say the things that Dennett says they say. The events involve a patient who is in therapy, often for several years, and who comes to say the things she says. The experiment is so strongly controlled that if she does not say those things, she may even be released from therapy for being too resistant, for denial. The question is not whether children are abominably treated. The question is not whether they will grow up with grave psychological difficulties if their childhood is vile. The question is: Is the subsequent prototypical multiple behavior one of nature's experiments? Or is it rather the way in which a certain class of adults in North America will behave when treated by therapists using certain practices, and having certain convictions? Nothing I have said calls into question the lucid and probing investigation of the multiple movement reported by Humphrey and Dennett. Nor does it take issue with any of the fundamental precepts of Dennett's philosophy of the human mind. They stand on their own, and that is my only point here. Multiple personality may furnish a graphic illustration of Dennett's philosophy, but nothing in the detailed phenomena of present-day multiple personality teaches us anything about his theory of subsystems. His philosophy is no more supported by the phenomena than is Whitehead's.

Humphrey and Dennett were careful observers, for a shortish time, of the multiple scene. Stephen Braude is more like a participant-observer. His book, *First Person Plural: Multiple Personality and the Philosophy of Mind*, was published in 1991, the same year as Dennett's *Consciousness Explained*, but its philosophy is exactly the opposite of Dennett's. Where Dennett heartily dismisses, or explains away, the idea of a single underlying self, Braude firmly believes in the necessity of such an entity. This already performs for us an important service by exactly reversing the inferences to be drawn from multiple personality. I have been urging that the illness has nothing to teach the philosophy of mind. But at least the very existence of the phenomenon must (it seems) be inconsistent with ideas such as a metaphysical soul, a necessarily unified self, or a transcendental ego. Hence (it seems) the existence of multiple personality *does* bear on traditional philosophical issues of great importance. So I'm wrong: multiplicity does bear directly on philosophical questions about the self? That was exactly what Ribot argued, and to some extent

Dennett too. But Braude argues the opposite way. He contends that the very phenomena of multiple personality demand a unity underneath the multiplicity. Starting with almost exactly the same suppositions as Ribot, he concludes that there must be a transcendental ego. Who is right, Ribot or Braude? One possibility is that one of the two men is right. The other is that both are wrong: no conclusions about the self can be derived from the phenomena of multiple personality. I take the latter view. Ribot and Braude cancel each other out, each reminding us how slippery is the argument favored by the other.

Braude thinks there is an underlying self, but he disowns the most obvious model for this idea. You might think that there is a true person waiting to be discovered, a true person who has been there all along, and who must be revealed in therapy. I have mentioned the debate on which was the true state of Azam's Félida: the first state or the second, the one she finally settled into. Early American writers, Prince and clinicians influenced by him, seem to have had a picture of the true personality. Which alter is the true Miss Beauchamp? Foster her, once she has been discovered, and tell the others to exit (Prince did just that with one alter, who obeyed). Braude argues that there need be no original person who split and is to be reclaimed.

One of Braude's arguments for an underlying ego—not the true self, but a central core of all selves—starts from the observation that the alters of one individual have a lot of overlapping basic skills. They can walk and cross the street and tie their shoelaces. Even those rare multiples who have had to do a great deal of relearning in each state retained nearly all ordinary skills. They relearned only what could be rather ostentatiously learned, such as penmanship, or piano, or Greek, or male athletics, skills that are themselves manifestations of a desired social status. The pert and lively person could do these things better than her normal inhibited self. Meanwhile, she could still make small talk, find change at the grocer's, or drive a car. Of course a child alter may be unable to do some of these things, but they are precisely the aspects of the grown-up world that the patient is trying to avoid. Unless she is making a scene, the child alter preserves the skills needed to cross a busy street. There must be some substratum that explains the overlapping skills of alters and enables the alters to interact when they become co-conscious. There is some underlying unified self in which this mental theater is engaged.

Braude is glad to say that there is more than one self per multiple person. Thus far, he and Dennett agree. After that, there's trouble. He calls Dennett's type of view "colonialist," in virtue of the termite colony metaphor. Colonialism, writes Braude, is a view according to which "there is no ultimate psychological unity, only a deep and initial multiplicity of subjects, 'selves' (or, for those smitten with recent work in cognitive science and artificial intelligence) 'modules' or subsystems within a person."[18] Dennett has himself protested against this description in terms of modules.[19] One of Braude's key points against colonialism is the network of overlapping basic skills partially shared from alter to alter. This observation is correct but does not seem as forceful a counter to Dennett's position as he thinks. For Dennett does not portray a multiple as several subsystems, each of which mysteriously has the same street-crossing capacity as every other. On the contrary, there may be a subsystem that handles street crossing for the one body, a body variously represented, at different times, by different subsystem "heads of state" that collaborate with the vast majority of street-crossing and business-conducting subsystems. After a palace revolution, the new head of state retains most but not all of the old bureaucracy of government.

So one must examine Braude's vision of the life of the multiple directly, and not as the result of a successful refutation of Dennett. As I have said, he does not think that the alters are splits off a one true person. He is willing to say that a multiple has a number of different selves, although he sees that we must improve on this terminology. He would do this as follows. Multiples are genuinely different from most people. They have distinct "centers of apperception." That is philosophical jargon with a long history, going back past Kant to Leibniz. The dictionary defines *apperception* as conscious perception with full awareness. To have different centers of apperception means, for Braude, having several "me's." Each me has a fairly ordinary collection of awarenesses, beliefs, memories, hopes, angers, and so forth; each me ascribes these beliefs itself to its own "I" in the first person: the beliefs are what Braude calls "indexical." That is another philosophical word from very recent linguistic philosophy. Words like "here" and "now" and "me" and "they" refer only in a context of utterance. They are called indexical. When I say "I went to town," I mean me; when you say it, you mean you.

Braude makes good use of this idea. He argues, for example, that there are not separate centers of apperception in hypnosis. In contrast, psychic mediums may have several distinct centers of apperception. They go into trances. They speak of beliefs, memories, and feelings in a thoroughly indexical way, associating different selves with the different voices that speak through them: the voice of your grandmother, Zoroaster, and so forth. Braude is therefore inclined to take the "disorder" out of multiple personality disorder: mediums are unusual; in some ways they resemble multiples, but they are not suffering from a disorder in need of treatment. And maybe some multiples could be just fine too. It should be said here that Braude published two previous books on psychical research about which he holds a careful but favorable opinion.[20] He was particularly fascinated by psychokinesis—the use of the power of thought to make accordions float, as in the golden days of psychic events around 1900, or nowadays to predict sequences of random numbers produced by sophisticated electronics. He also takes mediums very seriously, not as people gifted at communicating with spirits, but as people with multiple selves, not necessarily disordered.

His theory has the merit that it does not make dissociation into an artificial continuum. There I have agreed with him, but we do not need his semantic terminology to do the work. His use of words like "indexicality" sounds like deep logic. He argues that the way multiples use pronouns such as "we" reflects an underlying epistemological stance. Nothing as profound as that, alas, is in question. What helps keep all those "me's" going for a patient in a clinic or a medium in a séance may be nothing as logically fancy as the indexical use of "I" to refer to distinct centers of apperception. It is the old-fashioned practice of naming. We should replace Braude's importation of technical semantics with some down-home reflections on the use and abuse of proper names.

Braude's argument has grander ambitions than a mere refutation of colonialism. He holds that Kant was fundamentally correct, that there is a "transcendental unity of apperception" underlying all those distinct centers. Kant and Braude agree on the conclusion—a transcendental ego—but differ on the argument for it. Kant's argument is notoriously difficult, but I think I know how it goes. I cannot figure out how Braude's goes, so I must leave his version for the reader. Ribot and Braude start with essentially the same phenomena. From these data Braude wants to lead us to his conclusion, that there is a fundamental prior and perhaps transcendental ego. Ribot wanted us to reach the opposite conclusion, that there is no such thing. Neither one nor the other is correct. Multiple personality adds color to the arguments but furnishes no evidence for them.

Wilkes's *Real People* takes a tack very different from those of Dennett and Braude. Those two are trying to say what the self, the person, consciousness, or whatever really is. She writes in the tradition called ordinary language philosophy, aiming at conceptual analysis. She wants to understand not objects but our concepts of objects. She wants to know how we think about things. A familiar concept is articulated by the usage of words. Concepts can be limned not only by what we actually do say, but by what we would say in various circumstances. Sufficiently strange events may leave us speechless. Concepts that snugly fit the sorts of things that usually happen may fall apart when asked to sort out really weird events. When we notice that happening, we have found out something about the bounds of application for our ideas. Wilkes is, however, affronted by the practice of so many writers in her tradition. They invent stories. Personal identity is a favorite domain of philosophical fiction: "What would we say if. . . ." The lacuna is filled by various "bizarre, entertaining, confusing, and inconclusive thought experiments" that are supposed to push our concept of personal identity to the limit.

> To my mind, these alluring fictions have led discussion off on the wrong tracks; moreover, since they rely heavily on imagination and intuition they lead to no solid or agreed conclusions, since intuitions vary and imaginations fail. What is more, I do not think that we need them, since there are so many actual puzzle-cases which defy the *imagination*, but which we nonetheless have to accept as facts.[21]

Wilkes makes excellent use of a few famous reports of multiplicity, especially Morton Prince's most celebrated exemplar, Miss Beauchamp. She writes of puzzle-cases that we "have to accept as facts." We should be cautious about the facts, and about the belief that fact is not only stranger than, but also wholly distinct from, fiction. My worry occurs at almost every possible level. To begin with, there is lying. H. H. Goddard simply lied about his patient "Norma." This is a salutary reminder that "the facts" may not be exactly as they stand in the case record.

Morton Prince's prodigiously long book about Miss Beauchamp does not exhaust the facts. He never told us that his patient married a colleague of his who became a society psychiatrist in Palm Springs. We know a lot more about the shadowy Mr. Jones, probably Beauchamp's first husband, than Prince ever told us. We know many more things about a famous scene of gothic horror that precipitated Beauchamp's crisis. She was an assistant in a madhouse during a thunderstorm, when Jones appeared on a ladder at the window. That and more happened the day before a trial for "the crime of the century" opened in the next village, none other than that immortalized in verse: "Lizzie Borden took an ax / And gave her mother forty whacks. / When she saw what she had done / She gave her father forty-one." So truth is stranger than fiction? Or is it fiction, not imagination superseded, as Wilkes implies, but imagination heightened?[22] Some five hundred playwrights submitted scripts for the play of Prince's book.[23] The winning author's play, *The Case of Becky*, directed by David Belasco, ran for six months on Broadway and was also made into a silent movie. Are we dealing with Docudrama, or Drama Doc?

Wilkes also refers to *The Three Faces of Eve*. Eve presented three different faces in three different autobiographies. Wilkes is well informed about these stories and as skeptical as I am. I go on at length because of Wilkes's method. She proposes to try our various conceptions of the self, person, and so forth against what the title of her book calls "real people." In the multiple personality chapter, she works chiefly with the four personalities of Miss Beauchamp. How many persons are there? she asks. She explores various things that we might say. She urges that our notion of the person seems to fall apart. Early in the book she had offered "six conditions of personhood." She asks how well each of Beauchamp's personalities fits each condition. On balance, at least three of the alters fare rather well.

> The brunt of the argument suggests that we ought to conclude that during [a certain period of therapy] Prince had three people to deal with. Arguments in favour of affirming plurality are more numerous than those suggesting singularity. What we ought to say, and what we do say, however, may not always jibe.[24]

Note that this is the last conclusion that an up-to-date dissociative identity disorder clinician would encourage. Prince, they would say, was dealing with one person, three of whose alters were more integrated than the other three. But Wilkes's analysis is scrupulous.[25] I question only the presupposition that we are presented with one true story and asked to try out our language and our philosophical analysis upon that actual case, a real case, not a fictional one. In the few years since Wilkes published *Real People* the number of multobiographies and auto-multobiographies may well have doubled again.[26]

I do not make the weak point that it would have been equally good if Prince's case were fictional. I make the strong point that the whole language of many selves had been hammered out by generations of romantic poets and novelists, great and small, and also in innumerable broadsheets and feuilletons too ephemeral for general knowledge today. Prince knew exactly how to describe his patient so that she would be a multiple. Is it any wonder that scanning his interminable report we conclude that there are several persons in one body? This is not a test of how we use language in order to describe real people. It is a consequence of how the literary imagination has formed the language in which we speak of people—be they real, imagined, or, the most common case, of mixed origin. When it comes to the language that will be used to describe ourselves, each of us is a half-breed of imagination and reality. Karl Miller summed up the matter well in his wonderfully rich book about the European novels of doubling:

> Every life is made up, put on, imagined—including, *hypocrite lecteur*, yours. Sybil's life was made up by Sybil, by her doctor, when she became a case, and again, when she became a book, by her author. Sixteen selves were imagined, but it is not even entirely certain that there were as many as two.[27]

An Indeterminacy in the Past

IT WILL BE GOOD to conclude in a more analytic vein. Multiple personality, I argued, has nothing to teach philosophers about mind and body. But philosophical analysis, of an almost grammatical sort, may help us with memory and multiplicity. The title of the present chapter means what it says, which is hard, because we think of the past as fixed, final, and determined. I am not about to address that banal topic, the indeterminacy of memory. I mean an indeterminacy about what people actually did, not about what we remember them doing. I mean an indeterminacy about past human actions, where it is something about our actions, not our memories of them, that is indeterminate. The memories that most affect us are memories of scenes and episodes in which we or others do something or other. The repressed memories that have so fascinated psychiatrists have commonly been memories of sexual actions or of cruel actions. In recent times, they have been cruel sexual actions, whose epitome is sadistic sexual abuse of children. But actions are not simply activities, movements that show up on video. We are primarily concerned with intentional actions, things that a person intended to do.

Intentional actions are actions "under a description." The philosopher Elizabeth Anscombe gave this example. A man was moving a lever up and down. He was manually pumping water into the cistern of the house. He was pumping poisoned water into the country house where evil men met for planning sessions. He was poisoning the men who met in the house.[1] Certainly there were not distinct physical sequences of activities, moving the lever, pumping the water, poisoning the men. Should we, however, say that there was a number of distinct actions, pumping water, on the one hand, and poisoning the men, on the other? Anscombe argued that there was just one action, under various descriptions. Each successive description of the action involves a larger range of circumstances, but only one intentional action is being described. Since the publication, in 1959, of Anscombe's slim monograph on these topics, there has developed an entire academic discipline called "action theory." Some philosophers argue that although there was only one physical activity, only one sequence of relevant events that would show up on a video record, the man performed two distinct actions, pumping and poisoning. The idea is, in part, that since there are two different descriptions, and action is always "under a description," there are two distinct actions. Here I shall follow Anscombe: there is indeed more than one true answer to the question "What was he doing?" (or, asked of the man at the pump, "What are you doing?"). But there was just one action, under several descriptions.

Intention introduces another set of issues. I shall soon show how they bear on memory and multiplicity, but it is very important not to fix on sensational examples without being clear about very ordinary events, events in which we know perfectly well what's going on. Imagine, says Anscombe, that I am sawing a board. My board is on top of your table. Inadvertently, I not only saw my board but also, simultaneously and without noticing, saw into your table. I did not do so intentionally. My action of sawing my board was identical with my action of sawing into your table. There was just one action, but I did two things, saw my board and saw into your table. I intended to do only one of these things. To generalize: we can distinguish *acting with an intention, acting intentionally*, and *intending to act*.[2] Acting intentionally is acting with some intention—that is, performing an action under some description, such that one intends to act, under that description. But one may act intentionally, under description A, and also perform an action under description B, without intending to act under description B. On Anscombe's theory, in order for one's action to be an intentional action there must be some description A, such that one intended to act under A, but in doing A, one may also have been doing B, though not intentionally. I should also say that Anscombe, much influenced by Wittgenstein, crisply argues that an intentional action is not, for example, an organized sequence of doings plus an inner, private, mental, intention.[3] The intention under which an event is done does not refer to some entity in the mind.

The thesis that action is action under a description has logical consequences for the future and for the past. When I decide to do something, and do it, I am acting intentionally. There may be many kinds of actions with which I am unacquainted, and of which I have no description. It seems to follow from the thesis that I cannot intend to perform those actions. I cannot choose to do those things. I could of course choose to do something A, to which a subsequently constructed new description B applies; then by choosing to do A, and doing it, I did indeed do B, but I did not intend to do B. The limitation is not a physical constraint or a moral prohibition. It is a trivial, logical fact that I cannot form those intentions. This fact cannot make me feel confined, or make me regret my lack of power. I cannot feel limited by lacking a description, for if I did, in a self-aware way, feel limited, then I would have at least a glimmering of the description of the action and so could think of choosing it.

Anscombe's theses about action seem to have an unexpected corollary. When new descriptions become available, when they come into circulation, or even when they become the sorts of things that it is all right to say, to think, then there are new things to choose to do. When new intentions become open to me, because new descriptions, new concepts, become available to me, I live in a new world of opportunities.[4] Almost the opening words of my first chapter were "a multiple personality epidemic." We have had plenty of "epidemics" in the course of this book: child abuse, ritual abuse, recovered memories, recantings of recovered memories. Cynics about one or another of these say the epidemics are made by copycats. But even if there was a lot of copying, there is also a logical aspect to "epidemics" of this type. In each case, even with an illness such as multiple personality, new possibilities for action, actions under new descriptions, come into being or become current. Multiple personality provided a new way to be an unhappy person. Even many supporters of the multiple personality diagnosis are willing to agree that it has become, to use one popular phrasing, a culturally sanctioned way of expressing distress.

Consider the new terminology, which, if not quite part of everyday English, has become familiar to anyone interested in multiple personality: "switching," "alter," "personality fragment," "coming out," "going to another place," and even the use of the first person plural, "we." A hundred years ago there was a more parsimonious set of new phrases such as *condition seconde*. It is often observed, by cynics, that during all the waves of doubling or multiplicity, one of the ways in which alters became solidified was by being named. A certain range of behaviors, feelings, attitudes, and memories became invested with a proper name and then glued together to form a partial personality. Another solidifying agent behind this practice has been less noticed. The new descriptive vocabulary of alters, such as switching, provided new options for being and acting. Instead of mood swings there was something much more specific that a person could be doing, namely, switching to a persecutor alter; a persecutor alter could be taking executive control. I do not mean that doubles could not switch, or that an alter could not come out, before these words were available. Mary Reynolds switched; her vivacious alter came out. We are content to apply such descriptions retroactively to times when the descriptions were not available, were not part of the conceptual space of the day. But it is not clear that the vivacious alter could intentionally come out, could choose to come out, in 1816.

This example brings out a certain vagueness around the edges of the thesis that all intentional action is action under a description. Anscombe was interested in the intentions of whole people, responsible moral agents. Now under one account of what is happening in multiplicity, the switch is not intentional but involuntary. This may be the account that will be favored if the diagnosis and the name dissociative identity disorder succeeds. We have in effect "less than one person"; we have no well-organized person to form intentions. Contrast an account that was widespread during the 1980s and is still current among the rank and file of the multiple movement. When Esther switches to Stan, Stan comes out, takes over, dominates Esther and other alters of Daphne, the host personality. Stan is an agent; Stan is the personality who is responsible for the switch. The switch was not one of Esther's or Daphne's intentional actions, but it was one of Stan's. Stan has decided to come out. Until the new language and conceptions of multiple personality came into use, this was not an option for a personality fragment, not as something like an intentional action. But it was described in the manner of an intentional action, Stan's action, at least in the 1980s. As dissociative identity disorder becomes the official diagnosis, and personalities become less distinct in theory and practice, these opportunities for intentional action may fade away.

This puts quite a strain on Anscombe's theses about intention and action. One has to have a certain integrity, a certain wholeness, to have intentions at all. The language of alters was providing descriptions in which dissociated actions could be said to have centers, personalities, or at any rate personality fragments, which had enough of the features of a person that actions could be ascribed to them, fragment by fragment. Consider the famous law cases, not only the murderers and rapists, but also the South Carolinian woman who claims that she did not commit adultery and hence is entitled to alimony, even if an alter did commit adultery. Say Daphne was like her, and that Esther was Daphne's adulterous alter. Esther has an affair, of which Daphne has no knowledge. What could be a clearer case of attributing intentional action to an alter, to Esther? I am suggesting that with the new forms of description, new kinds of intentional action came into being, intentional actions that were not open to an agent lacking something like those descriptions.

Of the "epidemics" that I have mentioned, the least controversial is child abuse. It is a familiar fact that child abuse statistics keep growing and growing. No one can help but wonder if, in addition to better and better reporting, there is also more and more child abuse. That would be an appalling conclusion, given the immense amount of effort, money, publicity, and goodwill that has gone into the control of child abuse. The variety of activities covered by the description "child abuse" has radically expanded during the past three decades. Some types of behavior that previously passed almost unnoticed came to be seen as abusive. New ways to be abusive came into being. Adults who want to abuse, but who, thanks to well-instilled inhibitions, recoil from the more overt kinds of abuse, can now perform acts that they themselves could describe as abusive. And then of course they might move on to actions that previously they would have hardly dared to contemplate. There may be what I shall call *semantic contagion*. When we think of an action as of a certain kind, our mind runs to other acts of that kind. Thus, classifying an act in a new way may lead us on to others. Few people reason like this: "Now that I am doing things of this kind—child abuse—I may as well be hung for a sheep as a lamb." But once certain barriers are gone because many things have been lumped under one semantic heading, "child abuse," some previously repulsive acts may become less forbidding. One should not dismiss the possibility that some of the increase in child abuse is due to the publicity itself, in that it makes available new descriptions under which to act and then, by semantic contagion, leads on to yet worse actions. Opening new possibilities for a person to do something: that sounds wonderful. It is not always so great. Lead me not into temptation. One can open possibilities for evil just as one can open possibilities for good.

But may not the increased incidence have been due simply to a copycat effect? There is no way to draw a sharp line between copying behavior and acquiring a new concept of a kind of behavior. Each case must be examined on its own. Sensational suicide pacts, whether of Heinrich von Kleist on the Wannsee in 1811 or of a group of teenagers in the Middle West in 1991, apparently produce imitators. I would not say they were creating a new concept or making available a new description. Their imitators are, one thinks, simply inspired to imitate. But in the case of child abuse we should build into our understanding the way in which new kinds of actions opened up, became opportunities for evil, as new concepts and new descriptions became distributed by a massive drive to disseminate information and to catch or prevent child abuse.

In passing we should note how this idea bears on the censorship of egregious pornography. There are of course deontological arguments that distributing pornography is bad in itself, intrinsically wicked. Close to this is the argument that the availability of pornography is in itself insulting to women or even creates a self-image of worthlessness. And there is the argument that photographed (as opposed to written) pornography requires exploiting some women and children. But most arguments are utilitarian, consequential. Disseminating pornography encourages men to demean women and may lead to acts of violence and cruelty. Pornography of the vilest and most sadistic sort, it is argued, invites imitation. The evidence for this claim is poor, but it may be the wrong claim to examine closely. The real evil may lurk one stage higher up. Distributing pornography is distributing knowledge of new kinds of action. Most men, including many cruel and abusive men, are remarkably innocent, being simply unacquainted with the range of possible demeaning actions. One thing that some pornography does is to disseminate new modes of action, new descriptions, verbal or visual. This is assuredly a very abstract thought about wickedness, but wicked actions should be addressed with logical rigor as well as pious moralizing.

I have from time to time spoken of the looping effect of human kinds—that is, the interactions between people, on the one hand, and ways of classifying people and their behavior on the other. Being seen to be a certain kind of person, or to do a certain kind of act, may affect someone. A new or modified mode of classification may systematically affect the people who are so classified, or the people themselves may rebel against the knowers, the classifiers, the science that classifies them. Such interactions may lead to changes in the people who are classified, and hence in what is known about them. That is what I call a feedback effect. Now I am adding a further parameter. Inventing or molding a new kind, a new classification, of people or of behavior may create new ways to be a person, new choices to make, for good or evil. There are new descriptions, and hence new actions under a description. It is not that people change, substantively, but that as a point of logic new opportunities for action are open to them.

Thus far I have been discussing a person's choosing or deciding what to do or be. Now let us turn to the actions of other people. There is more reporting of child abuse now than there was twenty years ago, because there are more reporting agencies, and because authorities and lay people are more assiduous. That is a far more obvious effect of the making and molding of the concept of child abuse than the hypothetical effects on future abusers that I have been discussing. It is almost unproblematic. We describe, and hence report, more actions as in-stances of child abuse. As the concept of child abuse expands, more and more situations fall under the description "child abuse." So there is more child abuse to report. That is plain enough. We move on to more difficult territory when we think about what children themselves see and experience. After about 1978 there was a concerted effort to educate children about child abuse. Once upon a time, the generic warning was "Don't take candy from strangers; never go for a walk or take a ride with someone you do not know." Then children were educated, for example, about good touches and bad touches. They were presented with vi-gnettes, scenarios, and video clips to teach them about such differ-ences—and to furnish them with a new vocabulary, a new mode of de-scribing. There is some debate among psychologists as to whether the children could grasp what they were taught. The state of California rad-ically cut back on child abuse education because some experts argued, on developmental grounds, that six-year-old children were not yet suffi-ciently mature to understand. Now whatever be the merits and defects of this kind of education, the developmental criticism is suspect. It is a good maxim that, absent compelling evidence to the contrary, young children are very smart and know very well what's going on, even if they are sometimes confused (or simply shy, or sensibly distrustful of adults) when it comes to talking about such things.[5]

Children may end up being more aware than adults. Take less heinous forms of abuse. I quoted some of Cornelia Wilbur's kinds of sexual abuse. They included an adult's bathing or showering with a nine-year-old child, arranging for children to sleep in the parent's bedroom, as well as various kinds of washing of children after infancy. A child might be educated to see these actions as abusive, even though the parent would never categorize them that way. What did the father do? He showered with his nine-year-old daughter. The daughter not only felt uncomfortable, she felt abused. Asked what her father did, she could reply that he abused her. Such issues become inhumane; in real life one hopes that if the daughter is uncomfortable, the father will realize it. We do not have to categorize. If the father insists on showering with his daughter, knowing she is uncomfortable at some level of her being, then he is being abusive. Whether the abuse counts as psychological or sexual is too fine a point to worry about except in an adversarial courtroom. Nevertheless, the conceptual question "What was he doing?" remains perplexing. Even more puzzling is the case of today's adult, who did not have these descriptions when she was a child, but who now looks at her past and recalls episodes that, she now thinks, fall under those descriptions. She was abused, although not flagrantly, as a child. Even so, when she was a child, neither she nor adults around her were well able to conceptualize what was happening in the way that today's five-year-old can. The retroactive redescription and reexperiencing of human actions is the most difficult of topics. We need a little more spadework before addressing it directly.

Matters become less personal and less pressing when we go back into history. Since we can be disinterested about historical figures, in a way that we cannot be with the father and daughter in the shower, the logical difficulties may be seen more clearly. Here is perhaps the simplest possible example of a nontrivial retroactive redescription. The British parliament has a private member's bill before it, pardoning some 307 young British and Canadian soldiers who were court-martialed and shot during the Great War, 1914–1918. The most common charge was desertion during a military engagement, or refusal to obey orders and go to the front. Details of these secret trials were finally published in 1990; few of us now can feel much empathy for the officers who conducted the courts-martial. The author of the private member's bill states that today the men would be judged to be suffering from post-traumatic stress disorder, and to be in need of psychiatric help, not execution.[6] This is retroactive redescription with a vengeance. Even this example is not at all straightforward. It pathologizes old behavior. Does that matter? The bill is symbolic. It is part of an antiwar politics and is indeed modeled on a previous bill connected with Anglo-Irish politics, concerning 24 Irish volunteers who were executed during the same war. The bill also has personal meaning for a few descendants. If one of my forebears had been shot for desertion during that long-ago war, I'm far from sure I would be happy with this private member's bill. I think I might be proud that my ancestor had the wit and the guts to try to desert, the most rational thing to do, under the circumstances. From a logical point of view this proposed retroactive redescription is interesting because it does not increase the number of things that the soldiers might have done intentionally. It decreases them. The men are no longer said to have deserted, or at any rate, not said to have deserted "in the first degree." This is because if they were suffering from post-traumatic stress disorder, they were not, strictly speaking, acting voluntarily.

The bill before parliament is intended to save reputations; more often we encounter proposals to destroy or diminish historical figures. Such retroactive redescription, using modern judgments to vilify someone, can sometimes seem misguided. A famous Scottish explorer, Alexander Mackenzie (1755–1820), has been called not just a child abuser but a child molester.[7] Mackenzie was the first European to navigate the Mackenzie River north to the Arctic Ocean, and the first European to cross the Rocky Mountains to reach the Pacific Ocean. No saint he, and surely a racist, yet I still wonder if he should be called a child abuser or child molester on the sole ground that he married a fourteen-year-old girl when he was forty-eight years of age. The marriage was neither illegal nor totally exceptional in 1802. When a forty-eight-year-old man has any sexual contact with a fourteen-year-old today, that is child abuse. (Nabokov's *Lolita* reminds us that even now the label "child abuse" could be a trifle simplistic and moralistic, but that is not the issue for Mackenzie, whose life seems to have been, in the relevant senses, rather simple.) Should we retroactively apply terms such as child abuse so generously? Luckily we do not have to prosecute, for the question is purely conceptual.

Nevertheless, great passions can be aroused by just such questions. Philippe Ariès had a vision of earlier centuries of childhood as providing a freer, franker, less sexually cluttered life for humans before and shortly after puberty.[8] There was not much of an idea of the child, and still less of abusing. Humans in that age group were not harmed, were not conceptually capable of being harmed, in ways that we now harm children. The psychohistorian Lloyd DeMause considers that to be rubbish.[9] He says that the history of at least Western civilization is the history of child abuse. Things get worse and worse the further back in time we go. Ariès used the constant public playing with the genitals of the infant and child Louis XIII (1601–1663, king of France from 1610) as evidence of an absence of oppressive conceptualization. A royal physician provided ample description of the fun. DeMause takes the story as evidence of rampant child sexual abuse. So too, for his purposes, were ancient Greek pederasty and the so-called Children's Crusade of 1212. In the same vein Denis Donovan argues that Freud missed the boat on the Oedipus complex.[10] It is as if Freud did not even notice that Sophocles' Jocasta had maimed Oedipus and handed him over to a shepherd to be killed. Donovan would like us to see *Oedipus Rex* as a story of child abuse and its sequelae. Well, it is certainly a story about attempted infanticide. That crime is often captured by child abuse statutes today. Does it follow that we should describe the antique legend as a story that begins with child abuse? There are clearly problems about retroactive attribution of modern moral concepts.

To take a trite example, imagine some plain, but not entirely gross, case of sexual harassment that took place in 1950, behavior that contravened no law or custom of 1950, and which hardly even infringed the canons of taste then current, in the social milieu where the event took place. If you tell me about the episode in 1950 terms, you certainly will not use the expression "sexual harassment." What was the man doing? You answer by identifying the action, telling me what the man said to his secretary, perhaps, and the way in which he said it. But now you can also answer the question "What was the man doing?" with "He was sexually harassing his secretary." This is the same action as the one you first presented in a more neutral way, but it is that action under a new description. On the other hand, when we ask whether the man intended to harass his secretary, most of us are less sure what to say. Today, in many milieus, we hold in contempt the man who says he did not realize he was harassing. And if he will not stop behaving that way, he is finished. But when we reflect on the 1950s man, there is a certain diminishment to the accusation if the very idea of harassment was not available to him.

As a cautious philosopher, I am inclined to say that many retroactive redescriptions are neither definitely correct nor definitely incorrect. As political tactics it is nevertheless useful to impose new descriptions and awarenesses on the past. That is what DeMause and Donovan are doing. We should realize the logical consequences of their tactic. It is almost as if retroactive redescription changes the past. That is too paradoxical a turn of phrase, for sure. But if we describe past actions in ways in which they could not have been described at the time, we derive a curious result. For all intentional actions are actions under a description. If a description did not exist, or was not available, at an earlier time, then at that time one could not act intentionally under that description. Only later did it become true that, at that time, one performed an action under that description. At the very least, we rewrite the past, not because we find out more about it, but because we present actions under new descriptions.

Perhaps we should best think of past human actions as being to a certain extent indeterminate. Let us begin with that too easy example of sexual harassment. I do not think it was determined, in 1950, that there would come into being a pivotal American concept of sexual harassment. I asked you to imagine some plain, but not entirely gross, example of sexual harassment that took place in 1950. I am not at all sure that it was determinate, in 1950, that this was an intentional act of sexual harassment. Indeed some people, with whom I strongly disagree, will say

243

that it definitely was not sexual harassment, then. Others will insist that of course it was. In this case I do judge that it was intentional sexual harassment in 1950. I stop short of saying that Mackenzie was a child molester because he married a fourteen-year-old. Others will adamantly insist that he was, and I can understand what they mean. We will all draw our lines differently here, which I take to be a hint of indeterminacy. It is not a question of "say whatever you like," but of "understand why we are pulled in different directions." When it comes to retroactive redescription of the past, political rhetoric will influence many people more than argument and reflection will. I do not want to convince anyone to draw the line, in retroactive redescription, at any particular place. Rather I would urge that it may simply not have been very determinate, in the past, that certain future descriptions of past intentional action would apply or could be applied.

Now let us swing back and ask a related question about multiple personality. Earlier in this chapter I had a story of one Daphne whose alter Esther, unbeknownst to placidly and properly married Daphne, had a male lover. I described the case in the 1980s language of multiplicity. How well can we use such descriptions retroactively? In any age a Daphne could have had regular trysts with her lover, and yet have segregated the meetings and the emotions they called forth from her daily life. Suppose that she was not really conscious of that side of her world while engaged in her life as wife and mother. She did not notice the perfume and the undergarments she kept in a private place. She had, as the old penny novelists used to say, two lives, and she kept them totally apart, even to the point of deluding herself. She and her lover used the private name Esther during their secret encounters. When they parted she gruffly adopted the role of a disagreeable man, "Stan."

Daphne, we imagine, had her illicit affair in the antebellum South, rather than the 1980s Carolinas. Double consciousness was unknown at that time and place. On hearing her story, can we not, nevertheless, say what was really happening, even if she could not describe herself that way? Was she not a multiple who would switch to alter Esther during romantic interludes away from her tedious husband? Her father, we find, not content with abusing the children of his slaves, took up with his own daughter at a very early age. Does that not clinch the matter? I believe many advocates of the multiple personality diagnosis would urge that Daphne was a multiple. I do not want to take issue with that. It is the next step that counts. For if she was a multiple, all the language of multiplicity can be applied to her retroactively, can it not? No.

For example, during the 1980s, as I said above, Esther chose to come out on certain occasions, taking executive control from Daphne. But this was simply not possible for an "Esther" in 1855. There was no so-lidified alter; there was not even the self-conception of an alter; there was no Esther-as-alter. Likewise there was no description of an action, "coming out," for any personality or fragment. I repeat, this is a logical point about action, but it may cast a different, if perplexing, light on the effect of introducing new descriptions of kinds of behavior, of kinds of people.

I may seem shortsighted: after all, if Daphne had undergone 1980s treatment, then she might well have developed full-blown multiplicity. Esther and Stan would have been among her alters. Did she not have the alter "in her"? This is a new consideration. Daphne had (it might be urged) what philosophers call a "disposition" to develop into full-fledged multiplicity, just as a fragile teacup has a disposition to shatter when dropped. The disposition is part of or results from Daphne's inter-nal makeup, just as the fragility of the teacup results from its internal structure. So can we not sensibly talk about Esther as an alter?

To see why not, consider an actual case, H. H. Goddard's patient Bernice R., of 1921.[11] I have argued that she definitely fit the criteria of *DSM-III*.[12] She was a multiple. She had one child alter, Polly, and I do not hesitate to say, on the basis of Goddard's reports, that Polly came out and took over Bernice. (I am not so sure, however, that Polly was acting intentionally when she did so.) I think it very likely that if Bernice had been treated in 1991, in a clinic for multiple personality and dissoci-ation, she would have developed a substantial number of alters. There was certainly plenty of trauma in the family. Yet I believe it is wrong to project back onto the historical Bernice a personality structure that she (probably) would have developed under a certain kind of treatment. It is not simply that we do not know for sure what would have happened. It is not true that when Bernice entered therapy in 1921, she had a per-sonality structure with more than one or two alters. It is true that she had at least one alter in September 1921, namely, Polly. It is also likely that if she had undergone a 1991 course of treatment, she would have evinced a number of alters. Maybe multiples like Bernice have a nature that has the potentiality to evolve in that way, if suitably reinforced. But there is no "actuality" in Bernice except this potentiality. The only rele-vant determinate fact about Bernice is that she had one alter, and the hint of another, one Louise.

Compare this with another fact about Bernice. She repeatedly told

Goddard that her father had sex with her. Goddard was convinced this was a fantasy, which Bernice had picked up after spending some time in a home for wayward girls. He did not think this false memory was connected with Bernice's multiplicity. Like Janet, he thought he should make the incest-memory go away. He says that he convinced her it never happened. My guess, after reading Goddard and doing a little family history which has to be regarded as confidential, is that Bernice was recalling genuine incest (which, in her day, meant vaginal sexual intercourse) or, what I think may be more likely, sodomy. I believe she had an essentially true memory. I may be completely wrong. I may be half wrong; there may have been what we now call flagrant sexual abuse but without penetration. But there is a definite fact of the matter. Either Bernice's father had sexual intercourse with her, or he did not. That is an "actuality," although we shall never know for sure what was the truth of the matter. But there is no truth of the matter as to the real number of Bernice's alters, something in her inner nature like the physical structure of a teacup. That is not determinate. To repeat, the only determinate fact is that Bernice had a child alter, Polly.

Thus far we have discussed retroactive application of new descriptions to past people or past actions. I shall end by turning to the most difficult case of all, the coming to terms with our own past. The recovered memory people and the false memory people may seem completely at loggerheads, but they share a common assumption: either certain events occurred, and were experienced, or they did not and were not. The past itself is determinate. A true memory recalls those events as experienced, while a false one involves things that never happened. The objects to be remembered are definite and determinate, a reality prior to memory. Even traditional psychoanalysis tends not to question the underlying definiteness of the past. The analyst will be indifferent as to whether a recollected event really occurred. The present emotional meaning of the recollection is what counts. Nevertheless, the past itself, and how it was experienced at the time, is usually regarded as determinate enough.

Of course many of the events that are disputed between the two sides (recovered memory versus false memory) are determinate, in the banal sense that they would have shown up if there had been a camcorder there to make a video of the disputed scene. Either the man sodomized his five-year-old stepson, or he did not. That is a determinate part of the past. Either Bernice's memory of incest was fairly accurate, or it was not. Every case that has gone to court using evidence from recovered memories has been tried on allegations about completely determinate past events, usually monstrous, that either did occur or did not occur. Many other events recovered in memory are equally determinate. Notoriously, however, the vast amount of memory work does not end with such plainly cut-and-dried facts-or-falsehoods. Perhaps even Bernice's memory, had it been probed critically, might have yielded a shady feeling of sexual discomfort about her father but nothing as dramatic as the incest she first reported, using the old-fashioned sense of the word. Maybe Goddard was half right. Bernice's father did sexually abuse her, but in less flagrant ways than Bernice seemed to remember; when she acquired a set of new descriptions in the form of horror stories at the home for wayward girls, semantic contagion went to work. That is, on acquiring new ideas, she applied them to old actions.

Most people now accept the commonplace that memory is not itself like a camcorder, creating, when it works, a faithful record. We do not reproduce in memory a sequence of events that we have experienced. Instead we rearrange and modify elements that we remember into something that makes sense, or, sometimes, that has just enough structure to be puzzling or even incoherent. (Even incoherence demands enough organization for elements to be discordant.) We touch up, supplement, delete, combine, interpret, shade. There is still the conception that the past is the sort of thing of which a faithful record could have been made, had there existed an array of hidden cameras. But suppose I see (or remember) two people shaking hands to conclude a deal, and that I, on another occasion, see (or remember) two strangers meeting each other for the first time. The camera images of these two different scenes could well be indistinguishable, separable only when the full story came on the screen. The activities are recorded, but not the actions-under-a-description. Some theorists say that we interpret the scenes differently, but I do not find that helpful. We need considerable social savvy to know it is two entrepreneurs concluding a deal, but with that knowledge we do not, in the standard case, "interpret" what we see. We just see two men greeting each other, or two men concluding a deal. But for those who prefer an analysis in terms of interpretation, then what I see (or remember) is an "interpreted" scene, a meaningful episode. At any rate an image, whether it is in the mind or on the video screen, is not enough to furnish an answer to the question "What were the two men doing?"

The remembered past that interests us psychologically is precisely this world of human action, of greeting, or of agreeing to a deal. Thus the imaginary camcorder in the sky, which records everything that happens in a particular scene, does not of itself suffice to record what people were doing. Perhaps this bears on trauma research. There is at present something of an industry of interviewing, at intervals of time, victims of dreadful accidents. The recent earthquakes in California, the Buffalo Creek Dam disaster, the Oakland fire, the work of Scottish policemen sorting out the corpses from an oil rig disaster, or the episode in which some louts who were my former neighbors hijacked a school bus from Chowchilla, in the California desert, and buried the bus filled with children for a day and more. Only the last is even close to human action, although the relevant trauma was less the kidnapping, which, though scary, was also a bit of a lark, than the burial. Trauma experts are fascinated by these events and study the victims' memories (as well as the symptoms of post-traumatic stress) at various times. Pioneer in this field Lenore Terr, who studied the Chowchilla kidnapping, holds that victims of what she calls single-event trauma retain clear memories of what happened.[13] That would apply to most natural disasters as well as being buried alive. Yet I would point to another difference between such cases and recovered memories. The essential feature of the traumas was not human action. The traumatic events were what they were, and intention or acting under a description do not arise.

Thus I am urging caution in projecting results of trauma produced by impersonal conditions onto trauma produced by human actions. This is not because some different kind of memory is involved, but because of a logical difference between the events remembered. We describe earthquakes, but it makes little sense to talk about an earthquake under a description. It is just an earthquake. Of course Terr's difference (single-event as opposed to repeated trauma) and mine (impersonal as opposed to intentional human action) are not so much at odds as they may seem. For one of the ways in which human action falls under descriptions is in terms of the way the action fits into a larger scene. The man's hand on the pump is going up and down. Enlarge the scene. He is pumping water. Enlarge the scene. He is poisoning the men in the villa. As Anscombe makes so plain, the intentionality of an action is not a private mental event added on to what is done, but is the doing in context.

I have been speaking of redescribing old actions, especially with newly coined forms of description. There is something else that happens in recollection. The action-packed traumatic scenes of what people did may be invested with different meanings at different times. This phenomenon was well known to Freud, from quite early in his career. Before he had allowed full rein to infant sexuality, he was inclined to say that the primal scene, in which the infant or child witnesses parental intercourse, need not have had any sexual meaning at the time it was experienced. In adolescence or later, however, the same old scene became intensely sexual. Thanks to Freud and others, the nineteenth-century idea that children are asexual is no longer well entrenched—although it is partially retained in theories of child development, in the idea that certain experiences are "inappropriate" at a certain stage of development, and hence in the clinical diagnosis of child abuse on the basis of excessive interest in sex. Freud probably bought into the asexuality of infants and children more than many of his contemporaries, and hence his retraction was the more pronounced.[14] We can separate matters of Freud-history and Freud-exegesis from his initial insight. The idea, that the primal scene has a different meaning when experienced by the child from what it means when remembered or repressed by the adolescent, is of fundamental importance, even if founded on misleading presuppositions. We may think of it at the level of interpreting given events, or of acquiring new levels of feeling for what happened. I propose to go further.

Old actions under new descriptions may be reexperienced in memory. And if these are genuinely new descriptions, descriptions not available or perhaps nonexistent at the time of the episodes remembered, then something is experienced now, in memory, that in a certain sense did not exist before. The action took place, but not the action under the new description. Moreover, it was not determinate that these events would be experienced in these new ways, for it was not determinate, at the time that the events occurred, that in the future new descriptions would come into being. I should repeat that there are also lots of straightforward memories, suppressed or repressed, of perfectly determinate and thoroughly awful events. I am exploring memories that are on the fringe of these, memories that arise by mental mechanisms different from more straightforward recollection, whatever that may be.

Thus I am suggesting a very difficult view about memories of intentional human actions. What matters to us may not have been quite so definite as it now seems. When we remember what we did, or what other people did, we may also rethink, redescribe, and refeel the past. These redescriptions may be perfectly true of the past; that is, they are truths that we now assert about the past. And yet, paradoxically, they may not have been true in the past, that is, not truths about intentional actions that made sense when the actions were performed. That is why I say that the past is revised retroactively. I do not mean only that we change our opinions about what was done, but that in a certain logical sense what was done itself is modified. As we change our understanding and sensibility, the past becomes filled with intentional actions that, in a certain sense, were not there when they were performed.

There are people to whom such a preposterous conclusion is perfectly obvious, people who delight in dispensing with the old categories of fact, of truth, of reason, and of logic. I regret that what I say may appeal to such people. It will be evident from the way I have written this book, and from what I have already said in this chapter, that I myself take for granted that the ideas of truth and fact are both basic and relatively unproblematic. My paradoxical claims about a certain indeterminacy in some past human actions are serious precisely because they are set against a background of truth and falsehood. Theorists who write as if everything were indeterminate, and a matter of texts and descriptions, usefully shake up our preconceptions. Their examples often teach a great deal, but their general thesis does not tell us much. To cite an old adage, if all flesh is straw, then kings and cardinals are straw—but so is everyone else, and we have not learned much about kings and cardinals.

We had best put the idea of indeterminacy of the past together with two commonplaces about memory. One I have mentioned already. Memory is not like a video record. It does not need images, and images are never enough; moreover, our memories shade and patch and combine and delete. This thought leads to the second one: the best analogy to remembering is storytelling. The metaphor for memory is narrative. Novelists probably do better at these themes than any theoretician. In *The Good Terrorist* (from which I quoted at the end of chapter 5) Doris Lessing's protagonist Alice "was struggling to bring her memory to heel," but

> when her mind started to dazzle and to puzzle, frantically trying to lay hold of something stable, then she always at once allowed herself—as she did now—to slide back into her childhood, where she dwelt pleasurably on some scene or other that she had smoothed and polished and painted over and over again with fresh color until it was like walking into a story that began, "Once upon a time there was a little girl called Alice with her mother, Dorothy. . . ."[15]

The doctrine that memory should be thought of as narrative is an aspect of memoro-politics. We constitute our souls by making up our lives, that is, by weaving stories about our past, by what we call memories. The tales we tell of ourselves and to ourselves are not a matter of recording what we have done and how we have felt. They must mesh with the rest of the world and with other people's stories, at least in externals, but their real role is in the creation of a life, a character, a self. This vision of memory as narrative is usually presented as humane, humanistic, anti-scientistic. It is certainly at odds with the neurological program of understanding memory. That has been anatomical in character—different types of memory are to be located in different parts of the body, that is, different parts of the brain. The opposition between memory as anatomy and memory as narrative need not be complete. Thus the neurologist Israel Rosenfeld, in his book *The Invention of Memory*, traces the anatomical program of localization of brain function but urges something far more like a narrative analysis of the role of memory in the life of human beings.[16] There remains no doubt, however, that memory-as-narrative is often part of an antiscientific ideology. Yet it should never be forgotten that memoro-politics emerges precisely in the scientific context of positive psychology. It is part of the secular drive to replace the soul with something of which we have knowledge. Poets do not care for secular and scientific knowledge, but even they could not stand still. The humanistic reaction was to try an alternative: capture the soul not as science but as narrative. Proust's *A la recherche du temps perdu* is a response to the first wave of French scientistic memoro-politics. He wrote book after book of rewriting memories, retelling the same stories transformed. Proust is more Bergson than Janet, certainly, but the matrix is the same. A case described by Marcel's father will appear equally in *A la recherche* and in several different studies by Pierre Janet.[17] Bergson drew repeatedly on Janet, his exact contemporary, fellow student, and finally lifetime colleague. Memory as narrative and the sciences of memory are branches of the same stem, the secularization of the soul.

How strongly should we adhere to the picture of memory as narrative? Lessing, vividly connecting memory and storytelling, nevertheless writes of dwelling on a *scene*. I think that's right. I want briefly to suggest the merits of a vulgar point of view: memory is in some ways comparable to perception, so long as we do not demand images. I want, for a moment, to direct our attention away from narrative. Despite my insistence that action is action under a description, I am suspicious of our incessant verbalizing of the human condition. Gilbert Ryle, the doyen of postwar Oxford philosophy, was already connecting remembering and narrating in his discussion of memory at the end of his classic 1949 contribution to the philosophy of mind.[18] "Being good at recalling is being good at presenting. . . . It is a narrative skill." "Reminiscing, then, can take the form of a faithful verbal narration."[19] Ryle rightly says that *one* of the ways that we remember, recall, and reminisce is by narrating. It does not follow that remembering *is* narrating. Although Ryle usually wrote of recalling episodes, he, like Lessing, also spoke of scenes. To say that remembering is often of scenes, views, and feelings is not to imply that we remember in images or reproduce, internally, an image of a scene or an afterimage or interpretation of a feeling. We may do so, but we need not. Empirical psychology teaches that people are very different in the extent to which they (say they) visualize or form images.

The metaphor of the scene makes good sense of the experiences reported in the sudden recovery of painful memories. The most common expression now used is "flashback," a term taken from the movies. It is a scene or episode recalled, perhaps without provocation, unexpectedly. Sometimes it is only a glimpse, or a flooding with feeling. Yet there is a danger here. Theoreticians of repressed memories often urge that there is a difference between conventional memories on the one hand and flashbacks or sudden bursts of feeling on the other. They grant that our memories of the past are like stories, rearranged, repainted, full of invention and rife with omission. When memories result in straightforward narratives, they are often wrong in detail, tone, or substance. But the flashback and restored feelings—those are genuine reexperiencings. They are somehow privileged, or so it is implied.

Where does this supposed privilege come from? Undoubtedly from the sheer horror associated with a clear flashback, and the terrible misgivings and angst associated with a cloudy one. How can there be these oppressive floodings from the past, if they do not point to something that really happened? David Hume distinguished our immediate perceptions from our memory images on the ground that the former are more "lively" or "vivacious." Nothing, alas, is more lively than a fearful flashback, which may be felt more intensely than the original trauma. But in fact flashbacks are not so secure as all that. Recent memory therapy reinforces flashbacks, and they become stabilized. Janet and Goddard destabilized them and removed them, sometimes with a few words of hypnotic suggestion.

I do not intend to diminish the sheer reality-feeling of frightening flashbacks, but I would like to suggest a quite different element behind the idea that flashbacks of emotion or feeling point inexorably to the truth. The popular entrenchment of the idea of memory as narrative has something to do with it. The logical structure of the reasoning may be as follows. We agree that memory of type X has gaps and inventions. But there is a memory of type Y that is different in kind, spontaneous, uncontrolled. There is no reason to infer from the fact that X is prone to error that Y is prone to error. So, since memory of type Y is so powerfully experienced, we may assume that Y is not erroneous. Set out abstractly like that, the conclusion manifestly does not follow. But I would not let matters rest there. For the argument relies on a sharp distinction between X and Y. It already grants, as I do not, that there is a wide class of remembering best compared to narrative. That I deny, even though I agree with Ryle that recalling is a narrative skill—being good at recalling is being good at presenting. I suggest that our common conception of remembering, as encoded in grammar, is remembering of scenes, a remembering that is presented, often, by narrating but is nevertheless a memory of scenes and episodes. The flashback is no more than an unusually jolting scene. It is not peculiarly different from memory in general—and hence, not especially privileged.

Thus those who describe remembering as narrative often intend to undercut any privilege of memory as a means of getting at the truth about the past. But in fact they create a space for another kind of memory, a special kind of memory, which is then, by its advocates, given special rights. My approach says that the logical error begins when one identifies remembering with narration. That makes a flashback something whose very nature is different from other memory. But if recollection is to be compared to thinking of scenes and episodes (and describing or narrating them on occasion), then it is not intrinsically different from other remembering. There is no reason to believe that the flashback experience is better at getting at the unvarnished truth than any other type of remembering.

Flashbacks may be unusual because they are painful, terrifying, uncontrollable. But they are not very unusual. Many ordinarily recalled scenes are also painful, terrifying, and one wishes they would go away, but they won't. Nor should we forget the completely insignificant scenes that recur throughout our lives of remembering; they are annoying because they will recur, and the very act of trying to make them go away seems to make them the more ineradicable. Finally, a great many flashbacks are not painful at all. A few days ago I was at a spot where I have not been for years; a whole scene came back to me; I was speaking with someone whom I do not know well, but for whom I care a good deal; the flashback was suffused with feeling, mostly good, a little sadness. This was above all an ordinary experience. It happens to every adult, to every reader of this page. We should not let the ordinary be stolen away from us by ideologues of any stripe.

253

The old, and valuable, Freudian insight is that scenes that are recovered, whether it is in flashbacks, or through memory therapy, or through more ordinary reflective but unassisted recollection, become invested with meanings that they did not have at the time that they were experienced. Let me add that in our days of inflated psychological verbiage, the human actions which occur in those scenes are very often retroactively redescribed. That is, they become actions under descriptions that were not available at the time the actions were first performed. This is particularly true of the memories involved in the recent flurry of distressing accusations and counteraccusations. Our prototype is a woman in her thirties who recalls dreadful scenes from the age of five. If she was thirty in 1990, she was five years old in 1965, when the recognition of child abuse as battering babies had only barely got under way. Lessing spoke of smoothing and polishing and painting over and over again with fresh color until the memory of a scene was like walking into a story. That happens all the time, but at this moment in history there is an added feature. The colors with which we paint often did not exist when the episodes occurring in the scenes actually occurred.

I am determined not to be misunderstood. I have already said that I have little problem about applying present moral categories, such as child abuse, in the present meaning of the term, at least to events that occurred in the past generation or two. As we recede into the past, culture and norms become increasingly different, and I develop qualms about retroactive application. I also resist applying modern terms to old stories on the ground that the person in the story would have behaved or developed in a certain way today. In the case of a human action or condition, I will use modern epithets only for old actualities, not for old potentialities. I am not here preoccupied by the customary question, which in each case of importance must be settled by corroboration, of whether a memory accurately represents the past. I am concerned with the phenomenon of indeterminacy of human action in the past. In various ways it may not have been determinate, then, that an action fell under certain present-day descriptions. Thus the question of accuracy may not arise, at least not in any direct and simplistic version.

Next there is the phenomenon of contagion by words. Let a scene be recalled, an uncomfortable scene now recalled in terms of abuse. Although the scene may have some prominences, it is also clouded; it has long been buried. There is no conscious structure in which to encode it. But there is one generic description under which to categorize the central action of whoever created the discomfort: child abuse. How shall the scene be continued? The rubric is set out by the generic description. There is a retinue of possible events with which to flesh out (rather literally) the scene. This does not require overt suggestion on the part of a therapist, as is often alleged by the false memory movement. The spreading of the phrase "child abuse" upon the scene stems from deeper and more semantic mechanisms, ultimately linked to the notion of human action under a description. The scene is not merely "smoothed and polished and painted over," as happens in all memory of important events; it is painted from a particular palette, and that palette is called child abuse.

Semantic contagion is an effect that tends to go to extremes. If some events are described as of type A, then they may be redescribed yet again as extremely bad, or extremely good, events of type A. The fantasies of Doris Lessing's Alice made life with mother all glowing. Accusatory memories make the past horrible. There may also be a thoroughly non-logical element driving semantic contagion, namely, the recent popularity, among middle-class people who can afford therapists, of seeing oneself as victim. In conversation one African-American psychiatrist unkindly called this me-tooism; at a time when consciousness is being raised about real oppression, the confused and depressed take comfort in saying, "Me too."

The current (1994) wisdom in the multiple personality and recovered memory movements is that therapists must ensure that they do not suggest memories to their clients. Not only must there be no suggestion, but it must be seen that there is no suggestion. If necessary, tapes and even witnesses must be used as a safeguard against later lawsuits. (Alas, the public discussions that I have heard are over and over again about how to prevent lawsuits, not about how to avoid harming clients or their families.) I fear this is simplistic. We have very little grasp of the workings of "suggestion," a word that, as Nietzsche said of "psychological pain," so often stands for a question mark rather than for a clear idea. Many clients in therapy belong to numerous self-help groups or at least read the self-help books. After you have filled in the questionnaires and proved that you satisfy at least the minimum requirements for disorder X, it requires a certain robustness of mind not to suspect that you do have disorder X. The best cure is to complete all the questionnaires for every disorder. When you discover that you suffer from every dysfunction, a certain skepticism may set in. Few have the stamina for that type of cure.

Many more types of suggestion come from the milieu than from the therapist. The most difficult type of suggestion to grasp or grapple with is the type of internally prompted suggestion that I have called semantic contagion. Having recalled a scene, you begin to paint it, using the palette of the generic but retroactive redescription that came with the first intimations of memory, for example, of being abused. Multiple personality furnishes an especially interesting example, because of the way it links scenes with narrative. Someone who is severely depressed, incapable of forming stable friendships, and sexually troubled may turn to self-help or therapy, and may find solace after recovering memories and working through them. But there is no specific etiology. Freud's first forays into the psyche aimed at specific etiologies for hysteria, neurasthenia, anxiety neuroses, and the like. The current state of multiple personality theory resembles the earliest Freud. Stories call for causes. We weary of chronicles: this happened, then that. The Bible's "begats" may make a found poem, but as narration are a deadly bore. Fairy tales create fairy causes; Cinderella's coach did not change back into a pumpkin by chance. In real life the tighter the chain of causation—the more specific the etiology—the better the narrative. Multiple personality provides the best available narrative frame for recovered memory.

Early in the book I showed how the modern multiple movement has thrived in a milieu of heightened consciousness about child abuse. I have even ungraciously compared it to a parasite living upon a host, child abuse. But as ecologists teach us, parasitism is always a two-way relationship with the host. Aside from workers with a close affinity to psychoanalysis, clinicians who work with recovered memories are very receptive to signs of multiple personality. The intimate relationship connecting recovery of traumatic memories of child abuse with multiple personality is no accident. For although I fall short of saying memory simply is narrative, I agree with Ryle that one becomes good at recalling the critical part of one's past when one acquires the skill to cast it into a coherent narrative. That is precisely what is provided by the causal lore of multiple personality, for good stories use explanations. Dissociation is explained as a coping mechanism. The multiple comes to understand that she is as she is now because of the way she deployed coping mechanisms in the past. A narrative structure is available that can then be filled in with the appropriate scenes.

The models of suggestion and iatrogenesis are cavalierly invoked by skeptics about multiplicity. They are confidently rejected by advocates. I am urging that the models are skimpy and superficial. The multiple personality phenomenon directs us to phenomena that students of the human mind have hardly begun to address. One of them I call semantic, for lack of a better word. "Semantic" at least has the virtue of making plain that I am speaking more from the space of logic than from that overtilled country called "social construction." The semantic effect arises from the way in which we can apply present descriptions retroactively to actions in one's long-ago, less than determinate, past. Another semantic phenomenon, which feeds on the first, is semantic contagion. More actions come into memory, actions described by more and more specific descriptions that fall under the generic head of the first description. A third semantic phenomenon has to do with the way in which memory is most satisfying when it provides a narrative, and narrative is most tight when it has a clear causal structure. Multiple personality has succeeded, at least for the nonce, where Freud abandoned ship: in the realm of a specific etiology of a neurosis. The distressed person, casting about for self-understanding, becomes satisfied by a specific causal structure whose chief obligation is to be faithful to the memories that arise from the first two semantic phenomena. What must count first is whether she becomes happier, better able to live with friends and family, more confident, less terrified. That granted, and imaging that no one at all is harmed by any elements of falsehood or fantasy that may have crept into the cure, does it matter whether her reconstructed soul remembers her past and her self with some accuracy? Throughout this book difficult moral questions have been in the background. Now I want to bring one of them to the fore.

False Consciousness

DOES IT MATTER whether what we seem to remember really happened, more or less as we remember it? In daily life it matters most of the time. I thought I left my wallet in my raincoat pocket; it's not there. Panic. I (seem to) remember loaning you my copy of Putnam's book. Oh. I'm sorry, I loaned it to Lisa; I was confused. But what about seeming memories of long ago? They matter when our beliefs affect other people. That is the point of the false memory polemics. If someone cuts off all contact with her family, because she wrongly has come to believe that her father abused her and her mother knew but kept silent, then incalculable harm has been done to the family. In that case, the false beliefs, which seem to be memories, have terrible effects. But what about false beliefs that do not affect other people? What is wrong with mistaken memories that do no harm? I shall suggest an answer in terms of what I call false consciousness.

I mean something quite ordinary by false consciousness: the state of people who have formed importantly false beliefs about their character and their past. I argue that false consciousness is a bad state to be in, even if one is not responsible for being in that state. False memory—something of a contradiction in terms—is only a small part of false consciousness. This is because "false memory syndrome" usually refers to a pattern of memories of events in one's own past that never took place. It is not that the events are remembered inaccurately (for most events are). It is rather that nothing remotely like those events occurred. Indeed, the so-called syndrome might be called contrary-memory syndrome, for the seeming memories are not merely false but contrary to all reality. In the prototypical example, a "recanter" says that she seemed to remember being regularly raped by her uncle, but now she realizes that nothing of the sort ever occurred. Nobody ever raped her. Her uncle was gentle and caring. Her seeming memory that the abuser was her uncle does not cast him as a stand-in for someone else, for no one ever abused her. That is what I call a contrary-memory. That is the sort of "memory" that the False Memory Syndrome Foundation advertises. A person with contrary-memories of her own most intimate life would, in my terminology, have false consciousness. But there is more to false consciousness than that.

A merely-false-memory, in the same ballpark as the above example of a contrary-memory, would be one in which the uncle is, in memory, a screen for the father, the real perpetrator. Thus the memory is not contrary to all reality, but the past has been radically remolded. Another possibility is that the uncle did not rape her when she was six, but did fondle her improperly. The false memory syndrome people have expressed little interest in merely-false-memories like that. But such seeming memories could certainly feed what I call a false consciousness—for example, if the victim seems to remember vile treatment from her uncle, who was sweetness and light, in order to shield her father, and her own self-image.[1]

Another relevant defect in memory could be called wrong-forgetting. That is the suppression of central items from one's past that are integral to one's character or nature. I say suppression, not repression. Repression is a postulated mechanism whereby incidents are lost to conscious memory and drives or tendencies are lost to conscious desire. Part of the postulate is that the repression is itself not a deliberate and conscious act on the part of any moral agent. A purist, especially a psychoanalytic purist, might say that a person who has not worked through the past and liberated repressed memory suffers from false consciousness. Well, maybe a person with five years of free time and a great deal of money, who declines analysis out of fear, is afflicted with false consciousness. But ordinary mortals bringing up a family, and supplying its needs of love, care, and sustenance, are not suffering from false consciousness, in any important way, if repressing their memories keeps them on an even keel. If, however, some memories have been suppressed, deliberately, by whomever and by whatever means, then we may begin to think of false consciousness.

Contrary-memory, merely-false-memory, and wrong-forgetting by no means exhaust the possibilities. Let me group these and other possibilities under the heading of deceptive-memory. I am inventing compound words with hyphens to flag the fact that, strictly speaking, we are concerned not with memories but with seeming memories or the absence of memories. In deceptive-memory I include seeming memories, or absence of memory, of definite facts about the past. I am not referring to the indeterminacies about past human action discussed in the previous chapter. But of course if there is what I called semantic contagion, then a person may arrive at definitely false beliefs that seem to be incorporated in memory. If she passes from redescribing a past action as sexual abuse (an adult's obsessive attention to her genitalia when washing her as a child) to the seeming memory that her mother constantly forced a rubber duck into her orifices while bathing her, we have semantic contagion and deceptive-memory.

Since memoro-politics has largely succeeded, we have come to think of ourselves, our character, and our souls as very much formed by our past. Hence, in our times, false consciousness will often involve some deceptive-memories. It need not do so. The Delphic injunction "Know thyself!" did not refer to memory. It required that we know our character, our limits, our needs, our propensities for self-deception. It required that we know our souls. Only with the advent of memoro-politics did memory become a surrogate for the soul. Even today there are plenty of kinds of false consciousness that have nothing to do with memory. We all know those who genuinely believe that they are generous and sensitive, when in fact they are self-centered and indifferent. Kant held the maxim "He who wills the end wills the means," yet I know someone who is a living refutation of Kant. For he sincerely strives for worthy ends, but he is lacking in self-understanding and sensibility for other people; hence he does not comprehend what could serve as means to the ends for which he strives. He wills the end but seems incapable of willing the means. That too is a kind of false consciousness. Every reader will furnish other examples close to home, or closer: readers who are sure that they are free of any taint of false consciousness are perhaps the falsest of all.

Here, however, we are concerned with remembering, and hence with false consciousness that feeds on deceptive-memories. I say that it feeds on them, because it is not enough that we have deceptive-memories. In order for there to be false consciousness we must use the deceptive-memories as part of our sense of who we are. They must be part of the story that we tell about ourselves. They must be part of the way in which we constitute ourselves, or see our selves as constituted.

So much impassioned rubbish is now spoken and written about "false memory"—that is, contrary-memory—that we shall have a cleaner slate if we think instead about wrong-forgetting. No one, I think, so systematically cultivated deceptive-memory as Pierre Janet. He did so from the highest motives. His patients were in torment. Their symptoms were caused by ill-remembered trauma. His cures often relied on eliciting the trauma by discussion and by hypnosis. Once the cause of the distress had been brought to light, he hypnotized the patient into thinking that the events never happened. To recall two cases discussed earlier, Marie had been traumatized by her terror of her first menstrual period, and by standing in a barrel of freezing water in order to stop it. Her periods did cease, for a while, but later on she endured hysterical hypothermia, terrible fits of freezing cold every month. She did not understand why, and more and more hysterical symptoms appeared. When Marguerite was six she had to sleep beside a girl with a disgusting facial skin disease and had been made to put her hand on it to show she was not frightened by it. As an adult, she developed rashes, paralyses, insensitivity, and blindness on that side of her face and body. Janet hypnotized these women into believing that the events never occurred. Marie had never, on the occasion of her first menstrual period, stood for hours in a freezing water barrel. Marguerite had never had to sleep beside a girl with an appalling skin disease on her face. In both cases the hysterical symptoms vanished.

Marie and Marguerite did not suppress their memories, but Janet did. Hence, by my definition, they have wrongly-forgotten a critical event in their lives. Should we say that these women suffered from false consciousness? Not on the basis of what Janet told us. Marguerite's trauma is, so far as Janet has informed us, an accident, a mere incident in her life that repelled her. We may well suspect that a great deal has been left out. Why was she made to sleep beside the sick girl? Why did she have to touch the repugnant skin? What cruel mother or aunt did this to her? What else did that person do to her? What sort of family was this, anyway? Likewise with Marie we wonder why she was so terrified of her periods, why she took such desperate measures. There is a great deal to learn about both lives. We may suspect that after treatment by Janet both women were living in a state of thoroughly false consciousness. But we cannot prove that. It is a counsel of perfection that everyone should understand themselves to the core.

Now turn to another historical example of what was probably wrong-forgetting. Goddard's nineteen-year-old Bernice had an alter aged four, the obnoxious Polly. Bernice repeatedly told Goddard about incest with her father. Goddard convinced her, and I think hypnotized her, into believing this was a fantasy. Let us suppose that Bernice's memories of incest were pretty much correct. (That is only a hypothesis on my part, but assume it for this analysis.) Let us suppose also that Goddard succeeded in suppressing Bernice's memory. (This is dubious; we know, from letters written by the superintendent of the Columbus State Hospital for the Insane, that Goddard lied when he ended his account of Bernice by saying that he sent her off effectively cured.) I use these two suppositions not to present a "Real Person," in Kathleen Wilkes's sense, but to provide an example that in many ways resembles a real-life incident. Under the first supposition, Goddard induced wrong-forgetting. Under the second supposition, Bernice believed that she was not molested in any way by her father or anyone else. But, under the first supposition, she was.

This only slightly imagined Bernice certainly has deceptive-memory. Unlike Marguerite and Marie, I think that she also has false consciousness. For she has not forgotten an incident or pattern of behavior that we, or she, or people in her community, in 1921, would take to be a mere incident in her life. The incest was something deeply important about her growing up, her family, her young life.

But is there anything wrong with the false consciousness that Goddard induced and to which Bernice succumbed? There might be obvious, utilitarian, things wrong with it. It might have had terrible consequences. For example, in historical fact, in 1921 Bernice had a number of younger siblings, including a three-year-old sister, Betty Jane. Her father had died of tuberculosis three years earlier; her mother also died of TB soon afterward, and the family was broken up. Betty Jane was adopted by an upright family in the community, even changing her surname. Now if the father had not died when Bernice was sixteen—when Betty Jane was an infant—many experienced social workers would bet their bottom dollar that father would have been after Betty Jane in a while. If so, Goddard would have achieved an evil consequence. Bernice, who might have given the alarm, is now silenced. She no longer remembers what once she knew. But for the utilitarian, the false consciousness is not what is wrong. It is the fact that Bernice was deprived of a crucial piece of information that would have mattered to young Betty Jane.

False beliefs about one's past can have less dramatic bad consequences. Most of us find it embarrassing to be contradicted, even in matters of no significance. But in the story as told, there were no survivors to contradict Bernice. Even a twin sister, who may well have been assaulted, died at the age of eleven. In this story that I am adapting from historical fact, Bernice was simply insulated from all contradiction. It would have been different if all this had happened thirty years later. Bernice, aged nineteen in 1951 (rather than 1921), comes to believe that the incest never occurred. But by 1981, when she is forty-nine, she can hardly escape the media coverage of child sexual abuse and incest. We can certainly envisage a severe midlife crisis, to say the least, as she dimly feels her mind torn by a vague sense that something awful happened to her long ago.

In the story that is closer to the historical situation, however, Betty Jane is safe (we hope) in her adoptive home, and almost everyone else is dead. Given Bernice's health record, I expect that she died before incest became front-page news. There was no occasion for any cognitive dissonance. Thus I am deliberately telling a story in which there may be no utilitarian argument to show that Bernice's false consciousness in 1930, say, was a bad thing. There were no bad consequences. But perhaps we can find utilitarian objections to Bernice's state of affairs. There were still dangers. For example, the dead father may have been a member of a cult. That cult might go on harming children, and Bernice, with memories suppressed, would not be able to blow the whistle. Or even in 1930 there was the risk that Bernice's suppressed memories might, after all, resurface. Then, lacking adequate support, she might endure dreadful psychological self-torture. Janet himself was well aware of this danger and sometimes found it necessary to rehypnotize his patients into reforgetting their trauma. Only half in jest he said that he hoped he would outlive his patients, for without him to make the resurfaced memories go away again, they would be in trouble.

The utilitarian has to work harder and harder to find anything to object to in false consciousness. That is not surprising, for false consciousness is (I say) objectionable in itself, not in its consequences—and what utilitarians must object to is consequences. Suppose Goddard's therapy had worked. Bernice issued as a relatively whole person, able to carry on a life, perform light secretarial work (she was not a very well person), able to fulfill the societal norms of her day, marry, raise a family. What's wrong with that if there were no bad consequences?

Bernice, as imagined, certainly violates the ancient injunction "Know thyself." There is a sense in which she really does not know herself, how she came to be as she is, the dreadful episodes with her father that (according to today's etiology of dissociation) brought about her breakdown. So what? Bernice has achieved a coherent soul. It works, or so we are told. What better truth for her is needed? The therapist will say, perhaps, none. He is glad to get Bernice back to an almost normal life. There is a slight inconsistency in Goddard's reporting. He ended his article published in 1926 by saying that Bernice is quite happy working half-days. In the book published the next year, and closer to the historical truth, we learn that "it will be some time before she will be strong enough to earn her own living." Leave that aside. Suppose Bernice carried on well enough after Goddard released her. The pragmatist may say that there is no need for some "historical" truth: Bernice's soul worked.

I am not satisfied. We do have another vision of the soul and self-knowledge. What is its basis? It comes from deeply rooted convictions and sensibilities about what it is to be a fully developed human being. They are parts of the Western moral tradition—that of Bernice, Goddard, and myself. First, there is an old sense of teleology, fostered by Aristotle, a sense of the ends for which a person exists: to grow into a complete and self-aware person. Second, there is the nominalism, represented by John Locke, according to which memory is a criterion for personal identity, perhaps the essential one. Third, there is the idea of autonomy, that we are responsible for constructing our own moral selves; that is perhaps the most enduring aspect of Kant's ethics. Fourth, memoro-politics has recently taught us or coerced us to believe that a person, or in older language the soul, is constituted by memories and character. Any type of amnesia results in something's being stolen from oneself; how much worse if it is replaced by deceptive-memories, a nonself.

The third part of this inheritance is especially interesting in the example of Bernice and many other damaged women. Consider the kind of material that was and was not in the false consciousness of Miss Bernice R. She was reconstructed and built into the male-dominated world of Dr. Goddard, in which few fathers molest their daughters, and in which unwell young women are cured if they work as part-time secretaries. Bernice becomes a tidy and polite half-day clerk. Any possible autonomy of this already much weakened woman has been effectively annihilated.

Such a critique of what Goddard did has strong feminist overtones. But it also arises from basic "modern" moral theory, whether we take that to be characterized by Kant or by Rousseau or, for that matter, by Michel Foucault.[2] The thought of those men was dominated by the ideas of autonomy and freedom. They demanded awareness of how to take responsibility for one's own character, one's own growth, one's own morality. Those philosophers had overcome the ancient Greek idea that we, like all else in nature, have a fully defined end to which we as human beings naturally tend. No: in the modern image, it is we ourselves who must choose the ends. That is a stern creed: we can be fully moral beings only when we understand why we choose the ends. To be realistic, we do not expect Bernice to have been strong enough to satisfy the demands envisaged by Rousseau or Kant or Foucault. But Goddard absolutely precluded Bernice's having any freedom at all. He brutally reconstructed her and suppressed her past. He did so using patriarchal strategies, but one need have no special feminist alignment to see that what he did was wrong.

We should be under no illusions. Autonomy is not comfortable. A 1990s Bernice would not have her memories of incest simply quashed. Things are not so great today, either, for someone like Bernice. But at least with the consciousness that she would acquire now, and some serious sisterly support, there would be some possibility that she would find a self to which it would be worth her while to be true. Beware, however, of cant. One has no confidence that a 1990s Bernice is going to lead a happier or even better life in the rough-and-tumble of fuller knowledge than did my quasi-historical Bernice seventy years earlier. A truer consciousness may be a bed of thistles compared to which the real Bernice's false consciousness was a thorny rose garden.

Self-knowledge is a virtue in its own right. We value the way in which people can fulfill their own natures by gaining an unsentimental self-understanding. We think it is good to grow, for all our vices, into someone who is mature enough to face the past and the present, someone who understands how character, in its weaknesses as well as its strengths, is made of interlocking tendencies and gifts that have grown in the course of a life. The image of growth and maturing is Aristotelian rather than Kantian. These ancient values are ideals that none fully achieve, and yet they are modest, not seeking to find a meaning in life beyond life, but finding excellence in living and honoring life and its potentialities. Those values imply that false consciousness is bad in itself.

The idea of false consciousness may get at the heart of a nagging worry about multiple personality and its treatment. I began this book asking whether the disorder is real. That question, I said, was often a stand-in for a quite different type of question, about consequences. Clinicians need to know the best ways in which to help their patients. The immediate and pressing question is, what is the most helpful sort of therapy? Opponents, who say that multiple personality is not a real disorder, are often talking about treatment. They hold that it is a bad idea to encourage the development of alters associated with apparent memories of childhood trauma. They contend that other modalities of treatment will have better results. Proponents of the disorder believe that such "benign neglect" leaves the patient a permanent recidivist multiple. These seem like empirical questions, but there are no clinical trials that bear on them. Criticism and revision have come from within the multiple movement itself. The change in name, to dissociative identity disorder, is not merely nominal. It is an attempt to get away from solidified alters, agents who cope; it wants instead to emphasize disintegration, the loss of wholeness, the absence of person, that some of these patients exhibit.

Yet these internal debates are all about consequences. They are utilitarian. I suspect that there is also a deeper and what I might call moral issue. Some of those who are critical of the multiple movement are well informed, sensitive, and humble. They do not trumpet the evils of false memories, although they try to help individuals who have been poorly served by careless therapies. They are rather quiet about the issues, distrusting the stupid polemics that they hear around them. They will ask, late in the afternoon, in a corner, whether one thinks that multiple personality is real. But what worries them should not be put in terms of what is real. These cautious skeptics are concerned when they think of a patient who goes through multiple therapy, becomes intimate with more than a dozen alters, and believes that these alters were formed early in childhood as a way of coping with trauma, usually including sexual abuse.

Confident and blatant skeptics cheerfully dismiss all that as fantasy, but it is the less arrogant and more reflective doubters whom I have in mind. They accept that the patient has produced this version of herself: a narrative that includes dramatic events, a causal story of the formation of alters, and an account of the relationships between the alters. That is a self-consciousness; that is a soul. The doubters accept it as a reality. They are all too familiar with the fact that psychiatry is filled with pain and inability to help. They respect a clinician who can make a client feel more confident and able to get on with her life. Nevertheless, they fear that multiple personality therapy leads to a false consciousness. Not in the blatant sense that the apparent memories of early abuse are necessarily wrong or distorted—they may be true enough. No, there is the sense that the end product is a thoroughly crafted person, but not a person who serves the ends for which we are persons. Not a person with self-knowledge, but a person who is the worse for having a glib patter that simulates an understanding of herself. Some of the feminist writers who are critical of multiple personality appear to share this moral judgment. They add that too much multiple therapy implicitly confirms the old male model of the passive woman who could not hang in, who retroactively creates a story about herself in which she was the weak vessel.

Such tentative and cautious skeptics ask whether multiple personality is real. Not being philosophers, they feel that they have to continue their doubts in a utilitarian vein, raising questions about what is the most effective treatment. But since I am a philosopher, I should now speak for them. I say that in their hearts they suspect that the outcome of multiple therapy is a type of false consciousness. That is a deeply moral judgment. It is based on the sense that false consciousness is contrary to the growth and maturing of a person who knows herself. It is contrary to what the philosophers call freedom. It is contrary to our best vision of what it is to be a human being.

Notes

INTRODUCTION

1. Hacking 1986b.

CHAPTER 1
IS IT REAL?

1. Boor 1982.

2. American Psychiatric Association 1980, 257.

3. Horton and Miller 1972, 151. Such figures are always underestimates; more extensive literature surveys inevitably turn up more cases.

4. None: see Merskey 1992. Eighty-four: this is one count up to 1969; see Greaves 1980, 578. The 1791 case was noticed in Ellenberger 1970, 127.

5. Coons 1986.

6. Incidence rates are discussed in chapter 7. For the 5 percent figure, see Ross, Norton, and Wozney 1989. For "exponential increase" see Ross 1989, 45.

7. Brook 1992, 335. The first type of splitting involves dissociation. The second type is the splitting of objects and affects into those which are good and those which are bad, into objects of affection and objects of hostility. The third type is the splitting of the ego into an acting part and a self-observing part. Freud made comments about splitting throughout the whole of his forty-five years of writing about psychology and psychoanalysis.

8. World Health Organization 1992, 151–161. For critical comments on *ICD-10*, from members of the multiple movement, see the essays by F. O. Garcia, Philip Coons, David Spiegel, and W. C. Young in *Dissociation* 3 (1990): 204–221.

9. American Psychiatric Association 1980, 259. Kirk 1992 is a study of how *DSM* criteria become established, and how the manual itself achieved its present status as definitive.

10. 1987 criteria of *DSM-III-R* (American Psychiatric Association 1987, 272) were:

   A. The existence within the person of two or more distinct personalities or personality states (each with its own relatively enduring pattern of perceiving, relating to, and thinking about the environment and self).

   B. At least two of these identities or personality states recurrently take full control of the person's behavior.

11. This summary is from Putnam 1993 but was in force for the first survey of patients with multiple personality, Putnam et al., 1986.

12. Austin 1962, 72.

13. Ross 1989, 52. "True" is not the same word as "real." Austin held that "real" is the most general adjective of a class of which "true" was an instance. I am not sure he was right, but here it seems immaterial whether the APA or Colin Ross used the adjective "real" or the adjective "true."

14. For one review, see Wilbur and Kluft 1989, 2197–2198. The most usually addressed question about iatrogenesis is whether multiple personality is induced by hypnosis. The skeptic has something more general in mind and may observe with some justice that the most reliable predictor of the occurrence of multiple personality is a clinician who diagnoses and treats multiples.

15. For the phrase "benign neglect," see, for example, ibid., 2198. For the cautious approach see Chu 1991. Chu is not a skeptic; he is the director of the Dissociative Disorders unit at McLean Hospital, Belmont, Mass. He has written about how to help patients overcome their own resistance to the diagnosis of multiple personality; see Chu 1988.

16. For a proud statement of Dutch contributions, see van der Hart 1993a and 1993b. In 1984 and thereafter leading American advocates of multiple personality—Bennett Braun, Richard Kluft, Roberta Sachs—conducted workshops in Holland. For these and other events of the early days, see van der Hart and Boon 1990.

17. Frankel 1990. For the extraordinarily ambiguous relationships between hypnotism and psychiatry, especially in France, from 1785 to the present, see Chertok and Stengers 1992.

18. Braun 1993. This was the opening talk of the conference, in the first plenary session; I have quoted the first paragraph of Braun's abstract.

19. Ross, Norton, and Wozney 1989, 416. For a balanced discussion of the idea of superordinate diagnosis in this context, see North et al. 1993.

20. Merskey 1992, 327. Merskey's denunciation of multiple personality produced an outpouring of angry letters in subsequent issues of the journal in which he published. So did Freeland et al. 1993, an account of how Merskey and his colleagues treated four apparent cases of multiplicity.

21. One pioneering book which gives the impression that multiplicity is part of human nature is Crabtree 1985. Another work with a milder version of this idea is Beahrs 1982. For one patient who also rejects the idea that multiple personality is a disorder, see note 28, chapter 2 below. Rowan 1990 is a fascinating account of group therapies in which every member of the group creates a number of subpersonalities, expressing different aspects of character. Each individual's subpersonalities interact with other subpersonalities that emerge in group discussion. But although these subpersonalities acquire distinct names, there is no suggestion that they were "really there" as entities all along, waiting to be revealed by therapy.

22. Coons 1984, 53.

23. Braun 1986.

24. To get a sense of evolving opinions, notice how in 1989 Colin Ross agreed to this way of speaking: "I personally use the terms alter, alter personality and personality as synonyms. I call more limited states fragments, fragment alters, or fragment personalities." But in 1994 he opined that "although MPD patients are, by definition, diagnosed as having more than one personality, in fact they don't." And: "Much of the scepticism about MPD is based on the erroneous assumption that such patients have more than one personality, which is, in fact, impossible." Ross 1989, 81; Ross 1994, ix.

25. Putnam 1989, 161.

26. Putnam 1993; cf. Putnam 1992b.

27. Spiegel 1993b.

28. Lewis Carroll, *Alice's Adventures in Wonderland* (1865), the third to last paragraph of chapter 1.

29. Bowman and Amos 1993.

30. Spiegel 1993a.

31. Torem et al. 1993, 14. I have spelled out the abbreviation DD as Dissociative Disorders.

32. Spiegel 1993b, 15.

33. American Psychiatric Association 1994, 487. The addition of the amnesia condition C was the culmination of a decade-long debate.

34. *DSM-IV*, clause B, deletes the word "full" from the corresponding clause of *DSM-III-R*, note 10 above. An alter need no longer take full control—just control. This is because in the current phenomenology of multiple personality, an alter in control may still be forced to listen to the jabbering of another alter who is sitting just inside the left ear. The one in control is not in full control.

35. Spiegel 1993a.

CHAPTER 2
WHAT IS IT LIKE?

1. Hacking 1994.

2. For example, Ross 1989, 82–83.

3. Putnam 1993, 85.

4. Ross 1989, 83.

5. Whewell 1840, 8.1.4.

6. There are a number of different ways to understand Wittgenstein on family resemblances, and there is real reason to doubt that he would have been happy seeing his concept of family resemblance applied to dogs or multiple personality. But the phrase that he coined is so well known that it may help to fix ideas. For complete references to Wittgenstein, and detailed textual discussion, see Baker and Hacker 1980, 320–343.

7. See, for example, Rosch 1978.

8. The idea of a radial class is from Lakoff 1987, which provides a rich theory and also full references to Rosch's pathbreaking work on prototypes. Note that "prototype" is used in a semitechnical way. It refers to the examples of members of a class, like the class of birds or multiple personalities, that are most readily produced by people comfortable with using the name of that class, "bird," or "multiple personality." Prototypes are not to be confused with stereotypes, which are usually derogatory pictures of the people in a given class.

9. Spitzer et al. 1989.

10. Torem 1990a. For a workshop including recordings of an anorexic patient switching, consult Torem 1992.

11. For "contracting" see Putnam 1989, 144–150.

12. Schreiber 1973.

13. Ludwig 1972. Wilbur was a coauthor of this paper. She diagnosed and treated the patient; the other authors tested him in various ways.

14. Putnam et al. 1986. The results of this survey had been in circulation since 1983.

15. The *State*, Columbia, S.C., 11 February 1992, 1B. Dr. Nelson gave expert testimony that he had treated Carol R. since 1988, and that he had identified twenty-one of the twenty-two personalities in Carol. He also testified in court that Carol suffered from major depression, arthritis, hypothyroidism, nymphomania, and multiple personality disorder, a list that includes a more generous ration of psychiatric illness than most experts would want, plus one disorder, nymphomania, that is not to be found in the *DSM*.

16. Yank 1991.

17. Coons, Milstein, and Marley 1982. Coons 1988.

18. Putnam, Zahn, and Post 1990.

19. Bliss 1980, 1388.

20. Pitres 1891, 2: plate 1.

21. Wholey 1926; for stills, see Wholey 1933. The patient was in many ways like the recent prototype but had fewer alters. She was absolutely enamored of motion pictures and had fantasies of appearing on the silver screen. Wholey wrote up and showed the case as if it were a film, complete with a printed "Screen Presentation" including a list of dramatis personae, namely, the alters.

22. Smith 1993, 25.

23. This material is from *Dissociation Notes: Newsletter of North Carolina Triangle Society for the Study of Dissociation* 4, no. 3 (July 1994). Peterson's letter is on p. 1; the life story occupies pp. 3–4.

24. Some of the philosophical country, in its psychiatric and psychoanalytic context, is elegantly and accessibly mapped in Cavell 1993, 117–120.

25. Casey with Fletcher 1991.

26. From the flyleaf of the paperback edition of *The Flock* (New York: Fawcett-Columbia, 1992).

27. Dailey 1894.

28. This information is taken from Ms. Davis's intervention at the end of the taped conversation, Ross 1993.

29. Hacking 1986b, 233. At the time of this 1983 lecture I casually and wrongly referred to multiples as splits; I have corrected the wording here.

CHAPTER 3
THE MOVEMENT

1. Thigpen and Cleckley 1957.

2. Thigpen and Cleckley 1954.

3. Lancaster 1958.

4. Sizemore and Pitillo 1977.

5. Sizemore 1989.

6. Thigpen and Cleckley 1984.

7. Schreiber 1973.

8. For autobiography, see Wilbur 1991. For an interview of Wilbur with reminiscences, see Torem 1990b.

9. Wilbur 1991, 6.

10. For the number of other patients, see Schreiber 1973, 446.

11. For an account of uses of Amytal (amobarbitol) interviewing, see deVito 1993. On p. 228: "MPD patients experienced Amytal as bringing about a more profound narcosis and, hence, a stage in which alters could emerge with greater ease." Critics say this is an all too easy way to create alters, or any set of beliefs whatsoever. They say that Amytal is not a truth drug but a suggestibility serum. Herbert Spiegel, a distinguished emeritus psychiatrist from Columbia University, treated "Sybil" briefly. Recently he has said in interviews for television and *Esquire* that her alters are artifactual. Fifth Estate 1993, Taylor 1994.

12. According to Kluft 1993c. For the number of formal therapy sessions, see Schreiber 1973, 15.

13. Ellenberger 1970.

14. The man and his work have been affectionately described in Micale, ed. 1993. See especially the biographical and analytic introduction, 3–86.

15. Janet was initially receptive to Freud and Breuer's 1893 use of trauma, memory, and the subconscious. Even then he was careful to say he got there first: "We are glad to find that several authors, particularly Breuer and Freud, have recently verified our interpretation, already somewhat old, of subconscious fixed ideas in cases of hysteria." Janet 1893–1894, 2:290 (here and hereafter, translations are mine unless otherwise noted). He became increasingly disaffected; see Janet 1919, 2: chapter 3. What made the situation worse for Janet, French patriot and patrician, was being overwhelmed by a movement that was both Germanic and Jewish.

16. James 1890, chapter 10. Prince 1890.

17. He has stated that his own early enthusiastic reporting of success may have seriously misled other therapists and produced overly sanguine expectations of easy cures. Kluft 1993c.

18. Kluft 1993b, 88. I added the word "who" to make sense of the sentence as printed.

19. Ellenberger 1970, 129–131.

20. See my discussion in chapter 10, pp. 156–157 below.

21. Greaves 1980.

22. Fourteen cases are described or mentioned by name in Allison with Schwartz 1980. Another case is described in Allison 1974b. The total of thirty-six cases comes from Allison 1978b, 12.

23. Allison 1978a, 4. Personal letter, Allison, 21 November 1994.

24. Allison with Schwartz 1980. For a more recent sense of his enthusiasms, see his fruitless "search for multiples in Moscow," Allison 1991.

25. Allison 1974a.

26. Kluft 1993c, referring to Allison 1974b.

27. For example, "Psychotherapy of Multiple Personality," presented at the annual meeting of the American Psychiatric Association, Atlanta, May 1978.

28. Allison circulated his notes as "Diagnosis and Treatment of Multiple Personality" (Santa Cruz, 1977) and "Psychotherapy of Multiple Personality" (Broderick, 1977).

29. Allison with Schwartz 1980, 131–132.

30. Ibid., 161.

31. Allison 1978b, 12.

32. Putnam 1989, 202. For a literature survey of the ISH, see Comstock 1991.

33. Quoted in Putnam 1989, 203, from a paper "Treatment Philosophies in the Management of Multiple Personality," presented at the same session of the American Psychiatric Association as Allison's paper cited in note 27 above, Atlanta, May 1978.

34. Hawksworth and Schwartz 1977.

35. "Is Treatment of Inmates with MPD Possible in Prison?": printouts of debate between Ty Culiner (affirmative) and Ralph Allison (negative), 1994 ISSMP&D Fourth Annual Spring Conference, Vancouver, Canada, 6 May 1994.

36. Keyes 1981.

37. Essays by the expert witnesses are Allison 1984; Orne, Dingfes, and Orne, 1984; and Watkins 1984. For a bitterly ironic account of the trial by an opponent of multiple personality, see Aldridge-Morris 1989. Martin Orne, who argued for the prosecution, has become something of a bête noire in the multiple movement. He seems to have convinced the jury that the dissociative phenomena were a mix of acting and hypnotism. Orne is best known to the general reader as the psychiatrist of poet Anne Sexton. He kept, and allowed the publi-

cation of, some of the tapes of her therapy: Middlebrook 1991; see xiii–xviii for Orne's foreword. For the opinion of the multiple movement about this professional practice, see Faust 1991. On Sexton as multiple, mistreated by Orne, see Ross 1994, 194–215.

38. Azam 1878, 196. I have translated *aliénistes* by "psychiatrists."

39. Brouardel, Motet, and Garnier 1893. These three authors were the prosecution witnesses, respectively dean of the Paris Faculty of Medicine, doctor-in-chief of the House of Correctional Education, and doctor-in-chief of the psychiatric infirmary adjacent to the main Paris prefecture of police. They were opposed to the team of Charcot, Ballet, and Mesnet. There was a particularly vivid diagnostic confrontation between Paul Brouardel and a fourth defense witness, Auguste Voisin, a colleague of Charcot's. The loss of face by Voisin in the trial, and the corresponding challenge to his diagnoses, was worse than that experienced by any of the expert witnesses in the Hillside Strangler trial, but only in degree. The terminology of the debates is unfamiliar, being conducted in terms of somnambulism and latent epilepsy, but the terrain is very similar to that of the Hillside Strangler case.

40. See, for example, Ondrovik and Hamilton 1990, Perr 1991, Slovenko 1993, Steinberg, Bancroft, and Buchanan 1993, Saks 1994a and 1994b..

41. Lindau 1893. For discussion of the play by leading psychiatrists of the day, see Moll 1893 and Löwenfeld 1893.

42. *TV Guide*, 23 April 1994, 34.

43. For full milking of current multiple lore in the thriller department, try *A Great Deliverance* (George 1988). Runaway Gillian, whose Bible-toting father has been gruesomely decapitated, was a promiscuous tart for the village youths, but the sweetest and most innocent living thing for women and children. Her sister, who has a gross eating disorder, and who was the second to be molested by dad, did him in in order to protect a child who would soon come under his sway. We have to wade on for 298 pages before the psychiatrist reveals that Gillian dissociated; "taking it to its furthest extreme, it becomes multiple personalities."

44. *Time*, 25 October 1982, 70. The consultant expert on multiple personality was Nathan Rothstein of the William B. Hall Psychiatric Institute in Columbia, S.C. Neither he nor his present colleague Larry Nelson—cf. chapter 2, note 15—is a movement activist. When interviewed about Eric, Rothstein said that multiple personality is rare—he had seen five cases only and did not expect to see many more. Yes, he thought youthful trauma could be connected to the disorder, but it was connected to many other disturbances too. The *State*, Columbia, S.C., 7 November 1982, F1.

45. The psychologist in Daytona Beach who obtained consent was Malcolm Graham. The *State*, Columbia, S.C., 4 October 1982, 3A. Consent is obviously a real problem. See Greenberg and Attiah 1993 for current wisdom.

46. Greaves 1992, 369. Throughout this chapter I have been deliberately

commenting on the movement's self-image. From other perspectives other events might seem more important. For example, Margherita Bowers, writing in 1971, in a standard journal, set out many of the principles of subsequent multiple diagnosis and therapy. Her work has played no significant role in movement literature: Bowers et al. 1971; cf. Bowers and Brecher 1955. Confer 1983 was never taken up, although it has all the intellectual ingredients of an early textbook on multiplicity. From the point of view of psychiatrists not in the movement, Hilgard 1977 seems like the most important work reviving the concept of dissociation—see, for example, Frankel 1994. Movement writers do cite Hilgard, one of the great students of experimental hypnosis, but it is not clear that his work much influenced them. The canonization of certain works, and the exclusion of others, provides an important illustration for the social history of knowledge and power.

47. *American Journal of Clinical Hypnosis, Psychiatric Annals, Psychiatric Clinics of North America*, and *International Journal of Clinical and Experimental Hypnosis.*

48. Greaves 1987. He was apologizing for the fact that he could not answer all his telephone calls.

49. Kluft literally owns the journal, and Rush-Presbyterian-St. Luke's in a sense owned the annual ISSMP&D conference, according to Ross 1993.

50. Putnam 1993, 84.

CHAPTER 4
CHILD ABUSE

1. Herman 1992, 9.

2. Ariès 1962.

3. Wong 1993.

4. There is a vast literature on child abuse, to which I have contributed Hacking 1991b and 1992. Since both these essays include a great deal of documentation, I shall be sparing of notes here. I emphasize how child abuse has been molded into different shapes at different times. But perhaps it has simply been suppressed by interested parties. For this argument and references, see Olafson, Corwin, and Summitt 1993.

5. Briquet 1859.

6. Kempe et al. 1962, 23.

7. Braun 1993.

8. Belsky 1993, 415.

9. Kempe et al. 1962, 21.

10. Helfer 1968, 25.

11. Sgroi 1975.

12. Herman and Hirschman 1977 emphasized that the phenomenon had

been well known for decades, even in detailed statistics, but had passed without comment. For full discussion, see Herman 1981.

13. In published work (assume a lag of several years between the topic's initial currency and its publication) this extension of the concept starts about 1977, a watershed year for consciousness-raising about child abuse, comparable to 1962. See Browning and Boatman 1977, Forward and Buck 1978.

14. Wilbur 1984.

15. Kinsey 1953, 121. Landis 1956 obtained a 30 percent prevalence rate for males and 35 percent for females.

16. Finkelhor 1979 and 1984.

17. Browne and Finkelhor 1986, 76.

18. Kendall-Tackett, Williams, and Finkelhor 1993, 164, 175, 165. The authors conjectured that there may also be more evidence of post-traumatic stress disorder, but since that disorder was being formulated at the time of the studies it was not well incorporated into most research designs.

19. Malinosky-Rummell and Hansen 1993, 75.

20. Nelson 1984.

21. Belsky 1993, 424.

22. M. Beard, *Times Literary Supplement* 14–20 (September 1990): 968.

23. Greenland 1988.

24. *New York Times*, 28 June 1990, A13.

25. Romans et al. 1993.

26. O'Neill 1992, 121.

27. Pickering 1986.

28. Latour and Woolgar 1979.

29. Gelles 1975.

CHAPTER 5
GENDER

1. Goff and Simms 1993 analyze 52 cases reported in the English language, 1800–1965, and obtain 44 percent males, compared to 24 percent of 54 recent cases.

2. Bliss 1980 has a series of 14 patients, all of whom were women. Bliss 1984 has 32 patients, 20 of whom were female. Seven of the 8 patients of Stern 1984 were women. Horevitz and Braun 1984 have 33 patients, 24 of whom were women. Kluft 1984 has another 33, 25 of whom were women. We should not conclude that a quarter of diagnosed patients were men, because there was a conscious desire to include men in some of these series. Most individual reports are of females, and the prototype of multiple personality is female.

3. Putnam et al. 1986.

4. Ross, Norton, and Wozney 1989.

5. Wilbur 1985.

6. Allison with Schwartz 1980, in "Discovering the Male Multiple Personality," chapter 7.

7. Ross 1989, 97. The claim that men and women do not differ in dissociative experiences is based on measurement by the Dissociative Experiences Scale discussed in chapter 7 below.

8. In a short series of adolescents, 7 out of 11 were male (Dell and Eisenhower 1990). In a series of child multiples, 4 out of 6 were boys (Tyson 1992).

9. Brodie 1992.

10. Loewenstein 1990.

11. This is certainly true of great fiction. After each wave of multiples, the balance is to some extent corrected by soppy novels with female heroines. Thus in addition to Jekyll and Hyde, Ellenberger (1970, 165–168) summarizes eight stories published after the French wave of doubling. There were four doubled men and four doubled women. In our day we have, for example, Stowe 1991 and Clarke 1992, with female or child multiples.

12. Hoffmann knew G. H. von Schubert, whose lectures had ample accounts of doubling, as in Schubert 1814, especially 108–111. On Hoffman and Schubert, see Herdman 1990, 3. On the doubling relations between Hogg, author of *The Private Memoirs and Confessions of a Justified Sinner*, and Dr. Robert McNish, author of *The Philosophy of Sleep*, see Miller 1987, 9. Robert Louis Stevenson corresponded with Pierre Janet while writing *Dr. Jekyll and Mr. Hyde*. Dostoyevsky's Mr. Golyadkin of *The Double* seems to suffer from what was once diagnosed as autoscopy, seeing oneself from behind or at a distance. That was thought to be a condition of epilepsy, which afflicted Dostoyevsky. Autoscopy would now count as depersonalization disorder, which is still listed among the dissociative disorders in *DSM-IV*.

13. Kleist 1988, 265. The translator has brilliantly adapted the lines of scene 24: "Küsse, Bisse / Das reimt sich, und wer recht von Herzen liebt, / Kann schon das eine für das andre greifen." Kleist attended Schubert's lectures in Dresden; see Tymms 1949, 16. In a famous letter to his half sister he said that the play contained all the filth and brightness of his soul, but some have wondered whether when he wrote *Schmutz* (filth), he meant to write *Schmerz* (pain). There is no doubt that with the exception of Stevenson's rather trivial Jekyll and Hyde, most of the great doubling stories were about the pain of the author— *and* about his feeling of filth.

14. Berman 1974. Kenny 1986 urges a similar thesis for nineteenth-century American doubles.

15. Olsen, Loewenstein, and Hornstein 1992.

16. Rush 1980.

17. Rivera 1988.

18. Rivera 1991.

19. MacKinnon 1987.

20. Leys 1992, 168 and 204. Rose 1986.

21. Dewar 1823.

22. For example, a young married woman who falls in love with her physi-cian-hypnotist and has a child by him. This tale is dramatically told by Bellanger 1854. Parts are summarized in Gilles de la Tourette 1889, 262–268.

23. Rosenzweig 1987.

24. An alter in Dewey 1907 was lesbian. Male personality fragments appear in the first woman multiple to be portrayed in a movie, Wholey 1926 and 1933. The list of sixty-seven cases called multiple personality in a survey of Taylor and Martin 1944 includes some that are not a close fit with present-day *DSM* crite-ria, but it is striking that in those days of relative silence about homosexuality, there are nine instances of gender ambivalence involving either a homosexual alter or a male alter for a female host.

25. Schreiber 1973, 214.

26. Bliss 1980.

27. For a young woman with a ninety-year-old male alter, see Atwood 1978. Why stop at people? How about stereotypical animals for alters? I'm not making this up; see Hendrikson, McCarty, and Goodwin 1990 for birds, dogs, cats, and the panther. The childhood scenes described in this article are repulsive, but if one stands back for a moment, one notices the remarkable ease with which the authors' analysis can fit all too many slices of life, both vile and mundane. The animal alters may be traced to "(1) being forced to act or live like an animal, (2) witnessing animal mutilation, (3) being forced to engage in or witness besti-ality, or (4) experiencing traumatic loss of or killing of an animal. Clinical clues to the animal alter phenomenon that emerge during therapy are (1) over iden-tification with an animal, (2) hearing animal calls, (3) excessive fears of animals, (4) excessive involvement with a pet, and (5) cruelty to animals" (p. 218).

28. Rivera 1987.

29. Rivera and Olson 1994.

30. Ross 1989, 68.

31. Lessing 1986, 34.

32. Ibid., 146.

33. Ibid., 148.

CHAPTER 6
CAUSE

1. Greaves's "paraphrase" of a talk by Richard Loewenstein, "Dissociative Spectrum and Phenomenology of MPD," Paper presented at the First Eastern Conference on Multiple Personality and Dissociation, Alexandria, Virginia, 24 June 1989. Greaves 1993, 371.

2. For a classic modern statement of this old idea, see Davidson 1967. For a classic modern challenge to this doctrine, see Anscombe 1981.

3. Wilbur and Kluft 1989, 2198.

4. Greaves 1993, 375. Spiegel 1993a.

5. Wilbur 1986, 136.

6. Marmer 1980, 455.

7. There can be no such thing as the unequivocal psychoanalytic understanding of trauma and multiple personality, especially since Freud so wanted to distance himself from the phenomenon of multiplicity. For a perspective from the early days of the multiple movement, see Berman 1981. For a recent one, see the special issue of *Bulletin of the Menninger Clinic* (1993).

8. Saltman and Solomon 1982.

9. Coons 1984, 53. Cf. Coons 1980.

10. Kluft, ed. 1985.

11. Putnam 1989, 45. Quotations that follow are from pp. 45–54.

12. Van der Kolk and Greenberg 1987, 67.

13. See Hacking 1991c.

14. See, e.g., Cartwright 1983.

15. Putnam refers to Wolff 1987. He argues the comparison between infants and multiples in Putnam 1988.

16. *American Heritage Dictionary*, 3d ed. (1992). Donovan and McIntyre 1990 paraphrase and quote a good deal of Putnam's discussion on their pp. 55–70. Although they use Putnam's "normative," they relapse into "normal" with a section titled "Normal and Pathological Dissociation" (p. 58), which speaks of Putnam's first normal substrate—Putnam had written "normative substrate" (e.g., Putnam 1989, 51).

17. Donovan and McIntyre 1990. The longest exact quotation, on p. 57, of thirteen lines from Putnam's (1989) p. 51, has no qualifiers, although Putnam's next sentence begins "One can postulate that...."

18. Kluft 1984.

19. Peterson 1990. Reagor, Kaasten, and Morelli 1992. Tyson 1992.

20. Laporta 1992.

21. In a letter dated 9 September 1994, Denis Donovan has kindly granted me permission to print this paraphrase of his own précis of a confidential summary of the case.

CHAPTER 7
MEASURE

1. Putnam 1989, 9.

2. Ibid., 10, my italics.

3. Frankel 1990.

4. Bernstein and Putnam 1986, 728.

5. Ross 1994, x–xi.

6. The most recent edition of *Tests in Print* (Mitchell 1983) listed 2,672 English-language psychological tests that are published on their own for testing

purposes. The most recent edition of the *Mental Measurements Handbook* (Krane and Connoly 1992) reviews 477 tests. The forthcoming 12th edition will review the DES for the first time. For a recent review by psychologists not directly involved with multiple personality, see North et al. 1993.

7. Binet 1889 and 1892. For a selection of his papers prepared for an American editor, see his 1890.

8. Jardine 1988 and 1992. Jardine uses the idea of calibration more generally, for the way in which a new theory may substitute for an old one. We cannot simply have scientific revolution in the manner of Thomas Kuhn; an old theory, as Kuhn always insisted, must agree with many of the phenomena covered by a predecessor theory. A successful new theory is calibrated to an old one.

9. Carlson and Putnam 1993 explain their use of "construct validity" very clearly. They say it "refers to an instrument's ability to measure a construct, in this case dissociation." They continue, "The most obvious evidence of the construct validity of the DES is the fact that those who are expected to score high on the test do score high, and those who are expected to score low do score low." They also distinguish "convergent validity and discriminant validity." "To establish convergent validity, one shows that the new instrument correlates well with other measures of the same construct." "Discriminant validity is established by showing that scores on the new instrument do not correlate highly with variables thought to be unrelated to the construct of interest." In short: their research on the DES has to do with comparing scores on the DES against other judgments or measures of dissociation, and with making sure that irrelevant factors are not producing the scores.

10. Thus women scored better than men. This showed that the tests were defective. Questions on which women did better than men were deleted, while questions on which men did better than women were added (Terman and Merritt 1937, 22f., 34). More recently we have become familiar with debates about the culture and class discrimination built into the far more diverse body of tests now available.

11. Newer self-report questionnaires include QED, the Questionnaire of Experiences of Dissociation (Riley 1988), and DIS-Q, the Dissociative Questionnaire (Vanderlinden et al. 1991).

12. Putnam 1993, 84.

13. Braun, Coons, Loewenstein, Putnam, Ross, and Torem.

14. Carlson and Putnam 1993.

15. For each of the twenty-eight experiences we are asked to "circle a number to show what percentage of the time this happens to you." What percentage of *what* time? The first question is about the experience of suddenly realizing, on a trip, that you cannot recall part of the trip. What percentage of the time does that happen to you? Literally, the percentage of the time when I have the experience of "suddenly realizing" (anything) is minute. At most twenty seconds of my day are dedicated to sudden realizations. Sensible people charitably take the question to mean, during what proportion of the trips you take do you suddenly

realize you cannot recall part of the trip? Each question has to be made sense of it its own way.

16. Gilbertson et al. 1992.

17. Kluft 1993a, 1.

18. Carlson et al. 1993, 1035. The authors note that symptom learning is discussed in Putnam 1989 and Kluft 1991.

19. My own second-year undergraduate class most recently given the questionnaire on the first day of class is drawn about fifty-fifty from arts and sciences. Their average score was 17, with no significant differences between humanists and scientists.

20. Let N (≤ 100) be the highest dissociative score observed on any tested individual, and M (≥ 0) be the lowest. Then the no-gap hypothesis states that for any discriminable segment of scores between M and N, there are individuals whose scores fall in that segment. A discriminable segment is one that is meaningfully distinguished by the test, and that might be set in a test protocol at, say, 4 percent. Obviously on a test with twenty-eight questions scored in ten-percentiles, any two nonidentical scores must differ by $^{10}/_{28}$ of a percent, i.e., about 0.035 percent.

21. One needs to add that there is no discriminable threshold M such that the lowest scorers score either 0 or M, with none in between.

22. Frankel 1990, 827.

23. Actually Ross, Joshi, and Currie 1991, in a sample of 1,055 Canadians, found that almost 7 percent answered 0 to all twenty-eight questions. I do not interpret this to mean that 7 percent of my fellow citizens never daydream, get caught up in movies, or ignore pain (etc.), but that we are a cagey lot and, as has been determined on a larger scale by repeated constitutional referenda, many of us will say no to anything (thank goodness).

24. These commonplace notions of smoothness are naturally defined in terms of monotone increase, monotone decrease, and at most a single inflection point.

25. Bernstein and Putnam 1986, 728.

26. "Clearly this distribution is not normal, and statistical analysis of the data should be handled in a nonparametric fashion." Ibid., 732. There are two distinct technical issues, normality and the use of parametric tests. I say nothing of the latter and so omit this clause from the text. In their subsequent paper Carlson and Putnam (1993) allow use of parametric statistics for groups of more than thirty subjects. But they also may think that scores are normally distributed after all.

27. It makes no real-world sense. To use R. A. Fisher's parlance, one could consider the statistical distribution of scores in the hypothetical infinite population constituted by 5.3 percent normals, 6.2 percent schizophrenics, 9.1 percent agoraphobics (etc.)—the proportions chosen by Bernstein and Putnam for their study—but this population does not model anything in the real world whatsoever.

28. Ross, Joshi, and Currie 1990.

29. Ross, Heber, and Anderson 1990.

30. Ellason, Ross, and Fuchs 1992.

31. Steinberg 1985, 1993.

32. Draijer and Boon, 1993.

33. Carlson and Putnam 1993, 20, referring to a presentation at the eighth annual (1991) meeting of the ISSMP&D. They mention a "confirmatory study" presented at the same meeting by Schwartz and Frischolz.

34. Ross, Joshi, and Currie 1991.

35. Ray et al. 1992.

36. It also demands attention to technical detail. If scores on the DES really are skewed, then traditional factor analysis is problematic anyway.

37. Frankel 1990, 827.

38. Undergraduates furnish the fodder for a great many psychology tests. Bernstein and Putnam refer to their eighteen- to twenty-two-year-old "college students" as "adolescents." Compare the study of "college students" by Ross, Ryan, and colleagues: 385 were selected by a process stated to be random. The mean age of these randomly selected "college students" was twenty-seven (Ross, Ryan et al. 1992). On the basis of this sample Ross infers that 5 percent of all college students are pathologically dissociative (Ross 1989, 90–91, referring also to Ryan 1988), but in the 1992 paper suggests a higher incidence rate.

39. Ross 1990, 449. Fernando 1990, 150; I have slightly rearranged the grammar of Dr. Fernando's sentence.

40. See, for example, Chu 1988.

41. Chu 1991.

42. Diana L. Dill has published jointly with Chu; see, for example, Chu and Dill 1990.

43. Fogelin and Sinnot-Armstrong 1991, 123–126. "Self-sealing arguments," the authors write, "are hard to deal with, for people who use them will often shift their ground."

44. Root-Bernstein 1990.

45. The classic paper is Kahneman and Tversky 1973.

46. Carlson and Putnam cite figures from advocates of multiple personality ranging from 2.4 percent to 11.3 percent of psychiatric inpatient samples: Bliss and Jeppsen 1985; Graves 1989; Ross 1991; Ross et al. 1991.

CHAPTER 8
TRUTH IN MEMORY

1. Mulhern 1995.

2. Ganaway 1989, 211.

3. Van Benschoten 1990, 24.

4. Kluft 1989, 192.

5. Fine 1991.

6. Ganaway 1989, 207.

7. Notice in *FMS Foundation Newsletter*, 1 April 1992.

8. Ganaway 1993.

9. Bryant, Kessler, and Shirar 1992, 245.

10. Spencer 1989.

11. The book is Stratford 1988, reissued 1991; the exposé is Passantino, Passantino, and Trott 1990.

12. Fraser 1990, 60.

13. Young et al. 1991.

14. The challenge was Mulhern 1991b; the response was Young 1991.

15. Putnam 1993, 85. Cf. Putnam 1991.

16. Goodwin 1994 suggests that this is an important reason for the name change, but more seems to be at stake.

17. Abuse within a Malevolent Context: Identifying and Intervening in Severe Intra-Familial Abuse, sponsored by the Justice Institute of British Columbia, Vancouver, B.C., 23 September 1994.

18. Lockwood 1993.

19. Ibid., final print section of book (n.p.), containing a synopsis of prosecutions 1984–1992, prepared by Cavalcade Productions of Ukiah, Calif. Cavalcade, nestled in gorgeous California ranch land, makes instructional films about abuse.

20. The *Independent* (London), 3 June 1994. Emeritus professor of sociology Jean La Fontaine chaired the committee.

21. I think it possible that there have been and will be ongoing satanic rituals by organized sects in which children are viciously abused. I know that in my hometown, which has an undeserved reputation for being the most decent, safe, urbane, and dull large city in North America, goats are sacrificed to Satan on the roofs of warehouses only a few streets from my home. I fear that once any idea, no matter how depraved, is in general circulation, then someone will act it out. Even if a decade ago no goat-sacrificing satanists tortured children, my lack of faith in human nature leads me to think it possible that some do so now. When vile stories are rampant, minds that are sufficiently confused, angry, and cruel will try to turn fiction into fact. It is possible that some local secret society, with loose relationships to other groups in other places, has gone completely off the deep end. Perhaps somebody, somewhere, has used an adolescent to breed a baby for human sacrifice. I sadly do not think it is impossible for such things to happen—or even terribly unlikely. Hence in my view a person could in principle have rather accurate memories of such events.

22. Goodwin 1989.

23. Mulhern 1995 and 1991b.

24. P. Kael, *5001 Nights at the Movies* (New York: Holt, 1991), 462.

25. Condon 1959. The card was the queen of diamonds.

26. I have here had to abandon my resolve to use only matters of public rec-

ord. The following account is based on a report by an observer other than me but is consistent with observations that I have made.

27. For one of the first printed discussions of this, see Smith 1992 and the reply, Ganaway 1992.

28. The *Toronto Star*, 16, 18, and 19 May 1992.

29. Ibid., 28 May 1992.

30. Fraser 1987. Fraser had three personalities.

31. Krüll 1986.

32. She also attacked "syndrome" when she took on the foundation in a middlebrow monthly. *Saturday Night* 109 (March 1994): 18–21, 56–59.

33. *FMS Foundation Newsletter* 3, no. 1 (1994): 1.

34. P. Freyd 1991 and 1992.

35. J. F. Freyd 1993.

36. The quotation and all facts asserted in this paragraph are given by the *New York Times*, 8 April 1994, A1 and B16. There are endless cases and countercases in process.

37. According to Taylor 1994, Herbert Spiegel said that Sybil asked him if she was obliged to talk like alter Helen; Dr. Wilbur would want her to. Spiegel said no, and there was no further discussion of multiples. He described a row with Schreiber, the author of *Sybil*, when he refused the diagnosis of multiplicity. He did think Sybil had a dissociative disorder.

38. Fifth Estate 1993. Ross has referred to his book, tentatively titled *Satanic Ritual Abuse*, in several articles, but as we go to press in November 1994, there is definitely no projected publication date. On the same television show that we see a chapter from Ross's book, Spiegel is filmed saying almost exactly what he said to Taylor for the *Esquire* article, except that the alter he mentions is named Flora and not Helen. We also see an old clip of Spiegel hypnotizing an NBC correspondent; Spiegel showed this to Taylor as well.

39. Ofshe and Watters 1994.

40. Loftus and Ketcham 1994.

41. Van der Kolk 1993.

42. Comaroff 1994.

43. *Crime and Punishment*, part 6, chapter 5.

44. Tymms 1949, 99.

CHAPTER 9
SCHIZOPHRENIA

1. Bleuler 1924, 137–138.

2. Breuer and Freud, in Freud, *S.E.* 2:15f., 31–34, 37f., 42–47, 238.

3. Rosenbaum 1980.

4. Putnam 1989, 33.

5. Greaves 1993, 359.

6. Ellenberger 1970, 287.

7. Bleuler 1908.

8. Bleuler 1950 (1911), 8.

9. Ibid., 298–299.

10. Greaves 1993, 360.

11. M. Prince 1905, B.C.A. 1908.

12. For an informal account of Bonaparte, which uses the adjective "redoubtable" more than once, see Appignanesi and Forrester 1992, 329–351.

13. Even before the turn of the century there was talk of *so-called* multiplicity, or rather *dédoublement*—for example, Laupts 1898. The diagnosis is pretty much at the end of the road even by the time of Arsimoles 1906.

14. Micale 1993, 525f.

15. Janet 1889, 1893–1894, and 1907; 1909, 256–270.

16. Janet 1919, 3:125.

17. Hart 1926, 247. For a revised version of this article, see Hart 1939, vi: "It is hoped that the addition [of a chapter titled "The Conception of Dissociation"] will serve to amplify and make more intelligible the point of view that [I have adopted], particularly with regard to the respective contributions of Janet and Freud."

18. Jones 1955, 3:69.

19. Goettman, Greaves, and Coons 1991.

20. Absolute counts of numbers of articles per year in the *Index Medicus* can be misleading because the total number of published articles is increasing year by year. Using rounded numbers, in 1903 there were 100 articles on hysteria, and 140 in 1908. Then there was a steady drop to 20 in 1917, followed by a brief jump to more than 50 in 1920, and then steady decline. Articles on neurasthenia have the same pattern, with slightly smaller numbers, but no bounce up after the war. The bounce was caused by studies of shell shock that were still regarded as cases of hysteria. The only way in which Rosenbaum's counts for multiple personality do not shadow counts for hysterical articles is that hysteria was way down in 1917, and multiple personality had not yet started to plummet.

21. M. Prince 1920.

22. Hacking 1988.

23. Myers 1903.

24. W. F. Prince 1915–1916. Add in 216 pages on Doris's mother, W. F. Prince 1923, and you have some story.

25. Braude 1991.

26. Irwin 1992 and 1994.

27. Ross 1989, 181.

28. Adams 1989, 138.

29. Putnam 1989, 15. There is also a discussion of Breuer and Freud on 16–17.

30. Putnam 1992a presents Anna O. as a multiple. Like so many others of

Freud's cases, Anna O. has been amply rediagnosed; I know of more than thirty distinct diagnoses that have been advanced over the years.

31. Rank 1971.

32. Bach 1985, chapter 1.

33. Schreiber 1973, 117.

34. Laing 1959.

35. Zubin et al. 1983.

36. Lay opinion seems to divide; some of us think the drugs are miracles, and others of us think they are mind-control with gross side effects and irreversible brain destruction. Hence a few balancing remarks are in order. Some patients experience overactivity (extrapyramidal symptoms): muscular rigidity, tremors, rolling eyes, salivation and drooling, jerky movements, blurred vision, and a shuffling gait. Others experience underactivity (tardive diskeniesia). Between 5 and 20 percent of schizophrenics do not respond to the antipsychotic drugs at present prescribed, and another 5 to 20 percent have side effects that overwhelm any improvement in symptoms. The most recent drug, clozapine, after some lethal misdosage, is now available again in the United States and helps some of the patients who cannot be treated with other psychotropic medicine. For one survey, see Safferman et al. 1991.

37. Andreasson and Carpenter 1993.

38. Crose 1985.

39. This was implicit in R. D. Laing and the antipsychiatry movement; for a book-length exposition, see Boyle 1990.

40. Schneider 1959 (which includes a translation of Schneider's 1939 paper).

41. Kluft 1987.

42. Ross, Norton, and Wozney 1989.

43. Ross 1994, xii.

44. John P. Wilson, quoted on p. 2 of the eight-page brochure of the conference, presented by Kairos Ventures Ltd. and organized by Anne Speckland and Denis M. Donovan.

CHAPTER 10
BEFORE MEMORY

1. Völgyesi 1956; Völgyesi published in German in 1938. In Germany and Russia (where Völgyesi studied), a "praying mantis" is "one who prays to God."

2. Spiegel 1993a.

3. Darnton 1968.

4. Braid 1843.

5. Lambek 1981.

6. Douglas 1992.

7. Bourreau 1991 and 1993.

8. Hacking 1991a. My survey is incomplete but indicates the lay of the land.

9. *Encyclopédie ou dictionnaire raisonée* (Neufchatel: Faucher, 1765; facsimile reproduction by Readex Microprints), 15:340.

10. Azam 1876c, 268.

11. Gauld 1992a.

12. Crabtree 1993.

13. Mitchill 1817; from the issue of February 1816.

14. Breuer and Freud (1893), in Freud, *S.E.* 2:12 (emphasis in original), where despite identical spelling French is intended, not English.

15. Carlson 1981 and 1974. Kenny 1986.

16. Gauld 1992b.

17. Ward 1849, 457.

18. Wilson 1842–1843.

19. H. Mayo 1837, 195. Not in previous editions. Herbert Mayo has somehow escaped the notice of the modern multiple movement; his classic case is not cited in Goettman, Greaves, and Coons 1991. It was often referenced during the nineteenth century; "Dr. Mayo's case" refers to Herbert, and not to Thomas Mayo (1845) whose case has been picked up in the recent multiple literature as a case of "adolescent" multiplicity; cf. Bowman 1990.

20. Carlson et al. 1981, 669.

21. J. C. Browne 1862–1863. Globus is the sensation of a lump in the throat, then commonly taken to be a symptom of hysteria.

22. These concerns were fired by Alan Ladbroke Wigan 1844, esp. 371–378. The classic studies of the dual brain are Harrington 1985 and 1987.

23. It is to be remembered that on average nineteenth-century children were older at the onset of puberty than children are today. Thus a famous Scottish case of 1822 concerns a woman of sixteen, who became well only after her first period. Dewar 1823.

24. I quote this plea at length in chapter 16, p. 221–222 below.

25. Bertrand 1827, 317–319.

26. Despine 1838 (issued October 1839). This has less polish and less public-relations savvy than the piece usually cited, Despine 1840. For a fairly neutral resumé, see Ellenberger 1970, 129–131.

27. Shorter 1992, 160f.

28. Fine 1988.

29. Janet 1919, 3:86.

30. Janet 1893–1894.

CHAPTER 11
DOUBLING OF THE PERSONALITY

1. Azam 1893, 37–38. Azam republished his pieces in a number of forms. Azam 1893 contains all his main contributions to psychology, lightly edited. Azam 1887 contains slightly different editings of the same or related pieces up

to 1886. Azam's son-in-law, a Latinist at the Collège de France, published an annotated bibliography of 180 items: Jullian 1903. The books and the bibliography are quite hard to lay hands on. Hence I will cite both the books and the original journal articles, many of which are easy to locate in research libraries.

2. Janet 1907, 78.

3. See bibliography entries for Azam, 1876 to 1879.

4. Babinski 1889, 12. Cf. Didi-Huberman 1982.

5. For a deeply insightful essay, which refers back to a generation of work but is also an important contribution in its own right, see Showalter 1993. For two bibliographies of historiography of hysteria, see Micale 1991 and 1992.

6. Alam and Merskey 1992, 157.

7. Taine 1870, 1:372.

8. Taine 1878, 1:156.

9. Littré 1875, 344.

10. Ribot 1988, 107.

11. Janet 1888, 542.

12. Warlomont 1875.

13. Azam 1876a, 16. Warlomont's study was commissioned in 1874, not 1875.

14. Azam 1893, 90.

15. Egger 1887, 307.

16. And "pure metaphysics will become only a memory," he continued. Azam 1887, 92.

17. Ibid., 143–153.

18. Janet 1876, 574. Bouchut 1877. The most interesting contribution is Dufay 1876.

19. Ladame 1888, 314.

20. Hacking forthcoming.

CHAPTER 12
THE VERY FIRST MULTIPLE PERSONALITY

1. My free translation of "des cas d'hystérie fruste." Voisin 1886, 100. Cf. Voisin 1885.

2. Bourru's account appears directly after Voisin 1885. Cf. Bourru and Burot 1885 and 1886b.

3. A. T. Myers 1896, "The Life-History of a Case of Double or Multiple Personality." Myers's more famous brother used another name for the same case. F.W.H. Myers 1896, "Multiplex Personality."

4. Binet and Féré 1887.

5. Binet 1886. Binet was reviewing Bernheim 1886.

6. Babinski 1887. For a summary, see Babinski 1886.

7. For the road from metallotherapy to Luys, see Gauld 1992a, 332–336.

8. Ibid., 334f.

9. Bourru and Burot 1888. Crabtree 1993, 303.

10. Camuset 1881. Abstracted in Ribot 1882, 82–84.

11. Not my words but those attributed to the doctor in charge of l'asile St.-Georges; I translate *habilement* as "slyly." Bourru and Burot 1888, 24.

12. Voisin 1886, 105.

13. The conquest of Indochina was technically complete by 1883, but the north was in constant rebellion. According to Bourru and Burot, Vivet joined up to fight in Tongking; Azam speaks of him as just doing his obligatory military service. Certainly in one of his states he passionately did not want to go to Tongking. Perhaps he was arrested for yet another theft of clothes and effectively impressed into the military?

14. Bourru and Burot 1886a.

15. "Le premier soin qui s'imposait était d'essayer l'action des métaux et de l'aimant." Bourru and Burot 1888, 35.

16. Ibid., 39.

17. Gauld 1992a, 453.

18. Bourru and Burot 1888, 263.

19. Ibid., 299f.

20. Gauld 1992a, 365f. Myers 1903, 1:309.

CHAPTER 13
TRAUMA

1. Fischer-Homberg 1975, 79.

2. Micale 1990a, 389n.112.

3. Gilles Deleuze, "Zola et la fêlure"(1969), preface to Emile Zola, *La Bête humaine* (1889) (Paris: Gallimard, 1977), 21.

4. Fischer-Homberg 1972.

5. Schivelbush 1986, 134–149.

6. The lectures were published as Erichsen 1866.

7. Ibid., 127. He became more favorable to the comparison with hysteria in later work.

8. Reynolds 1869a, 378. Summary of the lecture's contents and discussion.

9. Reynolds 1869b. A fuller version of the paper.

10. Trimble 1981.

11. Charcot 1886–1887, lectures 18–22 and appendix 1.

12. In this and many other explanatory details I follow Micale 1990a.

13. But they were tainted with degeneracy, itself an inherited condition. *Degénerescence* was an all-purpose notion one of whose primary connotations was the decline of France compared to Britain and Germany. It was connected throughout the century with low birth rates, and hence with suicide, prostitution, homosexuality, alcoholism, insanity, vagrancy, and, after 1880 and abetted by Charcot, with hysteria. See Nye 1984.

14. Charcot 1886–1887, 335ff.

15. Pitres 1891, 28. A table for age at onset, classified by sex, is given on p. 15. The original lectures were given during the summer semester of the academic year 1884–1885. Notes taken by J. Davezac were published in serial form beginning 4 April 1886, in *Journal de médecine de Bordeaux*.

16. J. Davezac in his review-homage to Pitres in *Journal de médecine de Bordeaux* 20 (1891): 443.

17. Guinon 1889. Freud, *S.E.* 3, see index.

18. Fischer-Homberg 1971. Cf. Micale 1990a, 391n.118.

19. Lunier 1874.

20. From a French medical thesis of 1834, cited by Schivelbush 1986, 137.

21. Lunier 1874, cases 12, 111, 288, and 300.

22. Rouillard 1885, 87.

23. Ibid., 10.

24. Review by Camuset, *Annales médico-psychologiques* 44 (1886): 478–490. The *thèse* was 252 pp. long; most *thèses* for the Faculty of Medicine in Paris were only a little over 100 pp. in length.

25. Azam 1881. Azam 1893, 157–197.

26. Even Charcot, who usually preferred his own neologisms, uses Azam's terminology, 1886–1887, 442.

27. J. Janet 1888.

28. "Preliminary Communication" (1893), *S.E.* 2:12.

29. Crocq and de Verbizier 1989.

30. "Hysteria" (1888), *S.E.* 1:41–57.

31. Gelfand 1992; cf. Gelfand 1989.

32. "The Psychopathology of Everyday Life," *S.E.* 6:161.

33. *S.E.* 1:137 (emphases in original).

34. A more cautious statement of this analogy is to be found in Carter 1980.

35. *S.E.* 1:139.

36. "Further Remarks on the Neuro-psychoses of Defence" (1896), *S.E.* 3:162–190, 163 (emphasis in original) .

37. Kitcher 1992.

38. Van der Kolk and van der Hart 1989, 1537–1538.

39. Friedrich Nietzsche, *Zur Genealogie der Moral* (1887), pt. 3, sec. 16. I translate *seelische Schmerz* as "psychological pain," and, more freely, *eines sogar spindeldüren Fragezeichen* as "a skinny question mark."

40. Lampl 1988.

CHAPTER 14
THE SCIENCES OF MEMORY

1. Foucault 1972, 182. There are now many ways to read Foucault. For my take on *savoir* and *connaissance*, see Hacking 1986a.

2. Ellenberger 1970, 289–291. Although his own book is subtitled *The History and Evolution of Dynamic Psychiatry*, he notes that the word "dynamic"

was used in psychiatry "with a variety of meanings that often entailed some confusion."

3. Dr. Delannay, as reported in *Gazette des Hôpitaux*, no. 81 (1879): 645.

4. The classic modern studies are Rossi 1960 and Yates 1966.

5. Carruthers 1990, 71, prefers this term to the widely used name brought into currency by Frances Yates, Ciceronian mnemonic.

6. Carruthers 1990, 260.

7. John Locke, *An Essay Concerning Human Understanding* (1693), 2.10.7.

8. Broca 1861.

9. Lichtheim 1885. My periodization of early work on localization follows Rosenfeld 1988.

10. Danziger 1991, 142.

11. Ebbinghaus 1885.

12. Murray 1983, 186.

13. It should be clear from the text that I take "firsts" as markers, not as prizewinners. For an anticipation of Ebbinghaus on the use of nonsense units (digits) and of statistics, see Stigler 1978. Ebbinghaus was not the first to use probability in psychology. That palm goes to Fechner; see Heidelberger 1993. Fechner was nonstatistical; he used the Gaussian (Normal) distribution as an a priori model for psychophysics, whereas Ebbinghaus used empirical statistics, curve fitting, and measures of dispersion.

14. Ribot 1881, 1883, and 1885.

15. Brooks 1993.

16. Roth 1991a and 1991b.

17. Danziger 1991, 24–27.

18. Sauvages 1771, 1:157.

19. Associationist psychology had been his point of departure in psychology: Ribot 1870.

20. Ribot 1881, 107.

21. Hartmann 1869. For a brief but rich account of Hartmann and his intellectual surroundings, see Ellenberger 1970, 202–210.

22. Ribot 1881, 26–27.

23. Ibid., 82, italics in original. I have left *moi* in various passages because I cannot uniformly translate it as "self" or "ego," let alone "me."

24. Ibid., 83.

25. Ribot 1885, 1.

26. Ribot 1881, 94, 95 (emphasis in original).

27. "In the case of *general* dissolution of the memory, loss of recollections [*souvenirs*] follows an invariable course: recent events, ideas in general, feelings, acts. In the best known case of *partial* dissolution (forgetfulness of signs [aphasia]), the loss of recollections follows an invariable course: proper names, common nouns, adjectives and verbs, interjections, gestures. In both cases ... there is a regression from the complex to the simple, from the voluntary to the auto-

matic, from the least organized to the best organized." Ibid., 164, in the conclusion to the book, and which summarizes 90–98.

CHAPTER 15
MEMORO-POLITICS

1. Herman 1992, 9.
2. Foucault 1980, 139 (emphasis in original).
3. Comaroff 1994.
4. Functionalism is not in fashion. For criticism, see Elster 1983. For rebuttal, see Douglas 1983, chapter 3.
5. Hacking 1982.
6. For an early sketch of this idea, see Hacking 1983. The most systematic study of the relationship between the census and making up kinds of people is Desrosières 1993.
7. Plint 1851.
8. Goodstein 1988.
9. Briquet 1859.

CHAPTER 16
MIND AND BODY

1. McCrone 1994 (my emphasis).
2. Wakley 1843 (emphasis in original).
3. James 1890.
4. James 1983, 269.
5. James 1890, 384–385.
6. Ibid., 401.
7. Whitehead 1928, 141. On 147: "The point of a 'society', as the term is here used, is that it is self-sustaining.... To constitute a society, the class-name [the name for the entity or type] has got to apply to each member, by reason of genetic derivation from other members of the same society."
8. Ibid., 164.
9. Ibid. (my emphasis).
10. Humphrey and Dennett 1989, 77.
11. Whitehead 1928, 164.
12. Dennett 1991, 419.
13. Ibid., 422.
14. Ibid., 420.
15. Taylor and Martin 1944, 297.
16. Hilgard 1986, 24 (and cf. 18).
17. Wittgenstein 1956, for example I-80.
18. Braude 1991, 164.

19. Dennett 1992.

20. The second and more considered of these two books is Braude 1986. I have explained why I disagree with the main theses of this book in Hacking 1993.

21. Wilkes 1988, vii (emphasis in original).

22. There are many studies to help us learn more about Miss Beauchamp. One of the most informative is Rosenzweig 1987.

23. Moore 1938.

24. Wilkes 1988, 128.

25. She has been challenged by Lizza 1993.

26. North et al. 1993 have two appendixes about this genre. Appendix A (pp. 186–229) summarizes the plots of book-length accounts and discusses the symptoms described in those plots. Appendix B (pp. 231–251) gives the results in tabular form. The majority of books are written in the "as told to" or "with" format of authorship. Books per year in the eighties: 1981—2, 1982—2, 1985—1, 1986—1, 1987—3, 1988—1, 1989—2.

27. Miller 1987, 348.

Chapter 17
An Indeterminacy in the Past

1. Anscombe 1959, especially 37–44.

2. This is Donald Davidson's trio, slightly different in formulation from Anscombe's. Davidson tends to agree with Anscombe on the issues that matter to the present chapter, but differs from her on questions about the reasons for and causes of an action. She keeps them apart; Davidson argues that many reasons are causes. See Davidson 1980 for a sequence of essays commenced in 1963.

3. At first Davidson was of this opinion but later revised it. Thus in the first essay of *Essays in Actions and Events*, he thought (as he says on p. xiii of Davidson 1980), "that 'the intention under which an event was done' does not refer to an entity or state of any kind," but the fifth essay "partially undermined" that theme. These matters are far too complex to discuss here. I shall write like an Anscombian hard-liner.

4. I have discussed this in the final sections, "Old Worlds" and "New Worlds," pp. 223–230, of Hacking 1992.

5. See Reppucci and Haugaard 1989 for a discussion of prevention programs and how little we know about their efficacy.

6. *Globe and Mail* (Toronto), 5 July 1994, A6.

7. Joan Barfoot reviewing *Caesars of the Wilderness* by Peter Newman, *New York Times Book Review*, 20 December 1987, 9.

8. Ariès 1962.

9. DeMause 1974.

10. Donovan 1991.

11. Goddard 1926 and 1927.

12. Hacking 1991c. For the purposes of the present example, I shall treat Goddard's reports as accurate and reasonably complete. They are not.

13. Terr 1979 and 1994.

14. Carter 1983 notes that Freud can hardly be said to have "discovered" infant sexuality; the Viennese medical and psychological literature of his day was rife with the idea.

15. Lessing 1986, 454.

16. Rosenfeld 1988.

17. It was a case of fugue, but it was also described in the literature as double consciousness. A. Proust 1890. This story appears in "Le temps retrouvé"; see M. Proust 1961, 3:716. And in Raymond and Janet 1895.

18. Ryle 1949, 272–279.

19. Ibid., 279, 276.

CHAPTER 18
FALSE CONSCIOUSNESS

1. Early Freud is still the best read on screen memories. See "Screen Memories," *S.E.* 3:304–322. For secondary material my first choice is Spence 1982.

2. People are so busy calling Michel Foucault postmodern that they seldom notice how old-fashioned he was. For a brief remark about Foucault's Kantian construction of himself, see Hacking 1986c.

Bibliography

Adams, M. A.
  1989 Internal Self Helpers of Persons with Multiple Personality Disorder. *Dissociation* 2:138–143.

Alam, C. M., and H. Merskey
  1992 The Development of the Hysterical Personality. *History of Psychiatry* 3:135–165.

Aldridge-Morris, R.
  1989 *Multiple Personality: An Exercise in Delusion*. Hove, England, and London: Lawrence Erlbaum.

Allison, R. B.
  1974a A Guide to Parents: How to Raise Your Daughter to Have Multiple Personality. *Family Therapy* 1:83–88.
  1974b A New Treatment Approach for Multiple Personalities. *American Journal of Clinical Hypnosis* 17:15–32.
  1978a On Discovering Multiple Personality. *Svensk Tidskrift för Hypnos* 2:4–8.
  1978b A Rational Psychotherapy Plan for Multiplicity. *Svensk Tidskrift för Hypnos* 3–4:9–16.
  1984 Difficulties Diagnosing the Multiple Personality Syndrome in a Death Penalty Case. *International Journal of Clinical and Experimental Hypnosis* 32:102–117.
  1991 In Search of Multiples in Moscow. *American Journal of Forensic Psychiatry* 12:51–65.

Allison, R. B., with T. Schwartz
  1980 *Minds in Many Pieces*. New York: Rawson, Wade.

American Psychiatric Association
  1980 *Diagnostic and Statistical Manual of Mental Disorders*. 3d ed. Washington, D.C.: American Psychiatric Association. Called *DSM-III*.
  1987 *Diagnostic and Statistical Manual of Mental Disorders*. 3d ed., rev. Washington, D.C.: American Psychiatric Association. Called *DSM-III-R*.
  1994 *Diagnostic and Statistical Manual of Mental Disorders*. 4th ed. Washington, D.C.: American Psychiatric Association. Called *DSM-IV*.

Andreasson, N. C., and W. T. Carpenter Jr.
  1993 Diagnosis and Classification of Schizophrenia. *Schizophrenia Bulletin* 19:199–214.

Anscombe, G.E.M.
  1959 *Intention*. Oxford: Blackwell.
  1981 Causality and Determinism. 1971. In *Metaphysics and the Philosophy of Mind: Collected Papers*, 2:133–147. Minneapolis: University of Minnesota Press.

Appignanesi, L., and J. Forrester

1992. *Freud's Women*. Basic Books: New York.

Ariès, P.

1962 *Centuries of Childhood*. London: Jonathan Cape.

Arsimoles, L.

1906 Sitiophobie intermittente à périodicité regulière—Double personnalité coexistante. *Archives Générales de Médecine* 82:790–797.

Atwood G. E.

1978 The Impact of *Sybil* on a Patient with Multiple Personality. *American Journal of Psychoanalysis* 38:277–279.

Austin, J. L.

1962 *Sense and Sensibilia*. Oxford: Clarendon Press.

Azam, E.

1860 Note sur le sommeil nerveux ou hypnotisme. *Archives générales de médecine*, ser. 5, 15:1–24. In Azam 1887, 1–59; Azam 1893, 13–33.

1876a Amnésie périodique, ou dédoublement de la vie. *Annales médico-psychologiques*, ser. 5, 16:5–35.

1876b Amnésie périodique, ou doublement de la vie. *Revue scientifique*, ser. 2, 5:481–487. In Azam 1893, 41–65. [Published 20 May 1876.] Reprinted in *Journal of Nervous and Mental Disease* 3 (1876): 584–612.

1876c Le dédoublement de la personnalité, suite de l'histoire de Félida X***. *Revue scientifique*, ser. 2, 6:265–269. In Azam 1893, 73–86. [Letter dated 6 September 1876.]

1876d Névrose extraordinaire, doublement de la vie. *Mémoires et Bulletins de la Société de Médecine et de Chirurgie de Bordeaux*, 11–14. [Read on 14 January 1876.]

1877a Amnésie périodique, ou dédoublement de la personnalité. *Séances et travaux de l'Académie des Sciences Morales et Politiques. Comptes Rendus* 108:363–413. In Azam 1887, 61–144. [Read by an Academician in Paris, 6 and 13 May 1876.]

1877b Le dédoublement de la personnalité et l'amnésie périodique. Suite de l'histoire de Félida X . . . : relation d'un fait nouveau du même ordre. *Revue scientifique*, ser. 2, 7:577–581. In Azam 1887, 145–169, 221–229.

1877c La double conscience. *Association Française pour l'Avancement des Sciences*. Compte rendu de la 5ᵉ session, Clermont-Ferrand, 1876, 787–788. [Read on 23 August 1876.]

1878 La double conscience. *Revue scientifique*, ser. 2, 8:194–196. In Azam 1887, 176–186; 1983, 194–196. [Read on 26 August 1878.]

1879a La double personnalité. Double conscience. Responsibilité. *Revue scientifique*, ser. 2, 8:844–846. In Azam 1887, 191–202. [Letter dated 16 September 1878.]

1879b Sur un fait de double conscience, déduction thérapeutique qu'on peut tirer. *Mémoires de la Société des Sciences Physiques et Naturelles de Bordeaux*, ser. 2, 3:249–256. In Azam 1878, 203–213; 1893, 111–118.

1880 De l'amnésie retrograde d'origine traumatique. *Gazette hébdomadaire des sciences médicales de Bordeaux* 1:219–222. Included in Azam 1881.

1881 Les troubles intellectuels provoqués par les traumatismes du cerveau. *Archives générales de médécine*, February. In Azam 1893, 157–198.

1883 Les altérations de la personnalité. *Revue scientifique*, ser. 3, 3:610–618. In Azam 1887, 231–280; 1893, 119–141.

1887 *Hypnotisme, double conscience, et altérations de la personnalité.* Paris: Baillière.

1890a Le dédoublement de la personnalité et le somnambulisme. *Revue scientifique* 2 (August): 136–141.

1890b Les troubles sensoriels organiques et moteurs consécutifs aux traumatismes du cerveau. *Archives générales de médécine*, May.

1891 Un fait d'amnésie rétrograde. *Revue scientifique* 47:412.

1892 Double consciousness. In *A Dictionary of Psychological Medicine*, edited by D. Tuke, 401–406. Philadelphia: Balkiston.

1893 *Hypnotisme et double conscience. Origine de leur étude et divers travaux sur des sujets analogues.* Paris: Félix Alcan.

B.C.A. (Nellie Parsons Bean)

1908 My Life as a Dissociated Personality. *Journal of Abnormal Psychology* 3:240–260.

Babinski, J.

1886 Recherches servants à établir que certaines manifestations hysteriques peuvent être transferées d'un sujet à un autre sujet sans l'influence de l'aimant. *Revue philosophique* 22:697–700. This summarizes a longer essay with the same title, Paris: Publications du progrès médicale (1887).

1889 *Grand et petit hypnotisme.* Paris: Publications du progrès médicale.

Bach, S.

1985 *Narcissistic States and the Therapeutic Process.* New York: Aronson.

Baker G. P., and P.M.S. Hacker

1980 *Wittgenstein: Understanding and Illusion. An Analytical Commentary on the Philosophical Investigations.* Vol. 1. Chicago: University of Chicago Press.

Beahrs, J.

1982 *Unity and Multiplicity.* New York: Brunner/Mazel.

Bellanger, A.-R.

1854 *Le magnétisme: vérités et chimères de cette science occulte.* Paris: Guillermet.

Belsky, J.

1993 Etiology of Child Maltreatment: A Developmental-Ecological Analysis. *Psychological Bulletin* 114:413–434.

Berman, E.

1974 Multiple Personality: Theoretical Approaches. *Journal of the Bronx State Hospital* 2:99–107.

1981 Multiple Personality: Psychoanalytic Perspectives. *International Journal of Psychoanalysis* 6:283–300.

Bernheim, H.

1886 *De la suggestion et ses applications à la thérapeutique*. Paris: Doin.

Bernstein, E. M.

1986 Development, Reliability and Validity of a Dissociation Scale. *Journal of Nervous and Mental Disease* 174:727–735.

Bertrand, A.-J.-F.

1827 *Traité du somnambulisme et des différents modifications qu'il présente*. 1823. Paris: Dentu.

Binet, A.

1886 Review of Bernheim 1886. *Revue philosophique* 22:557–563.

1889 Recherches sur les altérations de la conscience chez les hystériques. *Revue philosophique* 17:377–412, 473–503.

1890 *On Double Consciousness, with an Essay on Experimental Psychology in France*. Chicago: Open Court.

1892 *Les altérations de la personnalité*. Paris: Baillière.

Binet, A., and C. Féré

1887 *Le magnétisme animal*. Paris: Alcan.

Bleuler, E.

1908 Die Prognose des Dementia Praecox: Schizophreniengruppe. *Allgemeine Zeitschrift für Psychiatrie* 65:436–464.

1924 *Textbook of Psychiatry*. Translated by A. A. Brill from the German of 1916. New York: Macmillan.

1950 *Dementia Praecox, or the Group of Schizophrenias*. 1911. Translated by Joseph Zinkin. New York: International University Press.

Bliss, E. L.

1980 Multiple Personalities: A Report of Fourteen Cases with Implications for Schizophrenia and Hysteria. *Archives of General Psychiatry* 37:1388–1397.

1984 A Symptom Profile of Patients with Multiple Personalities, including MMPI Results. *Journal of Nervous and Mental Disease* 172:197–202.

Bliss, E. L., and E. A. Jeppson

1985 Prevalence of Multiple Personality among Psychiatric Inpatients. *American Journal of Psychiatry* 142:250–251.

Boon, S., and Draijer, N.

1993 *Multiple Personality Disorder in the Netherlands: A Study on Reliability and Validity of the Diagnosis*. Amsterdam: Swets and Zeitlinger.

Boor, M.

1982 The Multiple Personality Epidemic: Additional Cases and Inferences

Regarding Diagnosis, Dynamics and Cure. *Journal of Nervous and Mental Disease* 170:302–304.

Bouchut, F.

1877 De la double conscience et de la dualité de moi. *Séances et travaux de l'Académie des Sciences Morales et Politiques. Comptes Rendus* 108:414–417.

Bourgeois, M., and M. Géraud

1990 Eugène Azam (1822–1899): Un chirurgien précurseur de la psychopathologie dynamique ("Hypnotisme et double conscience"). *Annales médico-psychologiques* 148:709–717.

Bourreau, A.

1991 Satan et le dormeur: une construction de l'inconscient au Moyen Age. *Chimère* 14:41–61.

1993 Le sabbat et la question de la personne dans le monde scholastique. In *Le sabbat des sorciers en Europe XVe–XVIIIe*, edited by N. Jacques-Chaquin. Paris: Jérôme Millon.

Bourru, H., and P. Burot

1885 Un cas de la multiplicité des états de conscience chez un hystéro-epileptique. *Revue philosophique* 20:411–416.

1886a *La suggestion mentale et l'action à distance des substances toxiques et médicamenteuses.* Paris: J. B. Baillière.

1886b Sur les variations de la personnalité. *Revue philosophique* 21:73–74.

1888 *Variations de la personnalité.* Paris: J. B. Baillière.

Bowers, M. K., and S. Brecher

1955 The Emergence of Multiple Personalities in the Course of Hypnotic Investigation. *International Journal of Clinical and Experimental Hypnosis* 3:188–199.

Bowers, M. K., et al.

1971 Therapy of Multiple Personality. *International Journal of Clinical and Experimental Hypnosis* 19:57–65.

Bowman, E. S.

1990 Adolescent Multiple Personality Disorder in the Nineteenth and Early Twentieth Centuries. *Dissociation* 3:179–187.

Bowman E. S., and W. E. Amos.

1993 Utilizing Clergy in the Treatment of Multiple Personality Disorder. *Dissociation* 6:47–53.

Boyle, M.

1990 *Schizophrenia: A Scientific Delusion?* London: Routledge.

Braid, J.

1843 *Neurypnology or the Rationale of Nervous Sleep.* London: J. Churchill.

Braude, S.

1986 *The Limits of Influence: Psychokinesis and the Philosophy of Science.* London: Routledge.

1991 *First Person Plural: Multiple Personality and the Philosophy of Mind.* London: Routledge.

Braun, B. G.

1986 Issues in the Psychotherapy of Multiple Personality Disorder. In *Treatment of Multiple Personality Disorder*, edited by B. G. Braun, 1–28. Washington, D.C.: American Psychiatric Press.

1993 Dissociative Disorders: The Next Ten Years. In *Proceedings of the Tenth International Conference on Multiple Personality/Dissociative States*, edited by B. G. Braun and J. Parks, 5. Chicago: Rush-Presbyterian-St. Luke's Medical Center.

Briquet, P.

1859 *Traité clinique et thérapeutique de l'hystérie.* Paris: Baillière.

Broca, P.

1861 Perte de la parole, ramollissement chronique et destruction partielle du lobe antérieur gauche du cerveau. *Bulletin de la Societé d'Anthropologie* 2:235–237.

Brodie, F.

1992 *When the Other Woman Is His Mother.* Tacoma, Wash.: Winged Eagle Press.

Brook, J. A.

1992 Freud and Splitting. *International Review of Psychoanalysis* 19:335–350.

Brooks, J. L., III

1993 Philosophy and Psychology at the Sorbonne, 1885–1913. *Journal of the History of the Behavioral Sciences* 29:123–145.

Brouardel, P., A. Motet, and P. Garnier

1893 Affaire Valrof. *Annales d'hygiène publique et de médecine légale*, ser. 3, 29:497–525.

Browne A., and D. Finkelhor

1986 Impact of Child Sexual Abuse: A Review of the Research. *Psychological Bulletin* 99:66–77.

Browne, J. C.

1862–1863 Personal Identity and Its Morbid Manifestations. *Journal of Mental Science* 8:385–395, 535–545.

Browning, D. H., and B. Boatman

1977 Incest: Children at Risk. *American Journal of Psychiatry* 134:69–72.

Bryant, D., J. Kessler, and L. Shirar

1992 *The Family Inside: Working with the Multiple.* New York: Norton.

Camuset, L.

1881 Un cas de dédoublement de la personnalité. Période amnésique d'une année chez un jeune homme. *Annales médico-psychologiques*, ser. 6, 7:75–86.

Carlson, Eve Bernstein, and Frank Putnam

1993 An Update on the Dissociative Experiences Scale. *Dissociation* 6:16–27.

Carlson, Eve Bernstein, F. W. Putnam, et al.

    1993 Validity of the Dissociative Experiences Scale in Screening for Multiple Personality: A Multicenter Study. *American Journal of Pyschiatry* 150:1030–1036.

Carlson, E. T.

    1974 The History of Multiple Personality in the United States: Mary Reynolds and Her Subsequent Reputation. *Bulletin of the History of Medicine* 58:72–82.

    1981 The History of Multiple Personality in the United States: 1. The Beginnings. *American Journal of Psychiatry* 138:666–668.

Carlson, E.T., et al., eds.

    1981 "Benjamin Rush's Lectures on the Mind." *Memoirs of the American Philosophical Society* (Philadelphia) 144:669.

Carruthers, M. J.

    1990 *The Book of Memory: A Study of Memory in Medieval Culture.* Cambridge: Cambridge University Press.

Carter, K. C.

    1980 Germ Theory, Hysteria, and Freud's Early Work in Psychopathology. *Medical History* 20:259–274.

    1983 Infantile Hysteria and Infantile Sexuality in Late Nineteenth-Century German-Language Medical Literature. *Medical History* 23:186–196.

Cartwright, N.

    1983 *How the Laws of Physics Lie.* Oxford: Clarendon Press.

Casey J. F., with L. Fletcher

    1991 *The Flock: The Autobiography of a Multiple Personality.* New York: Knopf.

Cavell, M.

    1993 *The Psychoanalytic Mind: From Freud to Philosophy.* Cambridge: Harvard University Press.

Charcot, J.-M.

    1886–1887 *Leçons sur les maladies du systêmes nerveux.* Paris: Progrès Medicale.

Chertok, L., and I. Stengers

    1992 *A Critique of Psychoanalytic Reason: Hypnosis as a Scientific Problem from Lavoisier to Lacan.* Translated by M. N. Evans. Stanford: Stanford University Press.

Chu, J. A.

    1988 Some Aspects of Resistance in the Treatment of Multiple Personality Disorder. *Dissociation* 1(2):34–38.

    1991 On the Misdiagnosis of Multiple Personality Disorder. *Dissociation* 4:200–204.

Chu, J. A., and D. L. Dill

    1990 Dissociative Symptoms in Relation to Childhood Physical and Sexual Abuse. *American Journal of Psychiatry* 149:887–893.

Clark, M. H.
  1992 *All Around the Town*. New York: Simon and Schuster.
Comaroff, J.
  1994 Aristotle Re-membered. In *Questions of Evidence: Proof, Practice, and Persuasion across the Disciplines*, edited by J. Chandler, A. I. Davidson, and H. Harootunian, 463–469. Chicago: University of Chicago Press.
Comstock, C. M.
  1991 The Inner Self Helper and Concepts of Inner Guidance: Historical Antecedents, Its Role within Dissociation, and Clinical Utilization. *Dissociation* 4:165–177.
Condon, R.
  1959 *The Manchurian Candidate*. New York: McGraw-Hill.
Confer, R.
  1983 *Multiple Personality*. New York: Human Sciences Press.
Coons, P. M.
  1980 Multiple Personality: Diagnostic Considerations. *Journal of Clinical Psychiatry* 41:330–336.
  1984 The Differential Diagnosis of Multiple Personality: A Comprehensive Review. *Psychiatric Clinics of North America* 7:51–67.
  1986 The Prevalence of Multiple Personality Disorder. *Newsletter. International Society for the Study of Multiple Personality and Dissociation* 4(3):6–8.
  1988 Psychophysiological Investigation of Multiple Personality: A Review. *Dissociation* 1:47–53.
  1993 The Differential Diagnosis of Possession States. *Dissociation* 6:213–221.
Coons, P. M., V. Milstein, and C. Marley
  1982 EEG Studies of Two Multiple Personalities and a Control. *Archives of General Psychiatry* 39:823–825.
Crabtree, A.
  1985 *Multiple Man: Explorations in Possession and Multiple Personality*. Toronto: Collins.
  1993 *From Mesmer to Freud: Magnetic Sleep and the Roots of Psychological Healing*. New Haven: Yale University Press.
Crocq, L., and J. de Verbizier
  1989 Le traumatisme psychologique dans l'oeuvre de Pierre Janet. *Bulletin de psychologie* 61:483–485.
Crose, T. J.
  1980 Molecular Biology of Schizophrenia: More Than One Disease Process. *British Medical Journal* 280:66–86.
  1985 The Two Syndrome Concept—Origin and Current Status. *Schizophrenia Bulletin* 11:471–486.

Dailey, A. H.
  1894 *Mollie Fancher: The Brooklyn Enigma*. Brooklyn: Eagle Book Printing Department.

Danziger, K.
  1991 *Constructing the Subject*. Cambridge: Cambridge University Press.

Darnton, R.
  1968 *Mesmerism and the End of the Enlightenment in France*. Cambridge: Harvard University Press.

Davidson, D.
  1980 Causal Relations (1967). In *Essays on Actions and Events*, 149–162. Oxford: Clarendon Press.

Dell, P. F., and J. W. Eisenhower
  1990 Adolescent Multiple Personality Disorder: A Preliminary Study of Eleven Cases. *Journal of the American Academy of Child and Adolescent Psychiatry* 29:357–365.

DeMause, L.
  1974 The Evolution of Childhood. In *The History of Childhood: The Untold Story of Child Abuse*, edited by L. deMause, 1–73. New York: Psychohistory Press.

Dennett, D. C.
  1991 *Consciousness Explained*. Boston: Little Brown.
  1992 Letter to the *London Review of Books*, 9 July, 2.

Despine, C.H.A.
  1838 *Observations de médecine pratique. Faites aux Bains d'Aix-en-Savoie*. Anneci: Aimé Burdet (dated 1838, issued October 1839).
  1840 *De l'emploi du magnétisme animal et des eaux minérales dans le traitement des maladies nerveuses. Suivi d'une observation très curieuse de guérison de névropathie*. Paris: Germer Baillière.

Desrosières, A.
  1993 *La politique des grands nombres*. Paris: Découverte.

deVito, R. A.
  1993 The Use of Amytal Interviews in the Treatment of an Exceptionally Complex Case of Multiple Personality Disorder. In *Clinical Perspectives on Multiple Personality Disorder*, edited by R. P. Kluft and C. G. Fine, 227–240. Washington, D.C.: American Psychiatric Press.

Dewar, H.
  1823 Report on a Communication from *Dr Dyce* of Aberdeen, to the Royal Society of Edinburgh. "On Uterine Irritation, and Its Effects on the Female Constitution." *Transactions of the Royal Society of Edinburgh* 9:365–379.

Dewey, R.
  1907 A Case of Disordered Personality. *Journal of Abnormal Psychology* 2:142–154.

Didi-Huberman, C.

1982 *Invention de l'hystérie: Charcot et l'iconographie photographique de la Salpêtrière*. Paris: Editions Macula.

Donovan, D. M.

1991 Darkness Invisible. *Journal of Psychohistory* 19:165–184.

Donovan, D. M., and D. McIntyre

1990 *Healing the Hurt Child: A Developmental-Contextual Approach*. New York: Norton.

Douglas, M.

1983 *How Institutions Think*. Syracuse: Syracuse University Press.

1992 The Person in an Enterprise Culture. In *Understanding the Enterprise Culture: Themes in the Work of Mary Douglas*, edited by S. H. Heap and A. Ross, 41–62. Edinburgh: Edinburgh University Press.

Draijer, N., and S. Boon

1993 The Validation of the Dissociative Experiences Scale against the Criterion of the SCID-D Using Receiver Operating Characteristics (ROC) Analysis. *Dissociation* 6:28–37.

Dufay, R.

1876 La notion de la personnalité. *Revue philosophique*, 2d ser., 5:69–74.

Ebbinghaus, H.

1885 *Über das Gedachtnis. Untersuchungen zur experimetallen Psychologie*. Leipzig: Duncker & Humblot.

Egger, V.

1887 Review of Azam's *Hypnotisme, double conscience et altérations de la personnalité. Revue philosophique* 24:301–310.

Ellason, J., C. A. Ross, D. Fuchs, et al.

1992 Update on the Dissociative Disorders Interview Schedule. In *Proceedings of the Ninth International Conference on Multiple Personality/Dissociative States*, edited by B. G. Braun and E. B. Carlson, 54. Chicago: Rush-Presbyterian-St. Luke's Medical Center.

Ellenberger H.

1970 *The Discovery of the Unconscious*. New York: Basic Books.

Elster, J.

1983 *Explaining Technical Change*. Cambridge: Cambridge University Press.

Engel, E.

1872 Beitrage zur Statistik des Krieges von 1870–71. *Zeitschrift des Königlich preussischen statistichen Bureaus* 12:1–320.

Erichsen, J. E.

1866 *On Railway and Other Injuries of the Nervous System*. London.

Faust, G. H.

1991 The Sexton Tapes, *News. International Society for the Study of Multiple Personality & Dissociation* 9(6):7–8.

Fernando, L.

1990 Letter. *British Journal of Psychiatry* 157.

Fifth Estate (Canadian Broadcasting Corporation)

1993 Multiple Personality Disorder (8 P.M., 9 November 1993). Toronto: Media Tapes and Transcripts.

Fine, C. G.

1988 The Work of Antoine Despine: The First Scientific Report on the Diagnosis of a Child with Multiple Personality Disorder. *American Journal of Clinical Hypnosis* 31:33–39.

1991 President's Message. *News. International Society for the Study of Multiple Personality & Dissociation* 9(1):1–2.

Finkelhor, D.

1979 What's Wrong with Sex between Adults and Children? Ethics and the Problem of Sexual Abuse. *American Journal of Orthopsychiatry* 49:692–697.

1984 *Child Sexual Abuse: New Theory and Research*. New York: Free Press.

Firschholz, E. J., et al.

1991 Construct Validity of the Dissociative Experiences Scale (DES): I. The Relationship between the DES and Other Self-Report Measures of Dissociation. *Dissociation* 4:185–189.

Fischer-Homberg, E.

1971 Charcot und die Ätiology der Neurosen. *Generus* 28:35–46.

1972 Die Büchse der Pandora: Der mythische Hintergrund der Eisenbahnkrankheit des 19 Jahrhunderts. *Sudhoff's Archiv* 56:296–317.

1975 *Die Traumatische Neurose: vom Somatischen zum sozialen Leiden*. Bern: Huber.

Fogelin, R., and W. Sinnott-Armstrong

1991 *Understanding Arguments: An Introduction to Informal Logic*. 4th ed. New York: Harcourt Brace Jovanovich.

Forward S., and C. Buck

1978 *Betrayal of Innocence: Incest and Its Devastation*. Harmondsworth: Penguin.

Foucault, M.

1972 *The Archaeology of Knowledge*. New York: Harper and Row.

1980 *A History of Sexuality*. Vol. 1, *An Introduction*. New York: Vintage.

Frankel F. H.

1990 Hypnotizability and Dissociation. *American Journal of Psychiatry* 147:823–829.

1994 Dissociation in Hysteria and Hypnosis: A Concept Aggrandized. In *Dissociation: Clinical and Theoretical Perspectives*, edited by S. J. Lynn and J. W. Rhue, 80–93. New York: Guilford.

Fraser, G. A.

1990 Satanic Ritual Abuse: A Cause of Multiple Personality Disorder. *Journal of Child and Youth Care*, Special Issue: 55–66.

Fraser, S.

1987 *My Father's House: A Memoir of Incest and Healing*. Toronto: Doubleday.

Freeland, A., et al.

1993 Four Cases of Supposed Multiple Personality Disorder: Evidence of Unjustified Diagnoses. *Canadian Journal of Psychiatry* 38:245–247.

Freud, Sigmund

1953–1974 *S.E.* (*The Standard Edition of the Complete Psychological Works of Sigmund Freud*). Translated from the German under the general editorship of James Strachey. 24 vols. London: The Hogarth Press and the Institute of Psycho-Analysis.

Freyd, J. F.

1993 Theoretical and Personal Perspectives on the Delayed Memory Debate. In *Proceedings: Controversies around Recovered Memories of Incest and Ritualistic Abuse*, 69–108. Jackson, Mich.: The Dissociative Disorders Program, The Center for Mental Health at Foote Hospital, 7 August 1993.

Freyd, P. (Jane Doe)

1991 How Could This Happen? Coping with a False Accusation of Incest and Rape. *Issues in Child Abuse Accusations* 3:154–165.

Freyd, P. (Anonymous)

1992 How Could This Happen? In *Confabulations: Creating False Memories, Destroying Families*, edited by Eleanor Goldstein with Kevin Farmer, 27–60. Boca Raton, Fla.: SIRS Books.

Ganaway, G. K.

1989 Historical Truth versus Narrative Truth: Clarifying the Role of Exogenous Trauma in the Etiology of Multiple Personality Disorder and Its Variants. *Dissociation* 2:205–220.

1992 On the Nature of Memories: Response to "A Reply to Ganaway." *Dissociation* 5:120–122.

1993 Untitled presentation. In *Proceedings: Controversies around Recovered Memories of Incest and Ritualistic Abuse*, 42–68. Jackson, Mich.: The Dissociative Disorders Program, The Center for Mental Health at Foote Hospital, 7 August 1993.

Gauld, A.

1992a *A History of Hypnotism.* Cambridge: Cambridge University Press.

1992b Hypnosis, Somnambulism and Double Consciousness. *Contemporary Hypnosis* 9:69–76.

Gelfand, T.

1989 Charcot's Response to Freud's Rebellion. *Journal of the History of Ideas* 50:293–307.

1992 Sigmund-sur-Seine: Fathers and Brothers in Charcot's Paris. In *Freud and the History of Psychoanalysis*, edited by T. Gelfand and J. Kerr, 27–42. Hillsdale, N.J.: Analytic Press.

Gelles, R. J.

1975 The Social Construction of Child Abuse. *American Journal of Orthopsychiatry* 45:363–371.

George, E.

1988 *A Great Deliverance*. New York: Bantam.

Gilbertson, A., et al.

1992 Susceptibility of Common Self-Report Measures of Dissociation to Malingering. *Dissociation* 5:216–220.

Gilles de la Tourette, A.

1889 *L'hypnotisme et les états analogues au point de vue médico-légale*. Paris: Plon.

Goddard, H. H.

1926 A Case of Dual Personality. *Journal of Abnormal and Social Psychology* 21:170–191.

1927 *Two Souls in One Body? A Case of Dual Personality. A Study of a Remarkable Case: Its Significance for Education and for the Mental Hygiene of Childhood*. New York: Dodd Mead.

Goettman, C., G. B. Greaves, and P. M. Coons

1991 *Multiple Personality and Dissociation, 1791–1990: A Complete Bibliography*. Atlanta, Ga.: G. B. Greaves.

1994 *Multiple Personality and Dissociation, 1791–1992: A Complete Bibliography*. 2d ed. Lutherville, Md.: Sidran Press.

Goff D. G., and C. A. Simms

1993 Has Multiple Personality Disorder Remained Constant over Time? *Journal of Nervous and Mental Disease* 181:595–600.

Goodstein, J.

1988 *To Console and Classify: The French Psychiatric Profession in the Nineteenth Century*. Chicago: University of Chicago Press.

Goodwin, J.

1989 Satanism: Similarities between Patient Accounts and Pre-Inquisition Historical Sources. *Dissociation* 2:39–44.

1994 Sadistic Abuse: Definition, Recognition and Treatment. In *Treating Survivors of Ritual Abuse*, edited by V. Sinason, 33–44. London: Routledge.

Graves, S. M.

1989 Dissociative Disorders and Dissociative Symptoms at a Community Health Center. *Dissociation* 2:119–127.

Greaves, G. B.

1980 Multiple Personality: 165 Years after Mary Reynolds. *Journal of Nervous and Mental Disease* 168: 577–596.

1987 President's Letter. *Newsletter. International Society for the Study of Multiple Personality & Dissociation* 5(2):1.

1993 A History of Multiple Personality Disorder. In *Clinical Perspectives on Multiple Personality Disorder*, edited by R. P. Kluft and C. G. Fine, 355–380. Washington, D.C.: American Psychiatric Press.

Greenberg, W. M., and S. Attiah

1993 Multiple Personality Disorder and Informed Consent. Letter to the editor. *American Journal of Psychiatry* 150:1126–1127.

Greenland, C.
    1988 *Preventing C.A.N. Deaths: An International Study of Deaths Due to Child Abuse and Neglect.* London: Routledge, Chapman & Hall.

Guinon, G.
    1889 *Les agents provocateurs de l'hystérie.* Paris: Progrès Medical.

Hacking, I.
    1982 Wittgenstein the Psychologist. *New York Review of Books*, 1 April, 42–44.

    1983 Biopower and the Avalanche of Numbers. *Humanities and Society* 5:279–295.

    1986a The Archaeology of Foucault. In *Foucault: A Critical Reader*, edited by D. C. Hoy, 27–40. Oxford: Blackwell.

    1986b Making Up People. In *Reconstructing Individualism: Autonomy, Individuality and the Self in Western Thought*, edited by T. C. Heller et al., 222–236. Stanford: Stanford University Press.

    1986c Self-Improvement. In *Foucault: A Critical Reader*, edited by D. C. Hoy, 235–240. Oxford: Blackwell.

    1988 Telepathy: Origins of Randomization in Experimental Design. *Isis* 79:427–451.

    1991a Double Consciousness in Britain, 1815–1875. *Dissociation* 4:134–146.

    1991b The Making and Molding of Child Abuse. *Critical Inquiry* 17:253–288.

    1991c Two Souls in One Body. *Critical Inquiry* 17:838–867.

    1992 World-Making by Kind-Making: Child Abuse for Example. In *How Classification Works: Nelson Goodman among the Social Sciences*, edited by M. Douglas and D. Hull, 180–238. Edinburgh: Edinburgh University Press.

    1993 Some Reasons for Not Taking Parapsychology Very Seriously. *Dialogue* 32:587–594.

    1994 The Looping Effects of Human Kinds. In *Causal Cognition: A Multidisciplinary Approach*, edited by D. Sperber, D. Premack, and A. J. Premack, 351–394. Oxford: Clarendon Press.

    Forthcoming *Les Aliénés voyageurs:* How Fugue Became a Medical Entity. *History of Psychiatry.*

Harrington, A.
    1985 Nineteenth Century Ideas of Hemisphere Differences and "Duality of Mind." *Behavioral and Brain Sciences* 8:617–660.

    1987 *Medicine, Mind, and the Double Brain: A Study in Nineteenth-Century Thought.* Princeton: Princeton University Press.

Hart, B.
    1926 The Conception of Dissociation. *British Journal of Medical Psychology* 6:247.

1927 *Psychopathology: Its Development and Its Place in Medicine.* Cambridge: Cambridge University Press.

Hartmann, E. von
1869 *Philosophie des Unbewussten.* Berlin: Duncker.

Hawksworth H., and T. Schwartz
1977 *The Five of Me.* Chicago: Regnery.

Healy, D.
1993 *Images of Trauma: From Hysteria to Post-Traumatic Stress Disorder.* London: Faber and Faber.

Heidelberger, M.
1993 *Die innere Seite der Natur: Gustav Theodor Fechners wissennschaftliche Weltaufassung.* Frankfurt: Klostermann.

Helfer, R.
1968 The Responsibility and Role of the Physician. In *The Battered Child*, edited by R. E. Helfer and C. H. Kempe. Chicago: University of Chicago Press.

Hendrikson, K. M., T. McCarty, and J. Goodwin
1990 Animal Alters: Case Reports. *Dissociation* 3:218–221.

Herdman, J.
1990 *The Double in Nineteenth-Century Fiction.* London: Macmillan.

Herman, J. L.
1981 *Father-Daughter Incest.* Cambridge: Harvard University Press.
1992 *Trauma and Recovery.* New York. Basic Books.

Herman J., and L. Hirschman
1977 Father-Daughter Incest. *Signs* 2:735–756.

Hilgard, E.
1977 *Divided Consciousness: Multiple Controls in Human Thought and Action.* New York: Wiley.
1986 *Divided Consciousness: Multiple Controls in Human Thought and Action.* Expanded ed. New York: Wiley.

Horevitz, R. P., and B. G. Braun
1984 Are Multiple Personalities Borderline? An Analysis of Thirty-Three Cases. *Psychiatric Clinics of North America* 7:69–88.

Horton, P., and D. Miller
1972 The Etiology of Multiple Personality. *Comparative Psychology* 13:151–159.

Humphrey, N., and D. C. Dennett
1989 Speaking for Ourselves. *Raritan* 9:68–98.

Irwin, H. J.
1992 Origins and Functions of Paranormal Belief: The Role of Childhood Trauma and Interpersonal Control. *Journal of American Society for Psychical Research* 86:199–208.

1994 Childhood Trauma and the Origins of Paranormal Belief: A Constructive Replication. *Psychological Reports* 74:107–111.

James, W.

1890 *The Principles of Psychology.* 2 vols. New York: Holt.

1983 Notes on Ansel Bourne. In *Essays in Psychology*, 269. Cambridge: Harvard University Press. The notes were taken in 1890.

Janet, J.

1888 L'hystérie et l'hypnotisme, d'après la théorie de la double personnalité. *Revue scientifique*, ser. 3, 15:616–623.

Janet, Pierre

1886a Deuxième note sur le sommeil provoqué à distance et la suggestion mentale pendant l'état somnambulique. *Revue philosophique* 22:212–223.

1886b Note sur quelques phénomènes de somnambulisme. *Revue philosophique* 21:190–198.

1886c Les actes inconscients et la dédoublement de la personnalité pendant le somnambulisme provoqué. *Revue philosophique* 22:577–592.

1886d Les phases intermédiaires de l'hypnotisme. *Revue scientifique* 23:577–587.

1887 L'anesthésie systematisée et la dissociation des phénomènes psychologiques. *Revue philosophique* 23:449–472.

1888 Les actes inconscients et la mémoire pendant le somnambulisme provoqué. *Revue philosophique* 25:238–279.

1889 *L'automatisme psychologique.* Paris: Alcan.

1892 Etude sur quelques cas d'amnésie antétograde dans la maladie de la désagrégation psychologique. In *International Congress of Experimental Psychology, Second Session, London*, 26–30. London: Williams and Norgate.

1893 L'amnésie continue. *Revue générale des sciences* 4:167–179.

1893–1894 *Etat mental des hystériques.* 2 vols. Paris: Bibliothèque médical Charcot-Delbove.

1903 *Les obsessions et la psychasthénie.* 2 vols. Paris: Alcan.

1907 *The Major Symptoms of Hysteria.* London: Macmillan.

1909 *Les névroses.* Paris: Flammarion.

1919 *Les médications psychologiques. Etudes historiques, psychologiques et cliniques sur les méthodes de la psychothérapie.* 3 vols. Paris: Alcan.

Janet, Paul.

1876 La notion de la personnalité. *Revue scientifique*, ser. 2, 5:574.

1888 Une chair de psychologie expérimentale et comparée au Collège de France. *Revue de deux mondes*, ser. 3, 86: 518–549.

Jardine, N.

1986 *The Scenes of Inquiry.* Oxford: Clarendon Press.

1991 *The Fortunes of Inquiry.* Oxford: Clarendon Press.

Jones, E.
  1955 *Sigmund Freud: Life and Work*. 3 vols. London: Hogarth Press.
Jullian, C.
  1903 *Notes bibliographiques sur l'oeuvre du docteur Azam*. Bordeaux:
    Gounouilhou. Reprinted from *Actes de l'Académie Nationale des Sciences
    et Belles Lettres de Bordeaux*, ser. 3, 63 (1901).
Kahneman, D., and A. Tversky
  1973 On the Psychology of Prediction. *Psychological Review* 80:237–251.
Kempe, C. H., et al.
  1962 The Battered Child Syndrome. *Journal of the American Medical Associ-
    ation* 181(1):17–24.
Kendall-Tackett, K.A., L. M. Williams, and D. Finkelhor
  1993 Impact of Sexual Abuse on Children: A Review and Synthesis of Recent
    Empirical Studies. *Psychological Bulletin* 113:164–180.
Kenny, M.
  1986 *The Passion of Ansel Bourne*. Washington, D.C.: Smithsonian.
Keyes, D.
  1981 *The Minds of Billy Milligan*. New York: Random House.
Kinsey, A. C.
  1953 *Sexual Behavior in the Human Female*. Philadelphia: W. B. Saunders.
Kirk, S.
  1992 *The Selling of DSM: The Rhetoric of Science in Psychiatry*. New York: de
    Gruyter.
Kitcher, P.
  1992 *Freud's Dream: A Complete Interdisciplinary Science of Mind*. Cam-
    bridge: MIT Press.
Kleist, H. von
  1988 *Five Plays*. Translated by Martin Greenberg. New Haven: Yale Univer-
    sity Press.
Kluft, R. P.
  1984 Treatment of Multiple Personality Disorder: A Study of Thirty-Three
    Cases. *Psychiatric Clinics of North America* 7:69–88.
  1987 First-Rank Symptoms as a Diagnostic Clue to Multiple Personality Dis-
    order. *American Journal of Psychiatry* 144:293–298.
  1989 Editorial: Reflections on Allegations of Ritual Abuse. *Dissociation*
    2:191–193.
  1991 Clinical Presentations of Multiple Personality Disorder. *Psychiatric
    Clinics of North America* 14:605–629.
  1993a The Editor's Reflective Pleasures. *Dissociation* 6:1–3.
  1993b The Treatment of Dissociative Disorder Patients: An Overview of
    Discoveries, Successes, and Failures. *Dissociation* 6:87–101.
  1993c The Treatment of Multiple Personality Disorder—1984–1993. Tape
    VIIE-860–93. Alexandria, Va.: Audio Transcripts.

Kluft, R. P., ed.
  1985 *Childhood Antecedents of Multiple Personality*. Washington, D.C.: American Psychiatric Press.
Krane, J. J., and J. C. Connoly
  1992 *The Eleventh Mental Measurements Handbook*. Lincoln, Nebr.: Buros Institute of Mental Measurement.
Krüll, M.
  1986 *Freud and His Father*. German ed. 1979. Translated by A. J. Pomerans. New York: Norton.
Ladame, P. L.
  1888 Observation de somnambulisme hystérique avec dédoublement de la personnalité, gueri par la suggestion hypnotique. *Annales médico-psychologiques* 46:313–320.
Laing, R. D.
  1959 *The Divided Self: A Study of Sanity and Madness*. London: Tavistock.
Lakoff, G.
  1987 *Women, Fire, and Dangerous Things: What Categories Reveal about the Mind*. Chicago: University of Chicago Press.
Lambek, M.
  1981 *Human Spirits: A Cultural Account of Trance in Mayotte*. Cambridge: Cambridge University Press.
Lampl, H. E.
  1988 *Flair du Livre. Friedric Nietzsche und Théodule Ribot, eine trouvaille. Hundert Jahre "Zur Genealogie der Moral."* Zurich: am Abgrund.
Lancaster, E. (i.e., Chris Costner Sizemore)
  1958 *The Final Faces of Eve*. New York: McGraw-Hill.
Landis, J. T.
  1956 Experiences of Five Hundred Children with Adult Sexual Deviation. *Psychiatric Quarterly Supplement* 30:91–109.
Laporta, L. D.
  1992 Childhood Trauma and Multiple Personality Disorder: The Case of a Nine-Year-Old Girl. *Child Abuse and Neglect* 16:615–620.
Latour, B., and S. Woolgar
  1979 *Laboratory Life: The Social Construction of a Scientific Fact*. London and Beverly Hills: Sage.
Laupts, Dr.
  1898 Les phénomènes de la distraction cérébrale et les états dits de dédoublement de la personnalité. *Annales médico-psychologiques*, ser. 8, 8:353–372.
Lessing, D.
  1986 *The Good Terrorist* (1985). New York: Vintage.
Leys, R.
  1992 The Real Miss Beauchamp: Gender and the Subject of Imitation. In

Feminists Theorize the Political, edited by J. Butler and J. Scott, 167–214. London: Routledge.

1994 Traumatic Cures: Shell Shock, Janet, and the Question of Memory. *Critical Inquiry* 20:623–662.

Lichtheim, L.

1885 On Aphasia. *Brain* 7:433–484.

Lindau P.

1893 *Der Andere*. Dresden: Teubner.

Littré, E.

1875 La double conscience: fragment de physiologie physique. *Revue de philosophie positive* 14:321–336.

Lizza, J. P.

1993 Multiple Personality and Personal Identity Revisited. *British Journal for the Philosophy of Science* 44:263–274.

Lockwood, C.

1993 *Other Altars: Roots and Realities of Cultic and Satanic Ritual Abuse and Multiple Personality Disorder*. Minneapolis: CompCare Publishers.

Loewenstein, R. J.

1990 The Clinical Psychology of Males with Multiple Personality Disorder: A Report of Twenty-One Cases. *Dissociation* 3:135–143.

1991 Psychogenic Amnesia and Psychogenic Fugue: A Comprehensive Review. *Review of Psychiatry* 10:189–222.

Loftus, E., and K. Ketcham

1994 *The Myth of Repressed Memories: False Memories and Allegations of Sexual Abuse*. New York: St. Martin's Press.

Löwenfeld, L.

1893 Paul Lindaus "Der Andere" und die ärztliche Erfahrung. *Medicinische Wochenschrift* 40:835–838.

Ludwig, A. M.

1972 The Objective Study of a Multiple Personality. *Archives of General Psychiatry* 26:298–310.

Lunier, L.

1874 *De l'influence des grands commotions politiques et sociales sur le développement des maladies mentales*. Paris: F. Savy.

MacKinnon, C.

1987 *Feminism Unmodified: Discourses on Life and Law*. Cambridge: Harvard University Press.

Malinosky-Rummell, R., and D. J. Hansen

1993 Long-term Consequences of Childhood Physical Abuse. *Psychological Bulletin* 114:68–79.

Marmer, S. S.

1980 Psychoanalysis of Multiple Personality. *International Journal of Psychoanalysis* 61:439–459.

Masson, J. M.

    1984 *The Assault on Truth: Freud's Suppression of the Seduction Theory.* New York: Farrar, Strauss and Giroux.

Mayo, H.

    1837 *Outlines of Human Physiology.* 4th ed. London: Renshaw.

Mayo, T.

    1845 Case of Double Consciousness. *London Medical Gazette, or Journal of Practical Medicine*, n.s., 1:120–121.

McCrone, J.

    1994 Don't Forget Your Memory Aide. *New Scientist*, no. 1911 (5 February): 32.

Merskey, H.

    1992 The Manufacture of Personalities: The Production of Multiple Personality Disorder. *British Journal of Psychiatry* 160:327–340.

Micale, M. S.

    1989 Hysteria and Its Historiography: A Review of Past and Present Writings. *History of Science* 27:223–261.

    1990a Charcot and the Idea of Hysteria in the Male: Gender, Mental Science, and Medical Diagnosis in Late Nineteenth-Century France. *Medical History* 34:363–411.

    1990b Hysteria and Historiography: The Future Perspective. *History of Psychiatry* 1:33–124.

    1993 On the Disappearance of Hysteria: A Study in the Clinical Deconstruction of a Diagnosis. *Isis* 84:496–526.

Micale M. S., ed.

    1993 *Beyond the Unconscious: Essays of Henri F. Ellenberger in the History of Psychiatry.* Princeton: Princeton University Press.

Middlebrook, D. W.

    1991 *Anne Sexton: A Biography.* New York: Houghton Mifflin.

Miller, K.

    1987 *Doubles: Studies in Literary History.* 2d ed., corrected. Oxford. Oxford University Press.

Mitchell, J. V.

    1983 *Tests in Print III.* Lincoln, Nebr.: Buros Institute of Mental Measurement.

Mitchill, S. L.

    1817 A Double Consciousness, or a Duality of Person in the same Individual: From a Communication of Dr. MITCHILL to the Reverend Dr. NOTT, President of Union College. Dated January 16. 1816. *The Medical Repository of Original Essays and Intelligence Relative to Physic, Surgery, Chemistry and Natural History* etc. 18 [or New Series 3] From the issue of February 1816.

Moll, A.

1893 Die Bewusstseinspaltung in Paul Lindaus neuen Schauspiel. *Zeitschrift für Hypnotismus, Psychotherapie, sowie andere psychophysiologische und psychiatrische Forschungen* 1:307–310.

Moore, M.

1938 Morton Prince, M.D., 1854–1929: A Biographic Sketch and Bibliography. *Journal of Nervous and Mental Diseases* 87:701–710.

Mulhern, S.

1991a Embodied Alternative Identities: Bearing Witness to a World That Might Have Been. *Psychiatric Clinics of North America* 14:769–785.

1991b Letter. *Child Abuse and Neglect* 15:609–611.

1991c Satanism and Psychotherapy. In *The Satanism Scare*, edited by J. T. Richardson, J. Best, and D. G. Bromley, 145–173. New York: Aldine de Gruyter.

1993 A la recherche du trauma perdu. Le touble de la personnalité multiple. *Chimères* 18:53–86.

1995 Deciphering Ritual Abuse: A Socio-Historical Perspective. *International Journal for Clinical and Experimental Hypnosis.*

Murphy, J. M., et al.

1987 Performance of Screening and Diagnostic Tests: Application of Receiver Operating Characteristic Analysis. *Archives of General Psychiatry* 44:550–555.

Murray, D.

1983 *A History of Western Psychology.* Englewood Cliffs, N.J.: Prentice-Hall.

Myers, A. T.

1896 The Life-History of a Case of Double or Multiple Personality. *Journal of Mental Science* 31:596–605.

Myers, F.W.H.

1896 Multiplex Personality. *Proceedings of the Society for Psychical Research* 4:596–514.

1903 *Human Personality and Its Survival of Bodily Death.* 2 vols. London: Longmans, Green.

Nelson, B.

1984 *Making an Issue of Child Abuse: Political Agenda Setting for Social Problems.* Chicago: University of Chicago Press.

North, C. S., et al.

1993 *Multiple Personalities, Multiple Disorders: Psychiatric Classification and Media Influence.* New York: Oxford University Press.

Nye, R. A.

1984 *Crime, Madness and Politics in Modern France: The Medical Concept of National Decline.* Princeton: Princeton University Press.

317

Ofshe, R., and E. Watters

  1994 *Making Monsters: False Memories, Psychotherapy and Sexual Hysteria.* New York: Charles Scribners' Sons.

Olafson, E., D. L. Corwin, and R. C. Summitt

  1993 Modern History of Child Sexual Abuse Awareness: Cycles of Discovery and Suppression. *Child Abuse and Neglect* 17:7–24.

Olsen, J. A., R. J. Loewenstein, and N. Hornstein

  1992 Mini-Workshop: Gender Issues and Influences in the Treatment of MPD. Ninth International Conference of Multiple Personality and Dissociative States, Tape E-770-92. Alexandria, Va.: Audio Transcripts.

Ondrovik, J., and D. M. Hamilton

  1990 Multiple Personality: Competency and the Insanity Defense. *American Journal of Forensic Psychiatry* 11:41–64.

O'Neill, P.

  1992 Violence and Its Aftermath: Introduction. *Canadian Psychology* 33:119–127.

Orne, M. T., D. F. Dingfes, and E. C. Orne

  1984 On the Differential Diagnosis of Multiple Personality in the Forensic Context. *International Journal of Clinical and Experimental Hypnosis* 32:118–169.

Passantino G., B. Passantino, and J. Trott

  1990 Satan's Sideshow: The True Laura Stratford Story. *Cornerstone* 18:24–28.

Perr, I. N.

  1991 Crime and Multiple Personality: A Case History and Discussion. *Bulletin of the American Academy of Psychiatry and Law* 19:203–214.

Peterson, G.

  1990 Diagnosis of Childhood Multiple Personality Disorder. *Dissociation* 3:3–9.

Pickering, A.

  1986 *Constructing Quarks.* Chicago: University of Chicago Press.

Pitres, A.

  1891 *Leçons cliniques sur l'hystérie et l'hypnotisme faites à l'hôpital Saint-André à Bordeaux.* 2 vols. Paris: Doin.

Plint, T.

  1851 *Crime in England: Its Relation, Character and Extent, as Developed from 1801 to 1848.* London: Charles Gilpin.

Prince, M.

  1890 Some of the Revelations of Hypnotism: Posthypnotic Suggestion, Automatic Writing, and Double Personality. *Boston Medical and Surgical Journal* 122:463–467.

  1905 *The Dissociation of a Personality: A Biographical Study in Abnormal Psychology.* New York: Longmans, Green.

1920 Babinski's Theory of Hysteria. *Journal of Abnormal Psychology*. 20:312–324.

Prince, W. F.

1915–1916 The Doris Case of Quintuple Personality. *Proceedings of the American Society for Psychical Research* 9:23–700; 10:701–1419.

1923 The Mother of Doris. *Proceedings of the American Society of Psychical Research* 17:1–216.

Proust, A.

1890 Automatisme ambulatoire chez un hystérique. *Bulletin de médecine* 4:107–109.

Proust, M.

1961 *A la recherche du temps perdu.* 3 vols. Paris: Gallimard.

Putnam, F. W.

1988 The Switch Process in Multiple Personality Disorder and Other State-Change Disorders. *Dissociation* 1:24–32.

1989 *Diagnosis and Treatment of Multiple Personality Disorder.* New York: The Guilford Press.

1991 The Satanic Ritual Abuse Controversy. *Child Abuse and Neglect* 15:95–111.

1992a Altered States: Peeling Away the Layers of Multiple Personality. *The Sciences*, November/December, 30–38.

1992b Are Alter Personalities Fragments or Figments? *Psychoanalytic Inquiry* 12:95–111.

1993 Diagnosis and Clinical Phenomenology of Multiple Personality Disorder: A North American Perspective. *Dissociation* 6:80–86.

Putnam, F. W., T. P. Zahn, and R. M. Post

1990 Differential Autonomic Nervous System Activity in Multiple Personality Disorder. *Psychiatric Research* 31:251–260.

Putnam F. W., et al.

1986 The Clinical Phenomenology of Multiple Personality Disorder: A Review of One Hundred Recent Cases. *Journal of Clinical Psychiatry* 47:285–293.

Rank, Otto

1971 Translated and edited by Harry Tucker, Jr. *The Double: A Psychoanalytic Sudy.* University of North Carolina Press.

Ray, W. J., et al.

1992 Dissociative Experiences in a College Population: A Factor Analytic Study of Two Dissociative Scales. *Personal and Individual Differences* 13:417–424.

Raymond, F., and Pierre Janet

1895 Les délires ambulatoires ou les fugues. *Gazette des hôpitaux*, 754–762, 787–793. [Notes taken by Janet of Raymond's lecture.]

Reagor, P. A., J. D. Kaasten, and N. Morelli
  1992 A Checklist for Screening Dissociative Disorders in Childhood and Early Adolescence. *Dissociation* 5:4–19.
Reppucci, N. D., and J. J. Haugaard
  1989 Prevention of Child Sexual Abuse: Myth or Reality. *American Psychologist*, October, 1266–1275.
Reynolds, J. R.
  1869a Certain Forms of Paralysis depending on Idea. *British Medical Journal* 2:378.
  1869b Remarks on Paralysis, and Other Disorders of Motion and Sensation, Dependent on Idea. *British Medical Journal* 2:483–485.
Ribot, T.
  1870 *La psychologie anglaise contemporaine et expérimentale*. Paris: Ladrange.
  1881 *Les maladies de la mémoire*. Paris: Baillière.
  1883 *Les maladies de la volonté*. Paris: Alcan.
  1885 *Les maladies de la personnalité*. Paris: Alcan.
Richards, D. G.
  1991 A Study of the Correlation between Subjective Psychic Experiences and Dissociative Experiences. *Dissociation* 4:83–91.
Riley, K. C.
  1988 Measurement of Dissociation. *Journal of Nervous and Mental Disease* 176:149–150.
Rivera, M.
  1987 Am I a Boy or a Girl? Multiple Personality as a Window on Gender Differences. *Resources for Feminist Research/Documentation sur la Recherche Féministe* 17(2):41–43.
  1988 "All of Them to Speak: Feminism, Poststructuralism, and Multiple Personality." Ph.D. diss., University of Toronto.
  1991 Multiple Personality Disorder and the Social Systems: 185 Cases. *Dissociation* 4:79–82.
Rivera, M., and J. A. Olson
  1994 Treating Multiple Personality in Its Social Context: A Feminist Perspective. Abstract for 1994 ISSMP&D Fourth Annual Spring Conference. Vancouver, Canada.
Romans, S. E., et al.
  1993 Otago Women's Health Survey Thirty Month Follow-up. I. Onset Patterns of Non-psychotic Psychiatric Disorder. II. Remission Patterns of Non-psychotic Psychiatric Disorder. *British Journal of Psychiatry* 163:733–738, 739–746.
Root-Bernstein, R. S.
  1990 Misleading Reliability. *The Sciences*, March/April, 44–47.
Rosch, E.
  1978 Principles of Categorization. In *Cognition and Categorization*, edited by E. Rosch and B. B. Lloyd, 27–48. Hillside, N.J.: Lawrence Erlbaum.

Rose, J.

1986 *Sexuality in the Field of Vision*. London: Verso.

Rosenbaum, M.

1980 The Role of the Term Schizophrenia in the Decline of Multiple Personality. *Archives of General Psychiatry* 37:1383–1385.

Rosenfeld, I.

1988 *The Invention of Memory: A New View of the Brain*. New York: Basic Books.

Rosenzweig, S.

1987 Sally Beauchamp's Career: A Psychoarchaeological Key to Morton Prince's Classic Case of Multiple Personality. *Genetic, Social and General Psychology Monographs* 113:5–60.

Ross, C. A.

1987 Inpatient Treatment of Multiple Personality Disorder. *Canadian Journal of Psychiatry* 32:779–781.

1989 *Multiple Personality Disorder: Diagnosis, Clinical Features and Treatment*. New York: Wiley.

1990 Letter. *British Journal of Psychiatry* 156:449.

1991 Epidemiology of Multiple Personality and Dissociation. *Psychiatric Clinics of North America* 14:503–517.

1993 Conversations with the President of ISSMP&D. Tape XIIE-860-93. Alexandria, Va.: Audio Transcripts.

1994 *The Osiris Complex: Case Studies in Multiple Personality Disorder*. Toronto: University of Toronto Press.

Ross, C. A., G. Anderson, W. P. Fleisher, and G. R. Norton

1991 The Frequency of Multiple Personality among Psychiatric Inpatients. *American Journal of Psychiatry* 148:1717–1720.

Ross, C. A., S. Heber, and G. Anderson

1990 The Dissociative Disorders Interview Schedule. *American Journal of Psychiatry* 147:1698–1699.

Ross, C. A., S. Heber, et al.

1989 Differences between Multiple Personality Disorder and Other Diagnostic Groups on the Structured Diagnostic Interview. *Journal of Nervous and Mental Disease* 177:487–491.

Ross, C. A., S. Joshi, and R. Currie

1990 Dissociative Experiences in the General Population. *American Journal of Pyschiatry* 147:1547–1552.

1991 Dissociative Experiences in the General Population: A Factor Analysis. *Hospital and Community Psychiatry* 42:297–301.

Ross, C. A., S. D. Miller, et al.

1990 Structured Interview Data on 102 Cases of Multiple Personality Disorder from Four Centers. *American Journal of Pyschiatry* 147:596–601.

Ross, C. A., G. R. Norton, and K. Wozney
  1989 Multiple Personality Disorder: An Analysis of 236 Cases. *Canadian Journal of Psychiatry* 34:413–418.
Ross, C. A., L. Ryan, L. Vaught, and L. Eide
  1992 High and Low Dissociators in a College Student Population. *Dissociation* 4:147–151.
Rossi, P.
  1960 *Clavis Univeralis: Arti Mnemoniche e logica combinatoria de Lulle a Leibniz.* Milan: Ricardi.
Roth, M. S.
  1991a Dying of the Past: Medical Studies of Nostalgia in Nineteenth-Century France. *History and Memory* 3:5–29.
  1991b Remembering Forgetting: *Maladies de la mémoire* in Nineteenth Century France. *Representations* 26:49–68.
  1992 The Time of Nostalgia: Medicine, History, and Normality in Nineteenth-Century France. *Time and Society* 1(2):271–286.
Rouillard, A.-M.-P.
  1885 *Essai sur les amnésies principalement au point de vue étiologique.* Paris: Le Clerc.
Rowan, J.
  1990 *Subpersonalities: The People Inside Us.* London and New York: Routledge.
Rush, F.
  1980 *The Best Kept Secret: Sexual Abuse of Children.* New York: McGraw-Hill.
Ryan, L.
  1988 Prevalence of Dissociative Disorders and Symptoms in a University Population. Ph.D. diss., California Institute of Integral Studies, San Francisco.
Ryle, G.
  1949 *The Concept of Mind.* London: Hutchinson.
Safferman, A., et al.
  1991 Update on the Clinical Efficiency and Side Effects of Clozapine. *Schizophrenia Bulletin* 17:247–261.
Sakheim, D., and S. E. Devine
  1992 *Out of Darkness: Exploring Ritual Abuse.* New York: Lexington.
Saks, E. R.
  1994a Does Multiple Personality Disorder Exist? The Beliefs, the Data and the Law. *International Journal of Law and Psychiatry* 17:43–78.
  1994b Integrating Multiple Personalities, Murder and the Status of Alters as Persons. *Public Affairs Quarterly* 8:169–182.
Saltman V., and B. Solomon
  1982 Incest and Multiple Personality. *Psychological Reports* 50:1127–1141.

Sanders, B.
1992 The Imaginary Companion Experience in Multiple Personality. *Dissociation* 5:159–162.

Sauvages, F. Boissière de la C.
1771 *Nosologie methodique* (Latin 1768). 3 vols. Paris: Hérissent et fils.

Saxe, G. N., et al.
1993 Dissociative Disorders in Psychiatric Inpatients. *American Journal of Pyschiatry* 150:1037–1042.

Schivelbush, W.
1986 *The Railway Journey*. Berkeley and Los Angeles: University of California Press.

Schneider, K.
1959 *Clinical Psychopathology*. Translated by M. H. Hamilton. New York: Grune and Stratton.

Schreiber, F. R.
1973 *Sybil*. Chicago: Regnery.

Schubert, G. H. von
1814 *Die Symbolik des Traumes*. Leipzig: Brockhaus.

Sgroi, S.
1975 Sexual Molestation of Children: The Last Frontier of Child Abuse. *Children Today*, May–June 1975, 18–21 and continuation.

Shorter, E.
1992 *From Paralysis to Fatigue: A History of Psychosomatic Illness in the Modern Era*. New York: Free Press.

Showalter, E.
1993 Hysteria, Feminism and Gender. In *Hysteria beyond Freud*, edited by S. L. Gilman et al., 286–344. Berkeley and Los Angeles: University of California Press.

Sizemore, C. C.
1989 *A Mind of My Own*. New York: Morrow.

Sizemore, C. C., and E. S. Pitillo
1977 *I'm Eve*. Garden City, N.Y.: Doubleday.

Slovenko, R.
1993 The Multiple Personality and the Criminal Law. *Medicine and Law* 12:329–340.

Smith, M.
1992 A Reply to Ganaway: The Problem of Using Screen Memories as an Explanatory Device in Accounts of Ritual Abuse. *Dissociation* 5:117–119.
1993 *Ritual Abuse: What It Is, Why It Happens, How to Help*. San Francisco: Harper.

Spence, D. P.
1982 *Narrative Truth and Historical Truth: Meaning and Interpretation in Psychoanalysis*. New York: Norton.

Spencer, J.

1989 *Suffer the Child*. New York: Pocket Books.

Spiegel, D.

1993a Dissociation, Trauma and *DSM-IV*. Lecture to the Tenth International Conference on Multiple Personality/Dissociative States, Chicago, 15–17 October; Tape VII-860-93. Alexandria, Va.: Audio Transcripts.

1993b Letter, 20 May 1993, to the Executive Council, International Society for the Study of Multiple Personality and Dissociation. *News. International Society for the Study of Multiple Personality & Dissociation* 11(4):15.

Spitzer, R. L., et al.

1989 *DSM-III-R Casebook: A Learning Companion to the Diagnostic and Statistical Manual*. 3d ed., rev. Washington, D.C.: American Psychiatric Press.

Steinberg, M.

1985 *Structured Clinical Interview for the DSM-III-R Dissociative Disorders (SCI-D)*. New Haven, Conn.: Yale University Graduate School of Medicine.

1993 *Interviewer's Guide to the Structured Clinical Interview for DSM-IV Dissociative Disorders; Structured Clinical Interview for DSM-IV Dissociative Disorders (SCI-D)*. Washington, D.C.: American Psychiatric Press.

Steinberg, M., J. Bancroft, and J. Buchanan

1993 Multiple Personality Disorder in Criminal Law. *Bulletin of the American Academy of Psychiatry and Law* 21:345–355.

Steinberg, M., B. Rounsaville, and D. V. Cicchetti

1990 The Structured Clinical Interview for *DSM-III-R* Dissociative Disorders: Preliminary Report on a New Diagnostic Instrument. *American Journal of Pyschiatry* 147:76–82.

1991 Detection of Dissociative Disorders in Psychiatric Patients by a Screening Instrument and a Structured Diagnostic Interview. *American Journal of Pyschiatry* 148:1050–1054.

Steinberg, M., et al.

1993 Clinical Assessment of Dissociative Symptoms and Disorders: The *Structured Clinical Interview for DSM-IV Dissociative Disorders (SCI-D)*. *Dissociation* 6:3–15.

Stern, C. R.

1984 The Etiology of Multiple Personalities. *Psychiatric Clinics of North America* 7:149–160.

Stigler, S. M.

1978 Some Forgotten Work on Memory. *Journal of Experimental Psychology, Human Learning and Memory* 4:1–4.

Stowe, R.

1991 *Not the End of the World*. New York: Pantheon.

Stratford, L.
   1988 *Satan's Underground*. Harvest House. Reissued. Gretna, La.: Pelican Publishing Co., 1991.
Suryani, L., and G. D. Jensen
   1993 *Trance and Possession in Bali: A Window on Western Multiple Personality, Possession Disorder, and Suicide*. New York: Oxford University Press.
Taine, H.-A.
   1870 *De l'intelligence*. 2 vols. Paris: Hachette. Vol. 1.
   1878 *De l'intelligence*. 2 vols. Paris: Hachette. 3d ed. Vol. 1.
Taylor, J.
   1994 The Lost Daughter. *Esquire*, March, 76–87.
Taylor, W. S., and M. F. Martin
   1944 Multiple Personality. *Journal of Abnormal and Social Psychology* 39:281–300.
Terman, L. M., and A. Maud
   1937 *Measuring Intelligence*. London: Harrap.
Terr, L.
   1979 Children of Chowchilla: A Study of Psychic Trauma. *Psychoanalytic Study of the Child* 34:547–623.
   1994 *Unchained Memories: True Stories of Traumatic Memories, Lost and Found*. New York: Basic Books.
Thigpen, C. H., and H. Cleckley
   1954 A Case of Multiple Personality. *Journal of Abnormal and Social Psychology* 49:135–151.
   1957 *The Three Faces of Eve*. New York: McGraw-Hill.
   1984 On the Incidence of Multiple Personality Disorder. *International Journal of Clinical and Experimental Hypnosis* 32:63–66.
Tissié, P.
   1887 *Les aliénés voyageurs*. Paris: Doin.
Torem, M. S.
   1990a Covert Multiple Personality Underlying Eating Disorders. *American Journal of Psychotherapy* 44:357–68.
   1990b A Dialogue with Dr. Cornelia Wilbur. *Trauma and Recovery* 3:8–12.
   1992 Mini-Workshop—Eating Disorders in MPD patients. Tape C-770-92b. Alexandria, Va.: Audio Transcripts.
Torem, M. S., et al. (ISSMP&D Executive Council)
   1993 Letter, 17 May 1993, to David Spiegel. *News. International Society for the Study of Multiple Personality & Dissociation* 11(4):13–15.
Trimble, M. R.
   1981 *Post-Traumatic Neurosis: From Railway Spine to the Whiplash*. New York: Wiley.
Tymms, R.
   1949. *Doubles in Literary Psychology*. Cambridge: Bowes and Bowes.

Tyson G. M.

1992 Childhood Multiple Personality Disorder / Dissociative Identity Disorder: Applying and Extending Current Diagnostic Checklists. *Dissociation* 5:20–27.

van Benschoten, S. C.

1990 Multiple Personality Disorder and Satanic Ritual Abuse: The Issue of Credibility. *Dissociation* 3:22–30.

van der Hart, O.

1993a Guest Editorial: Introduction to the Amsterdam Papers. *Dissociation* 6:77–78

1993b Multiple Personality in Europe: Impressions. *Dissociation* 6:102–118.

van der Hart, O., and S. Boon

1990 Contemporary Interest in Multiple Personality in the Netherlands. *Dissociation* 3:34–37.

van der Kolk, B.

1993 The Intrusive Past: The Flexibility of Memory and the Engraving of Trauma. Tape XIII-860-93A. Alexandria, Va.: Audio Transcripts.

van der Kolk, B. A., and B. A. Greenberg

1987 The Psychobiology of the Trauma Response: Hyperarousal, Constriction, and Addiction to Traumatic Reexposure. In *Psychological Trauma*, edited by B. A. van der Kolk. Washington, D.C.: American Psychiatric Press.

van der Kolk, B. A., and O. van der Hart.

1989 Pierre Janet and the Breakdown of Adaptation in Psychological Trauma. *American Journal of Psychiatry* 146:1530–1540.

Vanderlinden, J., et al.

1991 Dissociative Experiences in the General Population in the Netherlands: A Study with the Dissociative Questionnaire (DIS-Q). *Dissociation* 4:180–184.

Vibert, C.

1893 Contribution à l'étude de la névrose traumatique. *Annales d'hygiéne publique et de médecine légale*, ser. 3, 29:96–117.

Voisin, J.

1885 Un cas de grande hystérie chez l'homme avec dédoublement de la personnalité. *Archives de neurologie* 10:212–225.

1886 Note sur un cas de grande hystérie chez l'homme avec dédoublement de la personnalité. Arrêt de l'attaque par le pression des tendons. *Annales médico-psychologiques*, ser. 7, 3:100–114.

Völgyesi, F. A.

1956 *Hypnosis of Man and Animals.* Translated by M. W. Hamilton from the German edition of 1938. London: Methuen.

Wakley, T.

1842–1843 (Unsigned editorial). *The Lancet* 1:936–939.

Ward, T. O.

1849 Case of Double Consciousness Connected with Hysteria. *Journal of Psychological Medicine and Mental Psychology* 2:456–461.

Warlomont, J.C.E.

1875 *Louise Lateau: Rapport médical sur la stigmatisée de Bois-d'Haine fait à l'Académie Royale de Médecine de Belgique.* Brussels: Muquardrt; Paris: Baillière.

Watkins, J. G.

1984 The Bianchi (L.A. Hillside Strangler) Case: Sociopath or Multiple Personality. *International Journal of Clinical and Experimental Hypnosis* 32: 67–101.

Whewell, W.

1840 *Philosophy of the Inductive Sciences.* London: Longman.

Whitehead, A. N.

1928 *Process and Reality.* Cambridge: Cambridge University Press.

Wholey, C. C.

1926 Moving Picture Demonstration of Transition States in a Case of Multiple Personality. *Psychoanalytic Review* 13:344–345.

1933 A Case of Multiple Personality (Motion Picture Presentation). *American Journal of Psychiatry* 12:653–688.

Wigan, A. L.

1844 *The Duality of the Mind Proved by the Structure Functions and Diseases of the Brain and by the Phenomena of Mental Derangement, and Shown to Be Essential to Moral Responsibility.* London: Longman, Brown, Green and Longmans.

Wilbur, C. B.

1984 Multiple Personality and Child Abuse. *Psychiatric Clinics of North America* 7:3.

1985 The Effect of Child Abuse on the Psyche. In *The Childhood Antecedents of Multiple Personality*, edited by R. P. Kluft, 21–36. Washington, D.C.: American Psychiatric Press.

1986 Psychoanalysis and Multiple Personality Disorder. In *Treatment of Multiple Personality Disorder*, edited by B. Braun, 135–142. Washington, D.C.: American Psychiatric Press.

1991 Sybil and Me: How I Got to Be This Way. *Trauma and Recovery* 4:4–7.

Wilbur C., and R. P. Kluft

1989 Multiple Personality Disorder. In *Treatments of Psychiatric Disorders*, 3:2197–2234. Washington, D.C.: American Psychiatric Association.

Wilkes, K. V.

1988 *Real People: Personal Identity without Thought Experiments.* Oxford: Clarendon Press.

Wilson, J.

1842–1843 A Normal and Abnormal Consciousness Alternating in the Same Individual. *The Lancet* 1:875–876.

Wittgenstein, L.

1956 *Remarks on the Foundations of Mathematics.* Oxford: Blackwell.

Wolff, P. H.

1987 *The Development of Behavioral States and the Expression of Emotions in Early Infancy.* Chicago: University of Chicago Press.

Wong, J.

1993 On the Very Idea of the Normal Child. Ph.D. diss., University of Toronto.

World Health Organization

1992 *The ICD-10 Classification of Mental and Behavioural Disorders: Clinical Descriptions and Diagnostic Guidelines.* Geneva: World Health Organization.

Yank, J. R.

1991 Handwriting Variations in Individuals with Multiple Personality Disorder. *Dissociation* 4:2–12.

Yates, F.

1966 *The Art of Memory.* London: Routledge and Kegan Paul.

Young, W. C.

1991 Letter. *Child Abuse and Neglect* 15:611–613.

Young, W. C., et al.

1991 Patients Reporting Ritual Abuse in Childhood: A Clinical Syndrome. Report of Thirty-seven Cases. *Child Abuse and Neglect* 15:181–189.

Zubin, J., et al.

1983 Metamorphoses of Schizophrenia: From Chronicity to Vulnerability. *Psychological Medicine* 13:551–571.

Index